ADVANCE PRAISE FOR

NEW DAWN: The Battles for Fallujah

"In *New Dawn*, Richard S. Lowry presents not just a brilliant account of the battle for Fallujah, but also a useful overview of the history, economics and culture of the region. Lowry shows what's great about the US military: skilled and powerful but also humanitarian and ultimately peace-seeking. Lowry's book is a must-read for anyone interested in how we won in Iraq but also for anyone interested in the history and culture of the region."

— Newt Gingrich, bestselling author and
Former Speaker of the House of Representatives

"Today's readers and tomorrow's historians will be most thankful that Richard devoted years of his life to ensure *New Dawn* not only accurately documents these battles, but also rightfully gives the credit to those young Americans whose sacrifices made success possible."

— Lieutenant General Thomas Metz, US Army (Ret.)

"*New Dawn* is an historically accurate and riveting account of the heroic struggle for Fallujah. Lowry has captured our warriors' courage, determination and sacrifice. A must read to understand the War on Terror."

— Colonel Mike Shupp, USMC (Ret.)

"I just wanted to tell you with tears in my eyes, you are doing a great service to this Nation by telling the stories of our experiences at war. Thank you."

— HM2 (FMF) Juan Rubio (Ret.)

"The detailed accuracy of accounts gathered from countless interviews sets *New Dawn* apart and places the reader in the middle of the fight. Richard has magnificently captured history in this riveting tribute to the heroism of our American and Coalition forces."

— Sergeant Jason R. Arellano, USMC, 0311

"Richard Lowry has done a great service to thousands of families with *New Dawn*. Our grandchildren will have this account to better understand what was lost and what was achieved in the Battles of Fallujah."

— David Bellavia, author of *House to House: An Epic Memoir of War*

"I just want to say thank you for writing about this, it means a lot to both of us. This [*New Dawn*] helps me to understand a lot of what my husband has been through without him having to recount it with me and it means a lot to me to be able to read and know this part of my husband's life. I'm very grateful that my husband's story has been shared with so many people, I hope that it is helpful for other people in understanding what our troops are going through and what they have done for us. Thank you again for a job well done!"

— HM1 Jennifer Rubio, USNR

NEW DAWN

The Battles for Fallujah

Books by Richard S. Lowry

The Gulf War Chronicles (2003, 2008)
US Marine in Iraq: Operation Iraqi Freedom, 2003 (2006)
Marines in the Garden of Eden (2006 and 2007)

Consultant

Perfect Valor (David C. Taylor's award-winning documentary film
that earned Best Feature Documentary Award at the 2009 GI Film Festival)

NEW DAWN

The Battles for Fallujah

Richard S. Lowry

Savas Beatie
New York and California

Cataloging-in-Publication Data is available from the Library of Congress.

ISBN 978-1-932714-77-7

05 04 03 02   5 4 3 2 1
Second edition, first printing

SB

Published by
Savas Beatie LLC
521 Fifth Avenue, Suite 1700
New York, NY 10175

Editorial Offices:

Savas Beatie LLC
P.O. Box 4527
El Dorado Hills, CA 95762
Phone: 916-941-6896
(E-mail) editorial@savasbeatie.com

Savas Beatie titles are available at special discounts for bulk purchases in the United States by corporations, institutions, and other organizations. For more details, please contact Special Sales, P.O. Box 4527, El Dorado Hills, CA 95762, or you may e-mail us at sales@savasbeatie.com, or visit our website at www.savasbeatie.com for additional information.

For Vickye

"We make war that we may live in peace."

— Aristotle

Contents

Contents (continued)

Contents (continued)

Maps and graphics have been placed throughout
the text for the convenience of the reader.

A gallery of photographs follows page 162

Please Note: With all the efforts over the years to standardize our military services tactics, techniques, and procedures, each service has clung to its traditional method of abbreviating units and ranks. These differences make it more difficult to tell a "joint" story like *New Dawn*. I have taken great pains to use the correct abbreviations from each service, for Marines would fault the use of Army terminology, and soldiers would fault the exclusive use of Corps jargon. Please refer to the Military Ranks, Abbreviations, and Unit Hierarchy chart beginning on page xxii for a complete description of these differences.

Foreword

In this superbly written book detailing the battles for Fallujah, Richard Lowry focuses on powerful accounts of the tactical campaign. Braving the toughest urban combat since World War II, our Marines, soldiers, sailors, and airmen cleared the way for success at the operational and strategic levels of Operation Iraq Freedom (OIF-I). As the Multi-National Corps-Iraq (MNC-I) commander during Operation New Dawn, I was honored to observe the superb performance of our young men and women. Quite simply, their valiance turned the tide. Today's readers and tomorrow's historians will be most thankful that Richard devoted years of his life to ensure *New Dawn* not only accurately documents these battles, but also rightfully gives the credit to those young Americans whose sacrifices made success possible.

In the fall of 2001, I was already on orders to leave my assignment in the Pentagon as Vice Director of the J8 to command the 24th Infantry Division and Fort Riley, Kansas. On the afternoon of September 11, 2001—after the Twin Towers had collapsed, after American Airlines Flight 77 had slammed into the Pentagon, and after I saw firsthand the devastation that could be wrought by global terrorism—I knew that I would be focused on training and preparing soldiers for war. I had no vision of what that war would look like, but I knew that the Army in which I enlisted after high school graduation and had served ever since was going to be at war in the twilight of my career.

That afternoon, I could not have envisioned becoming the CENTCOM Chief of Staff during the final planning phases of Operation Iraq Freedom, nor of taking command of the III Corps, deploying it to Iraq, and becoming the senior commander of the ground forces there with the mission of helping its people hold their first free elections.

I had never heard of Fallujah, and I certainly could not envision developing a Corps Operation three years later to rid this city of the thugs, criminals, foreign fighters, insurgents, and Al Qaeda operatives whose occupation of Fallujah was a significant obstacle to Iraqi democracy. On the afternoon of September 11, I could not have imagined that my entire career would now point to one operation: an end to the enemy occupation of Fallujah, which was a malignant tumor that needed to be cut away and destroyed. Defeating the enemy there would be essential to Iraq's first successful elections in January 2005. Fortunately, we had the world's best warfighters, whom Richard has so aptly honored in his book.

On my pre-deployment sight survey prior to moving III Corps Headquarters to Iraq, I met with General John Abizaid and learned that LTG Ric Sanchez would remain in Iraq as the Coalition Joint Task Force-7 (CJTF-7) Commander focused on the strategic level of Operation Iraq Freedom. General Abizaid needed me to focus on the day-to-day operations. As colonels, Ric and I overlapped for a year at Fort Riley and were accustomed to working together. Based upon General Abizaid's guidance, I leaned into the operational fight and intelligence that supported it. With a career in the operational Army, I was ready to use my education, training, and experiences to successfully achieve our goals in Iraq.

Violence was down during the first three months of 2004 because of Saddam's capture, but that changed on March 31 when insurgents in Fallujah dragged four Blackwater contractors from their SUVs, beat them savagely, and set them on fire. The brutal desecration of their bodies—pictures of which were infamously broadcast around the world—prompted some leaders to advocate immediate retaliation. Although a response was justified, hindsight tells us a more carefully considered reaction would have better served our short- and long-term goals.

Two concurrent decisions proved also to be missteps: the capture of one of Muqtada al-Sadr's top deputies, and the closure of *Al Hawza*, a newspaper published by his supporters. For good reasons, many leaders—from Anbar, Baghdad, CENTCOM, DoD, and on to the White House—were focused on a battle of revenge in Fallujah. But because of these three uncoordinated, concurrent decisions with respect to Fallujah and Sadr, the Coalition was fighting extreme Sunni and Shia forces across almost the entire country of Iraq by the second week in April.

While LTG Sanchez and Ambassador Paul Bremer focused on Fallujah, I turned to the remainder of the country to help the Coalition's division and brigade commanders get the resources to successfully put down the uprising. The enemy destroyed about a dozen bridges on our main supply route from Kuwait, and ambushed convoys at will across the country. Battle was joined in neighborhoods across Baghdad. Large 5,000-gallon tankers could be seen burning from our headquarters. The British and coalition partners were holding their own in the south, but the Poles and coalition partners in south-central Iraq needed help.

All units took on the task of guarding logistics convoys, and notwithstanding the significant fight in which they found themselves in the northern part of the Sunni triangle, we carved a reserve out of the 1st Infantry Division. We increased this reserve by taking a Stryker Battalion from the Multi-National Brigade-North, which added risk to an economy of force operation—a risk that I believed had to be taken.

American, Iraqi, and international media were strongly criticizing Marine tactics in Fallujah, while supplies of ammunition, fuel, and water were running low. As a result of our inability to disrupt the enemy's effective use of information operations, the political support for continued operations was withdrawn and the Marines were ordered to pull out of Fallujah. The solution was to form an Iraqi unit, the "Fallujah Brigade," which would be tasked to control the city and bring the Blackwater contractors' murderers to justice. Although we all wanted the "Fallujah Brigade" experiment to be successful, very few coalition leaders were optimistic.

As we were transferring authority of Baghdad from the 1st Armor Division to the 1st Cavalry Division, young soldiers were being killed during their last and first weeks in-country. But we decided to keep the 1st Armor Division an extra ninety days to give the Coalition the combat power to put out the up-rising hot spots, especially in the central south part of Iraq. Working closely with leaders like Jim Conway, Jim Mattis, Marty Dempsey, Pete Chiarelli, John Batiste, and Carter Ham, the following critical lessons learned were seared into my professional heart during the spring of 2004:

- Information operations are critical to victory on today's battlefield; you must consider the IO effect of every lethal and non-lethal decision;

- Commanders must think through the second and third order effects of their actions or inactions, and never forget that failure to make a decision is a decision;

- Our doctrine demands a reserve, so follow the doctrine;

- Never take your eye off logistics;

- When fighting with a host nation in a counter insurgency, you must start together, stay together, and finish together;

- Our young leaders in brigades, regiments, and battalions know how to fight "jointly" and can do so with superior effectiveness on today's battlefield. Senior leaders must maneuver and support them effectively.

I promised myself that I would absorb these lessons and ensure that I learned from them. My gut told me that I would need them before my tour in Iraq was complete.

Behind the chaos of the April uprising, the plans for creating the Multi-National Force-Iraq (MNF-I) and its subordinate ground component command, the Multi-National Corps-Iraq (MNC-I), were taking shape. By June 2004, MNC-I was fully operational and MNF-I was in its initial operation capacity. CJTF-7 and CPA were inactivated, Iraq was a sovereign government, and the Fallujah Brigade experiment had indeed proven to be a terrible failure: its leaders were in full cooperation with our enemies. The experiment to let Iraqi forces control a city had failed, and our enemies had a safe haven from which to operate.

The density of our enemies in Fallujah gave our special operations forces a "target-rich environment." As these special operations attacks continued over the summer of 2004, and as I realized that the international media was not covering them as fully as they had, I coined the non-doctrinal term "IO Threshold." Simply put, the IO Threshold is the boundary below which the media is not interested and above which they are. This concept would play an important part of the second battle of Fallujah.

One evening while in an informal meeting with General Casey and his staff, I asked, "In how many Iraqi cities do we have to have successful elections for the total elections to be successful?" I answered my question: "Baghdad, Basra, Mosel" and then paused. My good friend General Casey picked up the idea and challenged his staff to develop an answer. I knew that if Fallujah was one of these cities, we would have to retake it from the enemy in the coming months.

Over the summer and fall as the Fallujah cancer grew, few leaders in MNF-I, in the Iraqi government, in the Coalition partners, or at home in America were willing to accept the status quo there. Too much violence from Fallujah was moving north to Mosel, east to Baghdad, and south to Sunni insurgents who were in a good position to impact our main supply route into Baghdad. Fallujah had to be taken before the election of January 2005.

From my earlier experiences, I insisted the retaking of Fallujah would be a Corps operation. When we eventually attacked the enemy there, we would have to be ready for the same kind of nationwide uprising that we experienced in April. The Corps is a resource provider, and I ordered that the fuel, water, and ammunition available inside Iraq be doubled. For example, we went from storing 7,000,000 gallons of diesel fuel in Iraq to almost 15,000,000 gallons. Subordinate commanders across the Coalition were brought into the planning process. Senior commanders and civilian leaders supported our planning process with very positive coordination. For once, the bureaucrats were prone to say "yes" instead of "no." The full power of the Coalition would be brought upon the enemy in Fallujah. My staff recommended that this operation be called "Operation Phantom Fury," and as the Commander of Fort Hood, Texas's Phantom Corps, I approved. Fury was a very good description of my intent.

Despite our resolve, we did have some lingering concern of the attack's timing and the US presidential election. On a secure videoconference outlining the attack to President George Bush, he assured us that he saw no connection between the American election that November and our mission in Fallujah. In addition, the president gave commanders in Iraq the guidance we needed to successfully take out the cancerous safe haven there.

With total support from the chain of command, our options grew. Special programs gave us valuable and timely intelligence. Iraqi battalions were recruited and trained. The 1st Cavalry's Blackjack Brigade Combat Team's early departure was delayed. After gaining the United Kingdom's support, we moved one of their battalions to just southeast of Fallujah to free more Marines for the Fallujah fight. General Casey won the confidence of Prime Minister Allawi and the support of the young Iraq government. As the battle neared, Prime Minister Allawi disbanded the Fallujah Brigade, established a 24-hour curfew, and prohibited the carrying of weapons in Fallujah—actions that were instrumental to success in Operation New Dawn (we agreed with the Iraqi leaders to rename the operation as an important concession to help win their support).

A dominate combat power force was planned, and this force began to train and ready itself for Operation New Dawn. The team work in preparation was splendid—from the tactical level to the strategic level all were aligned, but with one very subjective part unknown: Information Operations.

Doctrinally we were doing everything right in the Information Operations domain. Deception feints were successful. Psyops operations were also very successful, as almost 90% of the population departed Fallujah. And even with more than 200,000 moving out of the city, the exodus did not create the humanitarian problem many predicted. Our electronic warfare efforts were superb: we listened when we wanted to and jammed when we did not want the enemy to communicate inside or outside Fallujah. We knew the enemy remained convinced that we would not attack them and that if we did, they would prevail. We could not hide the movement of massive combat power, but our operational security supported our IO efforts, and the enemy remained confused before and during the battle. Computer network operations were managed well above the NMC-I/MNF-I levels. Doctrinally, we were on top of the Information Operations, but I saw one remaining challenge: "The IO Threshold."

Since the first battle for Fallujah was lost in some measure due to the enemy's use of information—albeit false information—General Casey could have imposed strict rules of engagement for the second battle of Fallujah. On the other hand, General John Sattler, MNF-W Commander, had every right to unleash as much combat power as he needed to protect his force and achieve the mission.

Relationships are as important in the military as they are in other professions; friendships make those relationships tight and loyal threads bind warfighters. And so it was with General George Casey, LtGen John Sattler, and me. George trusted his team to adhere to our standard rules of engagement and allowed his operational and tactical commanders to orchestrate this battle. I would go to John and tell him that we can't lose this battle before it starts, so his prep must stay beneath the IO Threshold. In turn, I'd go to George to gain his support for using all available combat power, regardless of what the media says, until the enemy was defeated. We were confident that our Marines and soldiers would defeat the enemy in Fallujah.

There were, of course, IO challenges we could anticipate and for which we could plan. We took control of the hospital the evening before the main attack on Fallujah, removing it from the enemy's IO platform. If the enemy uses a mosque, school, or hospital from which to fight, that structure loses its protection under the Fourth Geneva Convention and Rules of Land Warfare. But since a majority of our young men and women carry digital cameras in their pockets, I asked them to take a picture of the enemy's misuse of these facilities before rightly using overwhelming combat power against them. When I visited young commanders, I emphasized to them that to win this battle I needed digital pictures coming my way as much as they needed main gun tank rounds headed toward the enemy. I knew our Marines and soldiers were good enough to win the total information war.

We were ready with a plan to strike at the enemy's strength quickly with overwhelming combat power, political support from home, the Coalition Partners, and the sovereign Iraqi government, and an understanding of the "IO Threshold" by commanders and warfighters alike. The real burden then fell to Marines, soldiers, sailors, and airmen to get the job done. Richard Lowry has masterfully captured the hard, dangerous, personal fight these men and women waged in Operation New Dawn. His research and accuracy will not only be enjoyed by readers today, but also help historians for years to come. He has honored young leaders and warfighters as he covers their actions, often minute-to-minute, throughout one of the toughest urban combats in which Americans have fought.

I want to thank Richard for the honor of writing this Foreword because his book superbly records the major challenge of III Corps' success in Iraq. Each of the major units in the Corps fought numerous successful tactical battles. The operational success achieved in Operation New Dawn by MNF-W, MNC-I, MNF-I and the Iraqi Government then led to the strategic success of national elections in January 2005.

In *New Dawn: The Battles for Fallujah*, Richard Lowry has brilliantly set forth the successes of the young men and women of all the services who fought and supported Operation New Dawn. To them and Richard, we owe a debt of gratitude. God Bless them all and God Bless America!

— Lieutenant General Thomas F. Metz, US ARMY (Ret.)
First MNC-I Commanding General

Preface

As goes Fallujah, so goes Anbar Province; as goes Anbar, so goes Iraq. Fallujah has long been a Sunni Wahabi tribal hotbed and vital commercial crossroad. Islamic fundamentalism arrived in Fallujah hundreds of years ago via an ancient trade route, linking societies in the Arabian Peninsula with the people of Iraq. This austere, blue-collar city on the banks of the Euphrates River has long been regarded as a notorious home of malcontents. Even Saddam had problems controlling Fallujah's religious zealots.

American forces easily deposed Saddam's regime in 2003, but the fighting never ended in Fallujah. The first Americans in the city were besieged and forced to hunker down in fortified outposts. The situation there was a harbinger of events to come throughout Iraq. As they had in Baghdad, the enemy in Fallujah proved time and time again that America was not prepared to fight a counter-insurgent war. The United States Army was not trained or equipped to deal with anarchy and insurrection. A metamorphosis of mission would be needed to overcome the rising insurgency.

The American military was restructured in the middle of the 1980s. The Goldwater-Nichols Department of Defense Reorganization Act of 1986 changed our military structure forever. The Chairman of the Joint Chiefs was given operational authority over the service chiefs. He also became the principal military advisor to the president, National Security Council, and secretary of defense. The intent was to bring all of the military services closer together and to create a "joint" force that could train, communicate, and fight as one. The intent was not to homogenize our fighting forces, but to enable them to work together, bringing all the tools in the toolbox to any given campaign. However, while a modicum of jointness was achieved during the 2003 invasion of Iraq, for the most part the Army and Marine Corps operated independently for the first year of the war.

In March 2004, the 1st Marine Division relieved the Army's 82nd Airborne Division in Iraq's western province. The mindset of the Marine Corps was better suited to deal with third-world chaos. Years earlier, they had developed the concept of the "three-block war."[1] In its struggle to redefine its mission after Goldwater-Nichols, the Corps worked to position itself as America's 911 force. Marine Expeditionary Units were designed to remain afloat near potential hotspots in order to be the first in. The Marines have responded to America's security needs in Lebanon, Haiti, Grenada, Kuwait, Somalia, and other hotspots. As the U.S. Military's SWAT team, the Marines became proficient at maintaining order and dealing with civilians in lawless lands. In 2003-2004 the leadership in the Pentagon realized that the Marines were best suited to handle the chaotic situation in al Anbar Province. As a result, after less than one year's respite, Major General James Mattis and his 1st Marine Division returned to Iraq.

No sooner had the Marines arrived than four Blackwater security guards were attacked and brutally beaten, burned, and dragged through the streets of Fallujah. According to the account in Bing West's *No True Glory*,[2] the Marine commanders wanted to quietly hunt down the perpetrators of the gruesome killings. President Bush and Secretary of Defense Donald Rumsfeld, however, with visions of the 1993 "Blackhawk Down" incident in Mogadishu, Somalia, insisted the Marines attack to clear the entire city. On April 4, 2004, the Marines attacked into an insurgent hornets' nest. After only five days, President Bush ordered a unilateral suspension of offensive operations. Al Qaeda had won the first round of the battle for Fallujah.

How had they achieved that? Al Qaeda had cleverly goaded American forces into a fight and then expertly manipulated the world news media, igniting a worldwide diplomatic firestorm. Inaccurate stories and staged photos abounded of so-called Marine atrocities, convincing the world that Marines were indiscriminately killing women and children. The propaganda

---

1   General Charles Krulak, the 31st Commandant of the Marine Corps from July 1, 1995 to June 30, 1999, defined the Marines' mission as being able to fight a "three-block war." This included simultaneous all-out combat operations on one block, clearing operations on the next block, and humanitarian operations on the third block.

2   Bing West, *No True Glory*.

was so effective that the fledgling Iraqi government insisted that the operation be suspended. The British, America's closest ally, also demanded an immediate cessation of offensive activities. As a result, the Marines stopped their advance into the city and held their positions. Even after the Marines halted, the insurgents continued to probe their lines, hoping to kill Americans and elicit another violent response. They continued to build roadblocks and strongpoints in preparation for the next round of fighting.

Meanwhile, the Marines and the Iraqi Governing Council attempted to negotiate an end to the violence. By April 19, 2004, the U.S.-led coalition reached an agreement with Fallujah's community leaders. In an attempt to reestablish some sort of stability, the Marines agreed to patrol the city alongside Iraqi security forces. Initially the city streets remained calm, but violence erupted in less than twenty-four hours. Frustrated by the forced restraint, the Marines withdrew and turned over responsibility for security inside Fallujah to the newly established Iraqi-manned "Fallujah Brigade." This ended the first siege of Iraq's "Wild West" stronghold.

The Fallujah Brigade had been armed and trained in the hope that its members could take back their own city. It remains debatable whether the Fallujah Brigade ever really intended to deal with the violent element within the city; its officer corps and ranks were heavily populated with former members of Saddam's Republican Guard. Regardless of their intent, they never became an effective security force and the Brigade disintegrated. Control of the city fell back into the hands of the insurgents.

While tragic, the brigade's failure to maintain security was a necessary evolutionary step in the history of Fallujah. The United States had attempted to back away and let the Iraqis bring peace and stability to their own city. The Fallujah Brigade's failure emphasized the need for additional American action and galvanized support for action within the ranks of the Iraqi national government.

Otherwise, there could not have been a worse outcome to the first battle for Fallujah. The mightiest military in the world had seemingly been defeated by a ragtag band of criminal thugs (as indeed, Al Qaeda proclaimed its victory over the infidel). The Marines had been unable to quickly penetrate the insurgents' maze of roadblocks and IED-laced streets. They didn't have the heavy assets they needed to punch through those fortifications without flattening the city with bombs and artillery.

The first battle dashed the Marines' chances of winning the hearts and minds of the people; Al Qaeda won that battle, too. The insurgents used their victory in Fallujah to recruit fresh fighters from the local inhabitants and to attract jihadists from all over the world. The call went out: "Come to Fallujah, kill Americans, and defeat the Zionists." The city was left isolated, with nearly 100% unemployment. Few of Fallujah's military-aged men had anything better to do than fight the Americans who had brought chaos and destruction to their city.

By the end of April, the Marines had withdrawn to the edge of Fallujah. Mattis' only hope was to contain the growing insurgency within the city. Fallujah was again a base of operations and safe haven for the enemy and an American no-man's-land. Mattis was restrained during the summer of 2004 as Coalition leadership tried to get the Iraqis to solve the problem. Given the opportunity, Mattis would have moved to clear Fallujah, but it was not meant to be. The job of defeating the enemy there would fall to Major General Richard F. Natonski, the 1st Marine Division's next commanding general. A longtime advocate of joint operations, Natonski assumed command in August of 2004, and planning was undertaken for the largest joint operation of the war: *Operation Phantom Fury*. The Marines had learned much since their arrival in March. They would not be turned back a second time.

Acknowledgments: First and foremost, I must thank the men and women of our armed forces who risk their lives to serve their country during these turbulent times. Our soldiers, sailors, airmen, coast guardsmen, and Marines are the finest in the world. I would also like to express my undying gratitude to the families and friends of these servicemen and women. You are the real heroes of this global war. May God bless you one and all.

This book would not have come to fruition without the support and encouragement of Lieutenant General Richard Natonski. He suggested the project and then worked to help me speak with the soldiers, sailors, airmen, and Marines who fought to free Fallujah. Thank you for helping me to tell their stories. Lieutenant General Thomas Metz took time out of his busy schedule to write a brilliant Foreword that provides readers with a high-level overview that sharpens the context in which Operation Phantom Fury was fought; thank you, Tom. I would also like to thank all the men and women who took the time to speak with me about their individual experiences in Fallujah. Each of you helped me to paint the picture of this historic battle.

I would like to add a special thank you to Lieutenant Colonel Nicholas Vuckovich, USMC (Ret.). When he heard that I was having problems with my previous publisher, he put me in touch with his friend Gunnery Sergeant

Nicholas Popaditch, USMC (Ret). "Gunny Pop," who wrote the outstanding *Once a Marine: An Iraq War Tank Commander's Inspirational Memoir of Combat, Courage, and Recovery* (2008) hand-carried my book proposal to his publisher, Theodore Savas of Savas Beatie LLC. Thank you for hooking me up with Ted, Gunny. And thank you, Ted, for having faith in me and my work. This story would not be in print today had it not been for the efforts of Colonel Nick, Gunny Nick, and Ted. Sarah Keeney of Savas Beatie has worked tirelessly to help get the word out to the world. Her marketing skills are a tremendous asset to our team. I would be remiss if I did not thank Savas Beatie editor Rob Ayer, an instructor at the United States Coast Guard Academy. Rob spent many weeks combing through my work, correcting errors, and giving me guidance on the content of *New Dawn*. He turned a good manuscript into a great book.

Thank you to the men and women at the United States Marine Corps Headquarters Public Affairs Office, the Quantico Marine Base Public Affairs Office (Lieutenant Colonel Patricia Johnson and Second Lieutenant Joy Crabaugh), and the Marine Corps University in both the library and at the History Division. I would like to convey a special thanks and gratitude for the support of my friends Dr. Charles Niemeyer, Colonel Nathan S. Lowrey, USMCR, and Chuck Melson. They are true professionals who work every day to record the history of the United States Marine Corps, and they have always bent over backwards to help me in my research.

I would like to add many thanks to Matt Matthews of the United States Army Combat Studies Institute at Fort Leavenworth, Kansas. Matt helped me gather the information I needed to understand the Army's participation in Operation Phantom Fury, and he directed me to all the interviews he had conducted while collecting his Operational Leadership Experiences. Thank you for helping me weave the Army's story into *New Dawn*.

Geoffrey Thorpe-Willett risked his life to capture eleven hours of high-quality video footage of Kilo Company, 3d Battalion, 5th Marines' fight in the city. He lived and worked with the grunts on the ground for nearly three weeks, and he readily provided that video to me so that I could better understand what it meant to be a Marine fighting in Fallujah. Thank you, Geoff, you gave me invaluable insight.

And last, but certainly not least, thank you Vickye. I could not tell these stories without your love, understanding, and support.

Military Ranks, Abbreviations, and Unit Hierarchy

ARMY	RANK	PAY GRADE	MARINES
	OFFICER		
GEN	General	O-10	Gen
LTG	Lieutenant General	O-9	LtGen
MG	Major General	O-8	MajGen
BG	Brigadier General	O-7	BGen
COL	Colonel	O-6	Col
LTC	Lieutenant Colonel	O-5	LtCol
MAJ	Major	O-4	Maj
CPT	Captain	O-3	Capt
1LT	First Lieutenant	O-2	1stLt
2LT	Second Lieutenant	O-1	2dLt
	WARRANT OFFICER		
WO5	Master Warrant Officer Chief Warrant Officer 5	W-5	CWO5
WO4	Chief Warrant Officer 4	W-4	CWO4
WO3	Chief Warrant Officer 3	W-3	CWO3
WO2	Chief Warrant Officer 2	W-2	CWO2
WO1	Warrant Officer	W-1	WO
	ENLISTED		
SGM CSM	Sergeant Major Command Sergeant Major Master Gunnery Sergeant	E-9	SgtMaj MGySgt
1SG MSG	First Sergeant Master Sergeant	E-8	1stSgt MSgt

SFC	Sergeant 1st Class Gunnery Sgt	E-7	 GySgt
SSG	Staff Sergeant	E-6	SSgt
SGT	Sergeant	E-5	Sgt
CPL	Corporal	E-4	Cpl
PFC	Private 1st Class Lance Corporal	E-3	 LCpl
PV2	Private2 Private 1st Class	E-2	 Pfc
PV1	Private	E-1	Pvt

ARMY	*RANK OF* *COMMANDER*	*MARINE* *CORPS*
Corps	Lieutenant General	*MEF
Division	Major General	Division
Brigade/BCT	Colonel	Regiment/RCT
Battalion/Squadron	Lieutenant Colonel	Battalion
Company/Troop	Captain	Company
Platoon	Second Lieutenant	Platoon
Squad	Sergeant	Squad
Section	Corporal	Fire Team

BCT – Brigade Combat Team

RCT – Regimental Combat Team

*The Marines do not have a unit equivalent to the Army's Corps. The Marine Expeditionary Force could command multiple Marine divisions, but during Operation Phantom Fury it only contained the 1st Marine Division. In reality, the MEF was part of the Multi-National Corps—Iraq.

Note: In the Army, the term 'Regiment' is used for historical purposes only, i.e. 503rd Infantry Regiment or the 4th Cavalry Regiment.

Acronyms

AAV: Assault Amphibian Vehicle

ACE: Aviation Combat Earthmover

ADC: Assistant Division Commander

AMTRAC: Amphibious Tracked Vehicle (AAV)

AO: Area of Operations

APC: Armored Personnel Carrier

ASP: Alternate Supply Point

ASR: Alternate Supply Route

BAS: Battalion Aid Station

BCT: Brigade Combat Team

BLT: Battalion Landing Team

BRT: Brigade Reconnaissance Troop

CAAT: Combined Anti-Armor Team

CAS: Close Air Support

Casevac: Casualty Evacuation

Chop: Removing a unit from its parent unit and assigning it to another unit

CJTF: Combined Joint Task force

COP: Combat Outpost

CP: Command Post

CSSA: Combined Services and Support Area

CSSB: Combined Services and Support Battalion

CSSC: Combined Services and Support Company

DEA: Drug Enforcement Agency

DMZ: De-Militarized Zone

EOD: Explosive Ordinance Disposal

FAC: Forward Air Controller

FiST: Fire Support Team

FLA: Field Litter Ambulance

FO: Forward Observer

FOB: Forward Operating Base

GLDS: Ground LASER Designator System

GPS: Global Positioning System

HE: High Explosive

HEAT: High Explosive Anti Tank

HESCO: British Company that makes HESCO Barriers

HET: Human Exploitation Team

HMMWV: High Mobility Multi-Wheeled Vehicle

HQ: Headquarters

IED: Improvised Explosive Device

IIF: Iraqi Intervention Force

I MEF: 1st Marine Expeditionary Force

ING: Iraqi National Guard

IO: Information Operations

JDAM: Joint Directed Attack Munitions

JTAC: Joint Tactical Air Controller

KIA: Killed In Action

LAR: Light Armored Reconnaissance

LAV : Light Armored Vehicle

LAV-25: Light Armored Vehicle with 25mm Bushmaster automatic cannon

LAV-AT: Light Armored Vehicle – Anti-tank – TOW missile launcher

LRAS: Long Range Advanced Scout Surveillance system

LZ: Landing Zone

MARDIV: Marine Division

MAW: Marine Air Wing

MCRD: Marine Corps Recruit Depot

MEB: Marine Expeditionary Brigade

MEF: Marine Expeditionary Force

MEU: Marine Expeditionary Unit

MICLIC: Mine Clearing Line Charge

MNC-I: Multi National Corps-Iraq

MNF-I: Multi National Force-Iraq

MOUT: Military Operations in Urban Terrain

MPAT: Multi-Purpose Anti-Tank

MRE: Meal-Ready-to-Eat

MSR: Main Supply Route

NCO: Non Commissioned Officer

NVGs: Night Vision Goggles

PL: Phase Line

PSD: Personal Security Detachment

RCT: Regimental Combat Team

RIP: Relief in Place

ROE: Rules Of Engagement

RPG: Rocket Propelled Grenade

SAMS: School of Advanced Military Studies

SASO: Security and Stability Operations

SASS: Same Axis, Same Speed

SAW: Squad Automatic Weapon or School of Advanced Warfighting

SEAL: Sea, Air, and Land; U.S. Navy's elite commando unit

SMAW: Shoulder-fired Multipurpose Assault Weapon

SURC: Small Unit Riverine Craft

SUV: Sport Utility Vehicle

SVBIED: Suicide Vehicle-Borne Improvised Explosive Device

SWAT: Special Weapons and Tactics

TCP: Traffic Control Point

TF: Task Force

TOC: Tactical Operations Center

TOW: Tube-launched, Optically-tracked, Wire-guided, antitank missile

TQ: al Taqaddum

UAV: Unmanned Arial Vehicle

USA: United States Army

USAF: United States Air Force

USMC: United States Marine Corps

USMCR: United States Marine Corps Reserve

USNS: United States Naval Ship

VBIED: Vehicle-Borne Improvised Explosive Device

WIA: Wounded In Action

XO: Executive Officer

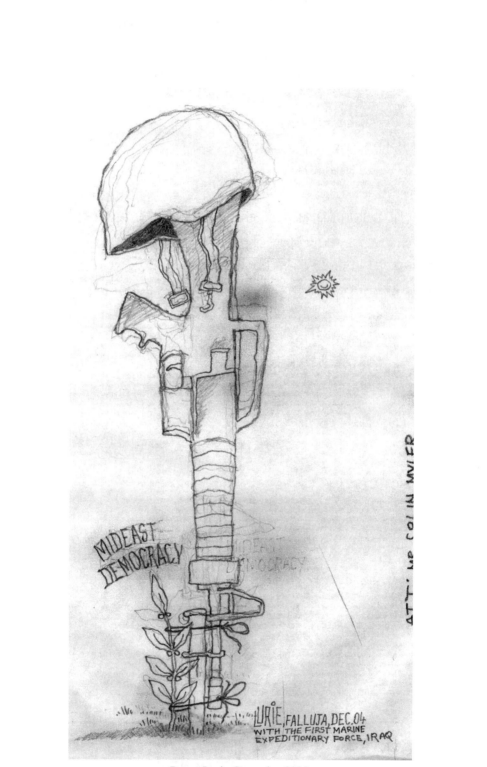

Ranan Lurie, December 2004

Chapter 1

Fallujah: The Most Dangerous City in Iraq

"Fallujah was a festering sore in al Anbar Province."

Colonel Gareth Brandl, USMC, November 20, 2007

Death to Americans

On the morning of March 31, 2004, three empty flatbed trucks snaked their way out of the heavily guarded north gate at Camp Fallujah. When Wesley Batalona reached the main road,[1] he turned left onto a modern, four-lane highway that stretched west toward the heart of the city. Soon Batalona saw freeway signs indicating a large intersection. A modern-day cloverleaf, much like you would find in America, lay directly ahead on the outskirts of the turbulent city. Batalona planned on meeting local Iraqi defense forces at the Cloverleaf. There, they would escort his handful of trucks through Fallujah. The tiny convoy drove under the overpass and rolled to a stop at the Marines' newly inhabited TCP-1.[2]

Batalona and three other private security contractors traveled in two Mitsubishi SUVs. They had been given the thankless assignment of

---

1   Main Supply Route (MSR) Michigan, or Highway 10.

2   Traffic Control Point. TCP-1 had been established months earlier by the paratroopers of the 82nd Airborne Division to control access in and out of the city.

protecting the flatbeds as they moved to retrieve old kitchen equipment from a base west of Fallujah. Wesley Batalona, a former sergeant in the elite U.S. Army Rangers, was in charge of security. Jerry Zovko, a 38-year-old Croatian-American and fellow former Ranger, rode shotgun in the lead vehicle with Batalona. Scott Helvenston, an ex-Navy SEAL,[3] drove the second SUV behind the three flatbeds, with Michael Teague, a Bronze Star recipient and veteran of the fighting in Panama, Afghanistan, and Grenada, riding as his gunner.

These four American Blackwater[4] contractors provided the only protection for this low-priority mission. Batalona's team was severely undermanned and under-armed. Before being relieved by the Marines, the U.S. Army would not enter the city with anything less than four heavily armored vehicles bristling with soldiers in full combat gear and weapons. Army and Marine forays into Fallujah were fraught with danger. More often than not the soldiers would withdraw under gunfire. Just a day earlier the Marines had fought a significant firefight in the city. Yet on this day the Iraqi escorts, traveling in two dilapidated pickup trucks, led the four lightly armed civilian security contractors and their 'thin-skinned' sport utility vehicles into the most dangerous city in Iraq. Trusting these Iraqis was like leaving the wolves to guard the sheep: their loyalties were, at best, questionable.

Batalona should have realized that he was approaching Hell the minute he entered the city. Unemployed military-aged men loitered on the garbage-strewn main thoroughfare. The deeper the convoy drove into the city, the worse things looked. Stares and frowns turned to jeers and hand gestures. As they snaked their way down the congested highway, traffic slowed to a crawl. The streets became eerily quiet. The Iraqi escorts slammed on their brakes, forcing Batalona to grind his vehicles to a stop.

The beleaguered convoy had driven almost two-thirds of the way through the city when all hell broke loose.[5] Gunfire, directed at the rear

---

3   Elite US Navy commandos. Their name is an acronym indicating the different ways they can be deployed: SEa, Air and Land.

4   Blackwater, Inc., was a North Carolina-based private security firm. Most of its employees were retired military. They have provided private security specialists since the beginning of the war in Iraq.

5   This account of the Blackwater ambush is taken from Patrick Toohay's article published on newsobserver.com, November 28, 2005.

vehicle, erupted from nearby buildings. Helvenston and Teague never had a chance to respond, as bullets ripped through their SUV. The first bursts of gunfire killed or mortally wounded them.

As soon as the shooting started, the two Iraqi escort vehicles sped away. Batalona made a quick U-turn and slammed his accelerator to the floor, but collided with an Iraqi civilian's Toyota, his SUV skidding to a stop. Another group of armed men rushed the scene of the collision, spraying his vehicle with automatic weapons gunfire. Batalona and Zovko slumped over, dead in their seats. The shooting stopped as quickly as it had begun, and the attackers slipped away into the city.

Insurgents with video cameras rushed to the bloody scene to film the carnage—evidence of their latest victory over the infidel. Young boys, teenagers, and old men swarmed the convoy, pouring gasoline on the vehicles. Flames erupted and both SUVs were soon engulfed, with thick black smoke rising from the inferno. The smoke drew an even larger mob to the scene and triggered a macabre frenzy. The cameras were rolling as the fire subsided. Four charred American corpses were pulled from the smoldering ruins. The mob beat the bodies repeatedly with sticks and shoes, kicking, mutilating, and dragging them through the streets. Two of the Americans were hoisted up on Fallujah's green steel footbridge and left to hang for the world to see. The celebrations continued until after dark.

Meanwhile, the Marines could only watch in horror the streaming video coming from their UAV.[6] The Marine commanders made the heartbreaking decision to not deploy troops to the ambush site. They knew that the American contractors were already dead, and that further intervention would only lead to more bloodshed. Instead, they decided to let the riot burn itself out.

The Perpetual Problem

The war had never really ended in Fallujah, even though Saddam's regime was quickly deposed in the spring of 2003. Subsequently the All Americans of the 82nd Airborne Division had been given the onerous mission of securing this restive town thirty miles west of Baghdad. Unfortunately, they never had enough combat power to clear the city of an

---

6 Unmanned Aerial Vehicle.

increasing number of enemy fighters. On April 28, 2003, a protest within the city turned violent and fifteen Iraqis were killed, further inflaming the local population.

The increase in violence throughout the summer and fall of 2003 prompted the American commanders to withdraw their forces to a series of camps outside the city. Fallujah became a safe haven and rallying point for hardened Saddam supporters, former Ba'ath party leaders, Republican Guard members, Iraqi Army diehards and, finally, Islamic fundamentalists. "These were hardcore insurgents who wanted nothing more than to kill Americans," explained a high ranking officer.[7]

The lightly armed paratroopers developed a "Fort Apache" mentality, only venturing into the city in heavily armed groups. They had not expected so much civilian discontent, but they quickly realized that the people were tied to centuries of local tribe and clan loyalties. Initially, the paratroopers were completely unprepared to deal with the people of Fallujah, but the soldiers worked hard to understand them and their history.

The Euphrates River cuts a swath through the Iraqi wasteland, bringing life-giving water to the Fertile Crescent. Vast barren plains lie to the north, east, and west of Fallujah. The city is an ancient crossroads and Euphrates River crossing connecting Saudi Arabia in the south with Syria and Turkey in the north. The river and roads are lifelines of trade. Fallujah has always been a hub of commerce, both legal and illegal. The main east-west road—Iraq's oldest and most important commercial artery—is its link to the western world and today known as Highway 10, connecting Baghdad with Amman, Jordan.

Because of Fallujah's location, control of the city has been contested since antiquity. In the 18th century B.C., Hammurabi expanded his Babylonian empire when he acquired the ancient city of Sippar.[8] During the 1st century A.D., the Romans, Trojans, Arabs, and Persians fought at one

---

7   LtGen Richard Natonski telephone interview, 10/11/07.

8   Sippar was roughly in the same geographic location as modern-day Fallujah. Georges Roux, *Ancient Iraq*, p. 197.

time or another for control of what is now known as Fallujah.[9] When the Mongols laid waste to Baghdad in 1258 A.D., Iraq's economy fell into ruin. Iraq's civilization lay dormant for centuries until the Iraqi people were conquered by the Ottomans in the 16th century. Control of the Fertile Crescent flipped back and forth between the Ottomans and the Persians for hundreds of years until the Turks reasserted their rule in the early 1800s.[10]

After the Ottoman Empire sided with the Germans in World War I, England fought a series of battles against the Turks along the Euphrates River valley. After the Allied victory in 1918, the British occupied what is now known as Iraq. In 1920 resistance to their occupation increased—and was uncannily similar to what America experienced in the months following the 2003 invasion. Fallujah, the divided city, was one of the flashpoints. The British learned quickly that reconciliation was the key to success in this ancient land. "Fallujah," explained a regional expert, "had become the symbol of the resistance and had to become the symbol of the reconciliation process."[11] Thus the British worked to woo the tribal and clan leaders, and Fallujah soon became a model for the nation. As a symbol of national pride, the British selected Fallujah as the site for the coronation of King Faisal, the new pro-British leader, on August 23, 1921.

Throughout the turbulent history of Anbar Province, daily life, business, and government have all revolved around its families, clans, and tribes. The province's rugged people depend upon one another to survive in an austere environment. Their ancestors learned that the only way to endure through the blistering summers, whimsical shifts in the Euphrates River, and even more whimsical changes in government, was by helping each other. The people are close-knit, fiercely loyal, radically independent, and distrusting of outsiders. They have been ruled by the leaders of their clans and tribes for as long as can be remembered. In 2003, the most prominent tribal leader was

9 Fallujah, www.globalsecurity.org.

10 Tore Kjeilen, "Iraq: History," *Encyclopedia of the Orient*, http://i-cias.com/e.o/iraq_5.htm.

11 NPR Interview – "Tracing the History of Fallujah," by Jennifer Ludden; interview with Annas Shallal 11/13/04.

Sheik Abdullah Al Janabi, the self-proclaimed leader of the city's governing Shura Council. Janabi's tribe was the most hostile to the Americans.

With the ever-shifting political climate, the tribes and clans have had little regard for the country's artificial international boundaries. To the people of Anbar, smuggling is all in a day's work, a necessity of commerce. As a result, Fallujah is peppered with trucking industry businesses. Flatbeds and long-haul trucks continually clog the main road. Truck stops, machine shops, and junkyards dominate the industrial area. If you need a tire changed, a chassis welded, a radiator soldered, or a new radio installed, Fallujahans stand ready to provide the service. Once the Americans arrived, the people of Fallujah had the talent, resources, and inclination to smuggle weapons and manufacture IEDs.[12]

Fallujah's main thoroughfare teemed with BMWs, donkey carts, and long-haul trucks. The road was lined with a mixture of magnificent mansions, majestic mosques, multi-storied concrete buildings, and mud-brick shanties. Throughout the city there were many poor neighborhoods, some middle-class areas, and enclaves with luxurious homes. More large mansions and estates lined the banks of the Euphrates River.

Like most Iraqi cities, Fallujah was built of cinder blocks. Nearly every building was surrounded by a wall. Some walls had been meticulously constructed, the obvious work of a proud stonemason. But many had the look of the repetitive cycle of destruction, repair, more destruction, and hasty reassembly, thrown together in a helter-skelter fashion with blocks stacked upon blocks with little or no mortar, just waiting to be pushed over again. Most houses were small, two- or three-story buildings with concrete slab floors and thick roofs. Others were large, with landscaped courtyards, marble floors, and ornate furnishings.

Fallujah's homes had been built to shelter their residents from the sweltering heat of the Iraqi summers. They also served to protect their residents from the continuous cycle of senseless violence. Concrete walls and roofs were sometimes three feet thick, with another three feet of dirt piled on the flat roofs. They were veritable bunkers. Most courtyard doors were made of sheet metal with two or three locks. Doors leading into homes were either metal or protected by a locked metal gate.

12 Improvised Explosive Device.

Because of this, Fallujah could not have been more attractive to the resistance. The population was distrusting of outsiders and naturally rebellious. Its workers provided the wherewithal to smuggle weapons, explosives, and foreign fighters. Its craftsmen provided the talent to build bombs, and every home was a mini-fortress.

As 2003 turned to 2004, the cancer inside Fallujah was growing. Most Fallujahans were unemployed. The insurgents launched attacks on nearby Baghdad to control commercial traffic. The city was home to gunrunners and smugglers. It seemed as if every storefront had a backroom full of weapons. Everyone knew who specialized in particular items: some sold machine guns, and others provided sophisticated night-vision devices. The local bazaars were crawling with merchants of death.

The Marines' Initial Response

Within hours of the Blackwater ambush on the last day of March 2004, the Marines moved to cordon off the entire city. Inside, the enemy prepared for the inevitable assault. Major General James Mattis and Lieutenant General James Conway, however, recommended restraint. The Assistant Division Commander, Brigadier General John Kelly, sought to temper America's response in the Division's daily report:

> As we review the actions in Fallujah yesterday, the murder of four private security personnel in the most brutal way, we are convinced that this act was spontaneous mob action. Under the wrong circumstances this could have taken place in any city in Iraq. We must avoid the temptation to strike out in retribution. In the only 10 days we have been here we have engaged the "good" and the bad in Fallujah everyday, and have casualties to show for our efforts. We must remember that the citizens and officials of Fallujah were already gathering up and delivering what was left of three victims before asked to do so, and continue in their efforts to collect up what they can of the dismembered remnants of the fourth.
>
> We have a well thought out campaign plan that considers the Fallujah problem across its very complicated spectrum. This plan most certainly includes kinetic action, but going overly kinetic at this juncture plays into the hands of the opposition in exactly the way they assume we will. This is why they shoot and throw hand grenades out of crowds, to bait us into overreaction. The insurgents did not plan this crime, it dropped into their

lap. We should not fall victim to their hopes for a vengeful response. To react to this provocation, as heinous as it is, will likely negate the efforts of the 82nd Airborne Division paid for in blood, and complicate our campaign plan, which we have not yet been given the opportunity to implement. Counterinsurgency forces have learned many times in the past that the desire to demonstrate force and resolve has long term and generally negative implications, and destabilize rather than stabilize the environment.[13]

The Marine commanders did not want to further disenfranchise the people of Fallujah. They told their corps commander, U. S. Army Lieutenant General Ricardo Sanchez, that they could find the perpetrators of the ambush and bring them to justice within two weeks. Sanchez passed on the Marines' recommendation. Secretary of Defense Donald Rumsfeld, however, was not impressed with the suggestion for a tempered response and ordered the Marines to attack. Conway and Mattis had delivered their recommendation as to how they thought they should respond, but when they received their orders, they—like any good Marines—unflinchingly obeyed them.

The Fight Begins: Operation Vigilant Resolve

On April 5, 2004, U.S. Marines charged into the city, destroying enemy positions and killing every enemy combatant who stood in their path. One of the Marines driving into Fallujah was Gunnery Sergeant Nicholas Popaditch. Angered by the heinous murders of the Blackwater contractors and the insurgents' claims that Fallujah was the graveyard of Americans, "Gunny Pop" couldn't wait to get into the fight. His tank platoon was one of only two armor platoons deployed around Fallujah. Popaditch's First Platoon was attached to Lieutenant Colonel Gregg Olson's Marines. With so few tanks, Captain Michael Skaggs, the 1st Tank Battalion's Charlie Company Commander, was forced to split up his platoons. His Second Platoon, under First Lieutenant Troy Sayler, was assigned to Lieutenant Colonel Brennan Byrne's 1st Battalion, 5th Marines. The Marine tanks

---

13 1MarDiv CC JJ04: 1 MarDiv Intentions 040401, S-3933-06\Intentions Mssg\Apr04.

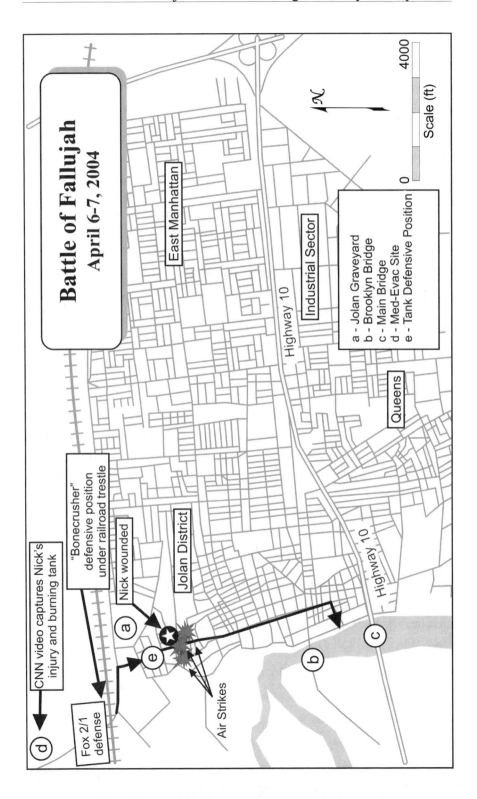

Battle of Fallujah
April 6-7, 2004

East Manhattan

Industrial Sector

a - Jolan Graveyard
b - Brooklyn Bridge
c - Main Bridge
d - Med-Evac Site
e - Tank Defensive Position

Highway 10

Queens

0   4000
Scale (ft)

Jolan District

Highway 10

"Bonecrusher" defensive position under railroad trestle

Nick wounded

CNN video captures Nick's injury and burning tank

Fox 2/1 defense

Air Strikes

would operate in sections of two tanks each, and would be sent out to support the infantry companies as they were needed.

Olson's 2nd Battalion, 1st Marines, moved into attack positions in the northwest corner of the city on April 5, 2004, and Byrne's Marines manned the cordon across town in the southeast corner of the city. On April 6, Captain Kyle Stoddard, 2/1's Fox Company Commander, sent a small squad-sized patrol into the northern edge of the city to assess enemy strength. The squad was attacked within the first few blocks, and one of the Marines was wounded in the initial bursts of gunfire. Outgunned and outnumbered, the squad called for reinforcements and a medevac.[14] As soon as Stoddard heard the call for help, he ordered, "Roll the QRT."[15]

Gunny Pop, Charlie Company's First Platoon Sergeant, was sitting in his tank under the railroad overpass in the northwest corner of the city, waiting as part of the QRT. Popaditch had been in Marine tanks his entire career. He had fought in southern Kuwait during Operation Desert Storm and had led the charge to Baghdad in 2003, where his tanks surrounded Firdos Square and toppled the large statue of Saddam. Straining at his leash, Popaditch asked Stoddard for permission to enter the city.

"Roll the tanks," ordered Stoddard.

Cleared for action, Gunny Pop ordered his two tanks into the fight. The armor rolled forward under the overpass, taking the gentle turn to the east along the road that skirted the northern edge of Fallujah. Popaditch's tanks drove east ahead of the QRT infantry, then quickly turned south, heading toward the embattled infantrymen. As soon as they turned into the city, Popaditch could see the wounded Marine being treated in the street.

Popaditch didn't like being buttoned up inside his tank. In an urban fight, his visibility was too restricted; he needed a 360-degree view to be able to react to the enemy on the ground. As a result, he rode with his tank commander hatch open and his head exposed to enemy fire. Peeking out, he found the other Marines, watched for a few moments to determine the direction they were firing, and then rotated his turret to point in the same direction. As his main gun slowly traversed, Popaditch scanned the rooftops, doorways, and alleys in search of the enemy.

---

14 Medical Evacuation – Medevacs encompass all sorts of medical evolutions, evacuating both battle-related casualties from the battlefield and non battle-related patients.

15 Quick Reaction Team.

He quickly found his first target—an insurgent firing from behind a wall about six blocks away. "Gunner, Coax,[16] troops. Fire and adjust,"[17] Popaditch ordered. Corporal Ryan Chambers, the tank's gunner, unleashed a deadly accurate burst of 7.62mm rounds, killing the distant enemy insurgent.

Popaditch drove his tanks forward beyond the Marines on the ground. He moved far enough out in front of the infantry to attract enemy fire. Stoddard's QRT infantry moved in behind Popaditch's tanks to medevac the casualty and relieve the small squad.

Once the casualty had been rushed out of the city, Second Platoon moved up to Popaditch's position and, in accordance with doctrine, swarmed out in front of Popaditch's two tanks. But with the Marines and enemy intermixed, the tankers couldn't employ their weapons. Popaditch radioed platoon commander Second Lieutenant Josh Jamison (Pale Rider 2) to ask if he would let the tanks take the lead. When the infantry pulled back they moved to the rooftops, which gave Popaditch forty sets of eyes looking for targets. As soon as the grunts were safely behind the tanks, Popaditch resumed mowing down insurgents in his path. He stayed busy all afternoon, killing the enemy as they rushed toward the fight.

Late that afternoon Popaditch moved to take the initiative, pushing forward to actively hunt down insurgents in the streets. He had rolled only a couple blocks when he discovered a fortified compound. The courtyard's entrance was blocked by two downed telephone poles and a web of wires. A gasoline tanker trailer was parked in the alley next to the compound. Popaditch could see sandbagged fighting positions throughout the courtyard and a wall of more sandbags at the front door of the building.

Sensing that the truck was rigged as a giant IED, Gunny Pop backed away. With this formidable fortress in his path, his tanks were stopped and the attack stalled. He had to reduce this position—but how? Popaditch came up with a plan. He would approach the courtyard entrance from an angle and push the poles out of the way with his tank. It wasn't the best plan (his tank could become mired in the kill zone, or it could throw a track) but it was better than sitting around and letting the enemy retake the initiative.

---

16 The 7.62mm Coaxial machine gun is mounted on the same axis as the main gun and is controlled by the tank's deadly-accurate fire-control system.

17 Nick Popaditch, with Mike Steere, *Once a Marine: An Iraq War Tank Commander's Inspirational Memoir of Combat, Courage, and Recovery* (Savas Beatie, 2008), p. 275.

Just as Popaditch was about to move out, Captain Stoddard came up on the net with a plan of his own. "Red 4, this is Pale Rider 6. I can get air on-station to breach your obstacle."[18]

The only downside to this idea was that Popaditch would have to wait for nightfall because AC-130 gunships only operated at night to avoid shoulder-launched anti-aircraft missiles. Since the enemy was not aggressively responding, Gunny Pop thought it better to wait for sunset than to plow his way into a potential hornets' nest.

"Roger that, sounds great," Popaditch replied.

As soon as it was dark, an Air Force Lockheed AC-130 Spectre gunship reported in, and Popaditch described his situation and the target to the airmen overhead. But he was not prepared to provide forward air control to the gunship—his maps were not precise enough and he had limited knowledge of the aircraft's capabilities. After talking for some time, the Marines on the ground and the airmen overhead came up with a new plan. Popaditch would drive his tank up next to the fortress and pitch an IR[19] chem-stick into the mass of wires at the entrance to target the position.

Popaditch ordered his driver to creep forward. Surprisingly, the approach of the massive M1A1 main battle tank did not draw enemy fire. As soon as they were close enough, Popaditch tossed the glowing stick into the obstacle at the entrance to the courtyard, and the airmen above reported a 'tally' on the target. Once the target was acquired, Popaditch reversed course and eased his tank away. The pilots warned Popaditch to back off 125 meters. Gunny Pop got 100 meters away from the barricaded courtyard. "That's far enough," he thought. "We're clear," he announced.

40mm high-explosive rounds blew the obstacle to pieces, sending a torrent of debris toward his tank. Seconds later the dark streets of Fallujah were quiet again.

The airmen asked for feedback on their accuracy: "Give us an adjust." No adjustment was needed. The first shots had been right on their target.

Popaditch thought that he should next take out the gasoline tanker truck. Gunny Pop had never worked with AC-130s before. "In what increments?" he inquired.

---

18 Popaditch, *Once a Marine*, p. 281.

19 Infra-Red.

"Five meter," the pilot responded.

"They've got to be kidding," the Gunny thought. "They can't do five-meter increments while flying around in the sky." It was then he remembered that he really should have given them 125 meters before.

"OK, give me 15 meters to the right."

A thunderclap followed and the gas truck exploded in a massive fireball. (Popaditch will never know if the truck was wired to explode, but it was full of gas.) Popaditch adjusted the aircraft's fire back to the building in the center of the courtyard, and the AC-130 turned that into a pile of smoking rubble.

The power and accuracy of the aircraft flying overhead blew Popaditch away. He was like a kid on Christmas morning with a new toy. The tank commander decided to press forward into the city with just his wingman. He wouldn't need the infantry to protect his flank and rear—he had an AC-130. With the enemy stronghold breached, the two tanks, Popaditch's and Sergeant Herbierto Escamilla's, drove south into the city on an armored rampage.

The pilots could see every movement on the streets below. They told Popaditch there were a dozen people standing in the street around the next corner, but the pilots could not determine if they were civilians or enemy fighters. Popaditch raced forward, rotating his turret to the left. As he cleared the corner building at the intersection, he found himself looking at a dozen armed and very surprised insurgents. They hadn't heard his tank because its approach was masked by the AC-130 engines. The first (and, for some, the last) thing they heard was the burst of Popaditch's coax machine gun.

The survivors rushed into a nearby building, which Popaditch peppered with machine gun fire to mark the target for the gunners overhead. The AC-130 gunners rained more 40mm rounds down, collapsing the building on top of the trapped enemy. This tactic worked so well that Popaditch and his wingman spent the rest of the night marauding down Fallujah's streets under the protective umbrella of their new friends in the AC-130.

Around 0400[20] Popaditch ran out of ammunition and was ordered to return to Stoddard's position at the northern edge of the city. Lieutenant Sayler tried to relieve Popaditch and Escamilla so they could return to the

---

20 The US military uses a 24-hour clock: 0100 is one in the morning, 1200 is noon; 1300 is one in the afternoon and 2300 is eleven at night. 0400 would be 4:00 A.M.

supply point outside the city to rearm and take on fuel, but Sayler's tank threw a tread entering the city. It was too dangerous to send supply and gasoline trucks in, so Popaditch was told that he would not be receiving fuel.

Stoddard's Marines stepped up to the plate to get Popaditch the machine gun ammunition he needed. Shortly after sunrise, Popaditch spotted a column of Marines to the north heading in his direction by twos. As they got closer he saw that each Marine had his weapon in one hand and the handle of an ammo crate in the other. Two-by-two, crate-by-crate, they were bringing ammo up to the tankers. The Marines who had been in the city all night now moved out of their buildings and pushed south to provide security for the resupply column. All the Marines worked together to rearm Popaditch's two tanks. Before long, both had all the machine gun rounds they could carry.

Popaditch was ready to take the initiative again. Stoddard's Marines had penetrated farther into the city than anyone else, if only a few blocks. With Gunny Pop's tanks low on fuel, they were ordered to hold their position. Stoddard's infantry moved back into their building strongholds, leaving Popaditch's tanks out in the street—alone.

It didn't take the enemy long to realize what was happening. The insurgents began moving through courtyards and alleyways to flank the Marines. Popaditch didn't like sitting still. He knew that every moment he sat there, the enemy was sneaking through the shadows to get closer for a shot. He knew that they wanted nothing more than to kill an American tank. It didn't take long for one of the insurgents to position himself between the buildings and pop out to unleash his rocket. The RPG[21] whooshed toward the lead tank, flying between Popaditch and his loader, Lance Corporal Alex Hernandez, who was manning his 240 machine gun. Popaditch felt the heat of the rocket exhaust as the projectile whizzed past his face. It could not have been a closer miss.

"Do you believe that?" Popaditch asked Hernandez.

More RPGs rained down on Popaditch's tank. Several detonated on impact but did no damage, while others whooshed by harmlessly and exploded in the distance. Some of the RPG teams were gunned down by the tankers, while others darted back in search of cover.

Popaditch was getting anxious. He was a sitting duck. He wanted to move back out on the attack. After a career of being a tanker, he knew that a

21 Rocket Propelled Grenade.

moving tank was much more effective than one that was standing still, and he had constantly drilled into his drivers' heads that if they got hit they should move. Popaditch wanted to take the fight to the enemy, but his orders were to stand his ground. He waited in the street all morning. Around noon, the Marines spotted a dozen insurgents gathering three blocks ahead outside a mosque. Popaditch radioed Stoddard and requested permission to go on the attack.

"Go get 'em," Stoddard radioed back.

"Red 3, this is Red 4, follow my move," Popaditch radioed Escamilla. "Driver," he ordered, "move out." Red 4 lurched forward, with Red 3 following close behind. After a morning of standing and taking punches, Popaditch's tanks were back in the hunt. The M1A1s ground forward alone, leaving the infantry behind.

Gunny Pop could see the mosque in the distance. As he approached, the insurgents scattered. He mowed half of them down with his guns. Popaditch didn't think twice about chasing down the survivors. Keeping the initiative went hand-in-hand with his philosophy of warfare. But as he drove deeper into the city, the streets started to close in around his tank. Within a short time the roadway was so narrow that he could not traverse his turret. Popaditch watched the remaining insurgents darting from doorway to doorway trying to flee. He continued to pursue them, grinding deeper and deeper into the narrow streets of Fallujah.

As Red 4 clanked into an intersection with an eight-foot-wide alley, an enemy grenadier was waiting only fifty feet from Popaditch's tank. The insurgent took careful aim and fired. Popaditch ducked down just as the RPG hit the side of his turret and exploded, leaving behind nothing more than a black scorch mark. Popaditch slewed his .50-cal cupola toward the grenadier. As he was doing so, another insurgent, this one unseen, fired a second RPG from a nearby rooftop slightly behind him. It was a point-blank shot onto the top of the tank.

Gunny Pop heard the hiss of the rocket a split second before it struck him on the side of his helmet. A blinding white flash of light "a thousand times brighter than a camera flash," followed instantly with a sledgehammer blow that knocked the tank commander to the floor of his turret. His world went dark and nearly silent. Still conscious, Popaditch pulled himself to his feet, holding on to steady himself. The inside of the turret was totally black, and there was a static-like humming in his ears "like an untuned radio turned up full blast." He reached up to feel a warm gooey wetness on his face.[22]

Popaditch reached out and grabbed Chambers. "You've got to get the tank moving," he calmly ordered.

Inside the turret, Chambers and Hernandez had also been wounded by flying shrapnel from the round that had nearly decapitated Gunny Pop. Realizing that Gunny had gotten the worst of it, Chambers acknowledged the order and took command of the tank. He told the driver to move out. Not knowing that his helmet had been blown off his head and that his intercom mic was gone, Popaditch commanded again, "Chambers, you've got to get the tank moving!"

When Popaditch felt the tank lurch forward, he knew that his crew was working to get out of the kill zone. The driver, Lance Corporal Christopher Frias, plowed through the ambush site.

"I know the way back," Frias told Chambers.

"Get us out of here!" Chambers ordered.

Frias raced forward, with Escamilla following in his tank. The trip was mercilessly short, and before long Popaditch's tank rolled under the train trestle from which it had departed the day before and ground to a stop.

Lance Corporal Hernandez was the first out. His left hand had been mangled by flying shrapnel and he was bleeding badly. Hernandez rushed to the front of the tank and jumped to the ground. Chambers climbed out next. When he spotted some personal gear burning on top of the tank, he yelled, "Give me a fire extinguisher!" to the Marines on the ground. They handed him a bottle of water, which he squeezed onto the flames, putting the fire out. Gunny Pop, meanwhile, had struggled to the open hatch. He was sleepy, and he knew that wasn't good. He had to remain conscious. His energy, however, was quickly draining away. Unable to get out of the tank, he cradled his head on the top of the tank as if he was about to take a nap.

"All right Gunny, Gunny, I'm right behind you, I'm right behind you," Chambers told Popaditch. Chambers grabbed him under his armpits and pulled him from the hatch.

Corpsmen jumped up on the tank and placed a field dressing on Popaditch's face, loaded him onto a stretcher, and carried him down.

Popaditch was still conscious, but he couldn't see and could barely hear. A short time later, something happened: the corpsmen were piling something on top of his body. It felt as if he was being buried. Because the enemy was still trying to get Popaditch's tank, mortar rounds were falling on the train trestle. The corpsmen had taken off their body armor and piled it across their wounded comrade, risking their own lives in the process. The barrage proved short-lived, and within minutes Gunny Pop was loaded into a waiting ambulance and rushed to Bravo Surgical at Camp Fallujah. The RPG round had blown his right eye out of his head and his left eye into his sinus cavity. Other pieces of shrapnel had penetrated his head and neck. The surgeons worked for hours to save his remaining eye. Gunny Pop was out of the fight for good.

But his fellow Marines were not, and they would continue the attack. There was no question as to the military outcome of Operation Vigilant Resolve: in a gunfight, the Marines always prevailed.

Despite the overwhelming firepower advantage, in the politically charged international environment that was Fallujah in the spring of 2004, an American victory was not certain for a host of reasons. The enemy controlled the international media presence on the battlefield. The Marines had not been allowed sufficient time to properly plan the incursion nor to clear the city of its civilian population. The fledgling Iraqi government lacked the will to continue support for the American assault. Finally, America lacked international support for the war in general, and specifically for the attack to clear Fallujah.

The enemy had an uncanny understanding of Information Operations. They invited Arab news organizations into the city and continually fed them misinformation. They posted propaganda on the internet and spread rumors throughout the city of Marine atrocities. The Western news media, under threat of kidnappings and beheadings and with little time for the Marines to embed reporters, stayed away from Fallujah. They were forced to use the video shot under insurgent control. This helped to spread the claims that the Marines were killing innocent civilians. The cumulative effects rattled the foundations of support within the Iraqi national government and the support of the few American allies in the world.

Unable to evacuate civilians from the city, the Marines had to fight among the population. This was especially difficult because the enemy used civilians as cover, fighting from mosques, schools, and hospitals. They even used Red Crescent ambulances to transport fighters. These tactics placed the Marines on the horns of a dilemma. If they held their fire, the enemy would slip away, but if they returned fire, they could wound or kill civilians or destroy mosques and schools. And every civilian casualty and damaged mosque was fodder for more insurgent propaganda.

The street fighting was bloody. The enemy moved throughout the city among the population using hit-and-run tactics, while the Marines had to try to isolate and neutralize them without causing much damage to the city's infrastructure. It was like playing rugby in a china shop.

All the while, the enemy wanted to kill as many Americans as possible and drag out the fighting in an effort to force a ceasefire. They knew they could never defeat the Marines, but they could force a draw. As it turned out, they only had to hold on for five days. Under mounting pressure at home and abroad, President George W. Bush ordered a ceasefire on April 9. The Marines immediately stopped their attacks and assumed defensive positions inside the city.

The skirmishes and all-out firefights, however, continued for weeks. During this initial twenty-six days of fighting, 600-700 insurgents were killed and an unknown number wounded. Up to that time, eighteen Marines had died in the fighting, and ninety-six—including Nicholas "Gunny Pop" Popaditch—had been injured.

On April 30, the Marines withdrew from Fallujah to allow the "Fallujah Brigade" its opportunity to return peace to the city.

Summertime Standoff

Sunni-dominated Fallujah had been home to many of Saddam Hussein's elite followers. Now it was filled with former Iraqi Army, Republican Guard, and Ba'ath Party officials who had all been cronies of Saddam. All these Iraqis had been put out of work with the dissolution of the Ba'ath Party and disbanding of the Iraqi Army; many wanted to continue the struggle to return the jailed Saddam to power. The disgruntled bureaucrats and soldiers wanted to reestablish the privilege, power, and prestige they had enjoyed during Saddam's reign. Some former officers saw the violence in Fallujah as an chance to regain their influence, so they formed the "Fallujah Brigade."

The brigade was made up primarily of out-of-work Iraqi soldiers. Its officers were corrupt and bore no loyalty to the fledgling, Shia-dominated Iraqi government. They hated the Americans and, in most cases supported the insurgents. At best the Fallujah Brigade was ineffective, and at worst it was part of the problem. But in April of 2004, the brigade was a necessary evil. American military leadership wanted to put an Iraqi face on the solution to the violence in Fallujah. The Marines sincerely hoped the Fallujah Brigade could start the much-needed reconciliation process between the powers-that-be in Fallujah and the Iraqi central government. "We tried to get the Iraqis to help us solve the problem," recalled LtGen John Sattler.[23] As it turned out, the Fallujah Brigade's dismal failure would finally show the government in Baghdad that it needed help in curing the ills within Fallujah. Prime Minister Iyad Alawi and his leadership finally understood that the Iraqis themselves were not yet prepared to solve this vexing problem.

Within months, the Fallujah Brigade melted away and the city again became an enemy sanctuary. Into it poured both local and foreign Islamic extremists who allied themselves with local criminals and warlords. There were scores of neighborhood gangs and a dozen key leaders. Emboldened, the insurgents spread terror, using Fallujah as their safe haven. Roving gangs attacked convoys, and the foreign jihadists spread violence throughout a 100-mile radius in the form of kidnappings, torture, and murder.

Most of the tribal sheikhs viewed the Americans as usurpers of their authority. Sheikh Abdullah al-Janabi—cleric, chieftain, and mystic, the foremost insurgent leader, head of the town's governing council, and general mover and shaker—viewed the Americans as invaders and wanted to drive them out of Iraq. But Janabi was not the kind of guy to get his own hands dirty. He was a rabble rouser, but he was not a fighter. Residents said Janabi never carried a weapon in public, but was frequently seen during the April fighting talking to front-line Mujahedeen,[24] exhorting them to fight on and telling them that those who died fighting Islam's enemies would be rewarded with eternity in paradise.

23 LtGen John Sattler telephone interview, 12/3/07.

24 Islamic holy warrior.

Janabi's principal enforcer and henchman was local electrician- turned-jihadi Omar Hadid. He had allied himself with Janabi and Abu Musab al-Zarqawi in the early days of the Fallujah insurgency and had become a front-line leader during the first fight. Hadid was a dangerous man, ready and willing to die in the fight to rid his land of the infidel.

Abu Musab Zarqawi was probably the most famous of Al Qaeda in Iraq's leaders. Born in Jordan, he had fought with Osama bin Laden in Afghanistan and was wounded there in 2002. He fled to Baghdad, where he was treated in an Iraqi hospital before dropping out of sight. The militant leader built the largest terrorist training camp in the world on a small finger of Iraqi land near Muqdadiyah, surrounded by Iranian mountains on three sides.[25] When American Special Forces chased Zarqawi out of his mountaintop stronghold in March of 2003, he fled and eventually ended up in Fallujah, where he became the head of Al Qaeda in Iraq.

In April 2004, Janabi and Zarqawi claimed victory over the hated Americans, and then used those claims to recruit more jihadists from around the world. The call went out: come to Fallujah and kill Americans.

No matter what the insurgents were claiming, they knew the fight was not over. Inside the city, they set out to fortify their positions in anticipation of the return of the Marines. They built bunkers, roadblocks, and obstacles. They set up ambush sites and buried thousands of mines and IEDs. They dug trenches and fortified fighting positions. They knocked holes in walls that were just large enough for a man to crawl through. These "rat holes" allowed insurgents to slip from compound to compound within the city without having to go out into the streets. They did everything they could to prepare to kill as many Americans as possible in the next round of fighting.

If the Marines could overcome these defenses, crush the resistance inside the city, and break the enemy's grip on the people of Fallujah, it would herald the beginning of the end for the insurgency. Victory in Fallujah would bring a new dawn of hope to the people of Iraq.

25 Linda Robinson, *Masters of Chaos – The Secret History of the Special Forces* (New York: Public Affairs, 2004), pp. 320-323. Operation Viking Hammer.

Chapter 2

New Leaders, New Plan

"Fighting house-to-house is the dirtiest of all fighting."

— Major George (Ron) Christmas, USMC, February, 1977

Starting at the Top

Major General Richard F. Natonski assumed command of the 1st Marine Division in a small ceremony at al Asad Air Base on August 20, 2004. Natonski is a gentleman general, a towering, genuine leader. "Everybody wanted to please him," remembered one of his officers.[1] This was Natonski's second tour in Iraq. After surviving the 9/11 attack on the Pentagon, he had led the 2nd Marine Expeditionary Brigade (MEB) during the 2003 invasion of Iraq as it fought the first major battle of the war in the dusty desert city of An Nasiriyah.

Major General John F. Sattler was in command of the 2nd Marine Division when Natonski was the MEB commander, and the two men had become neighbors and friends. Then, just before the beginning of Operation Iraqi Freedom, Sattler assumed command of the little-publicized Combined Joint Task Force–Horn of Africa, where America was fighting the

---

1   LtCol Joe L'Etiole telephone interview, 10/29/07.

little-publicized war on terror in Somalia, Yemen, and Ethiopia. Within two weeks of Natonski taking command of the 1st Marine Division, now-Lieutenant General Sattler relieved Lieutenant General James Conway as the 1st Marine Expeditionary Force commander. Sattler and Natonski were back together again in Iraq.

The generals inherited insurgent-controlled cities and a province that has been described as a cross between the "Wild West" and Mad Max.[2] Armed men ranged every road in Anbar Province. Every turn in the highway, roadside shed, or stand of palm trees posed a threat of ambush. Traveling anywhere "outside the wire"[3] was dangerous, and the city streets were downright deadly. Ramadi, Habbaniyah, Haditha, and Fallujah were by now all enemy strongholds. Marine bases in the area were regularly subjected to rocket and mortar attacks. The enemy had nearly complete freedom of movement, while American forces were vulnerable to attack anywhere and everywhere.

The enemy had been focusing on the Main Supply Routes (MSRs), the vital life-lines for the Marines. Insurgents continually tried to interdict MSR TAMPA, the main route running north out of Kuwait, and MSR MICHIGAN and MSR MOBILE, the two east-west routes connecting Fallujah with Baghdad. These three routes were under continual threat of hidden IEDs, ambushes, or both.

In addition to the dangers along the highways, the enemy tried to take advantage of the Marines' light footprint around their Forward Operating Bases (FOBs). Camp Fallujah, DELTA, al Asad, al Taqaddum (TQ), and Blue Diamond were regularly mortared or rocketed.

Al Anbar was unquestionably the most dangerous province in Iraq, and Fallujah was the most dangerous city in Anbar. American commanders in Baghdad and members of the Iraqi government feared that the instability in Anbar, and particularly in Fallujah, posed a threat to the upcoming national elections. Insurgents were using the town as a base of operations for

---

2   LtCol Christopher Starling, USMC, personal comment to author in June 2005.

3   Most American military bases were protected by a barbed wire fence. "Outside the wire" is anywhere outside the protected American military bases.

bombings, kidnappings, ambushes, and killings in nearby Baghdad and throughout central Iraq. The enemy planned their operations, built their bombs, and launched their attacks from Fallujah, returning to the safe harbor to rest and rearm. Many at the Multi-National Force headquarters and in Washington, D.C., believed that the upcoming Iraqi national elections could not succeed under the threat of bombings, murders, and reprisals from the insurgents in Fallujah.

As a result, the new Multi-National Corps–Iraq (MNC-I) commander, Lieutenant General Thomas F. Metz, ordered the 1st Marine Expeditionary Force (I MEF) to prepare for a new offensive against the insurgent stronghold of Fallujah. In turn, General Sattler ordered General Natonski to complete the preparations for the new assault. The operation was code-named Phantom Fury.

The MEF and Division staffs worked closely together. General Sattler coordinated the operation with the commanders in Baghdad and ensured that the 1st Marine Division had the resources it needed. The ultimate responsibility for the fight, however, rested with General Natonski, whose first challenge was to pull together a force capable of accomplishing the mission. Phantom Fury would not be an isolated fight in the city streets. By this time it was obvious that a much larger operation was needed. Natonski maintained responsibility for all of Anbar Province, and he could not ignore the Division's commitments outside of Fallujah. Forces would be needed to isolate the city, protect the Marines' existing infrastructure, keep the MSRs open, and maintain a modicum of security throughout the rest of western Iraq.

Brigadier General Joseph Dunford, Natonski's assistant division commander, was a veteran of the march to Baghdad in 2003 as commander of Regimental Combat Team-5 (RCT-5). Dunford was an inspirational leader, affable, and intelligent. He always had a line of Marines at his door seeking guidance, advice, and consent. Dunford's task was anything but easy: he was responsible for operations within the division's Area of Operations (AO) but had limited resources to accomplish his goals. Natonski needed most of the Marine assets for the actual assault on the city. This left Dunford with severely understrength units throughout his AO. While Dunford concentrated on the big picture across Iraq's largest province, Natonski focused on the planning for the second assault on Fallujah.

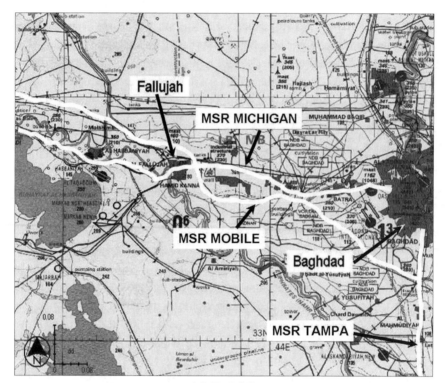

AO Raleigh

Planning

Major General Natonski assembled an operational planning team with representatives from throughout the Marine Air-Ground Task Force[4] (MAGTF): 3rd Marine Air Wing (MAW), 1st Marine Logistics Group, the MEF and the Army. They all congregated to help the 1st Marine Division staff plan for the upcoming fight. "This was an all-star cast," confirmed BGen Dunford.[5] Months of groundwork conducted by General Mattis and his staff provided the foundation for Natonski's plan.

---

4   Marine formations deploy as integrated Marine Air-Ground Task Forces (MAGTFs) of various sizes: Marine Expeditionary Unit (MEU), Marine Expeditionary Brigade (MEB), and Marine Expeditionary Force (MEF). These task forces contain air, ground and logistic assets, all working together on a three-dimensional battlefield.

5   BGen Joseph Dunford telephone interview, 11/16/07.

Lieutenant Colonel Joe L'Etiole had served as Mattis' deputy operations officer (G3) during the first fight for Fallujah in April of 2004. With his tour not yet complete, L'Etiole became Natonski's Operations Officer. He brought the painful lessons learned that April to Natonski's planning table.

In fact, all involved in the planning relied heavily on the lessons learned in previous fights. From the fight in Nasiriyah, Natonski brought memories of confused communications and a tragic friendly-fire incident. Dunford brought lessons learned during his march up to Baghdad and the first fight in Fallujah. Many in the staff carried with them lessons from the fight in Najaf during the sweltering summer of 2004. And, they had all learned much about the enemy in Fallujah during the preceding months.

In Vietnam, Major George (Ron) Christmas[6] had been wounded in the fighting in Hue City and awarded the Navy Cross for his heroism while leading Hotel Company of Second Battalion, Fifth Marines in the largest urban fight of that war. He later became young Marine Lieutenant Natonski's company commander at The Basic School.[7] Major Christmas wrote several articles about the dangers of fighting house-to-house and building-to-building. He impressed upon his peers and students that urban fighting is a dirty business, requiring attention to detail and overwhelming firepower. Many on Natonski's staff dug through the archives to retrieve Ron Christmas' words of wisdom. They studied his lessons from the last time the Marines had conducted large-scale urban combat. They were determined to apply the lessons learned in Hue City to the fight before them.

The planning for Phantom Fury began with mission analysis. The mission was simple: destroy the enemy within Fallujah, so as to create conditions in which Fallujahans could regain control of their city. One of the biggest concerns was the "Information Operations (IO) Threshold": what was the level of death and destruction the people of Iraq, America, and even

6 Now LtGen (ret) George (Ron) Christmas.

7 The USMC Basic School at Quantico, Virginia, is unique to the Marine Corps. Its mission is to train and educate newly commissioned or appointed officers in the high standards of professional knowledge, esprit-de-corps and leadership required to prepare them for duty as company-grade officers in the operating forces, with particular emphasis on the duties, responsibilities and warfighting skills required of a rifle platoon commander.

the world was willing to see and still allow the battle to continue? The IO Threshold had been exceeded in the first fight, and General Metz did not want a recurrence of the spring failure. So restraint during the preparation and speed of execution were of the essence. The window of violent action had to be small and the enemy had to be defeated as quickly as possible. This is part of what drove the development of Natonski's plan.

Natonski also understood Ron Christmas' classic concerns regarding urban combat. He needed to isolate the insurgents inside Fallujah, including denying them re-supply and reinforcement. He needed to select an entry point. He needed to select the appropriate strategy: would the Marines swarm, surge, or fight house-to-house?

The combined staff members planned several different scenarios, and then war-gamed each course of action. Eventually they decided to attack from the north. They would need to pull two RCTs and a LAV-heavy[8] task force into the Fallujah fight. But the operation could not be conducted in a vacuum. The city would have to be isolated, and the MSRs and FOBs would have to continue to be protected. Sattler, Natonski, and Dunford would have been hard-pressed to isolate and attack Fallujah with only the Marine forces on hand. Fortunately, all three officers were advocates of joint operations.

Once Dunford isolated the battlefield, the Marines would have to enter the city to destroy the enemy. First, however, they would have to hunt them down. In the wild, bears and lions drink with their heads down; they have no need to look around because they are the meanest predators around. But there were few bears or lions in Fallujah. This city was a den of jackals: Islamic extremists, disenfranchised former soldiers, Ba'ath Party leaders, foreign fighters, and young thugs—all there to kill Americans. Unlike bears or lions, the jackals were constantly looking over their shoulders and moving, wary of everything around them. Getting in position to kill them would not be easy. General Natonski needed a hunter to run his intelligence-gathering, someone to get inside these jackals' heads, someone to prepare the battlefield. For that task he inherited Lieutenant Colonel George Bristol, a real-life hunter and martial arts expert, as his G2 Intelligence Officer.

Beyond leaders, planners, and a plan, however, Natonski needed fighters.

---

8   Light Armored Vehicle.

Chapter 3

The 1st Marine Division

"There is 'No Better Friend, No Worse Enemy' than a U.S. Marine."

— MajGen James Mattis, USMC, April 2003

The 1st Marine Division was activated on February 1, 1941, and is the most-decorated division in the United States Marine Corps. During World War II, 1st Division Marines fought on Guadalcanal, Pelileu, and Okinawa, winning Presidential Unit Citations in all three engagements. In Korea, these Marines conducted the surprise landing at Inchon and fought at the Chosin Reservoir. During the Vietnam War, the Division saw heavy fighting in the Tet Offensive, and it led the charge through the "Saddam Line" during Operation Desert Storm in 1991.

In March of 2003, Major General James Mattis led the 1st Marine Division's attack up the Euphrates River Valley toward Baghdad. Once he had secured the Iraqi capital, Mattis sent some of his Marines to secure Saddam Hussein's home town of Tikrit, 100 miles north of Baghdad. When all was said and done, units of the 1st Marine Division had penetrated nearly 400 miles into the Iraqi heartland, attacking farther into enemy territory and moving faster than any other Marine unit in the history of the Corps. And in the process it completely crushed the Iraqi Army.

A little more than one year later, Major General Natonski was preparing to lead the 1st Marine Division into the history books once again.

The First Marine Regiment: RCT - 1

Natonski had two Marine regiments at his disposal for the attack into the city. The first, Regimental Combat Team–1 (RCT-1),[1] was responsible for the eastern portion of the 1st Marine Division's AO. The regimental command post was located just east of the city in Camp Fallujah. Of its main components, Third Battalion, First Marines was operating out of Abu Ghraib along MSR MICHIGAN, and Third Battalion, Fifth Marines would soon relieve Gregg Olson's Second Battalion, First Marines along MSR MOBILE.

Sometimes, fate plays a role in history. It certainly helped decide who would lead the 1st Marine Regiment.

Colonel Michael Shupp, a veteran of the fight for Kuwait International Airport during Operation Desert Storm and a graduate of the School of Advanced Warfighting (SAW), arrived in Iraq at the end of May. Shupp had been slated to take command of RCT-1, but in June he received a message from the Red Cross that his wife Sherrye had taken ill with cancer. Colonel Shupp returned home to be by her side during her extended treatment, not knowing whether she would survive the ordeal.

Colonel Larry Nicholson had been selected to take the 5th Marine Regiment in early 2005 and was already working in Iraq, so Mattis decided that Nicholson, a Citadel graduate, would take Shupp's regiment and Shupp would get the 5th Marine Regiment, if and when he could return.

Mike and Sherrye Shupp spent several months fighting her cancer with chemo treatments and radiation. Miraculously, no surgeries were needed. By late summer the cancer was in remission and Sherrye was on the road to becoming a cancer survivor. Her recovery was so thorough that Colonel Shupp was able to return to Iraq on September 9.

---

1   The 1st Marine Regiment, in its purest form, would be comprised of 1st Battalion, 1st Marines; 2nd Battalion, 1st Marines; 3rd Battalion, 1st Marines; and several supporting units. But the modern-day Marine Corps combines battalions and capabilities, adding tanks, LAR, AMTRACS and artillery to form a Regimental Combat Team, or RCT-1 (see Appendix 1 – Order of Battle).

When he arrived, he thought he would be on staff for the rest of his tour in Iraq. Colonel Nicholson ran into Shupp on the 14th of September as they were both walking to Nicholson's change-of-command in Camp Fallujah. Until they met, Nicholson had not known that Shupp had returned to Iraq. He felt a little awkward as he prepared to take command of the regiment that was originally meant to be Shupps'. Nonetheless, as Shupp looked on, Nicholson assumed command of the 1st Marine Regiment.

Colonel John Toolan had served as the Regiment's commanding officer since relieving Colonel Joe Dowdy during the march to Baghdad. He had also been a central figure in Mattis' first assault on Fallujah. Toolan had tucked away a bottle of French wine for a special occasion. Since the drinking of alcoholic beverages was not permitted in Iraq, today seemed like a good time to pass the wine on to Colonel Nicholson. "Drink this on your last day in Iraq,"[2] Toolan told Nicholson as he handed him the bottle.

During the first fight in April, Camp Fallujah had been pummeled repeatedly with indirect fire. Rocket and mortar attacks continued randomly during the summer. After the change of command and a short celebration, Colonel Nicholson went to work in his new office. He placed the bottle of wine on a shelf and began to settle into his new command.

One of the first items on his agenda was to set up his computer with his passwords and email accounts. Nicholson asked Major Kevin Shea to send a Marine over to get his computer squared away. Shea was one of only a few Marines who had graduated from the Air Force Academy. At the time he was the Regiment's communications officer. Shea was a mountain of a man and a model Marine. He had played defensive end in college and, unlike many communication officers, was a consummate warrior. Shea offered to set up Nicholson's computer himself and sat down at Nicholson's desk to do so. The colonel was moving around to the side of the desk when a rocket screamed through the sandbagged window, hit Shea in the back, and slammed into the far wall.

Nicholson went down. So did his bottle of Bordeaux. The wine tumbled from its perch and bounced on the concrete floor—but did not break. Colonel Nicholson did not fare as well. Marines know that if they hear the explosion, they are going to be OK. Nicholson didn't hear a thing. He staggered around the office, bleeding profusely as the room filled with flame

---

2   BGen Larry Nicholson telephone interview, 3/10/08.

and smoke. He could smell the cordite and see exposed rebar and small fires igniting all around him.

It seemed like an eternity, but within seconds Marines appeared to pull the colonel from the destruction. Lieutenant Colonel Patrick Malay and Colonel Robert Coates had been standing outside the building when the rocket screamed in and exploded, knocking them to their knees. Malay and Coates rushed inside and headed for the point of impact—the Regimental Commander's office. The moment they entered the room they knew that Kevin Shay was beyond help. Bob Coates grabbed a pressure bandage and slapped it on Colonel Nicholson, who was phasing in and out of consciousness. He awoke again as he was being placed on a stretcher. As pain shot through his back and shoulder, he turned to Malay and the others and said, "I'll be back, damn it. I'll be back."[3]

Malay was not so sure. Looking at Nicholson's wounds, he thought to himself, "You'll be lucky if you live to see tomorrow."[4]

The morning after the rocket attack on Nicholson's office, Natonski told Shupp, "Pack up your gear; you're going to Fallujah to take command of your regiment."[5] Colonel Shupp moved from Camp Blue Diamond to Camp Fallujah and immediately assumed command of the 1st Marine Regiment, to include the 3rd Battalion, 1st Marines and 3rd Battalion, 5th Marines.

The 3rd Battalion of the 5th Marine Regiment, Darkhorse,[6] had recently started arriving in Iraq and was at full strength by the time Colonel Shupp assumed command of RCT-1. "Three-Five" was the most decorated battalion in the Marine Corps, with one of the most respected commanding officers.[7] Lieutenant Colonel Patrick Malay hails from a traditional western New York Irish-American family, one with a long heritage of military

---

3   Col Patrick Malay telephone interview, 10/5/07.

4   *Ibid.*

5   Col Mike Shupp telephone interview, 9/3/07.

6   Korean War call sign used by LtCol Robert D. Taplett, USMC when he was the 3rd Battalion, 5th Marines commander.

7   "I can't think of a more courageous war fighter of all the commanders out there." Colonel Mike Shupp during telephone interview, 9/3/07.

service. His great-uncle died in the trenches in World War I. His father and four uncles all served in the military at various times during World War II, Korea, and Vietnam. His three older brothers have also served, or continue to serve, their country in the Navy and Marine Corps. They are all cut from a similar bolt of cloth. Service to their country is an important tradition in the Malay family.

Pat Malay enlisted in the Marine Corps in May of 1981. Upon completion of recruit training at the Marine Corps Recruit Depot (MCRD) at Parris Island, South Carolina, he was assigned to I Company, 25th Marines, United States Marine Corps Reserves (USMCR) in Buffalo, New York. After earning his Bachelor's Degree in Sociology from the University of Buffalo in 1984, he was commissioned a Second Lieutenant via the Platoon Leaders Course. He has served in the infantry, the light armored infantry, and as a Recon Marine. He has instructed Marines in Military Operations in Urban Terrain (MOUT) and mountain-warfare techniques. The Darkhorse Marines would be hard-pressed to find a better battalion commander.

This was Colonel Malay's second tour in Iraq. He assumed command of 3/5 in the summer of 2003. Following the charge to Baghdad it moved into central Iraq to conduct what is known as Security and Stability Operations (SASO), and Malay became the military governor of Diwaniyah.

The province was relatively quiet, but it wasn't unusual to see the local civilians firing weapons into the sky during weddings and other celebrations. The gunfire was sparse and usually concentrated in a single point in the city. That changed on the day the people in the primarily Shia-inhabited city learned of the death of Saddam's sons, Uday and Qusay. Intense celebrations started immediately, and the first trickle of shooting into the air quickly increased to a volume of fire that Malay had never seen before. "If an airplane had flown over the city," explained Malay, "it would have been shot to pieces."[8] One Marine was hit by a falling bullet, and in the city scores of civilians were injured and some killed by rounds coming back to earth. As Malay watched the massive demonstration of celebratory gunfire emanating from Diwaniyah, he thought to himself that if that amount of fire were ever directed in anger at his Marines, the enemy would have shot the walls down and the Marines would have had everything they could do to

8   Col Patrick Malay telephone interview, 10/5/07.

get out of there alive. That night Malay thought to himself, "We have not seen the end of this yet."[9]

Haunted by images of Diwaniyah, Patrick Malay intently followed the rise in violence in Iraq. In early 2004, when he learned that his Marines would return to Iraq, he had a feeling in his gut that his next deployment was going to get ugly.

Malay immediately began to prepare for another fight. He wanted his Darkhorse Marines to be as ready as possible for what they would face. They trained from before dawn until after dark.

First, they concentrated on the basics: assault, security, and support. Malay believed in Ron Christmas' mantra that attention to detail would save lives in urban fighting. He stripped his infantry of their supporting arms, forcing them to train without machine guns, mortars, or rockets. Squad leaders prepared their Marines to fight as if they would be the only ones on the battlefield. They trained for combat as an independent team—no Marine would make an uncovered move or operate alone. The Marines worked day and night to hone their basic infantry skills, clearing jammed weapons, bandaging wounds, and sharpening their marksmanship.

Colonel Malay knew that the coming fight would be placed squarely on the shoulders of his infantry squads, so he initiated a qualification process for each of his squad leaders. He trained them, tested them, and hand-picked them. No one would lead a squad without first having proven his abilities to his peers and to Malay. Final approval came only after a personal interview.

The Marine Corps' training centers were strained to capacity when it came time to conduct MOUT training. In fact, the Darkhorse Marines could not even find a facility to conduct their urban warfare training. Ever resourceful, Pat Malay turned to Stu Segall Productions, San Diego's only full-service TV and movie studio.

Stu's studio had almost gone under after the 9/11 attacks when Hollywood producers decided they were no longer interested in producing "shoot-'em-up" pieces, which were Segall's specialty. Stu had special effects experts, actors, and make-up artists who were masters at simulating

9 *Ibid.*

violent explosions and wartime scenarios for the camera. Rather than perish after Al Qaeda's terror attacks on America, Stu Segall Productions reinvented itself.

It took some time, but Stu managed to attract the attention of the U.S. Drug Enforcement Agency (DEA). The DEA contracted with Stu to use his 20-acre facility as a training ground for its agents. Stu began by supporting search-and-arrest training for federal agents, but some of the DEA agents who trained at Stu's studio were also Marine Corps reservists. Colonel Malay heard about this TV studio-turned-training-ground through some of these Agent-Marines. As a result, Malay met with Segall and before long his Marines were attending training exercises on Stu's Mean Arab Street.

To the surprise of many, Stu's actors started out beating Malay's Marines in the faux urban fights. How could a handful of actors and truck drivers repeatedly win these firefights? The shock of actors defeating Marines could have caused a lesser leader than Malay to discontinue the exercises, but it only made the colonel and his staff stand up and take note. The Darkhorse Marines could learn much in this environment. Malay expanded the training at the studio, and everyone in the battalion was included.

Stu broke out his makeup artists and amputee-actors. He found Iraqi immigrants who lived in the San Diego area, and together they created Hyper-Realistic[10] environments in which the Marines had to deal with distressed civilians, gruesome casualties, and enemy fighters—all at the same time.

Some of the Marines did not do well under the pressure of the exercises; others excelled beyond expectations. Assignments were adjusted accordingly: Marines who excelled, such as Corporal Terrence van Doorn, were given additional responsibilities; those who didn't do as well were moved to tasks for which they were better suited.

Before long the Darkhorse Marines were running scenarios—and winning. They began moving through the urban environment on muscle memory. They dealt with insurgent fighters, civilians, and casualties in a professional manner. They adjusted to situational changes with little or no conversation, and the squads and fire teams worked in concert with only a nod or a hand gesture directing a change in focus.

10 Hyper-Realistic training is a phrase coined by Stu Segall Productions.

Stu Segall's facility provided the venue to hone Malay's Marines into a capable urban fighting force. The training psychologically prepared them for what they were going to see and do. Malay credits this training with saving uncounted Marine lives.

Having prepared as well as they could, the Marines of 3/5 returned to Iraq in September. Lead elements began arriving in Camp Fallujah on September 10, but most of the Marines left San Diego on 9/11.

Three of Malay's best Marines—Corporal Jason Arellano and Sergeants Elber Navarro and Jeffrey Kirk—together with many more, left loved ones behind to endure months of waiting and uncertainty. Kirk had recently married the love of his life, Navarro was leaving a young wife behind, and Arellano had a girlfriend he already knew he wanted to marry.

Arellano had mixed emotions about the pending deployment. When the call came that he was going back, Jason's mom told him, "I wish you wouldn't have to go anymore."[11] He hated worrying his mother and father, and he hated leaving Lindsey. But Jason was dedicated to his men and his job. As hard as it was for him to leave Lindsey and his family and for them to see him go, they understood that this was where Jason belonged. Prior to leaving, he recorded a home video with a farewell to his sweetheart. "This is it. I'll be leaving tomorrow. Goodbye. You know, I'm only going to be gone for a little bit. I'll see you sooner than you know."[12] Arellano turned his camera on his friend, Jason Clairday. Clairday was lying on his bunk in a T-shirt, fatigue pants, and boots. He looked into the camera and smiled, speaking to Lindsey. "Just want you to know you don't need to worry about Arellano." Clairday tapped his heart. "I've got him taken care of."[13]

Jason and his family were not alone. Sergeant Navarro had already started his own family. Saying goodbye to his young wife was the hardest thing he had ever done. Many more Darkhorse families braced for the jolt of their Marine's departure. Marines savored their final moments at home.

11 Sgt Jason Arellano telephone interview, 03/10/08.

12 Perfect Valor, 2009.

13 *Ibid.*

With a final hug and departing kiss, they turned and boarded the plane for the long flight that would carry them halfway around the world into harm's way. For some, this was their final farewell.

Arellano, Clairday, Kirk, Navarro, and all the Marines in Malay's battalion were in place by September 14. They quickly started relieving Lieutenant Colonel Gregg Olson's 2nd Battalion, 1st Marines, veterans of the first Fallujah fight. It was "game on" from day one for the Darkhorse Marines. They immediately assumed responsibility for TCP-1 and twenty-two miles of MSR MOBILE.

RCT–1's second main component was 3rd Battalion, 1st Marines. When it came to fighting in Iraq, the Thundering Third was the most experienced battalion in the Corps. It had suffered the first insurgent attack of the war on Faylaka Island in 2002, during which it lost Corporal Antonio Sledd.[14] When the invasion started in March 2003, the 3rd Battalion led the 1st Marine Regiment through Nasiriyah and on to Baghdad. After a short time back in the States, its members returned to Iraq in June of 2004. Lieutenant Colonel Willie Buhl, a stout history major, former enlisted Marine, Bronze Star recipient, and veteran of Desert Storm, commanded the Thundering Third.

Buhl's Marines began fighting the enemy in Eastern Anbar Province from the day they returned, and by the time of Operation Phantom Fury had been engaged in the counterinsurgent fight for five months. They had a huge sense of violence of action, as if they were single-handedly fighting this battle. "Every mission was conducted with full-force, hard-on, full combined arms," recalled one Marine tank officer. "They were very aggressive and very tough."[15]

The battalion worked very hard. Buhl's Marines developed a battle rhythm consisting of a full rotating schedule: they conducted their share of security operations and patrols; took time to rest; and continually trained to sharpen their fighting skills. They even built their own MOUT training

14 O'Donnell, *We Were One*," p. 24. Of the more than 4,000 service members who have lost their lives in Iraq, Antonio Sledd is the first on the list.

15 Maj Rob Bodisch telephone interview, 1/8/08.

ground in Camp Abu Ghraib. They were the best prepared for the coming fight, and they were by far the most experienced battalion in the Marine Corps.

Captain Brian Heatherman's Lima Company was stationed at Camp Abu Ghraib, a former Iraqi military camp located just east of the infamous prison; Captain Brett Clark's India Company and Captain Timothy Jent's Kilo Company were both at Camp DELTA, just south of the insurgent bedroom community of Karmah and three and one-half miles north of Camp Fallujah. Jent had been a Russian linguist as an enlisted Marine before he obtained his college degree at Texas A&M in 1996. Heatherman, a native of San Diego, hailed from a military family. He was one of only a few Marine officers to have graduated from the Army's Ranger School.

In addition to the two regular infantry battalions, RCT–1 included several, more specialized, components.

Light Armored Reconnaissance (LAR) units are unique to the Marine Corps. Their highly mobile amphibious Light Armored Vehicles (LAVs) pack a heavy punch with their 25mm Bushmaster automatic cannons. They are agile and deadly. During Desert Storm, Marines mounted in LAVs repelled Saddam's attack into Saudi Arabia near Khafji, defeated an Iraqi Mechanized Brigade in the Kuwaiti oilfields, and rolled through Kuwait International Airport. Lieutenant Colonel Eddie S. Ray's 2nd Light Armored Reconnaissance Battalion led the charge to Baghdad in 2003. The LAR was the perfect unit for working in the vast expanses of Anbar Province.

Lieutenant Colonel Steve Dinauer, a soft-spoken and methodical eighteen-year veteran of the Marine Corps, had served in a provisional rifle company from 8th and I during Operation Desert Storm and, like Natonski, had been working in the Pentagon when it was attacked on 9/11. He had taken command of the 3rd Light Armored Reconnaissance Battalion (Wolfpack) in July of 2003. By August of 2004 he was back on the ground in Kuwait preparing to move his Marines into Anbar Province. The Wolfpack moved into Iraq with RCT–7, to the far western reaches of Anbar Province. Their fast-moving, rapid-fire vehicles were ideal for use in the open desert.

As the Marines began to shuffle their resources in preparation for the fight in Fallujah, Dinauer started building an agile fighting force around elements of his LAR battalion: Task Force Wolfpack. His command element and a LAR company were chopped[16] from RCT–7 to RCT–1 along with an infantry company from 1st Battalion, 23rd Marines.

Natonski attached the 2nd Division's Small Craft Company to the Wolfpack. The Company Commander, Major Dan Wittnam, was a battle-hardened Marine who took care of his men, so much so that they would follow him to the gates of Hell. And on March 23, 2003, they did. Wittnam, at the time a Captain, had led Charlie Company, 1st Battalion, 2nd Marines through the streets of Nasiriyah to take the northern bridge. Although they encountered heavy resistance, they secured their objective and held it until they could be relieved hours later. They accomplished their mission but at a high cost, losing eighteen Marines to enemy and friendly fire.

Now Wittnam's new company ranged the Iraqi waterways in twenty Small Unit Riverine Craft (SURC). These were the modern-day version of the Vietnam-era riverboats. The SURCs were nearly forty feet long and 20,000 lbs, yet they had only a nine-inch draft. Each boat was powered by twin 440-hp waterjet engines that could propel the craft at speeds exceeding forty knots. [17] These powerful boats could also turn on a dime. In addition to being both fast and agile, they packed a powerful punch. Each boat had 240G and .50-caliber machine guns as well as MK-19 automatic grenade launchers. Some even carried the GAU-17, 7.62mm mini-gun. In addition to all this, each boat could transport sixteen battle-ready Marines.

Juan Rubio joined the Navy in 1999. By 9/11 he was working as a junior corpsman at Bethesda Naval Hospital. Rubio had been trained as a member of one of four critical care teams, ready to respond to any emergency. Early on the morning of the September attack, Rubio was called into a meeting and told that a plane had hit the Pentagon and that he would be part of a medical team dispatched to the site. Members of two emergency response teams gathered their equipment and were hustled onto a waiting Coast Guard helicopter to be flown to the Pentagon.

---

16 Short for Change of Operational Control. When a military unit is shifted from its parent command, it is said to be 'chopped' to a new command.

17 1 knot = 1.151 miles per hour.

Rubio arrived within two hours of the attack. When he stepped off the helicopter he found an unimaginable scene. Smoke was rolling out of the huge building and the parking lot was swarming with emergency workers and dazed victims. To Rubio it looked like the ultimate emergency assistance drill. The medical teams were working like a well-oiled machine, and Rubio and his team immediately joined in.

After the casualties were transported, Rubio returned to Bethesda, then was sent on to the hospital ship USNS *Comfort*, which was dispatched to New York City to aid the victims of the most deadly attack in the history of our country. Rubio quickly realized that there would be no injured to care for. Once ashore, he found himself standing in front of a seemingly endless wall of photographs. That wall changed his life. Rubio stood transfixed, gazing at photos of sons, daughters, husbands, wives, mothers, and fathers. A block-long collage of fearful messages left by loved ones hoping that their family member would be found. A chill brushed his soul. He knew these people would not be found alive.

Rubio also knew that the world would never be the same, and that he would be needed to care for the servicemen who would be wounded in the coming fight. He vowed then and there to become a Marine Corpsman. By March of 2003 Rubio was humping it with his Marines through the muddy streets of eastern Nasiriyah. He fought with Task Force Tarawa's 1st Battalion, 2nd Marines in Bravo Company.

While he was caring for wounded Marines in Iraq, Rubio's estranged wife was filing for full custody of their two children. Rubio's company commander interceded and petitioned the court to postpone the legal proceedings until Rubio could return to Texas from his overseas deployment. When he eventually made it back to the United States, Rubio was faced with another battle against his ex-wife's attempt to take his children away from him.

When Rubio returned to Camp Lejeune, he heard that the Marines were putting together a company of small boats to go to Iraq. The unique assignment intrigued him, but he was not willing to volunteer until he heard that Dan Wittnam would be the CO. He knew Wittnam from Nasiriyah, so he sought out his chief to request the assignment.

"Do you have any idea what you are volunteering for?" Chief Reynolds asked.

"If Captain Wittnam's name is on it, I want to be there," Rubio declared. "This man is awesome!"[18] Rubio reported to the Small Craft Company at 0630 the next morning.

At the Small Craft Company, most of the Marines were in their teens or early twenties. They looked up to Rubio, who was thirty-one, as an older brother. One of those Marines was nineteen-year-old Lance Corporal Brian P. Parrello. Rubio and Parrello hit it off from the start, even though they were from very different backgrounds: Parrello grew up in West Milford, New Jersey, while Rubio was from San Angelo, Texas. But Rubio and Parrello had one thing in common: Parrello also decided on 9/11 to join the Marines, though he was only a sophomore in high school when our country was attacked.

Brian grew up in the shadow of his popular twin brothers, desperately searching for his own identity during high school. He wanted to be the best at everything he did and wanted to make a difference. He dreaded the thought of a long and meaningless life of mediocrity. He wanted to prove himself, and he wanted to do it quickly. So he volunteered for the Marines in February 2003 and his dreams quickly came true. Everyone doted on him, commenting how proud they were of him for volunteering to go off to fight instead of attending college like his older brothers. He started his active duty on September 22, 2003, three months after his high school graduation.

Brian Parrello would indeed make a difference early in his life: he was a Marine. Captain Wittnam's Small Craft Company was his first duty assignment.

The Seventh Marine Regiment: RCT-7

Colonel Craig Tucker, a big man and a hard Marine, was a graduate of the School for Advanced Military Studies (SAMS), one of the Marine Corps' best tacticians, and a veteran of Operation Vigilant Resolve.[19] When Natonski arrived Tucker was already in command of RCT–7, which was responsible for patrolling Iraq's Wild West. The 7th Marines[20] were

18 HM2 Juan Rubio telephone interview, 11/15/07.

19 General Mattis' first fight in Fallujah in April 2004.

20 See Appendix 1, Order of Battle, for RCT-7's composition.

home-based in Twentynine Palms, California, and were familiar with living, working, and fighting in the desert. They were perfectly suited for their assignment in al Anbar's barren western frontier. They had fought in Desert Storm as an infantry task force, breaching the Saddam Line in southern Kuwait as Task Force Ripper. Colonel Tucker proudly maintained the distinction gained in Desert Storm, carrying the radio call sign Ripper 6.

RCT–7 was based out west at al Asad Airbase. The Regiment was responsible for route and border security all the way to the Syrian and Jordanian frontiers. First Battalion, 7th Marines was stationed along the Syrian border; First Battalion, 23rd Marines, a reserve infantry battalion from Texas, was stationed in Hit, Iraq; Lieutenant Colonel Gareth (Gary) Brandl's 1st Battalion, 8th Marines was working in and around Haditha.

One-Eight had been chopped from Camp Lejeune's 2nd Marine Division. Brandl, a longtime friend of Willie Buhl, commanded the only East Coast Marine battalion in Natonski's assault force. Brandl was an imposing figure—intense, focused, and a man who rarely cracked a smile. As the commanding officer, he maintained a distance from his subordinates and men, leaving his XO,[21] Major Mark Winn, to handle the personal aspects of command. Brandl, a native of Passaic, New Jersey, loved the outdoors and, like George Bristol, Natonski's G-2, was an avid hunter—so much so that he had named his daughter Remington, and had taken the radio call sign Hunter 6.

Like most Marine battalions, the 1st Battalion, 8th Marines has a storied lineage. It fought from Guadalcanal to Iwo Jima in World War II and was garrisoned in the Beirut barracks that was bombed on October 23, 1983. Some consider the Marine Corps barracks bombing the actual beginning of our current war on terror. The Marines of 1/8 certainly do: 220 Marines, fifteen sailors, three soldiers and a Lebanese custodian were killed in that attack.[22] Brandl and his Marines viewed the upcoming fight as their opportunity to strike back for their fallen comrades.

---

21 Executive officer.

22 Jadick, *On Call in Hell*, p. 4

Tucker needed to leave 1st Battalion, 7th Marines and 1st Battalion, 23rd Marines out west, and he needed another infantry battalion for the assault on Fallujah. When Colonel Lee Miller and the 31st Marine Expeditionary Unit (MEU) arrived in Kuwait in September, Miller's Marines became part of the gathering storm. Lee Miller and his MEU command group relieved Craig Tucker in the west; Miller chopped his Battalion Landing Team (BLT), 1st Battalion, 3rd Marines, over to RCT–7.

The Hawaii-based Marines of 1/3 made their way from Kuwait to Camp Fallujah, arriving by the 19th of October. Lieutenant Colonel Michael Ramos, a veteran of Somalia, was an intelligent commander but not generally open to discussion or suggestions on how his battalion should be run. Coming from a West coast MEU, Colonel Ramos had little opportunity to train his Hawaii Marines in MOUT warfare or prepare for the coming assault on Fallujah. As a result, the Marines of 1/3 would enter the fight as the least experienced of the four Marine infantry battalions. But what they lacked in experience they made up for with enthusiasm; they were almost too eager to get into the fight.

Once Lee Miller settled into and assumed command of the western AO, Colonel Tucker moved his RCT–7 command element from al Asad to Camp Fallujah on October 21st, leaving most of his Marines in place. Two days later, Gary Brandl joined Tucker with all of 1/8.

Colonel Ron Johnson's 24th MEU (BLT 1/2) and the British Black Watch were moved in to protect the main supply routes east and south of Fallujah, thereby freeing up 3rd Battalion, 1st Marines and 3rd Battalion, 5th Marines to become part of Natonski's attack force.

Colonel Gary Patton's 2nd Brigade Combat Team of the U.S. Army's 2nd Infantry Division continued to have responsibility for Ramadi, Anbar's provincial capital and the second most violent city in Iraq. Second Battalion, Fifth Marines was under Patton's command. The battalion maintained a presence in Ramadi at Hurricane Point on the west side of town and at a small, company-sized Combat Out Post (COP) on the east side of Ramadi. Patton's 1st Battalion (Air Assault), 503rd Infantry Regiment (1-503) held the Shark's Fin west of Fallujah, and 1st Battalion (Air Assault), 506th Infantry Regiment (1-506) was responsible for security in Habbaniyah and the surrounding area.

General Natonski's two main Marine Regimental Combat Teams and their associated elements were now assembled and in place. But even with four reinforced infantry battalions and a Light Armored Reconnaissance Battalion at his disposal, Natonski needed more forces to accomplish the mission of clearing Fallujah and returning peace and security to the city. He needed heavy armor to punch through the enemy's defenses, more manpower to cordon the entire urban area, and Iraqi forces to take over the responsibility of maintaining security once the battle ended. He would have to reach out beyond the Marines Corps to the U.S. and Iraqi Armies to finish assembling his force.

Chapter 4

Task Force Blue Diamond

"The future is not the 'son of Desert Storm,' but the
stepchild of Somalia and Chechnya."

— General Charles C. Krulak, USMC

Welcome to Fallujah

Ever since the Marines' arrival in March, they had been building up
Camp Fallujah. In response, the enemy had been fortifying the entire eastern
edge of the city. This "Al Qaeda Maginot Line,"[1] as one officer described it,
faced eastward toward the Marines in Camp Fallujah. By October, Fallujah
had become an armed camp, with hundreds of prepared fighting positions,
most oriented toward TCP-1 and Camp Fallujah in the east. "They had
mined it, they had booby trapped it, they had rockets that literally lined the
roofs of the buildings," remembered one eyewitness.[2] It was impossible for
the Marines to enter Fallujah without the use of massive force.

---

1 Matt Matthews, interview with LTC Peter A. Newell, Operational Leadership
Experiences, Combat Studies Institute, Fort Leavenworth, Kansas, p. 6.

2 *Ibid.*

If anywhere could be considered the front line, it was MSR MOBILE at the eastern edge of the city. The terrain around TCP-1 was a killing field. TCP-1 was a small bunkered firebase, built from HESCO[33] barriers by John Toolan's Marines just west of the Cloverleaf. Pat Malay had assigned a platoon of Marines and a section of tanks to man the outpost around the clock. The enemy continually shot at the Marines with big rockets, little rockets, and mortars. There were periodic ground assaults against the strongpoint and sporadic yet persistent sniper fire. This was a no-shit war zone.

New insurgent recruits moved to the eastern side of the city to get their first taste of combat. If they survived the encounter with Darkhorse, they were sent to other parts of the city to dig in. Marine tankers repelled attack after attack. They killed enemy insurgents on a daily basis with devastating accuracy at unbelievable distances. Before long, they called their main guns "120mm sniper rifles."

TCP-1 may have been the focal point, but the entire eastern side of the city was a shooting gallery. Any vehicle attempting to drive MSR MOBILE from the Cloverleaf to the northern edge of the city came under fire from enemy gunners perched in the buildings at the edge of the city. The Marines bulldozed a dirt road east of the elevated main supply route to counter the danger. The gravel road, named the Military Bypass, lay in defilade behind the raised highway.

The Plan

The Fallujah attack plan started to gel as more details fell into place. Task Force Wolfpack would open the attack at sunset on the 7th of November. A lightning advance up the western peninsula would deny the enemy's flank, and would include an assault on the hospital and National Guard barracks west of town. With this stone Colonel Shupp could kill many birds: Lieutenant Colonel Dinauer would silence an enemy propaganda machine inside the hospital and deny the enemy the two bridges as routes for

---

3   HESCO barriers, named after the British company that manufactures them, are made of a collapsible wire-mesh container and a heavy-duty fabric liner. Easily erected and then filled with sand, they provide semi-permanent protection against small-arms fire and shrapnel.

retreat or reinforcement—all the while conducting a convincing diversion to the real assault.

The rest of the 1st Marine Division would attack Fallujah twenty-four hours later at H Hour (1900) on D+1 (November 8, 2004) from the north to destroy Anti-Iraqi Forces (AIF) in Fallujah. Natonski, L'Etiole, and Bristol wanted their infantry to penetrate quickly and get behind the string of barricades and IEDs at the edge of the city. The planners reasoned that a quick thrust down the eastern edge of Fallujah and another splitting the city in half would upset the enemy's command-and-control and dislocate any coordinated defense. They knew this move would disorient the individual combatants and demoralize most of the enemy. The Marines wanted to knock the enemy off balance and keep them disoriented, unable to regroup to stand and fight in large numbers.

Speed was of the essence. If the Marines could quickly get behind the enemy's outer barricades and IED-laced streets, the grunts on the ground would have a much easier time of it. To accomplish this, the point of the spear needed to be armor. The lead vehicles needed to be able to take a hit because they were going to draw intense fire.

On the other hand, achieving surprise would be difficult. With the majority of the 1st Marine Division converging on Fallujah, the enemy knew that an attack was coming. What they didn't know was where and when the Marines would attack.

Colonel Shupp's RCT–1 would attack in the northwest as Natonski's main effort.[4] Everyone believed that the enemy's core was located in the Jolan District in northwest Fallujah; Three-One and Three-Five would slug their way through the narrow streets of that byzantine neighborhood. Tucker's RCT–7, meanwhile, would sweep south through the less dense and more modern eastern neighborhoods. Tucker's main effort would be a north-to-south attack with two initial objectives: Brandl's Marines would

---

4 The Marine Corps Doctrinal Publication 1 – *Warfighting* defines the "main effort" as an important tool for providing unity and then goes on to require the commander to recognize the "single most critical effort to success at any given moment. The *unit* assigned responsibility for accomplishing this key mission is designated as the main effort—the focal point upon which converges the combat power of the force. The main effort receives priority for support of any kind. It becomes clear to all other units in the command that they must support that unit in the accomplishment of its mission…the main effort becomes a harmonizing force for subordinate initiative. Faced with a decision, we ask ourselves: *How can I best support the main effort?*

first secure the Hydra Mosque before moving south to take the Government Center along MSR MICHIGAN, thus splitting the northern half of the city in two; One-Three would assault on the eastern side of Fallujah.

Everyone knew that back-clearing would be necessary after the initial push into the city. In other words, the Marines would have a 360-degree fight. But the two regimental commanders couldn't have had a more different take on how they should deal with the enemy in their portions of the city. Tucker planned to move fast and capture his key objectives quickly. His Regimental Combat Team would intentionally bypass buildings and enemy fighters. In contrast, Colonel Shupp planned a deliberate sweep through the Jolan. RCT-1 would attempt to clear house-to-house from the opening moments of the fight. Shupp and his staff did not believe they could just focus on the objectives, which were nothing more than physical terrain features with suspected enemy activity. The focus of this fight had to be the enemy, and the enemy had to be destroyed to prevent them from destabilizing Al Anbar Province. They were the heart of the fight.

Bring in the Army - Plus

It had been clear from early on that Natonski would need additional forces. The Marines needed help in isolating the entire Fallujah battlefield, and they needed heavy units to lead the assault. They knew that they were at least a Brigade Combat Team (BCT) short in Anbar Province. At best, the Marines would be able to muster only two dozen tanks to share among four infantry battalions and Task Force Wolfpack. "[We] were clearly short of Armor," explained LtCol L'Etiole.[5] General Natonski turned to General Sattler for help. "I need Army. . . . We need a mech battalion—two mech battalions—to lead the attack, and we need an Army Cav unit to seal the south."[6]

There had been a recent American change in focus, structure, and command in Baghdad. Up until the summer of 2004, Lieutenant General Ricardo Sanchez had led the Coalition Joint Task Force 7 (CJTF–7) alongside career diplomat Lewis Paul Bremer. Responsibility for operations

---

5   LtCol Joe L'Etiole telephone interview, 10/27/07.

6   LtGen Richard Natonski telephone interview, 10/11/07.

in Iraq was divided between the Departments of Defense and State. When it became clear that this arrangement was not working, Sanchez, Bremer, and the U.S. Army's V Corps were all brought home.

In their place, Army Lieutenant General Thomas F. Metz' III Corps— The Phantom Corps—deployed to Iraq, and Army General George Casey was sent to lead the entire effort. General Casey became the first Multi-National Force–Iraq (MNF-I) Commanding General and Metz assumed the title of Multi-National Corps–Iraq (MNC-I) Commanding General.

Sattler had worked with Metz in the past and they were good friends. With Natonski at his side, Sattler turned to General Metz and asked for three Army battalions to support the Fallujah operation. General Metz leaned across the table and looked Sattler in the eye.

"You can't have them," he replied before pausing for effect. "You'll take a brigade HQ[7] and five [battalions]."[8]

Sattler would take all the help he could get. "Can we have 2-7?"

Lieutenant Colonel James Rainey's 2-7 Cavalry had fought with the Marines in Najaf only months before. The Marines were very impressed with Rainey's troopers and tankers. Sattler knew that Rainey's tanks and Bradleys could provide the armored punch the Marines would need in the deadly urban environment.

The Army doesn't work that way, Metz replied. Sattler would have to define the capabilities he needed to accomplish the mission, and the Army would determine the best unit to fill the requirement.

"OK," Sattler clarified, "we need two armored battalions with the capabilities of 2nd Battalion, 7th Cavalry Regiment."

Metz winked. "I got it."[9]

The general issued orders for 2-7 and the First Infantry Division's 2nd Battalion, 2nd Infantry Regiment to be chopped to the 1st Marine Division, which now became Task Force Blue Diamond. To further bolster Natonski's force, Metz also provided the Black Jack Brigade—1st Cavalry Division's 2nd Brigade Combat Team. The brigade brought to the fight the 1st Battalion, 5th Cavalry; 1st Battalion, 5th Infantry; and the 759th Military

7 Headquarters.

8 LTG Thomas Metz personal interview, 5/20/08.

9 LTG Thomas Metz personal interview, 5/20/08.

Police Battalion. The upcoming battle would be a joint affair: the Army, Navy, Air Force, and Marines would all fight side-by-side for victory in Fallujah.

Natonski could now wield a giant hammer onto an iron anvil. Led by two Army armored task forces, the Marines' RCT–1 and –7 would hammer the enemy in the north onto Colonel Michael Formica's Black Jack Brigade anvil pushing up from the south and east. Marines and soldiers would sweep from north to south, pinning the enemy against an impenetrable joint Army-Marine screen.

The Fight for Hearts and Minds

Warfare in the 21st century is not limited to kinetic operations. Everyone in the American command knew the importance of winning the IO fight, too. No one wanted a protracted period of high-intensity combat, so the rules of engagement were meticulously developed. At first, the rules hampered the regimental and battalion commanders, who would have to get clearance to attack known targets in the city. These limitations were intentional because the Multi-National Corps wanted early restraint. Its commanders wanted the Marines to stay well below the IO threshold. Natonski and Sattler also wanted to give civilians time to flee the city before the Americans unleashed their onslaught. This time, the enemy would not be given the opportunity to claim that the Americans were intentionally killing innocent civilians. "Do not fire until fired upon by the enemy" became the first rule of engagement.

Unlike Vigilant Resolve, Operation Phantom Fury would be conducted like a cancer surgery: Task Force Blue Diamond would rid the city of the enemy while limiting the amount of damage to the infrastructure. As a result, another rule of engagement was developed: "Employ progression of force." Natonski did not want his Marines calling in an artillery barrage to level a city block just because they received a single potshot from a window. Every commander was instructed to try to use appropriate force to deal with a threat and escalate to their heavier weapons only when absolutely necessary.

General Natonski put it this way:

> As you prepare for the fighting ahead, remember to set your sights on the rebuilding that will follow. As this Division has done many times before, we will shift our focus to civil affairs and humanitarian assistance even while desperate pockets of insurgency remain in the city. I am well aware

that to "do no harm" entails the assumption of personal risk. I have complete confidence that you and your Marines and soldiers will know how and when to switch off the killing instinct while limiting collateral damage to the greatest extent possible.[10]

Finally, Natonski wanted to sweep through the city quickly to minimize the duration of violent action. "We did not want a prolonged battle," was how he explained it later.[11] Instead, he wanted to get the attack over as soon as possible, as if yanking off a Band-Aid instead of peeling it slowly away from the skin. Orders were issued to engage all squad-sized enemy units and above, but to bypass individuals or groups of two or three.

The commanders did everything they could to make sure that Operation Phantom Fury would be anything but a fair fight. Task Force Blue Diamond had grown into a formidable fighting force made up of two Marine Regimental Combat Teams, two Army Brigade Combat Teams, two Marine Expeditionary Units, two Army mechanized battalions, the Army's first Stryker battalion, Navy SEALS, Army Green Berets, and Air Force tactical air control teams. Natonski and his staff had planned a "techno-blitz" to be followed by brute-force door-to-door fighting. The enemy would be ejected from Fallujah with GPS-guided bombs, UAVs, AC-130 gunships, Harrier jump jets, Apache, Kiowa, and Cobra attack helicopters, M1 tanks, Bradley fighting vehicles, Marine Light Armored Vehicles, D9 bulldozers, 155mm artillery, and digitally controlled, GPS-oriented, 120mm mortars.

Even with all of these tools in his toolbox, Natonski knew that the battle would boil down to a house-to-house fight, and that his soldiers, sailors, and Marines would have to clear every one of the 50,000 buildings in the city. All of the technology in the world couldn't guarantee what his troops would find behind the next locked door. American casualties could be horrific— and as high as thirty to forty percent.

10 MajGen Richard F. Natonski's letter to the leaders of the 1st Marine Division, November, 2004.

11 LtGen Richard Natonski telephone interview, 10/11/07.

A Joint Operation: "Some Assembly Required"

Preparation for a battle of this magnitude was no small affair. The Multi-National Corps, the Marine Expeditionary Force, the Marine Air Wing, and the 1st Marine Division were all involved in the planning in one form or another. Forces were drawn from all across Iraq, and others were shifted to fill vacuums left by units headed toward the fight. The Army's 1st Cavalry as well as the 1st and 2nd Infantry Divisions all became involved. While the MEF and 1st MARDIV built the assault plans, other headquarters labored to break units free to support the fight while continuing to maintain the security in their own areas of responsibility. If Operation Phantom Fury degenerated into a national "whack-a-mole" match, General Metz wanted to be able to thump anyone who popped up—hard and fast. At the very least, every unit throughout Iraq would be on alert.

Unit commanders converged on Fallujah from all over the theater. The 1st Cavalry Division sent Colonel Michael Formica, commander of the Black Jack Brigade. When he arrived he told General Dunford, "I'm here, and we will help in any way we can."[12]

Colonel Gary Patton did the same thing, offering up some of his 2nd Infantry Division soldiers.[13] The Division's 2nd Brigade Combat Team had recently arrived from a decade-long commitment in the Demilitarized Zone (DMZ) in Korea. Colonel Patton eagerly provided a mechanized company team with fourteen Bradleys and four M1 tanks to Task Force Wolfpack—even though his brigade still had its hands full in Ramadi.

The 1st Infantry Division sent Lieutenant Colonel Peter Newell's 2nd Battalion, 2nd Infantry Regiment. 2-2 would reinforce RCT–7 as the third, tank-heavy, mechanized infantry battalion, providing Colonel Tucker with

---

12 BGen Joseph Dunford telephone interview, 11/16/07.

13 The 2nd Infantry Division's soldiers have a special place in their hearts for the Marines. General John A. Lejeune had commanded the 2nd Infantry Division when his Marines fought under the division's Indian Head banner at Belleau Wood in World War I. It was there that the Germans labeled Lejeune's Marines "*Devil Dogs*" for their ferocious determination in battle.

the heavy punch he needed for rapid penetration into the city. Newell was an unflappable commander with steely blue eyes and a disarming smile. His experience as a former Ranger and longtime infantry officer was perfectly suited for the coming fight.

As his soldiers were preparing to become part of the Fallujah assault force, Newell approached his brigade commander, Colonel Dana Pittard, with an unusual request. Mine Clearing Line Charges (MICLICs) are used to clear breach lanes through minefields. A MICLIC is basically a 350-foot-long tube of C-4 explosives. A 5-inch rocket pulls the explosive cable out of its storage trailer onto the minefield. Once the explosive is pulled taut, engineers ignite the 1,750 pounds of C-4, detonating any mines nearby. A single MICLIC will clear a strip 300 feet long and 25 feet wide. While they are effective against enemy minefields, they are anything but guided weapons; you sort of point them and hope they go in the right direction. A MICLIC is like an explosive rope attached to a giant bottle rocket.

Newell saw Fallujah's IED-laced city streets as just another minefield. He wanted to precede his attack into the city with a MICLIC shot down the main thoroughfare. A MICLIC explosion on a city street would be like shooting an M1 main gun down a supermarket aisle: the over-pressure would destroy any IEDs on the avenue, and scare the shit out of anyone it didn't kill or knock silly. Newell thought the benefits of using MICLICs in an urban environment far exceeded the risks. Pittard agreed and approved Newell's request.[14]

The Army's 7th Cavalry Regiment, once commanded by Colonel George Custer, today is part of the famous 1st Cavalry Division—The First Team. 1st Battalion, 7th Cavalry, reinforced by 2nd Battalion, 7th Cavalry, had been the first to fight in Vietnam under Lieutenant Colonel Hal Moore at LZ X-ray in the Ia Drang Valley in November 1965.[15] Now, 2-7 would provide the main effort to RCT–1's main effort by leading the assault into the heart of Fallujah with a classic armored penetration.

The modern-day 2-7 CAV is a mechanized infantry battalion, in this case made even more powerful when the battalion commander added a tank company to build an armor-heavy Task Force. Task Force 2-7 was

14 LTC Peter Newell CSI Interview, p. 6.

15 The fight at Ia Drang was dramatized in the major motion picture We Were Soldiers (2002.)

completely mechanized, made up of the Army's most modern M1A2 tanks and Bradley fighting vehicles. Its soldiers could roll through the fight without ever having to leave their vehicles. They were an unstoppable armored juggernaut and exactly what was needed to lead the charge through the streets of Fallujah.

Lieutenant Colonel James Rainey was the task force commander. He had been a paratrooper, Ranger, and cavalry trooper. Rainey started his military career as an infantryman before switching to command mechanized units. He, too, was a graduate of the School of Advanced Military Studies (SAMS). The school, along with the School of Advanced Warfighting, provides a postgraduate education in the art and science of war to America's finest military officers. These schools bring officers from all the services together to learn the same tactics and, more importantly, to learn how to "talk the same language." Graduates of SAMS are proudly dubbed "Jedi Knights." When asked, Lieutenant Colonel Rainey's operations officer, Major Tim Karcher, also a SAMS graduate, downplayed his "Jedi Knight" status ("We can use a laser pointer better than most").[16] Jokes notwithstanding, Rainey and Karcher were among America's most highly qualified commanders.

In recent months, Rainey and Karcher had perfected the mechanized urban fight. Rainey viewed his job as a manager of chaos. "My job was to synchronize," he explained.[17] He worked hard to give good, clear, task-and-purpose orders to his company commanders and then stood back. Once the fighting started, he would monitor the action and try to minimize the fog and friction so that his soldiers could focus on killing the enemy. Rainey understood that his job would be to give his commanders the information and resources they needed to run their companies. After that, he would let them do their jobs.

Colonel Michael Formica's Black Jack Brigade of the 1st Cavalry Division had fought the pivotal battle in the Wadi al-Batin during Operation Desert Storm[18] and did not return to Iraq until January of 2004. In the middle of October they were told that they would be extended. Most everyone in the

16 LTC Tim Karcher telephone interview, 2/15/08.

17 COL Jim Rainey telephone interview, 11/7/07.

18 Lowry, *The Gulf War Chronicles*, p. 121.

brigade believed the extension would last until after the January elections. They did not anticipate being called in to help the Marines at Fallujah.

Formica started planning to move his entire Brigade Combat Team to Fallujah as soon as the call came down. The 1st CAV Division Commander told Formica, "Take artillery and Apaches too."[19] Formica asked Colonel James McConville, the commander of 1st Cavalry Aviation Brigade, to contribute aviation assets. "I will make sure you have four aircraft around the clock to take care of you," McConville assured his close friend. Lieutenant Colonel Ron Lewis, Attack 6, would be the one tasked with making good on McConville's promise. Formica also chopped a Paladin battery, with its supporting counter-battery RADAR, to the growing force.

Natonski now commanded units from the Army's 1st and 2nd Infantry as well as the 1st Cavalry Division, and every division in the Marine Corps.

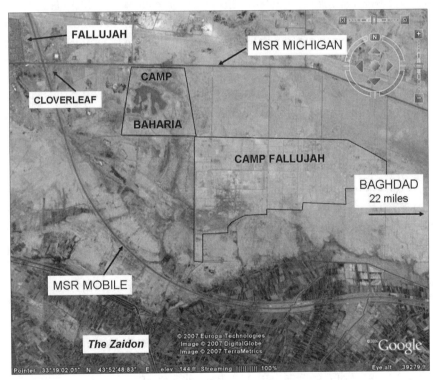

Camps Fallujah and Baharia

---

19 Col. Michael Formica telephone interview, 11/06/08.

They hailed from Kansas, Korea, Texas, and every stateside Marine facility from Camp Lejeune to Twentynine Palms. The integration of Army and Marine units was seamless. There were Army units embedded in Marine units, and Marine units embedded in Army units. There were Navy SEALS, corpsmen, and chaplains, and Air Force dog, combat-camera, and ground-control teams, along with nearly every aircraft in the U.S. military's inventory.

For the first time since the 2003 invasion, a significant number of Iraqi forces were involved in the operation.

Abdul Qadir was one of the first Iraqi officers to rejoin the new Iraqi Army. He had been one of the few Shiite senior leaders in Saddam Hussein's army. Now, as a two-star general, he commanded the Iraqi forces attached to Task Force Blue Diamond. He led five battalions from the rejuvenated Iraqi 1st Army Division. Some had fought the American onslaught in Desert Storm and others had faced General Natonski in 2003 at Nasiriyah. Now these soldiers (most of them, anyway) were extremely proud to be fighting alongside United States Marines.

The Iraqi forces were evenly distributed among the Marine line battalions. 36 Commando went to Task Force Wolfpack. It was made up mostly of Kurdish soldiers who were very competent and had excellent Special Forces leadership. Recently they had distinguished themselves in their limited participation in the summertime fight in Najaf. Each of the other Marine infantry battalions received three companies of Iraqi soldiers. 3rd Battalion, 1st Marines and 3rd Battalion, 5th Marines each had a battalion of Iraqi National Guard attached to them, while 1/3 got a battalion of Iraqi Army infantrymen.

When 3/1 arrived in country, Camp Abu Ghraib and Camp DELTA both had a company of Iraqi National Guard forces. The two companies could not have been more different. India Company, 1st Battalion of the Iraqi National Guard (ING) was based at Camp Abu Ghraib, in Nassir Wa Salam. They were primarily Shiites who had been transplanted from the south to work in the granaries and steel mills. Many had family members who had been imprisoned in Abu Ghraib during Saddam's reign. They hated the old regime and were eager to assist Buhl and his Marines. The Marines assigned a Combined Action Platoon[20] (CAP INDIA) to train and mentor the Iraqi soldiers from the time they arrived in the province. These Iraqi soldiers would prove themselves to be an effective resource in the coming fight.

On the other hand, Buhl had the second Iraqi National Guard company, based north of Fallujah at Camp DELTA in Karmah. These Iraqi National Guardsmen were all Sunni. These guys were completely different. At best they were completely undependable. Often they cooperated with the enemy. At worst, they were a threat to the Marines.

Natonski and his staff had established their strategy, planned the campaign, designed the force structure, and assigned the most varied joint and capable array of forces they could assemble. Now it was time to put it all to the test.

Not wishing to show his hand, General Natonski ordered his forces to begin congregating within Camp Fallujah and the adjacent Camp Baharia. Camp Fallujah had been a military base during Saddam's reign. Before the 2003 invasion, Saddam's sons Uday and Qusay had used Baharia as a lakeside getaway. On the west side of Fallujah, Task Force Wolfpack would bivouac outside Habbaniyah; ten miles west of the Shark's Fin.

When the Marines moved into Anbar, they adopted an Arabic phrase for their new camp: Mushaat al-Baharia, whose loose translation is "walkers of the navy," or naval infantry—i.e., Marines. The new camp name symbolized a new day in Iraq. The Marines had landed, and they were in control.

---

20 Combined Action Platoons were first employed at the end of the Vietnam War. They were quite effective at helping the Vietnamese maintain security in small villages across the countryside.

Chapter 5

Phase I: "Ready, Set..."

"It's hard to hide a mechanized battalion."

— Colonel Jim Rainey, USA, November 7, 2007

Modern Warfare—And Not So Modern

In the coming fight for Fallujah, there would be no reliance on a 20th-century, win-from-the-sky mentality. Instead, Generals Sattler, Natonski, and the Marine Air Wing Commander, Major General Keith Stalder, had embraced the boots-on-the-ground-but-support-from-the-sky, Marine MAGTF mantra. The plan was to overwhelm the enemy in a three-dimensional blitzkrieg.

Air Force, Navy, and Marine fixed-wing aircraft would loiter in holding patterns 18,000 feet above the city, waiting for a call to drop their deadly GPS-guided bombs onto unsuspecting enemy fighters. Marine AV8 Harriers would orbit at 13,000 feet, waiting to support Marines on the ground. Air Force AC-130 gunships from their Special Operations Squadron would circle at 10,000 feet every night. Unmanned Aerial Vehicles would buzz over the city, flying between 1,500 and 6,000 feet, watching and reporting the enemy's every move. US Army Kiowa, Apache, and Marine Cobra helicopters would provide scouting and close air support below 1,500 feet.

While Colonel Formica's soldiers and Marines isolated the battlefield, Natonski would pulverize the enemy on the ground with two unstoppable armored thrusts deep into the city, followed by the relentless onslaught of four Marine infantry battalions. The Iraqi Army and National Guard units would fill in behind the Marine infantry to hold captured ground and conduct more searches for stragglers and weapons.

As part of their preparation, the Marines exposed and destroyed as many command-and-control nodes and defensive fortifications as Metz' IO threshold would allow. These actions heightened the state of paranoia and anxiety within the enemy's rank and file. In addition, they tried very hard to confuse the enemy in an effort to keep the insurgents guessing as to where the actual attack would be launched.

The Marines also succeeded in driving a wedge between the anti-Iraqi forces and the local populace, convincing the majority of the civilians to leave the city. Everyone who could do so locked up their shops and homes and fled. As families streamed out of the besieged city, word leaked out of the insurgents' reign of terror inside Fallujah. Civilians were being beaten and beheaded for the most innocent of offenses. Thugs commandeered homes, businesses, food, and vehicles. Zarqawi and his Al Qaeda hoodlums had seized an entire neighborhood in the southern reaches of the city. Anyone who resisted was dragged off and beaten or killed on the spot.

Containment

Formica viewed his assignment of isolating Fallujah as a classic cavalry mission—a guard operation to protect the main body. The Black Jack Brigade had two tasks. First, to provide freedom of maneuver for the Marines, and second, to prevent the enemy from entering or leaving Fallujah. Now that most of the civilians had left the city, the Black Jack Brigade could move in. From that point forward, no one would be allowed in or out.

On this multi-layered battlefield, Formica would establish a dynamic cordon to control the battle space outside Fallujah, with static positions tied into the terrain at key locations. His soldiers and portions of Gary Patton's 2nd Brigade Combat Team would establish their outer cordon from Karmah to the Syrian border in the north and west, and Abu Ghraib to Al Amariyah in the east and south. Task Force Wolfpack would secure the "Shark's Fin," while Lieutenant Colonel Myles Miyamasu mechanized battalion (1-5

CAV) would establish blocking positions along MSR MOBILE from the Euphrates River east toward Karmah, manning two fortified outposts along the route.

This would not be the first time Colonel Miyamasu fought alongside Marines. As a young lieutenant, Miyamasu had rolled into Kuwait in 1991 with the Second Armored Division's Tiger Brigade. The brigade had been chopped to the 2nd Marine Division to provide the Marines with additional armored assets to punch through Saddam's defenses in Kuwait. Now Miyamasu would tie in with Lieutenant Colonel Todd McCaffrey's 1-5 Infantry. Together they would control the areas east and north of Fallujah, past Karmah all the way to Abu Ghraib.

To the south, Formica would build Natonski's anvil, a formidable fighting force formed around Lieutenant Colonel Darric 'Spike' Knight's Second Reconnaissance Battalion by adding a Bradley platoon, a LAR Company, and a few Marine tanks. By the first week in November, Knight's force would grow to more than 600 soldiers, sailors, and Marines.

Knight assigned Captain John Griffin's agile, fast-moving Apache Company from 2nd LAR Battalion to the industrial area and "Queens," the Al Qaeda stronghold in the southeast section of the city. Griffin worked out of a couple of outposts in the swampy wasteland and rough terrain south of the city, one at the Dam Bridge and the other named OP ROCKPILE. Knight established roadblocks to keep the enemy from coming out of the Zaidon into the rear areas. "We knew the Zaidon area was just a bad place," explained Colonel Formica.[1]

The Zaidon, just south of Camp Fallujah and southeast of the city, was one of the most dangerous parts of the region. This low-lying agricultural area was crisscrossed with irrigation canals and impassable terrain perfect for ambushes. While on patrol in the Zaidon, one of Griffin's LAVs was attacked by a Suicide Vehicle-Borne IED (SVBIED). Fortunately no Americans were killed, but the blast seriously wounded the LAV's driver. The explosion was so powerful that the bomber's engine block was thrown 100 meters from the point of the blast, and little was found of his body. The

---

1   COL Michael Formica telephone interview, 11/06/07.

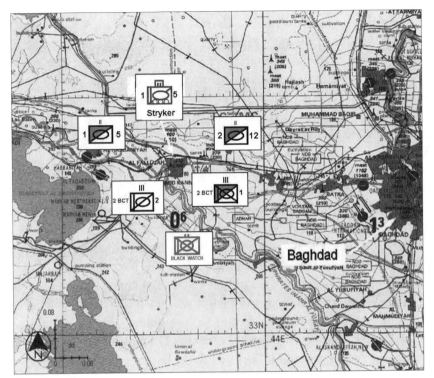

The Cordon Around Fallujah

Marines radioed Colonel Knight to report, "Sir, we found his balls in the road."[2]

Probing the Battlefield

As all the forces were converging around Fallujah in September and October and making their preparations for the attack, the 1st Marine Division conducted feints and short-term raids from every corner of the city. Natonski continued to run patrols and operations in the area to stretch his muscles, but without showing his hand. The forays remained small and never more than company-sized operations. Colonel Shupp conducted shaping operations every four days to keep the enemy off balance. One night he peppered the city with an artillery barrage of flares, turning night into day.

2 LtCol Darric Knight telephone interview, 3/3/08.

Next, he flew a standard Marine Corps C-130 over Fallujah to simulate AC-130s. (At night, Shupp's Marine transport plane sounded exactly like the Air Force's deadly gunship.) Natonski wanted to make the enemy believe that the attack would come from east to west, but careful not to overplay his hand, he periodically probed from the north and south as well.

Each new event excited and confused the enemy. Every incursion or probe prompted insurgent leaders to grab their cell phones and radios and fill the airwaves with expectant chatter. "This is it!" they would exclaim back and forth. "They are coming tonight! Prepare everyone!"

Colonel Bristol gathered intelligence during each outing. This created a loop in which the information gathered during one operation led to a new operation, and that information provided new intelligence for the next one. For example, one night F/A18s buzzed the city at supersonic speed, blowing out windows with a boom loud enough to wake the dead, while UAVs watched for enemy movement and the Radio Battalion listened for their reaction. When an enemy concentration was identified, a Joint Directed Attack Munition (JDAM) was dropped on the building, triggering additional movement and chatter. The Marines then simply followed the insurgents as they moved to their next site. They could run, but they could not hide.

General Metz cautioned the Marines not to exceed the IO threshold, so their feints and raids had to be conducted with some restraint. There would be no heavy artillery barrages and few air attacks. The focus was on low-risk targets, with a goal to keep civilian casualties to a minimum. The Marines ran large and small patrols, sometimes encountering IEDs or ambushes. They ran company-sized feints, cordon, and search operations, and triggered several firefights as a result. The Marines kept the enemy guessing as to where the real attack would come.

The Marines demonstrated less restraint on the eastern edge of Fallujah. The Askari neighborhood, dubbed the "Military District," was a newly constructed area. Its single-family homes were larger and the streets were wider than in the older neighborhoods farther west. The Marines had been sparring with the enemy along the eastern side of Fallujah for many months. Few, if any, civilians remained in the homes along the eastern edge of town. Most of the buildings were enemy bunkers, riddled with bullet holes and pockmarked by larger caliber rounds. Attacks on the eastern edge of Fallujah would not impose significant new damage or endanger civilians, so with platoon- and company-sized operations the Marines reinforced the enemy's belief that they would attack from the east.

On the night of September 24-25 (Colonel Shupp's birthday), RCT–1 conducted a large shaping attack. Under cover of darkness, Shupp moved tanks and armored vehicles to the northeast corner of Fallujah to destroy captured HESCO barriers the insurgents had used to block entrance into the city along the north-south streets. Shupp had two companies of Marine Corps tanks, Alpha and Charlie companies of the 2nd Tank Battalion. Captain Chris Meyers, the Alpha Company commander, conducted a tank attack with infantry support from Olson's 2/1 and Malay's 3/5 Marines. Shupp watched the operation from the Potato Factory, an agricultural facility with refrigerated storage capability at the northeast corner of the Cloverleaf. At one point he looked toward the city with his night-vision goggles and spotted small flickers of light. It reminded him of the Super Bowl or an Olympic Stadium, complete with thousands of camera flashes. But the flashes were not from cameras, but from hundreds of enemy fighters firing on his Marines.

The enemy had spent months erecting barricades and planting IEDs all over the Military District. Insurgents had stolen Jersey barriers (like you see on interstate construction projects) and HESCO barriers from ambushed American convoys. When no stolen barriers were available, they plowed earthen berms across major thoroughfares inside the city. Bombs were buried in the streets and mines were sowed in the courtyards. Entire homes were transformed into massive booby traps, with explosives stacked from floor to ceiling.

On one occasion, an American aircraft dropped a bomb on a suspected cache in the Military District. The bomb triggered secondary explosions, confirming the Marines' suspicions. Then, to everyone's amazement, a series of IEDs exploded along the street for about two blocks. Another five or six explosions erupted on an adjacent street, one right after the other. The discovery of so many IEDs planted around the edge of the city reinforced Natonski's belief that he needed to get his Marines past these urban minefields quickly. He needed to disrupt the enemy's command and control and not allow them time to blow any other strings of explosives. If a two-block-long string of IEDs had blown while Marines were in the street, an entire company could have been lost in the blink of an eye.

The Marines constantly shifted their focus to keep the enemy off balance. On October 14, 2004, Captain Meyers' Alpha Company, 2nd Tanks conducted a daylight feint in the northwest corner of the city. At 2200 Colonel Patton's 1st Battalion of the 503rd Infantry Regiment attacked up the Shark's Fin, while 3/5 and Captain Robert Bodisch's Charlie Company, 2nd Tank Battalion attacked to clear and seize the Soda Factory in the southeast. The Marines wanted to make the enemy believe this was the beginning of their advance to retake Fallujah, whereas in reality they were just trying to expose more enemy positions.

Captain Meyers' friend, Robert Bodisch, grew up near Austin, Texas. He joined the Marine Corps Reserves right after high school, completed his degree at Texas A&M, and was commissioned as a Marine Second Lieutenant. Bodisch's first assignment was as a tank platoon commander at Twentynine Palms. He served a stint as an intel officer but returned to tanks at Camp Lejeune to become the Charlie Company Commander in the 2nd Tank Battalion.

Bodisch attacked from the southeast in the lead tank and pushed forward across the sandy desert into the Industrial District, followed by twelve AMTRACs carrying India Company, 3/5. The enemy responded to the oncoming armor vehicles with direct and indirect fire from AKs, RPGs, machine guns, and mortars. Colonel Shupp had set up his Regimental mobile CP in the desert between the city and Route MOBILE, but discovered his view of the fight was blocked from that position. He called Major Arnold and told him he wanted to move. As soon as they pulled up stakes and displaced, a mortar barrage peppered their just-abandoned site. Once Shupp set up in his new CP, the enemy started firing 120mm rockets by lying them on sand ramps and shooting them toward the Marines on a flat trajectory. The rockets screamed above Shupp's head like line drives at Wrigley Field.

Bodisch's tanks knocked down a wall and Captain Brian Chontosh's infantry charged through and overran the buildings in the Soda Factory. Chontosh's infantry didn't stay long; they cleared the buildings and withdrew before sunrise. The next day, October 15, the Darkhorse Marines waged a six-hour battle along MSR MOBILE, during which eleven men were wounded.

The final shuffling continued. Ten miles west of Fallujah, Lieutenant Colonel Dinauer arrived in Habbaniyah on the 24th. He brought with him one of his battalion's LAR companies and two-thirds of his headquarters and maintenance Marines. The rest of his Wolfpack stayed behind to continue patrolling the border in western Anbar Province. Those Marines Dinauer arrived with immediately came under the command of Gary Patton's 2nd Brigade Combat Team. Dinauer's first task was to conduct a relief-in-place on the peninsula with the soldiers of the 1st Battalion, 503rd Infantry Regiment. As soon as Task Force Wolfpack was in place, 1-503 moved to Ramadi. Dinauer's staff, meanwhile, set to work planning its attack on the Shark's Fin.

Within days, the Kurds of the Iraqi 36 Commando Battalion showed up in a convoy of thin-skinned Toyota pickup trucks. Dinauer's Executive Officer was Major Ken Kassner, an infantryman by profession and a grunt by trade who grew up in San Antonio and attended the University of Houston. Kassner managed to convince a Marine artillery battalion at the Marine base at al Taqaddum to offer up its platoon of 7-ton trucks to the Iraqi commandos.

On the afternoon of October 25, RCT–1 conducted one of its final feints, a leader recon[3] of the northern approaches, the attack positions, the railroad station, and the regimental breach site 300 meters north of Fallujah. Colonel Shupp's commanders traveled in nine M1 Abrams tanks and eight LAVs. At MSR MOBILE's Check Point 84, due north of Fallujah, the reconnaissance patrol split into two groups. Lieutenant Colonel Jeffrey Chessani and the LAVs drove west cross country to identify approach routes and reconnoiter each of the battalion's anticipated attack positions. Bodisch and his VIP loaders (Shupp, Malay, Buhl, Piddock, Griffin, and Captain Russell from the Combat Engineers) drove south on Sichir Road, a hardtop route running from MSR MOBILE into the center of Fallujah. Shupp rode in the lead tank with Second Lieutenant Joe Cash. The plan was to turn right just north of the

---

3 Prior to any operation, senior officers like to see the battleground for themselves. Seeing the 'lay-of-the-land' helps them make critical decisions in the heat of the fight. So they try to go out on a personal reconnaissance, or "leader recon."

cemetery halfway between CP84 and the northern edge of the city, then along dirt roads across open terrain to the western side of the railroad station.

As Cash drove south, Shupp thought something was wrong: he could see the cemetery on his right. "Cash, you just missed your turn, buddy," Shupp commented over the tank's intercom.

"Naw, sir, we're alright," Cash replied, just as the tank rolled to a stop at the Sichir Road railroad crossing. Not only had they missed their turn, they were now fewer than 300 meters from the edge of Fallujah. Shupp thought to himself, "This is just supposed to be a recon. I don't want to start the fight now." He ordered Cash to backtrack. As Cash was reversing, Shupp spotted wires on the railroad bridge. The structure was mined.[4]

Bodisch's tanks found the right route and again moved to within 300 meters of the city, this time just west of the railroad station so that the commanders and engineers could survey their breach site. Within fifteen minutes enemy mortar rounds started falling on the Marines, followed by small arms fire and RPGs aimed at the tanks. The tankers remained exposed just long enough for the commanders and engineers to view the breach site before withdrawing.

Tanks would prove to be a critical asset in the coming attack. Captain Christopher Meyers, the Alpha Company, 2nd Tanks commander and the son of a former Marine, had spent his entire career in Marine tanks. He was well-versed in armor tactics and logistics. Alpha Company, however, was shorthanded. Meyers had only two platoons and the two tanks in his headquarters section—he had left his other platoon out west to support operations along the border. Alpha Company had been supporting 3/1 and RCT–1, but as RCT–7 arrived in Camp Fallujah, Meyers' ten tanks were chopped to Tucker's regiment.

Meyers' BLUE (3rd) Platoon commander was a former Gunnery Sergeant-turned-officer, 2nd Lieutenant Jeffery Lee. Married, 36-years-old, and with three children, Lee had been in the Marines since his high-school graduation in 1988. He, too, grew up in tanks, first as a driver, then a loader, a gunner, and finally a tank commander. After spending fourteen years as an

4 Col Mike Shupp telephone interview, 9/3/07.

enlisted Marine, Lee decided that he wanted to become a decision-maker—an officer. Now, on the eve of the Marines' largest tank fight since Vietnam, Second Lieutenant Lee had a tank platoon of his own. There were few Marines in the entire Corps more qualified to lead a platoon of tanks into the fight in Fallujah.

On Saturday, October 30, 2004, some of Meyers' tanks and Light Armored Vehicles supported Ramos' Hawaii Marines as they conducted an operation in the southeast corner of Fallujah. It was "only" a large feint, but it involved nearly the entire battalion. While some of Ramos' Marines attacked across rugged terrain into the southeast corner of the city, others conducted a sweep through the Zaidon—even though Shupp had warned Ramos, "Whatever you do, don't go into the Zaidon."[5] Meyers' tanks pressed forward in broad daylight with infantry support from 1/3 to an earthen berm one kilometer from the southeast edge of the city. Gil Juarez' LAVs attacked on the left flank into the southern part of the town. Some of the less intelligent enemy fighters revealed their positions by firing on the advancing Marines, who responded with nine artillery missions and rockets, bombs, and mortars. D9 bulldozers worked behind the advancing Marines, clearing lanes and building defensive berms as if they were preparing for a much larger attack.

Late that afternoon, Ramos ordered Meyers' tanks through the berm. Lieutenant Lee's tank led the advance and hit a mine on the far side, blowing one of his tracks off the road wheels. Meyers and Sergeant Jose Ducasse (Lee's platoon sergeant and wingman) raced to Lee's aid, pulled their tanks alongside the crippled M1A1, and began firing into the city while Lee and his crew abandoned the tank. The tankers called for their M88 tank retriever to rescue the stricken vehicle. The enemy continued firing at the stationary tank during the entire retrieval operation. The sun had set by the time the tank was dragged out of the line of fire and moved to the rear for repair.

Just as Ramos was disengaging and starting to wrap up the operation, he got word that Captain Jay Garcia's Bravo Company Marines had been hit by a suicide bomber. Garcia was completing his operation in the Zaidon and had already mounted up his Marines in 7-ton trucks for the ride back to Camp Fallujah when disaster struck. Garcia was riding in the lead vehicle over a small bridge when he looked right into the eyes of the driver of an

5 Col Mike Shupp telephone interview, 9/3/07.

approaching SUV—and knew immediately what was coming. The suicide bomber, his white Suburban loaded to the roof with explosives, raced past Garcia's vehicle, swerved sharply and rammed into the first 7-ton truck. The explosion was tremendous and killed eight Marines: Lance Corporal Jeremy D. Bow, Lance Corporal John T. Byrd II, Sergeant Kelley L. Courtney, Lance Corporal Travis A. Fox, Corporal Christopher J. Lapka, Private 1st Class John Lukac, Private 1st Class Andrew G. Riedel, and Lance Corporal Michael P. Scarborough. The blast wounded ten more and left the truck a mangled, burning wreck.

The enemy followed up with the ultimate in drive-by shootings. As the truck burned and the column was responding to the chaos, insurgents raced cars onto bridges and past the convoy, grenadiers and gunners firing RPGs and spraying automatic gunfire toward the crash scene. Gil Juarez raced to the site with some of his armored vehicles to stamp out the remaining enemy resistance and aid in the recovery mission. The casualties were evacuated and every Marine body was recovered. The survivors didn't get back to Camp Fallujah until well after midnight.

A Bit of Housekeeping

Ever since the brutal beating and murder of the Iraqi National Guard's leader Lieutenant Colonel Suleiman al Marawi[6], many of his Fallujahan guardsmen had become corrupt. The Marines kept them at arm's length, but had continued a dialogue in hopes they would clean up their act. By now one thing was certain: the Marines did not want them armed and roaming their rear area north of Fallujah during the coming fight.

On the first day of November, a Darkhorse patrol drove to the Iraqi National Guard camp at Saqlawiyah. Members of the patrol told the Iraqis that they had a Marine who wanted to be promoted in front of his Iraqi

---

6   Lieutenant Colonel Suleiman al Marawi was the only reliable Iraqi military leader in the area, commander of the 506th National Guard Battalion. He had been a Ba'ath Party member and had served in the Republican Guard, but was an honest man. Suleiman was legitimately concerned about his soldiers and the future of Fallujah, but he walked a fine line, keeping his distance from the Marines and the leaders inside the city. Suleiman's strategy was to bide his time on the Shark's Fin, allowing the Americans to deal with the insurgents inside the city. But he was kidnapped on August 9th, beaten, tortured, and finally beheaded by Omar Hadid. Days after his capture, his mutilated body was found, left to rot in the streets.

brothers, and called the Iraqis into formation. Jason Arellano was promoted to sergeant in front of a formation of less-than-enthusiastic Iraqi National Guardsmen. During the ceremony, Lieutenant Michael Cragholm positioned his handful of Marines to cover the sketchy Iraqis. Afterward Cragholm moved to the armory and spent several minutes visiting with the officer in charge. He told the Iraqi that he had to inspect their weapons. After some coaxing, the Iraqis opened their armory for the Marines.

"These weapons are in terrible shape," the Marine armorer explained to the soldiers. "We need to take them back with us to repair whatever we can. We have new weapons back at Camp Fallujah," he continued. "If we can't repair yours, we'll replace them with brand-new weapons."[7]

Through his interpreter, Lieutenant Cragholm directed the Iraqis to gather up the weapons and load them into his trucks. The handful of Marines then drove off with all the rifles, 102 in all. This was one Iraqi National Guard unit that would no longer pose a threat during the attack.

Final Preparations

The forces under Formica, Rainey, and Newell began shifting their attention to Fallujah in the first week of November. Newell sent an advance party to Camp Fallujah to participate in the continuing planning process. Once Rainey's 2-7 Cavalry troopers received their warning order, he sent some of his staff officers, including Major Tim Karcher, the Battalion's Operations Officer, to Camp Fallujah to get acquainted with the Marine commanders and to integrate themselves into the planning process.

In the pre-dawn hours of an early November morning, 2-7 left the enormous military compound at Taji. 2-7 moved south to Baghdad, hooked up with Formica's vehicles near Baghdad International Airport, and drove west to Camp Fallujah. The Black Jack Brigade rolled west on Highway 10 from Baghdad on a tactical road march, with Colonel Lewis' Kiowa and Apache helicopters flying cover overhead. The endless stream of armored vehicles was a massive show of force.

Rainey's troopers were itching for a fight. Their tanks and Bradleys were locked and loaded and every soldier in every vehicle was ready for battle. If insurgents decided to attack this convoy, they would be obliterated.

7   Capt Michael Cragholm telephone interview, 03/01/08.

Captain Edward Twaddell III, A/2-7's Company Commander, a United States Military Academy graduate, began his Army career as a paratrooper before becoming a cavalry trooper. Twaddell had been in command of Alpha Company since November of 2003. Captain Peter Glass, a Citadel graduate, led Rainey's armor company, commanding fourteen M1 tanks in C Company/3-8. According to Rainey, "Captain Pete Glass is about as aggressive a dude as there is in the Army."[8] Glass and Twaddell had swapped a platoon, so Twaddell had two Bradley platoons and one tank platoon, while Glass had two tank platoons and one Bradley platoon. Captain Chris Brooke, another Texas Aggie, led Rainey's other mechanized infantry company, C/2-7, which was understrength with only ten Bradleys in all.

Jim Rainey's Ghost Troopers and the Black Jack Brigade arrived at their positions outside Fallujah in early November. They were all in place within seventy-two hours of the attack. Under the cover of darkness Formica conducted a seamless transition with RCT–1, while 2-7 slipped into Camp Fallujah to take its place as one of the clouds of the gathering storm. When the enemy woke up the next morning, they faced the Black Jack Brigade in the south. Formica had a considerably larger force and completely different weapons systems than the commands it replaced.

Once the Black Jack Brigade was in place, no one got out of the city in any vehicle. Spike Knight knew where all the ratlines were. It is debatable whether or not they got there in time: if the brigade occupied these positions just a few days earlier, Zarqawi and other insurgent leaders might have been trapped inside the city. Regardless, the time for leaving Fallujah had passed. Any insurgents still inside would either surrender or die.

On Thursday, November 4, 2004, Task Force Wolfpack officially came under Colonel Michael Shupp's control. Lieutenant Colonel Dinauer was ready for the fight. Some of his Marines had built a mockup of Fallujah and the Shark's Fin on the floor of their command post. They were very creative, using broken glass, bricks, spray paint, and anything else they could get their hands on to create their objective. Shupp visited the Wolfpack only days

8   COL Jim Rainey telephone interview, 11/8/07.

before the battle. All of the Wolfpack leaders, including Juan Rubio and Major Wittnam's boat captains, were summoned to the final briefing.

When Rubio and Brian Parrello walked through the front door of Wolfpack's headquarters and saw the assembly of majors and colonels and the elaborate mock-up on the floor, it sank in that this operation would be unlike any other. This was a big deal. This one would make the history books.

"Holy shit!" Parrello said to Rubio. "This is really happening."[9]

Dinauer's staff briefed the soldiers, sailors, and Marines in the room on the entire plan one last time. Afterward, Shupp stood to give a final pep talk. He, too, confirmed to his men that they were all about to become a part of history, and that victory was certain. He left them with a final thought: "Take the fight to the enemy, but fight with firmness, dignity, and respect. You are warriors, not criminals."[10]

Colonel Newell's 2nd Battalion of the 2nd Infantry Regiment was stationed at Forward Operating Base Normandy near Muqdadiyah, 75 miles northeast of Baghdad in Diyala Province. These soldiers had the longest trek to Fallujah. Task Force 2-2 traveled from Muqdadiyah to Camp Fallujah in several serials.[11] Their tanks and Bradleys were hauled on low-boys, with the crews in their vehicles ready for action.

Captain Sean Sims, A/2-2's Company Commander, led the first serial. Sims was an inspirational leader, another graduate of Texas A&M and friends with Chris Brooke, one of his counterparts in 2-7. Sims loved the Army and his men loved him. Alpha Company was the only full-strength company going to Fallujah in Task Force 2-2. Like most of the other units converging on the fight, Colonel Peter Newell had to leave a portion of his command behind to maintain the operational tempo in Diyala Province. Still, Sims had the full complement of his mechanized infantry company at hand. He had two Bradley platoons, one tank platoon, and a platoon of

---

9   HM2 Juan Rubio telephone interview, 11/15/07.

10 Col Mike Shupp, *We Were One*, p. 61.

11 A *serial* is one of several small military convoys, traveling to the same destination, one after the other.

engineers. Captain Paul Fowler led Alpha Company of 2-63 armor. He had a full complement of men but only two platoons of tanks. His third platoon rode in HMMWVs. Captain Kirk Mayfield had only one platoon of Bradley fighting vehicles in his Brigade Reconnaissance Troop (BRT), F Troop, 4th CAV.

Newell's Battalion Surgeon, Major (Dr.) Lisa DeWitt, and her medical team were traveling in Sims' serial in their M113 and HMMWV ambulances. DeWitt had been in the military less than a year. She was an experienced emergency room trauma physician who decided to join the Army to do her part in the global war on terror. The Army had sent her to Kuwait to bandage cuts and treat automobile accident victims. When her tour there was finished, she decided that she wanted to get closer to the action, so she hitchhiked her way into the heart of Iraq and volunteered to become 2-2's surgeon. Sims was one of her favorites. He was easy to talk to, and it was clear to her that he cared about the well being of his men.

One of Sims' finest squad leaders, 29-year-old Staff Sergeant David Bellavia, rode into battle with his men. Bellavia was just an average American guy who grew up in New York. Just like Brian Parrello, he had aged in the shadow of older brothers. Bellavia struggled in college and in his effort to find the man within himself. He joined the Army in search of that man and evolved into a modern-day American warrior. Bellavia had already acquired the reputation as a "go-to" guy—always in the thick of the fight, always trying to become a better soldier and leader, and, like Sims, always concerned about the welfare of his men. Bellavia rode into this fight with both the bravado of an untested soldier and the apprehension of a combat veteran. Sims, Dewitt, Bellavia, and Task Force 2-2 arrived at the last rest stop before Hell—Camp Fallujah—on the 5th of November.

Task Force Blue Diamond conducted a dress rehearsal on the night of November 5 to validate the battalions' movement routes and identify some of the enemy's positions. The rehearsal lasted all night and ended at sunrise the following morning. Colonel Tucker wanted to go out during the rehearsal on a leader recon to personally view his regiment's planned breach site. The colonel, Brandl, Ramos, and Newell spent a couple hours training as tank crew loaders before Meyers' tankers drove them to the northern edge of the city.

Similarly, when the 1st Marine Regiment started its infiltration on November 6, Captain O'Palski's Force Recon Platoon took 3rd Battalion, 5th Marines' company commanders out on foot for a leader reconnaissance of the approach to the apartment complex northwest of Fallujah. Starting after sunset, they walked all the way to the railroad berm and then worked their way back through the apartment complex, moving in so close that they could see Iraqi families watching television in their living rooms.

All in Place

Fallujah was like a filthy window that hadn't been cleaned in a hundred years. Colonel Mike Shupp knew that the city had to be completely cleared, or the cancer of ruthless insurgency would return.

RCT–1 was to conduct a rapid penetration to disrupt and defeat the enemy. "We knew this was going to be a full-on fight," Shupp explained later, "and that the enemy was well prepared."[12] Shupp also knew that if the city was not cleared, the cancer of ruthless insurgency would return. So, he tasked Colonel Rainey's mechanized battalion with conducting the penetration down PL HENRY, and his Marines with the deliberate clearing behind Rainey's troopers.[13] Rainey wanted to concentrate his forces, using Glass' Cougar tanks to conduct the rapid penetration, and Twaddell's Apache tracks to attack through the city to seize Jolan Park. Rainey's troopers would not stop to clear each building. Instead, they would conduct a mounted attack, leaving the follow-up to Colonel Buhl's 3rd Battalion, 1st Marines, which would sweep behind Rainey's soldiers on foot and search every room in every house.

Next to Buhl, Pat Malay's Darkhorse Marines would attack into the northwest corner of the city, clearing from 3/1's right flank to the Euphrates

---

12 Col Michael Shupp telephone interview 9/3/07.

13 For ease of identifying locations within the city, the Marines developed a grid of Phase Lines that roughly corresponded to the streets of Fallujah. There were a series of PLs running north/south and another series running east/west. The north/south PLs were given male names and ran alphabetically from east to west. The farthest east was ABE, and KEN ran along the Euphrates River; in between were BILL, CHARLES, DAVE, ETHAN, FRANK, GEORGE, HENRY, ISAAC and JACOB. HENRY was the main north/south road that divided the city. It was the regimental boundary. The east/west PLs were named after women, with APRIL in the north and JENNA in the south. FRAN was MSR MICHIGAN (Highway 10), and ran through the center of the city.

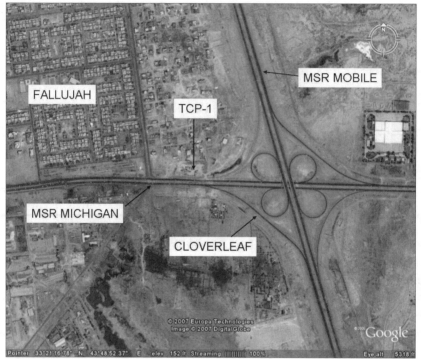

The Cloverleaf and TCP1

River, all the way down to MICHIGAN. Malay, Major Piddock, his S-3, and the Gunner believed that the enemy would hunker down. Darkhorse Marines would have to root them out, house-to-house and room-to-room. Malay and Piddock planned to move their Marines through the city like a giant squeegee across the filthy windows, and then backtrack to clean off the remaining specks.

Colonel Tucker had a slightly different view of how he should attack. He knew the importance of a quick penetration and did not want a recurrence of the April stalemate. The last thing Tucker wanted was to give the enemy an opportunity to regroup or set up new defenses. Getting bogged down in urban ambushes inside Falluhah was simply not on his agenda. As a result, Tucker planned a three-pronged, objective-driven penetration. Army Lieutenant Colonel Peter Newell was ordered to race forward on RCT–7's left flank along the eastern edge of the city with Task Force 2-2's Bradleys and M1 tanks. Most of the eastern side of Fallujah was already in ruins from months of skirmishes with the Marines along MSR MOBILE, so Newell's armored thrust would do little additional damage. But it would kill anyone who resisted and bypass hundreds of buildings and hunkered-down enemy fighters.

Tucker ordered his Marines to charge forward to seize critical objectives, only entering the buildings they needed for rooftop observation positions. Gary Brandl would attack down PL ETHAN and Mike Ramos would drive into the enemy's Askari neighborhood stronghold. The men of 1st Battalion, 8th Marines and 1st Battalion, 3rd Marines would rapidly seize critical enemy command-and-control positions, weapons caches, and enemy strongpoints, leaving most buildings in their path untouched. "They had to move," explained Colonel Vuckovich. "They had a timeline."[14]

The options boiled down to meticulous deliberation versus speed of advance. The coming days would reveal which approach was the best course of action.

Charlie Company, 1st LAR, which had been part of Ramos' Battalion Landing Team, provided Colonel Tucker's Marines with their only heavy punch. Captain Gilbert Juarez commanded the LAR Company. He was the type of commander who wouldn't ask his Marines to do anything he wasn't willing to do himself. He trained his Marines well, then trusted them to get the job done. To give Tucker more firepower to lead the infantry assault, Meyers' tanks were chopped to RCT–7 as well. With very few days left before D-Day, Brandl and Ramos had little time to train their Marines in tank-infantry operations. Meyers' men took a few minutes to introduce the grunts to the tank-infantry phone mounted on the back of the tank and tried to impress upon the young Marines how dangerous it was to stand anywhere close to the main gun when it was fired: the concussion alone, they explained, could kill a man if he stood too close.

Buhl's Marines had been constantly training and fighting for five months, making them the best prepared Marines in the attack. Malay continued to train his Marines as well. Now he included tanks, AMTRACs and gun trucks to practice tank-infantry techniques. Because Malay's Marines would move into the city with armored vehicles, they worked on a World War II technique called Same-Axis-Same-Speed (or SASS). The grunts worked with the tankers to establish procedures to move down Fallujah's narrow city streets in support of one another. Other training

14 LtCol Nicholas Vuckovich personal interview, 05/22/08.

involved communications and safety issues. Contrary to established doctrine, the infantrymen were directed to stay behind the tanks.

M1 Abrams tanks would be used to support the infantry on the wider streets, while AMTRACs, with their .50-cal machine guns and MK-19 grenade launchers, supported Marines moving along the narrower streets. Combined Anti-Armor Team (CAAT)[15] gun trucks would be used in the narrowest streets and alleys. Malay had trained his Marines to fight alone, but now he was going to give them as much firepower as he could. Tanks, tracks, and gun trucks would provide heavier firepower, and D9 Bulldozers would be used to smash in walls and topple insurgent-filled buildings.

Malay's planning maestro, Major Robert Piddock, was the son of a former Marine Staff Sergeant. Piddock stood 6'4," weighed 230 pounds, and was a tremendous athlete. He had been a 3rd Battalion, 5th Marines company commander in Operation Iraqi Freedom before becoming the Battalion's Operations Officer. He was a brilliant S3 with excellent interpersonal skills and worked easily with higher headquarters and subordinates alike. The major was the kind of planner who would actively participate in the development of plans at all higher levels of command, and then turn around and involve his company commanders in his own planning process.

Piddock rotated units out of the line and sent them through a final training package that Bodisch and the tankers had put together to refine the tank-infantry team. Meanwhile, Piddock brought in the Darkhorse company commanders to help him write the operation order. Once the Black Jack soldiers took over responsibility for MSR MOBILE's security, 3rd Battalion, 5th Marines went back to Camp Fallujah to rest, eat, sleep, clean their weapons, and make a final call home prior to taking up their attack positions north of the city.

Malay and Piddock had done everything they could to prepare the battalion. They had trained their Marines and planned the attack. Soon they would have to let go and trust their unit commanders, much like parents unleashing their children on the world.

As Colonel Malay put it: "You got to plan and then you create an order. You tell the men what to do, not how to do it. You push that stewardship and

---

15 The teams employ "hardback" HMMWVs with ring mounts for .50-caliber or M240 machine guns, TOW missile launchers and MK-19 automatic grenade launchers.

empowerment—that decision-making—down to the lowest level and give them their boundaries, give them an end-state and then turn them loose. They will usually do stuff much, much better than you would have ever envisioned."[16]

After long weeks of planning and preparation, the pieces of Operation Phantom Fury were finally locked in place. At that stage, remembered General Dunford, "All we needed was a green light."[17]

The Iraqi government assumed responsibility for what was about to transpire, and code-named the operation "al Fajr," after a passage in the Qur'an. The loose English translation is "The Dawn" or "Daybreak." The religious passage talks about wrongdoers returning to the grace of Allah and the approaching New Dawn.

16 Col Patrick Malay telephone interview, 11/4/07.

17 BGen Joseph Dunford telephone interview, 11/16/07.

Chapter 6

D-Day: Sunday, November 7th

"They really thought they could defeat us."

— LtGen Richard F. Natonski, USMC, March 11, 2008

Fallujah had become a ghost town. Many insurgents and their leaders had slipped away with the fleeing civilian population, leaving only hardcore enemy fighters roaming the deserted streets. Those civilians who had not escaped holed up inside their homes.

New Dawn would have to wait for sunset; General Natonski wanted to attack under cover of darkness, thick clouds, and a light winter rain. His first assault was designed to further confuse the enemy and divert attention from the main effort. Dinauer's Task Force Wolfpack would kick off the New Dawn with an attack up the western peninsula at 1900.

As Task Force Wolfpack attacked up the Shark's Fin, Natonski's regiments and brigades would move into their own attack positions. They staged in Camp Fallujah as if they were lining up for Chicago's St. Patrick's Day Parade: tanks, trucks, and armored vehicles parked in their order of march. For hours the soldiers, sailors, airmen, and Marines of Task Force Blue Diamond did what they have done best for decades: they waited. Eventually, painfully slowly, they began their journey to war. Each in its turn, the 1,000-plus vehicles rolled out of Camp Fallujah into position north of the city. The highways around Fallujah were jammed with bumper-to-bumper traffic that included tanks, Bradleys, LAVs, Amphibious Tractors (AMTRACs), High Mobility, Multi-Wheeled Vehicles (HMMWVs) and trucks—all laden with soldiers and Marines in full "battle rattle."

Recon Marines and scouts rolled out ahead of the enormous convoy in search of IEDs along the route. MOBILE stretched north from the Cloverleaf atop a thirty-foot berm, then leveled out and ran west. The berm offered cover from the city, blocking the enemy's view, and the Marines' as well. The terrain fell off to the north toward MOBILE, affording even more cover. RCT-1 and RCT-7 would approach and stage unseen.

Attack on the 'Shark's Fin'

The first evening, all eyes were on Task Force Wolfpack. Dinauer's soldiers and Marines roared up the roads into blocking and attack positions in a two-pronged attack toward the Fallujah Hospital and Colonel Suleiman's former Iraqi National Guard headquarters, a known enemy strongpoint. Dinauer's main effort came out of Habbaniyah, led by Wolfpack's mechanized Army team (C/1-9), followed by Dinauer's small command group. Behind it rolled Iraqi 36 Commandos in their borrowed 7-ton trucks. Major Ken Kassner led the eastern prong of Wolfpack's attack. Kassner's supporting attack came out of ASP ROCK, south of al Taqaddum. Dinauer's reserve Marine infantry company (Bravo 1/23) and engineers, in their 7-ton trucks and HMMWVs, moved into their attack positions on the east side of the peninsula along with a company of LAVs.

At 1900 they all moved out to secure the entire peninsula and the hospital. Bravo, 1/23 sprinted to block the Euphrates River bridges on the peninsula, while Wolfpack's Armored Combat Earthmovers (ACEs) scooped up dirt and dumped it on each bridge and, under sporadic fire from across the river, Marine engineers rushed up to string concertina wire across the berms. Traffic across both crossings was completely stopped by 2100.

While the Marines were working to block the bridges, the Iraqi soldiers of 36 Commando assaulted the hospital at the tip of the Shark's Fin. American and European film crews were present as Iraqi forces cleared the facility. The "hospital" was a complete pigsty, and not a place any American would go for treatment. In fact, it was little more than a nest of insurgent propagandists. That April they had used the facility to issue claims of non-existent civilian casualties. No propaganda would be spewed from this

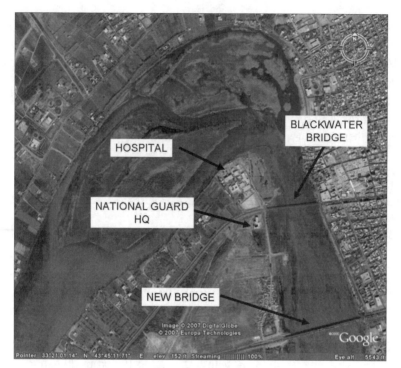

The Shark's Fin

facility during al-Fajr; the hospital was secure by 2300. Aircraft were called in to destroy Suleiman's Iraqi National Guard Building on the bank of the Euphrates River. Task Force Wolfpack's objectives 1, 2, and 3 were secure by 0140 of the 8th of November.

As Dinauer worked to secure the peninsula, Dan Wittnam moved five of his boats into position north and west of the Shark's Fin to block enemy movement across the river. Staff Sergeant Joshua Iversen was captain of the lead boat. He had been ordered to hold at the 843 Easting, just out of sight of the enemy in the city. Iversen killed his engines at 8429, but his boat drifted around the bend.[1] He gazed forward into the black night.

---

1 The Military Grid Reference System (MGRS) uses a Universal Transverse Mercator (UTM) zone designator to identify a unique 100km square on the surface of the earth. The

"Oh, shit! There's the Blackwater Bridge!" he exclaimed.[2]

Iversen called Sergeant Andrew Vasey to come alongside in the second boat. As Parrello pulled Vasey's boat alongside, the night exploded in gunfire, with enemy shots spewing from fortified positions inside the city. Third in line, Wittnam watched his first two boats get lit up like Christmas trees.

"Break contact, break contact!"[3] Wittnam ordered.

To Juan Rubio and Gunnery Sergeant Vinciguerra riding in the fourth boat, it looked as if Iversen and Vasey had run into a buzz-saw. Parrello and the other coxswains quickly spun their boats around and hauled ass to cover, dodging small arms, heavy machine gun, and anti-aircraft gunfire. It seemed to them as if everything was moving in slow motion. The boats pirouetted in the water, their .50-caliber machine guns blazing and MK-19s spitting out grenades. Rubio watched as muzzles flashed on the bank of the river and bullets snapped past his head. The enemy had a multi-barreled gun and recoilless rifles trained on the bend in the river from the eastern bank. Luckily for Wittnam's Marines, the enemy gunners were extraordinarily poor shots. Rubio leveled his M16 at the flashes in the night and opened fire, stopping now and again to make sure he had his medical bag with all of his supplies ready to jump boats to care for casualties—which seemed inevitable given the intense gunfire.

Rubio shouted a question to his boat captain, "Is everybody OK?" An answer shot back almost immediately, "Doc, everyone is fine."[4]

Gentlemen, Start your Engines

Almost everyone moved on the night of November 7-8. "We wanted to move two regimental combat teams and a brigade in one cycle of darkness,"

UTM zone designator is followed by an even number of numeric characters representing a point within that square with easting and northing values. Ten numeric characters provide a 1 meter precision. Six characters (three for the north coordinate and three for the east coordinate), such as 843 East, would indicate a resolution of 100 meters.

2 SSgt Josh Iversen telephone interview, 10/27/07.

3 Maj Dan Wittnam telephone interview, 10/8/07.

4 HM2 Juan Rubio telephone interview, 11/15/07.

remembered Colonel L'Etiole.[5] More than 1,000 vehicles moved out of Camp Fallujah and into their attack positions. It sounded like an approaching freight train when 2-7 thundered into its assembly area early on the morning of November 8. Having the farthest to travel, Malay's 3/5 Marines moved out first, their initial serial of 37 vehicles traveling under cover of darkness and in blackout conditions.

Lieutenant Colonel Willie Buhl's Marines piled into their AMTRACs and left Camp Abu Ghraib at 0200 on November 8, moving toward their attack positions northwest of the city. Their bumpy ride lasted for more than an hour. They were the last RCT-1 battalion to arrive at the attack positions north of Fallujah, which they reached by 0345.

While Buhl's Marines were closing on the battlefield, a Task Force Wolfpack bulldozer accident killed two Marines. After blocking the bridges, Dinauer's ACEs started digging fighting positions in the palm groves along the western bank of the Euphrates for the task force's tanks and Bradleys. During the work, Corporal Joshua Palmer drove his bulldozer onto an unstable section of the riverbank. The armored earthmover sank into the mud. Palmer jumped from his mired machine and sank beneath the surface. Lance Corporal Jeffrey Lam, who was guiding Palmer from the ground, watched in horror as his teammate disappeared. Lam stripped off his body armor and leaped in to save his friend. Both men drowned.

Rainey's troopers were already in their assembly area when Colonel Shupp called Bodisch on the radio to ask him to come pick up Lieutenant Colonel Rainey. Shupp wanted to use a section of his tanks for a staff ride to the railroad tracks and breach site. Bodisch called his wingman and they headed over to the Army assembly area. Rainey drove his company commanders and key staff members to the breach point for a final leader's reconnaissance in the light of day. Rainey had five or six vehicles. Ed Twaddell and his wingman rode to the breach in their Bradleys, Pete Glass and his wingman drove their M1s, and Bodisch's Marine tanks led the small armored convoy. Mortar rounds began falling around them within five minutes of their arrival at the railroad tracks. The soldiers and Marines returned fire, killing several Iraqis before backing off and returning to the battalion's attack position.

When General Metz and the MNC-I lifted all targeting restrictions, the coalition forces began pulverizing targets within the city. AC-130 gunships and 155mm artillery pounded the battlefield for twenty-four hours, from 1900 on D-Day right up until the breaching of the attack north of the city at 1900 the next day. The Air Force gunships attacked command-and-control centers and pounded insurgent concentrations and suspected IED locations in the city streets. On more than one occasion these attacks triggered a succession of sympathetic detonations up and down major thoroughfares, the IEDs erupting like a string of deadly Black Cat firecrackers.

Basher and Slasher[6] provided surgical firepower with their sensor-controlled, side-firing weapons. The AC-130 has been upgraded continuously since it first saw action in the skies above Vietnam. It has been employed in Kuwait, Grenada, Panama, Somalia, and Bosnia. The gunships were moved to exclusive nighttime operations after one was downed by a handheld anti-aircraft missile during Desert Storm.

The heavily armed C-130 is nearly 100 feet long and carries a World War II-vintage 40mm cannon (half of one of the Navy's historic pom-pom guns), a 105mm howitzer, and a 25mm Gatling gun—all controlled by sophisticated sensors and a state-of-the-art fire control system. Its crew consists of five officers and eight enlisted men. Everyone, from loader to pilot, is focused on the mission of supporting the troops on the ground with deadly-accurate firepower and unparalleled surveillance capabilities.

Gary Brandl's Broncos[7] led RCT–7 out of Camp Fallujah and into its attack positions east of RCT–1. The ground shook as the deadly parade continued rolling in Sunday morning's windy winter rain. Ramos' Marines of 1/3 rolled out of Camp Fallujah behind Gary Brandl's infantry battalion.

---

6   *Basher* and *Slasher* were the radio call signs for two of the AC-130s over Fallujah.

7   LtCol Gary Brandl's call sign was *Bronco 6*.

Lieutenant Colonel Newell's 2-2 was the last to leave Camp Fallujah in the early morning light. Newell had selected an attack position north of Fallujah and east of MOBILE. Task Force 2-2's armored vehicles staged in the open desert, only a short drive from their breach site.

By the time 2-2 Infantry was in place, two complete Regimental Combat Teams (the six battalions of RCT–1 and RCT–7) lined the northern edge of the city, from Malay's Marines in the west to Newell's tankers and infantrymen in the east. South and southeast of the city, the Black Jack Brigade had shifted into outer and inner cordons, blocking roads in the Zaidon and establishing more blocking positions in the south. Gary Patton moved his soldiers in to isolate the city from the north and northwest. Task Force Wolfpack would soon have a stranglehold on the western peninsula. By the middle of the day, the enemy fighters inside Fallujah were completely trapped.

The intermittent drizzle continued throughout the day, just enough precipitation to muddy windshields and make everyone miserable. The Marines of 1/8 waited in their attack positions astride Sichir Road north of the train station, where the enemy harassed them with intermittent mortar, rocket, and sniper fire. Fortunately, the muddy earth swallowed many of the mortar rounds, and the rocket and sniper fire was haphazard at best.

Prelude to the Main Attack

Enemy fighters lined every rooftop and lurked in every window facing the Euphrates, bracing for an attack that would never come. As the sun rose, Major Kassner could see insurgents moving from window to window and running through alleyways across the river in the Jolan District. When the Iraqis of 36 Commando tied an Iraqi flag to a pole and raised it at dawn on the 8th of November, small arms and machine gun fire erupted from every building lining the eastern bank. Once the enemy opened fire, Dinauer unleashed his wolves of war. Task Force Wolfpack opened with artillery, tank machine guns, and 25mm Bushmaster chain guns.

As the fighting intensified, Kassner radioed Dinauer, "Sir, I think I need to spend some time at the hospital."[8] Dinauer agreed, and Kassner raced to the Fallujah Hospital compound with his driver, Lance Corporal Tim

8 Col Steve Dinauer personal interview, 9/24/07.

Hutchinson. As soon as they pulled into the area, an RPG whooshed over their hood and hit a palm tree next to their vehicle.

Captain Adam Collier, the Marine liaison officer and commander of 36 Commando, was busy reinforcing his perimeter along a brick wall surrounding the compound. Kassner moved from machine gun position to machine gun position, helping to direct the fight. The enemy's fire was sporadic and ineffective, while Task Force Wolfpack's was deadly accurate, sending streams of fire into the buildings across the river. Every so often an enemy mortar round would explode in the hospital compound. One of the rounds knocked Kassner off his feet and peppered his arm with shrapnel. The major shook it off and continued his work. It wasn't until later that day that he would seek medical attention for a wound he considered minor.

The fight along the river reinforced the enemy's belief that the attack would come across the two bridges. Shupp's diversion at the Shark's Fin had worked. In the Jolan District, the enemy began shifting forces toward the river to brace for the coming American thrust.

It was time for Shupp's next move.

Movement to Attack Positions

ASR GOLDEN ran from the rural town of Saqlawiyah into the northwest corner of the city. Skirting a complex of eight four-story apartment buildings, GOLDEN ran under a railroad overpass and into Fallujah. Once south of the railroad tracks, the road made a gentle turn to the east and continued parallel to the railroad tracks along the northern edge of the city.

At 1000, Lieutenant Colonel Malay sent Kilo Company down GOLDEN to secure Shupp's next objective: the apartment complex in the northwest corner of the city. The rooftops of the southern-facing buildings would make an ideal perch for Shupp's forward command post and provide an important vantage point to watch the entire city. The adjacent soccer field and school buildings could be used as a helicopter landing zone, 3/5's Battalion Aid Station, and a logistics resupply point.

An hour later at 1100, with Comanche tanks in the lead, Captain Andrew McNulty's Team Samurai moved out to attack and seize the apartment complex. Sergeant Arellano and the rest of Kilo Company's Marines rolled into the compound, dropped their 80-pound assault packs, and maneuvered on foot to isolate the buildings. Once the westernmost structure was surrounded, First Platoon rushed into it. The complex was nearly deserted. Some Marines took a knee at the foot of the first stairwell while others sprinted up four flights of stairs to secure the roof.

After scouts were posted, the Marines moved down to the fourth floor to clear each apartment. They paused to catch their breath after the adrenalin-filled charge up the stairs. Four apartment doors were on each floor, two on the left and two on the right. Every door was locked. Most of the families who lived there had departed days earlier, leaving their household effects locked behind heavy wooden doors. With weapons at the ready, some Marines prepared to provide covering fire while others tried to kick in the first door. It refused to give way. The Marine kicked again and again. Still, nothing. Undaunted, they broke out crow bars, axes, and bolt cutters. Other Marines fired single, carefully aimed, M16 rounds point-blank into the locks. Many doors withstood repeated abuses before finally giving way to the persistent Marines.

Eventually each apartment was thoroughly searched. Before moving on, the Marines tagged each front door with a red spray-painted X. First Platoon Marines moved from the fourth floor to the third floor, then to the second and first floors, clearing every room as they descended.

Meanwhile, more of McNulty's Marines had moved up to surround the second building. The process was repeated as Marines once again rushed to the roof. Each of the eight buildings was cleared top-down in this methodical manner. Only a few remaining civilians were found in the entire complex. After being given food, blankets, and $300 cash they were trucked out of the area.

The apartment complex was a perfect site for command posts because the entire city could be seen from the rooftops. The southernmost building was only 150 meters from the railroad tracks and 500 meters from the edge of the city. Colonel Shupp set up his regimental CP within the apartment complex, and Colonel Malay set up his battalion CP in a building next door. Shupp could easily see 3/1's breach site at the railroad station, fewer than 1,500 meters to the east. Marine and Navy SEAL snipers lined the rooftops of the four-story buildings.

Learning from Ron Christmas' Vietnam experiences, Malay decided to put even more firepower on his roof, which sparked a machine gun and mortar duel with the enemy at the northern edge of the city. Kilo Company pounded the enemy positions in the northwestern corner of Fallujah with fixed-wing and Cobra air strikes, machine guns, artillery, mortars, and snipers. The buildings within the first few blocks were beaten into rubble, forcing the enemy to fall back deeper into Fallujah. While a section of Bodisch's tanks and McNulty's Marines established support-by-fire positions at the apartment complex, Captain Brian Chontosh's India Company moved to route GOLDEN, with more tanks in the lead. The Marines reached their assault position by 1400. Captain Eduardo Bitanga's Lima Company Marines rolled up behind McNulty's Kilo Company and cleared the buildings behind the apartments, while Major Todd Desgrosseilliers' men blocked ASR GOLDEN north of the complex.

Each of Malay's company commanders were hard-charging Marines. Bitanga, the son of a career Marine, was just as intense as Chontosh and McNulty but much more jovial. Andrew McNulty was a by-the-book Marine, well-liked by his men and dedicated to his job. Brian Chontosh had recently made captain.

Chontosh had already distinguished himself in combat. As a lieutenant and CAAT Platoon commander, he had become a hero during the march to Baghdad in 2003. When his platoon was ambushed on Highway 1, Chontosh attacked, ordering the driver of his gun truck to charge an enemy machine gun position. When they overran the stronghold, Chontosh jumped into an enemy trench with his M16 and 9mm pistol, killing enemy fighters as he worked his way down its length. When he ran out of ammo, Chontosh picked up enemy rifles and continued the fight. By the time he was finished, Chontosh had single-handedly killed twenty enemy soldiers and cleared 200 meters of enemy trench line. He was awarded the Navy Cross for his bravery. With the Marines' facing their largest urban fight since Hue City in Vietnam, Captain Brian Chontosh ignored his transfer orders and used his thirty days of leave to remain with his men so he could participate in the battle. His India Company would be used as Darkhorse's main effort.

The Desgrosseilliers family had started the Hudson Bay Company in the 17th Century in the North American wilderness and later settled in the northeastern part of the United States. After high school, Todd enlisted in the Marines and became an officer after receiving his bachelor's degree. As the Executive Officer of 3rd Battalion, 5th Marines, Desgrosseilliers was Lieutenant Colonel Malay's second-in-command.

Desgrosseilliers and Malay knew full well they were in for the fight of their lives, clearing 1,000 buildings in the narrow winding streets of the oldest and most dense section of Fallujah. In order to accomplish his difficult task, Desgrosseilliers pulled together his own unit by cherry-picking

Marines from around the battalion. He drew his men from Weapons and the Headquarters and Support (H&S) Companies, assembling administrators, supply clerks, truck drivers, intel guys, and engineers, as well as military working dogs, Explosive Ordnance Disposal (EOD) teams, and two D9 bulldozers. Desgrosseilliers' Task Force Stryker would move in to set up Malay's CP, service support area, Battalion Aid Station (BAS), and the helicopter landing zone. Later renamed Task Force Bruno, Desgrosseilliers' group of disparate Marines would enter the city behind Darkhorse's infantry companies to clean whatever mess remained behind.

Farther east, Lieutenant Jeffery Lee's Third Platoon tanks, along with Captain Gil Juarez' thirteen LAVs, headed south at 1400 to secure 1/3's breach site on the east side of Sichir Road. Juarez' LAVs were not heavy enough to lead the attack, so they were tasked with supporting the breach from behind the railroad berm, using their 25mm Bushmaster cannons as needed and Fire Support Team (FiST)[9] to call in artillery and air strikes. Lieutenant David Klingensmith, a Marine "Mustang,"[10] led 1/8's movement to the breach with his Second Platoon tanks. Captain Meyers stayed back with his headquarters section and Brandl's Alpha Company as the battalion reserve. It wouldn't be long before Meyers' HQ tanks were in the fight.

Just after noon, Captain Kirk Mayfield's Brigade Reconnaissance Troop (BRT), F Troop, 5th CAV from Task Force 2-2, and Newell's Fire Support Officer, Captain James Cobb, drove their two tanks and two Bradleys into position atop the MSR MOBILE Bridge that crossed the railroad tracks northeast of Fallujah. Once there, they immediately began engaging enemy observers and RPG teams with artillery fire. From Cobb's elevated position,

---

9   Each Marine company has a FiST team, led by the Weapons Platoon Commander. The team is equipped with communications and targeting equipment and manned with an artillery Forward Observer and Forward Air Controller. The team coordinates artillery and close air support.

10 The term 'Mustang' denotes an officer with prior enlisted service.

his team commanded a view of the entire northeast quadrant of the city, using their high-tech Long Range Advanced Scout System (LRAS) and Ground Laser Designator System (GLDS) to good effect. Cobb, Mayfield, and the BRT shot at anything that moved within 1,000 meters of the planned breach site. They used everything at their disposal—120mm mortars, 155mm artillery, close air support, direct fire from their M1 tanks and Bradleys, and precise fire from the two snipers riding with their troop.

Nearly four miles to the west of Cobb's BRT, a flight of four Marine F/A-18s dropped a pair of 2,000-lb. JDAM bombs at 1400 on each of Malay's breach lanes along the railroad tracks in the far northwest corner of Fallujah. One of the pilots was Major General Stalder, and it was his fighter that dropped the first bomb. After the initial strikes, the Marine pilots zeroed in on Rainey's and Buhl's breach lanes just west of the railroad station and dropped four more bombs. The ordnance mangled the railroad tracks, left small craters, and knocked the dirt loose atop the berm.

Lieutenant Michael Cragholm, McNulty's First Platoon commander, was standing outside one of the apartment buildings about 1,000 meters away from the impacts when the second set of bombs started falling. The explosions were tremendous, hurling debris high into the air. When Cragholm heard a loud whistling sound, he asked the Marine standing next to him, "What the hell is that?" The words were barely out of his mouth when a piece of shrapnel the size of a helmet slammed into the wall not ten feet from where they were standing.[11]

Cragholm winced and exclaimed, "Oh my God!" All of the Marines around him started laughing.

"You assholes!" Cragholm retorted.

"Sir, you should probably come inside," one of the Marines recommended.

"That's a great idea," replied the young lieutenant, who calmly walked into the breezeway of the apartment building.

The early stages of the battle for Fallujah were proceeding apace. Task Force Wolfpack was on the Shark's Fin, Dan Wittnam's boats were blocking

11 Capt Michael Cragholm telephone interview, 03/01/08.

the river, and now 3/5 had taken the apartment complex in the northwest corner of the city. This is exactly what the enemy had expected. In April's fight, Olson's Marines, along with Gunnery Sergeant Nick Popaditch's tanks, had charged into the cemetery in the northwest corner of the city. Shupp's initial movements had completely focused the enemy's attention to the west and northwest. Little did the insurgents know that they were about to be inundated all across their northern front.

Task Force Blue Diamond—On the Brink of Battle

Two US Army mechanized task forces and four reinforced Marine infantry battalions were preparing to attack all along the northern edge of Fallujah. Pete Newell would assault Fallujah's Maginot Line at the eastern edge of its northern flank, just as the Wehrmacht had done at the beginning of World War II. Jim Rainey's cavalry troopers prepared to split the city in half with an attack down HENRY, followed by the relentless onslaught of more than 2,000 Marines on the ground. Just east of Colonel Shupp's position, another 2,000 Marines of RCT–7 moved south from MSR MOBILE down Sichir Road (DAVE). Colonel Tucker's two Marine battalions prepared to attack into the city with two more piercing thrusts. One under 1/8 would drive down Fallujah's second largest north-south street (ETHAN) while Ramos' 1/3 would bound south between Newell and Brandl. 1/8 assumed its attack position as RCT–7's main effort on the west side of DAVE, and 1/3 moved south on the east side of DAVE behind Meyers' tanks. Unlike the April fight, Task Force Blue Diamond was about to overwhelm the enemy with a well-planned and deliberate attack.

Around 1700, Lieutenant Colonel Brandl took an opportunity to fly his Dragon Eye UAVs into the city for one final bird's eye view of his battle space before night fell. Two of his aircraft were shot down, but one survived its flight down ETHAN. Brandl's commanders gathered around the display and watched intently as the drone beamed back video of the ground they would soon be traversing. They examined their routes all the way past the Braxton Complex down to the Hydra Mosque and on to the Government Center. The Braxton Complex was a walled military compound three blocks down ETHAN. The complex contained barracks and a suspected suicide-bomb factory and training center. Newell also had his UAVs up, and at one point the vehicles got their signals crossed. Newell's soldiers watched as

Fallujah Phase Lines and Districts

their video feed suddenly switched to the Marine UAV. Within a short time the soldiers lost control of their vehicle and it crashed.[12]

At 1800, Lieutenant Colonel Brandl moved his tanks, engineers, and Charlie Company (riding in Amphibious Assault Vehicles) down DAVE to the breach points along the railroad tracks. When they spotted an unusually large number of Marines approaching, the enemy opened with rockets and mortar fire. Instead of trying to cut the rails, Brandl's engineers moved to the berm and began bulldozing a ramp over the tracks while the enemy lobbed RPGs at them from within the city.

---

12 LTC Peter Newell's interview with Matt Matthews, Combat Studies Institute, 03/23/06.

All along the northern edge of the city, Marine tanks climbed the berm and perched themselves atop the railroad tracks. The silhouetted tanks immediately drew more enemy fire. The tankers responded with main gun rounds and .50-caliber and coax machine gun fire, joining the aircraft and artillery that had been raining havoc on the enemy positions.

Around dusk, Bodisch and his XO, First Lieutenant Aaron Smithley, led the attack on the railroad station together with six more Charlie Company tanks. Captain Brian Heatherman's Lima Company Marines mounted up in their tracks and rolled forward toward the station behind Bodisch's armor, leading 3rd Battalion, 1st Marines and the Iraqi National Guard to support the attack.

The immediate goal was for the Marines to clear the area from the water treatment plant to the railroad station. There was a large water tower at the train station open to the sky—a perfect place for enemy lookouts. As the Marines approached, the lookouts in the tank started shooting. Smithley returned fire with a single main gun round, killing the two insurgents and blowing a large hole in the bottom of the tank. Under the covering fire of the Marine tanks and infantry, the Iraqi soldiers from Nassir Wa Salam and CAP India seized the station. While Heatherman's Marines and Bodisch's tankers attacked the train station, Jent's Kilo Company moved to the breach site. Now RCT–1 had three bases of fire: the train station, the apartment complex, and the western bank of the Euphrates River.

Once the train station was secure, Rob Bodisch's two headquarters tanks moved up onto the railroad tracks to join the other Marine tanks firing on the city. They pivoted and drove east on the rails until they were in position to fire directly down HENRY. Opening up with their main guns, they destroyed barriers at the edge of town.

At the far western edge of Fallujah, two more M1 tanks had climbed the fifty-foot berm at 1700. They straddled the railroad there while First Lieutenant Brian LaPointe's engineers raced to the top and set metal cutting charges on the tracks. LaPointe had done his homework. He had scouted the berm a couple of nights before with a group of recon Marines, and visited the same tracks far enough away from the city to take the time to carefully measure the thickness of the rails. When he returned to Camp Fallujah, LaPointe calculated the size and shape of charge he would need to cut through the metal tracks. His research paid off. His Marines set the charges and scampered back down the north side of the berm. Once the charges detonated, Lance Corporals John Pflager and Daniel Gadd II drove their D9 Bulldozer up to the top of the berm.

The D9 bulldozer is a militarized version of one of Caterpillar's largest commercial earthmovers. It is 26.5 feet long, 14.7 feet wide, and 13 feet high. It is virtually unstoppable and weighs nearly sixty tons. The seven-foot tall front blade can rapidly excavate mountains of dirt and even push over a house. It was the Israeli Army that first modified the commercial bulldozer for urban combat by adding armor and bullet-proof glass to protect the operators, who sit in a cockpit ten feet above the ground.

As soon as the bulldozers came into view, the enemy in the city started firing RPGs and machine guns. Unfazed by the gunfire and grenades, the dozer operators plowed across the top. The rails came loose and fell to the southern side of the hill. As the engineers worked, Marines atop the apartment complex returned the enemy fire with their MK-19s, .50-caliber machine guns, and sniper fire. It took Pflager and Gadd, and two other Marines plowing a second passage, exactly two hours to reduce the berm and clear a path for the battalion's vehicles.

Natonski's hammer was just about ready to come crashing down onto the Black Jack Brigade's anvil.

Chapter 7

"Let's Roll"

"We leave an apocalyptic landscape."

— Major Tim Karcher, USA, November, 2004

At 1900, the sky lit up on the eastern horizon and a distant rumble rolled in from Camp Fallujah. A white phosphorous smoke barrage shrouded the entire northern edge of the city. More 155mm howitzer rounds came screaming in like freight trains, exploding on enemy targets and shaking the ground a mile from their point of impact. Then, at last, the main attack was launched, with several coordinated breaching operations at key points along the railroad tracks.

General Natonski had planned to throw the enemy off balance by conducting a pair of deep and rapid mechanized-armor thrusts into the city. Rainey's tanks and Bradleys would form the vanguard of Colonel Shupp's main effort, while Lieutenant Colonel Newell's mechanized infantry would charge into the city on the division's eastern flank.

Rainey's soldiers were tasked with breaching the enemy stronghold just west of the train station, followed by Willie Buhl's Thundering Third Marines. RCT–7 moved toward its breaches at three separate points east of the train station: First Battalion, Eighth Marines entered between the railroad station and Sichir Road; First Battalion, Third Marines advanced into its

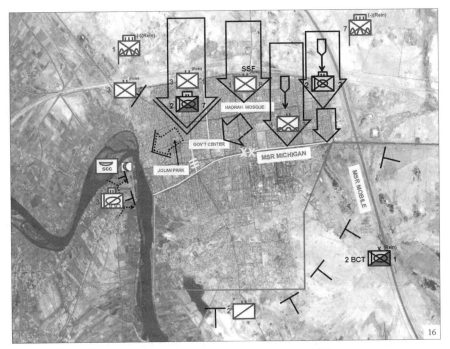

Operation Phantom Fury – Initial Battle Plan

Graphics obtained from LtGen Richard F. Natonski's
PowerPoint presentation, and used with his permission.

breach lane in the regiment's center, east of Sichir Road; and Newell's soldiers rolled forward at the far eastern edge of the city.

Captain Brian Chontosh pushed his India Company Marines through LaPointe's breach hard and fast, bypassing the IED-laced no-man's-land between the railroad tracks and the northern edge of the city. The Darkhorse Marines charged into the northwest corner of Fallujah in their AMTRACs, with Bodisch leading the way. Chontosh's Marines dismounted and occupied several isolated buildings. Once he established a foothold, Chontosh faced his company east and moved to secure the Ma'ahidy Mosque and adjacent cemetery that had been so bitterly contested in Mattis' first assault—the area where Captain Stoddard's squad-sized patrol had first encountered the enemy in April. They were rolling toward the cemetery in the northwest corner of the city by 1930. Any enemy fighters who had survived the relentless air attacks, artillery barrages, and machine gun duels fell back into buildings in the tangled web of streets and alleys of the Jolan

District. Remembering Nick "Gunny Pop" Popaditch's bloody rampage six months earlier, the enemy wanted nothing to do with Bodisch's tanks.

Colonel Formica had a box seat for the unfolding show at his Tactical Command Post (TAC CP) atop a small bridge that crossed MSR MOBILE, two and a half miles south of Mayfield's BRT.[1] As the sky darkened, one by one the lights inside the city switched on. Shorly thereafter, large sections of the city faded to black, one after the other, as if some huge natural disaster had befallen Fallujah. Soon only a few lights in the taller minarets remained illuminated. Eventually even their generators failed, and the last few lights flickered out, bathing Fallujah in complete darkness. Aircraft roared overhead and AC-130s circled in a deadly aerial ballet, pounding targets on the ground. Mesmerized by the scene, Formica watched through his night vision as the flying gun crews pounded targets ahead of the advancing troops.

The railroad berm in Newell's area of operations was only three to five feet high, while Ramos and Brandl faced a six- to twelve-foot berm plus a tank ditch on the far side. Newell's lead tanks pushed to the berm and let loose a volley of fire into the buildings at the edge of the city. Task Force 2-2's engineers raced forward with bulldozers to push an earthen ramp up onto the three-foot berm.

Sean Sims' Alpha Company was the first through the breach with a 2-2 plow tank. Newell's two heavy mechanized teams pushed into the city while Cobb's Fire Support Team moved south along MSR MOBILE like the chain crew at a football game, leading the battalion's advance. They stayed up on the raised highway, looking down into the embattled city. When the enemy tried to reposition or fall back, Cobb hit them with mortars, artillery, and tank and Bradley fire. Often only a single sniper shot was necessary. The raised road along MSR MOBILE afforded Kirk Mayfield's BRT a perfect overview of the fight and a unique opportunity to direct fire. Unable to safely move, the smarter insurgents in the Military District went to ground. Newell's mechanized infantry raced over the berm across the no-man's-land and into the northeast corner of the city.

---

1 COL Michael Formica telephone interview, 11/06/07.

The infantry dismounted in the midst of a 21st-century urban battlefield. It looked as though they had stepped out onto a Terminator movie set. After months of fighting, most of the buildings were piles of rubble. Debris of every description, from broken televisions to cinder blocks, from sofas, clothing, and twisted metal gates littered the streets. Telephone poles were snapped like toothpicks and wires dangled everywhere. Few buildings had emerged from the day's bombardment unscathed, let alone the weeks of abuse from the Marines who had been firing into the city. Newell's soldiers started working their way south amongst the evidence of the unforgiving destructive power of the United States military.

Lieutenant Colonel Ron Lewis enjoyed a bird's-eye view of the attack as he orbited in his Apache helicopter north of the city providing over-the-shoulder close air support to Lieutenant Colonel Rainey's 2-7 Cavalry troopers.[2] Lewis watched the air strikes, the smoke barrage, the artillery rounds impacting, and M1 main gun rounds hitting buildings at the edge of the city.

Then, as if an Olympic starter had fired his pistol, several giant explosions engulfed the railroad tracks. Anyone within earshot immediately knew this was no feint: the Americans were coming.

Ramos pushed Captain Thomas Tennant's Charlie Company up to the berm through a light rain and blowing sand. Charlie Company was tasked with leading the attack as 1/3's main effort. Ramos' Weapons Company gun trucks moved up close to the railroad tracks alongside Lee's tanks and Juarez' LAVs. They stood in overwatch as Charlie Company's Marines prepared to race through the breach in their amphibious tractors. Lee's tanks pushed up to the power lines at 1900, but the enemy had their heavy mortars dialed in on that spot, with rounds impacting all around Lee's pair of tanks. The tankers pushed forward closer to the berm, where they waited for the sappers to complete the ramps. Ramos continued to call in artillery on targets in the city.[3]

But the engineers had problems. They had fired a MICLIC across the berm, but it only mangled the railroad tracks without breaking them. A second MICLIC also failed to sever the tracks. In an effort to break the stalemate, the engineers sent their bulldozers forward to reduce the berm, but

2   COL Ronald Lewis telephone interview, 02/15/08.

3   Capt Jeffery Lee telephone interview, 07/10/08.

the first D9 got stuck in the mud and tipped onto its side. The second D9 caught the railroad track with its giant rear ripper and pulled the section of rail up from the ground. Unfortunately, all that did was create a raised metal barrier across the breach. Someone decided to employ satchel and cutting charges, to no avail. Try as they might, the engineers were unable to clear the mangled obstruction. The only solution was to start a new ramp.

Captain Tennant's Marines, meanwhile, were waiting nervously inside their tracks as more problems arose at the breach—all the while enduring mortar and machine gun fire that was thankfully sporadic and ineffective.[4] Tennant, a native New Yorker from Long Island and the son of a New York City cop, ended up waiting for hours with his Charlie Company Marines.

Lieutenant Colonel Brandl's Marines preceded their movement with a ten-minute artillery and mortar barrage, and some of Juarez' LAVs drove right up to the berm to provide breach security. Knowing that the Sichir Road railroad overpass was mined, Brandl ordered his engineers to breach the railroad tracks on the west side of DAVE.[5] He didn't move anyone under the bridge until his engineers had cleared Sichir Road.

Brandl had few problems at his breach site. First, he bulldozed a pair of lanes over the top. When one of the breaches became impassable, all of Brandl's Marines moved over to the second, clear breach lane. Lieutenant Klingensmith's White Platoon, A Co., 2nd Tanks was the first unit through, led by Corporal Anthony Gantt's White 3 tank.[6] They engaged enemy snipers from their support-by-fire positions while Brandl fired the first of two MICLICs into the open field between the railroad tracks and the city. Captain Read Omohundro's Bravo Company infantrymen charged through on foot to gain a foothold at the northwest end of ETHAN.

Captain Theodore Bethea's Charlie Company moved forward at 2200 on foot behind Omohundro's company. Charlie Company became the battalion's main effort. Brandl attacked south with two companies abreast, one on either side of ETHAN. Captain Cunningham's Alpha Company remained north of the breach, standing by as Brandl's reserve while Bethea attacked the Braxton Complex.

---

4   Maj Thomas Tennant telephone interview, 02/19/08.

5   Col Gareth Brandl telephone interview, 11/20/07.

6   Cpl Anthony Gantt telephone interview, 06/10/08.

Brandl's company commanders could not have been more different. Captain Aaron Cunningham, a tall, slender Georgian, was an intelligent leader with nerves of steel and a fantastic company commander. Bethea, Charlie Company's commander, hailed from Louisiana. Both were Southerners, but while Cunningham was deliberate and determined, Bethea was more gung-ho and gregarious. Everyone Bethea saw got, "Good to go! Good to go! Glad to see ya!" Bethea was like Shupp on steroids, a poster-perfect Marine. Omohundro was one of those Marines who excelled in combat but was not well liked by his men. That didn't bother him. Omohundro was a stern leader who made decisions and led with little consultation. Colonel Tucker had almost relieved him prior to the fight, but ended up recommending him for a Silver Star after it was all over.[7]

Brandl moved another MICLIC vehicle forward and fired another line charge straight down ETHAN, but it failed to explode. Marines rushed out and re-primed the charge. On their second attempt, nearly a ton of C4 detonated, lighting the night sky and sending a massive shock wave into the city. White Platoon tanks followed the shock wave down ETHAN. Charlie Company's 200 sailors and Marines swarmed down the thoroughfare toward the Braxton Complex behind Klingensmith's advancing tanks.

The Braxton Complex was three blocks into the city down Brandl's narrow avenue of attack. Bethea secured the complex with little resistance and set up his company mortars. Once his new position was secure, he turned his attention south toward his next objective: the Hydra Mosque.[8]

From his CP on the apartment roof, Colonel Shupp could see glowing chem-lights on Bodisch's tanks as they moved from right to left inside the city. As the Marines approached the cemetery, enemy fighters retreated into the mosque located at the northeast corner of the graveyard. The enemy made its first feeble stand in three buildings: a school, an old barracks, and the mosque where Janabi had imprisoned, tortured, and killed Lieutenant Colonel Suleiman.

---

7   Col (ret.) Craig Tucker telephone interview, 01/10/08.

8   Maj Theodore Bethea II personal interview, 05/20/08.

Chontosh's attack was so violent and overwhelming that the enemy fled south. India Company pushed all the way to 3/5's eastern boundary, forcing the insurgents out of the cemetery and buildings and into Willie Buhl's area.[9] Bodisch and Chontosh had taken their first objective so quickly that the regimental staff feared they might be in the line of fire when 3/1 detonated its MICLIC on the railroad tracks.

Bitanga's Lima Company raced through the berm behind Chontosh's Marines. Even after all of the work to reduce this obstacle, the berm was still fifteen feet high. When Bitanga's track went up the near side, all he could see was the darkening night sky. As his track hit the crest, its underbelly was exposed to the enemy. "Whoa—this is not good," Bitanga thought just as the front end dropped like a shifting teeter-totter.[10]

Suddenly, the city was right in front of him. Lima Company's twelve tracks slammed over the berm and headed for the buildings on the right. Bitanga's mission was to get to a small palm grove on the banks of the Euphrates River and guard the regiment's western flank. The Marines moved through the first few buildings until they found a good position to defend. Because Colonel Malay wanted to keep the battalion online, Bitanga did not want to move too far out in front. He held up just north of the "Palm Grove," waiting for Kilo Company to get into the city. Not long after they assumed their new position, Bitanga's men started taking fire.

Into the Breach

3d Battalion, 1st Marines was still having problems breaching the railroad tracks at the northern edge of the city. Its MICLIC didn't sever the steel rails, and bulldozers could not plow through until the mangled rails were removed. Engineers moved forward and placed a four-pound stick of dynamite under each track, and the resulting explosions finally cut them free. After this delay, a D9 bulldozer clanked forward and pushed the twisted metal aside. Only then could the engineers began the back-and-forth work of clearing a breach.

9　Capt Brian Chontosh telephone interview, 12/08/07.

10　Maj Eduardo Bitanga telephone interview, 2/15/08.

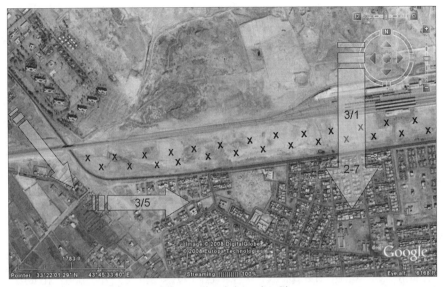

RCT-1's Attack into the City

Precious darkness slipped past as Lieutenant Colonel Rainey's 2-7 cavalry troopers waited for nearly six hours for the engineers to open a passage. Exasperated by the delay, Rainey decided to send his tracked vehicles into the city even though the Marines had not finished clearing their breach lanes. He attacked into the breach at 0030 on November 9, with C/3-8 leading the way, followed by A/2-7.[11] Rainey's troopers moved to secure HENRY and seize the enemy's command-and-control point at Jolan Park.

Staff Sergeant Matthew Smith led the battalion through the breach with a tank-mounted plow. Staff Sergeant Anibal Reyes followed Smith with a roller attached to the front of his tank. Once across no-man's-land, Smith rammed into the two-foot curb and dropped his plow. Reyes' roller, however, would not drop. Hoping to jar the roller loose, he continued forward until he rammed the cemetery wall; still the roller wouldn't budge. Reyes climbed out of his tank, jumped to the ground, and attacked the stubborn bolt with a sledge hammer. Tracers were flying over his head as he pounded on it metal. "Oh man," he thought, "I'm gonna get shot any

11 COL James Rainey telephone interview, 11/07/07.

minute."[12] Finally the bolt came loose and the roller fell with a heavy thud to the ground.

Smith and Reyes turned their tanks east on Route GOLDEN and raced toward HENRY. Their orders were to drive south into Fallujah and press down the city's main artery. But Bodisch's tanks had not destroyed all the Jersey and Hesco barriers at the intersection of HENRY and GOLDEN. Even after all the pounding they had received, the remaining obstructions looked to Reyes—passing by, in his buttoned-up tank in the dark of night—like a solid wall. So he missed the blockaded road and drove right past his turn. But Smith noticed the barricades, stopped, and radioed for Reyes to return.

While he waited, Smith opened fire on the remaining obstructions at point-blank range. His main gun rounds blew open a path wide enough for his tank to squeeze through. Reyes followed, snaking his tank through in an attempt to widen the breach. The enemy scattered like cockroaches discovered in a filthy kitchen. More than 100 AK-47s opened fire on Smith and Reyes. RPGs streaked through the darkness. The two tanks sprayed the area with machine gun fire, scaring off any insurgents they didn't mow down.

Sergeant Smith radioed to Reyes, "What is your pucker factor now?" he asked.

"If I had a lump of coal up my ass," Reyes replied, "it would be a diamond."[13]

Even as the enemy insurgents scrambled to cover, a continuous hail of gunfire pelted the two lead tanks. The enemy was unleashing everything they had with the mistaken assumption that they could take on the tanks and win. The tankers responded with coax machine gun fire that spewed streams of steel into insurgent strongpoints. The tank's main guns belched fireballs the size of a house, momentarily lighting the street as if it were daytime and shaking the ground as the supersonic projectiles shattered buildings and killed any insurgent in or close to their path.

Smith and Reyes were ordered to push forward to make room for the rest of Cougar's tanks. Slowly the two M1s ground forward into the maelstrom.

---

12 SSG Anibal Reyes telephone interview, 2/12/08.

13 *Ibid.*

Both tank commanders waited nervously at BETH for the battalion's tanks and Bradleys to fill in behind them. Lieutenant Colonel Rainey and Tim Karcher followed directly behind Cougar's tanks in their Bradleys with the battalion's command section.

Karcher was positioned fifty meters behind Rainey. Just as Rainey and Karcher turned down HENRY, shots rang out. Karcher's gunner peppered the back of Rainey's vehicle with 7.62 rounds. "What the hell are you doing?"[14] Rainey radioed to Karcher.

Unbeknownst to Rainey, an enemy fighter had jumped out behind Rainey's Bradley with an RPG on his shoulder. Karcher's gunner spotted him and opened fire, cutting the insurgent down before he could level his weapon on Rainey's vulnerable back ramp.

"I thought you wanted me to kill the enemy," Karcher calmly replied.

Swarms of insurgents tried to maneuver around to get behind the tanks, only to find more tanks and Bradleys pushing into the city through the gap in the barricade. From their perspective, it must have seemed as though there was no end to the armored juggernaut.

Apache 2-7 followed Rainey and his tanks through the breach on HENRY and fanned out to the west. Any enemy fighters remaining at the HENRY/APRIL intersection must have been scared silly as they watched an entire mechanized battalion roll through their flimsy barricade: tank after tank, Bradley after Bradley, the Americans just kept pouring into the city. Some insurgents were foolish enough to stand and fight. Their RPG rounds bounced harmlessly off the tanks and their bullets bounced off the armor like rain on a tin roof.

Captain Chris Brooke's Comanche Company was the last through the breach. C/2-7 moved in behind C/3-8 in its ten Bradley Fighting Vehicles. Brooke's mission was to keep HENRY open behind Rainey's armored attack.

Marines Lead from the Front

Colonel Shupp had been monitoring the progress of the attack from his perch atop the apartment complex. He had Dinauer clearing the Shark's Fin

---

14 COL Jim Rainey telephone interview, 11/8/07.

in the west, the train station under attack from the north, and 3/5 attacking in the northwest. Now, Rainey was slamming into the city.

But 3/1 seemed to be having problems getting through the breach. Buhl was running the attack from his own CP and couldn't update Shupp as to what was happening at the breach. A concerned Shupp sought out Major Bill Arnold, his security chief. "That's it!" he told Arnold. "Take me to the breach. I gotta see what's going on!"[15]

Major Bill Arnold, a high school history teacher, commanded a Marine reserve scout platoon from Amarillo, Texas. His platoon became the regimental scouts for 1st Marines, and Arnold personally led Shupp's security detachment. They moved the colonel and a squad of scouts around in six HMMWVs, four armed with .50-caliber machine guns and MK-19 grenade launchers.

Shupp, accompanied by Major Arnold and his Personal Security Detachment (PSD), drove up and over to the site of the breach in the railroad tracks. They stopped a little to the north and jumped from their vehicles to walk down to see what was causing the congestion. "It was deuce dark," remembered Shupp, who noted he could barely see five meters ahead in the blackness of the night.[16] Shupp's radio operator nearly got lost trying to keep up with the colonel. By the time Shupp reached the breach site Rainey had already moved into the city and a Marine D9 Bulldozer was working in the breach lane. The D9 driver was trying to make the breach lane perfect.

Lieutenant Colonel Dave Bellen and Gunner Charles Colleton started throwing rocks at the D9 cab. Once they got the driver's attention they waved him out of the lane, screaming at the top of their lungs, "Get the hell out of the way."[17] Finally, 3/1 was able to start moving through, but one of the Marine HMMWVs blew a tire in the effort. While they were changing it, the truck fell off the jack, pinning a Marine. As others worked to extricate the trapped warrior and clear the accident, the entire battalion waited in the dark north of the breach point.

Now Shupp was starting to get concerned. There was no way he wanted Rainey's tankers in the city without infantry support. Without infantry, the

15 Maj Bill Arnold telephone interview, 1/9/08.

16 Col Michael Shupp personal interview, 9/25/07.

17 *Ibid.*

enemy could swarm the armored vehicles and hit them from all sides with RPGs and drop fire bombs and IEDs on the tanks from rooftops. Without infantry support they could take heavy casualties. He had to get his men moving.

Shupp knew that Rainey's tanks had crossed the open field between the railroad tracks and the city with a plow and rollers. If he stayed in the tanks' tracks, he would not have to worry about mines. Even so and just to be safe, Shupp ordered the D9 Bulldozer to get in front and plow through again. Next, he told his staff, "Get that infantry company down here!" When he had Major Arnold and Lima Company's infantrymen in tow behind him, Shupp set out to lead his Marines across no-man's-land on foot. The bulldozer plowed all the way to GOLDEN, and when Shupp reached the edge of the city Rainey was there waiting for him.

"Colonel, what are you doing here?" Rainey exclaimed.

"I had to come see ya," Shupp calmly replied.

The Marines encountered the same two-foot tall concrete median running down the center of ASR GOLDEN as had Smith and Reyes. "Sir," one of the Marines told Shupp, "we are not going to be able to get our HMMWVs through this."

"Get the Goddamned bulldozer and come down here and take that thing out!" he replied.[18]

The D9 slammed into the median, ripped an eight-foot section out, and pushed it all the way across GOLDEN, crashing what was left into the wall of a house.

By leading from the front, Colonel Shupp broke the logjam and 3/1's Lima Company Marines began pouring into the city. Lieutenant Colonel Buhl moved into Fallujah with his Marines. He would not leave the city for seventeen days.

With 3/1 behind them, Rainey's 2-7 CAV attacked down three streets with Apache/2-7 as the battalion's main effort and HENRY as its eastern boundary. Twaddell attacked through crowded streets and open fields filled

18 *Ibid.*

with trash and abandoned cars. It was a mounted attack south toward Jolan Park (objective PENNSYLVANIA), with two platoons up and one back.

The cavalry troopers moved methodically forward in box formations (four vehicles, one at each corner) with UAVs and Lewis' Apache helicopters providing overwatch. This formation allowed the troopers to protect each other in all directions. If they came under attack, two of the other three vehicles in the box could easily reinforce the vehicle under fire.

Because Twaddell's Bradleys were moving south at a slower pace through the narrow streets and urban clutter, Rainey had to rein in Captain Glass and his tankers as they were rolling south on HENRY. He had to keep Cougar/3-8 on line with Twaddell. Glass stopped his advance down HENRY at DONNA around four in the morning, and Brooke's fighting vehicles rolled to a stop behind him.

The regiment had prepared this area with air strikes, artillery, and AC-130 gunship runs, during which strings of IEDs were detonated by a single 500-lb bomb. They exploded one after another down city streets like giant firecrackers on the Chinese New Year. The explosives would have inflicted heavy casualties on the Marines if they had gone off as the insurgents had hoped. Shupp wanted Rainey to move through as fast as he could to break through what was left of the IED belt and get behind the enemy's command-and-control nodes. With the enemy disrupted, his Marines could get into the city on foot without taking mass casualties in the streets.

Bodisch's tanks led Buhl's Marines, killing anything larger than squad-sized formations. Shupp had ordered them not to stop for smaller elements unless they had to fight through them. The immediate goal was to keep moving to get through the defenses and unhinge the enemy.[19] The last thing Shupp wanted was an urban war of attrition. He also knew that when everyone else left, RCT–1 was going to take control of Fallujah. His men would have to go back and clear every building. Driving ahead now was the only option. And so Shupp's Marines followed Rainey's devastation, shock, and violence of speed with a wave of infantrymen on the ground, moving through the city like a giant steamroller.

19 *Ibid.*

Captain Jent's reinforced Kilo Company Marines passed through the breach at 0400 and entered the city just before sunrise.[20] Kilo Company would be 3/1's main effort throughout the entire fight. It moved online with Clark's India Company (the sturdiest company in the battalion) on its left and Chontosh's Darkhorse Marines on its right. By this time a line of Marines stretched from the Euphrates River to HENRY, with Bitanga in the west and Clark in the east. Chontosh, Clark, and Jent pushed forward relentlessly.

Attack in the East

With Mayfield and Cobb up on MSR MOBILE killing everything that moved, Task Force 2-2's tanks, Bradleys, and infantry bounded relentlessly forward into the Askari District. On the ground, Captain Sean Sims' infantry moved from building to building, attacking south through the streets. Not far into the city and after not meeting the expected resistance, Sergeant David Bellavia's soldiers (wearing Night Vision Goggles) noticed a lone Iraqi walking down the street. The man was strolling north carrying a car battery with an AK strapped over his shoulder. Bellavia's men dropped the insurgent in the middle of the street with a short, well-placed burst of gunfire.[21]

Bellavia's men pushed forward and moved into one of the houses in their path. Once inside, they found it loaded with bombs and other explosives, all wired to explode. Before he was killed, the car battery-carrying insurgent had been walking toward this building. Bellavia believed the dead insurgent intended to hook up the battery to detonate the "house bomb" after Bellavia's men entered the trap. Natonski's strategy was working: Bellavia and his men had driven inside the city so quickly that at least this insurgent had been unable to detonate his booby trap as planned.

By 0400, some of the Iraqi soldiers supporting Lieutenant Colonel Newell had gone through the breach on foot, but their 5-ton trucks got hung up and slowed their progress. The Iraqis, who were supposed to be filling in behind 2-2's lightning advance, were falling farther and farther behind. Task

---

20 Maj Timothy Jent telephone interview, 03/24/08.

21 SSG Bellavia telephone interview, 07/18/09.

RCT-7's Attack into the City

Force 2-2's 49-year-old Command Sergeant Major, Steve Faulkenburg, was with the Iraqi soldiers. When he climbed out of his HMMWV to encourage them to move through the breach, he was hit in the head by a single bullet. Faulkenburg was the first Task Force 2-2 soldier killed in Operation al-Fajr. Unfortunately, he would not be the last.

The Hydra Mosque was a known enemy command-and-control center a little more than half a mile from the northern edge of the city on the southeast corner of the intersection of two major streets, ETHAN and CATHY. Bethea had a quarter mile of houses and open fields to negotiate before he reached CATHY. Omohundro advanced toward his objective on Bethea's right along the west side of ETHAN. The Community Center was across the street from the Hydra Mosque, and Brandl wanted both buildings attacked simultaneously.[22]

Markley and Meyers in their tanks led the two-company attack down ETHAN, advancing slowly to allow the Marines on the ground to keep pace. Bethea pushed forward behind the tanks in a tight formation, never more

22 Col Gareth Brandl telephone interview, 11/20/07

than two houses wide, with his Second Platoon in the lead. The enemy fought the Marines' advance openly in the streets all the way to the mosque.

Around midnight, just as the Marines pushed south from the barracks at the Braxton Complex, the enemy counterattacked. More than thirty insurgents charged Charlie Company head on firing RPGs, machine guns, and AKs from the buildings and open fields between Bethea and the Hydra Mosque. Bethea verified that Meyers' tank was south of his position and ordered his Marines to throw IR beacons out in front of their lines.

High above, Basher was watching. Bethea approved the strike, and the AC-130 gunners opened up with their 40mm cannon.

Boom! Boom! Boom! Boom!

The rounds slaughtered the attacking insurgents.

THUD! A 105mm howitzer round exploded right on target. Bethea ordered Basher to fire for effect.

Boom! Boom! Boom! THUD! Boom! Boom! Boom! THUD!

The enemy's attack was stopped cold. C Company moved forward and found thirty-one bodies, all victims of Basher's deadly-accurate fire.

The AC-130s were busy all night, slaughtering insurgents ahead of Task Force Blue Diamond's advance. They alternated between pounding OBJ VIRGINIA in front of Rainey's troopers and killing insurgents positioning themselves to defend against Newell's advance in the east.

Two of RCT–7's battalions were attacking into the city by 2200, but 1/3 was still bogged down at the breach. Lieutenant Lee had been talking on the radio with Captain Juarez as the tanks and LAVs waited to attack. Finally, just before midnight, Lee got fed up. He couldn't contact the battalion S3, so he asked Juarez to tell Major Pfeuffer that he was going to take his two tanks east and try to get through 2-2's breach about 800 meters to his left.[23]

As Lee and his platoon sergeant, Sergeant Ducasse, were moving east, one of Captain Thomas Tennant's tracks hit a string of anti-personnel mines. Bang! Bang! Bang! Boom! The last blast was next to the AMTRAC. One of the Marines sitting on top of the track, Corporal Johnson, took the brunt of the explosion that severed one of his arms and a leg. Tennant called for a

23 Capt Jeffery Lee telephone interview, 07/10/08.

casevac,[24] which stopped the advance. Once Johnson was evacuated, Charlie Company dismounted and pushed through the minefield on foot.[25]

Lee and his wingman, Ducasse, drove through 2-2's lane and south to APRIL, where they turned west and drove back down to where they belonged. Lee left Ducasse up near APRIL so that Tennant's Marines could find them, while he turned south toward their first objective, the al Tafiq Mosque. He drove twenty-five meters into the city and stopped. The enemy immediately opened fire at Lee's tank from the surrounding buildings and the mosque. Lee held his ground, waiting for Charley Company to come across the railroad tracks.

Once Tennant's Marines arrived, Lee and Tennant waited at their foothold for the rest of the battalion. Tennant's Marines were chomping at the bit. "Just sit tight, sit tight," he advised his Marines.[26]

Within minutes, Bravo Company came into the city and moved to Tennant's left, and Alpha Company came in right behind them. Once the entire battalion was in place, two companies up and one back, the S3 gave the go-ahead to push south. Ramos' Marines finally started slowly moving forward toward the al Tafiq Mosque. Insurgents were running in and out of the building and Lee's gunner, Corporal Ricardo Rios, was cutting them down with his coax machine gun as fast as he could.

When Lee and Ducasse's tanks reached the open field north of the mosque, the enemy started firing RPGs. The anti-personnel warheads hitting the M1 tanks was no different than as if someone had thrown a rock at them. The charges exploded harmlessly, leaving nothing more than a black scorch mark on the armor. Lee responded with twenty rounds from his main gun, filling the street with bone-jarring concussions and clouds of billowing dust. Those insurgents still inside the mosque scattered, and Tennant's Marines cut them down as they fled. By the time the Marines reached the mosque it was empty. Tennant's Iraqi Intervention Force rushed in to clear the site.

The al Tafiq Mosque was secure by 0300.

---

24 A casevac is specifically a Casualty Evacuation from the battlefield. Casevac is a subset of the more generic Medical Evacuation or medevac.

25 Maj Thomas Tennant telephone interview, 02/19/08.

26 *Ibid.*

Chapter 8

The First Day in the City

"I love tanks."

— Colonel Pat Malay, USMC, October 5, 2007

Fighting in the Askari District

Task Force 2-2 advanced one-half mile into the Askari District with tanks, Bradleys, and infantry squads bounding through the enemy positions like boats through water. The smarter insurgents let the armored vehicles and infantry flow right past them by simply moving aside or hiding until the juggernaut was well behind them.

Alpha Company, 2-2 reached the Imam al Shafi Mosque before the sun came up. The mosque, only 500 meters from MICHIGAN, was a major command-and-control center, aid station, and weapons cache for the Askari District. With 1/3's Marines slowed by their problems at the breach and 2-2 pushing forward, a large gap developed along the boundary between RCT-7's Marines and Newell's soldiers. As a result, A/2-2's infantrymen moved back north to set into defensive positions across the street from the mosque. From Lieutenant Joaquin Meno's Third Platoon, Staff Sergeant Colin Fitts moved his squad into a house due north of the mosque, while Sergeant Bellavia's 2nd Squad moved to the end of the block to occupy the corner house. While Fitts kept his squad hidden inside their house, Bellavia moved his men to the roof.

They were in position for only a short time when one of Bellavia's squad members noticed movement in a window in the house next door. Bellavia radioed Fitts to make sure that it wasn't one of his men. It wasn't. When the shadow appeared again in the window, Bellavia's soldiers opened fire, wounding the insurgent.

The injured enemy lookout stumbled down the stairs and out of the house next door as Bellavia's men lobbed grenades into the courtyard. Trapped, the now-dying insurgent called out for his friends. Voices in the dark answered their wounded comrade, first from the east, then the west, and even the north. The enemy was all around Bellavia's squad on its rooftop fortress, and his Bradleys were a block away: the squad was surrounded and isolated from their armored vehicles. The sun was just starting to glow in the early morning sky when a whistle blew, followed by another and then another.

"These fucking dudes are about to charge us," Bellavia told his squad. "Okay, get your ammo out, SAW ammo at your knees. Line your mags up where you can get to 'em quick. We're not leaving this roof. We're not moving. We'll stand and fight right the fuck here."[1]

The first attack came from the northwest as the sun rose. A half-dozen insurgents charged across the street right in front of Fitts' hidden squad. First Squad mowed them down before they knew what hit them. Now that his position was compromised, Fitts decided to pull his squad back and consolidate with Bellavia on the rooftop stronghold. "I'm coming to you," Fitts radioed to Bellavia. Moments later Fitts' First Squad streamed onto Bellavia's roof, reuniting Lieutenant Joaquin Meno's Third Platoon. Fitts and Bellavia set their fields of fire and prepared for the next assault.

The second attack came from the windows, rooftops, and alleyways all around Third Platoon's position. The insurgents attacked with everything they had: AKs, machine guns, and RPGs. Bullets chipped away at the walls and rockets whizzed overhead. The soldiers returned fire with their 240 machine guns, SAWs, and M4s.

Although they were outnumbered, for now Meno's men were holding their own in this hellish gunfight. Meno called for his Bradleys to bring in more firepower. Sergeant Chad Ellis was parked in Meno's track at an intersection southeast of the fight, but his Bushmaster and 240 were both

---

1   Bellavia, *House to House*, p. 145.

down and he was just trying to stay out of the way. It was Staff Sergeant Cory Brown's Bradley that answered the call for help. Brown's track rumbled up the street, firing at anything that moved. When the insurgents sensed that Ellis' track was compromised, they attacked. Ellis fought back by picking off charging insurgents with his only working weapon—his M16.

Brown continued to rake the street below, blasting windows with his Bushmaster cannon as more machine gun fire peppered the wall atop Bellavia's fortress. Bellavia's men took the enemy machine gun out with two AT4[2] rockets. By this time Bellavia's men were running low on ammunition, but they continued to drop insurgents in the streets. When a group of enemy fighters moved to engulf Brown's Bradley, he fired a TOW missile into them, killing most of the group and dispersing the rest.

The determined enemy refused to give up the attack. Reinforcements crossed MICHIGAN and charged north out of the industrial district. First they crouched behind a concrete barrier and started lobbing RPGs at Ellis. Sergeant First Class James W. "JW" Cantrell pulled up in his Bradley to protect Ellis. As soon as he rounded the corner, he let loose another TOW missile that whooshed down the road toward Ellis' attackers, blowing the corner off a building.

One of the company's M1 tanks clanked in behind Cantrell. The M1 gunner blew the enemy's Texas barrier at MICHIGAN apart with main gun rounds, and Cantrell's gunner blasted the dozen insurgents as they scattered. Cantrell and the Abrams tank finally broke the enemy's attack. Three and one-half hours had passed since Bellavia shot the insurgent in the window.

While Bellavia's soldiers were fighting for their lives, Captain Tennant's Charlie Company, 1/3, was preparing to push south from the al Tafiq Mosque. Before the Hawaii Marines moved out, the attached Army psyops detachment started broadcasting surrender pleas from the mosque's loudspeakers. As soon as they started, the entire block south of the mosque erupted in gunfire: RPGs and mortar rounds harmlessly rained down on the Marines waiting in the mosque courtyard.

2   The AT4 is a portable, one-shot, 84mm, anti-tank rocket.

Tennant moved his machine gunners and rocket teams to the roof of the mosque, and then dispatched his Third Platoon into the gauntlet. The Marines moved south, engaging in a house-by-house street battle with the insurgents. Corporal David Willis could see a gun barrel or muzzle flash in every window. One by one the Marines fired at each, either killing or scaring away its occupant; building by building, the infantry pushed past each house. They didn't take the time to fully clear the buildings. Their mission was to get to MICHIGAN as fast as they could. They fought their way deeper and deeper into the city, leaving scores of enemy fighters in the buildings behind them.

Lee's tanks and Tennant's Marines pushed south toward the next objective, the Mujareen Mosque located a block north of "Dave's Field." Dave's Field covered an entire city block, 400 x 200 meters along MSR MICHIGAN. It had once been the site of a large soccer facility that boasted at least three fields. In recent months the insurgents had used it as a makeshift graveyard.[3]

Fighting in the Jolan District

As the sun rose in the morning sky, the city's dingy-gray buildings slowly turned to the color of sand. Despite the spreading light, the morning was cold and wet, a low-lying fog on the city streets. With nearly all of the city's civilians having fled, only enemy combatants were left in a what was now a giant ghost town. Goats, chickens, and dogs roamed the rubble-strewn streets.

The Darkhorse Marines moved on line facing south and prepared to move into the Jolan District. Captain Brian Chontosh's India Company remained on the battalion's eastern boundary. Andrew McNulty's Kilo Company prepared to move into the city to fill in between Chontosh and Edward Bitanga's Lima Company, which held the western flank up against the Euphrates River.

Bitanga's Marines were still taking fire from the first block of buildings by the Palm Grove; so while they waited for McNulty's Kilo Company Marines to fill in on their left, Bitanga brought up his section of tanks and

---

3 Capt Jeffery Lee telephone interview, 07/10/08.

started wearing out the first row of houses with main gun rounds, TOW missiles, and Cobra gun runs.[4]

Once the men of Kilo got into the city, both India and Kilo companies advanced side by side, moving in unison like a giant squeegee. Initially there was little contact, for the enemy had fallen back to positions deep within Fallujah. As a result, the morning's advance was largely uneventful. Lima Company held north of the Palm Grove, waiting for McNulty and Chontosh to catch up.

Led by Bodisch's fourteen Comanche tanks, Colonel Shupp's entire regiment advanced six infantry companies abreast. Chris Brooke's ten Bradleys guarded the left flank along HENRY, and Wittnam, Parrello, Rubio, and the Small Craft Company guarded the river on the right. The tank-infantry teams went to work, grinding forward and defeating every enemy attempt to stand and fight. It was the Marine Air Ground Task Force at its best. "If you get Marine Corps firepower pointed in the right direction," observed Colonel Malay, "whoever is on the other end is in big, big trouble."[5]

Sergeant Jason Arellano and his squad were right in the center of Malay's squeegee. Arellano knew that Marines would die in the coming days, but he hoped that he could bring all of his Marines safely through the coming fight. His worst fear was that someone in his squad would fall due to some mistake on his part. He vowed to focus on each engagement and take one day at a time. He couldn't let his men down. He knew that if something happened to him, his guys would be ready to step up and take his position. They were ready; but was he?[6]

Early that morning, Colonel Shupp met with the troops of the Iraqi 1st Battalion as they were preparing to enter the city. He could tell they were scared, so he took his personal security detachment and went to the head of the formation to greet the Iraqi brigade commander. He then proceeded to

---

4   Maj Eduardo Bitanga telephone interview, 02/15/08.

5   Col Patrick Malay telephone Interview, 11/4/07.

6   Sgt Jason Arellano telephone interview, 03/10/08.

march the infantry into the city. Shupp wanted the Iraqis to see they were all in the fight together. He walked them into position alongside Captain Brooke's Bradleys that were lining HENRY, guarding the road with their 25mm Bushmaster cannons. Shupp's leadership and the armored vehicles gave the Iraqi soldiers the confidence they needed. They immediately started erecting barricades and concertina. It was the perfect mission for them. They put up tetrahedrons and they blocked HENRY across the whole eastern side of the city. Nothing could get through.

There comes a point in time when the well-planned operation gives way to actual combat, and for many soldiers and Marines that experience took place on November 9. For some, it would take a series of events—seeing a dead body, a severed foot, or a blood-stained room. For others, it was a single traumatic event, like the realization that the enemy was shooting at them. For Captain Rob Bodisch, that moment came around 0830 when a guy in a "man-dress" popped out into the street in front of his M1 tank and launched an RPG at nearly point-blank range.

Bodisch, who had been leading Captain Jent's Kilo Company down the claustrophobic streets of the Jolan District, returned fire with his main gun. The tank rocked and was immediately enveloped in a cloud of dust and debris. His main gun round and the enemy RPG whizzed past each other in flight, each heading for its target. Bodisch had no clue where his MPAT[7] round impacted, but the RPG hit his tank with a loud boom. As soon as the dust settled, Bodisch fired again—and watched in amazement as his second round clanged out of the muzzle and fell to the ground in front of the tank. The RPG detonation had damaged the main gun, taking it out of action.

Captain Chris Brooke was tasked with protecting route HENRY down to CATHY during the first day of fighting. As the commander of Rainey's trailing company, he also had to be prepared to respond as the battalion reserve. Brooke devised a strategy that would conserve his ammunition and enable him to complete his mission.

---

7   The Multi-Purpose Anti-Tank round is a high-explosive munition designed to destroy lightly armored ground targets, such as bunkers or buildings.

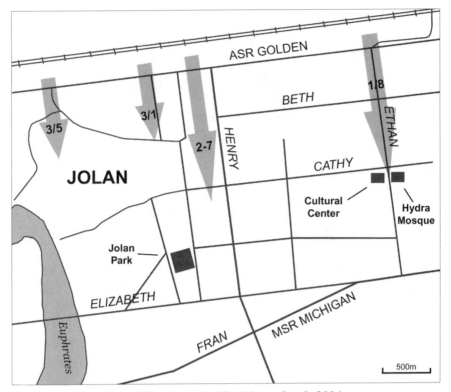

Initial Push into the City, November 9, 2004

Brooke only had ten Bradleys and little infantry, so he broke his company up into two-vehicle sections. On his left flank there was a 500-meter gap between HENRY and GEORGE, between his Bradleys and RCT–7's units; on his right was the entire 1st Marine Regiment. Brooke decided to devote all of his attention toward that 500-meter no-man's-land. Glass and Twaddell had bypassed a lot of stuff in their charge south, so Brooke's first task was to make sure the buildings along HENRY were clear. He had his Bradley sections drive up and down HENRY, and his men clear suspected buildings on the east side of the street.

Once he was comfortable that HENRY was clear, Iraqi security forces started moving in and Brooke began concentrating on the blocks to his east. His method was to send a section of Bradleys driving east on one of the side streets until they were fired upon. In most cases, the Bradleys would almost immediately come under coordinated salvos of RPGs and heavy small arms fire. In response, the Bradley gunners would return fire into the offending building, while Brooke's Fire Support Team called in either artillery or an air strike. As soon as the indirect fire mission was set up, the Bradleys would withdraw, the bombs and mortars would fall on the target, and the Bradleys would push forward again. The process was repeated every time they encountered an enemy position.

Brooke kept this up all morning, venturing farther into the gap between RCT–1 and RCT–7 and deeper south toward CATHY.

1/8's First Big Fight

For most of the night, Captain Theodore Bethea's Charlie Company and Captain Read Omohundro's Bravo Company had been fighting their way down ETHAN, with Meyers and Klingensmith's tanks in the lead and Basher flying overhead. There was heavy fighting from the Braxton Complex all the way down to CATHY. By sunrise, Brandl was ready to attack the al Hydra Mosque Complex.

At first light Bethea called in a barrage of white phosphorous to screen Charlie Company's movement. Marine artillery shells screamed in from the east and giant air bursts hurled hundreds of four-inch smoking balls to the earth. When some of the burning balls landed around the Marines in the street, the infantrymen had no choice but to run for shelter in nearby buildings. Some of the fireballs also landed on the tanks, where they burned and burned, but did no damage to the armored vehicles. None of the Marines were injured.

It was a dark and gloomy morning, with fog and smoke obscuring Meyers' gunner's view. Still, Sergeant Jonathan Ball could make out silhouettes in the distance: insurgents were running in and out of the Hydra Mosque dead ahead at the next intersection. Without warning, five Muj fighters ran into the street and into Ball's view directly in front of Meyers' tank. Ball flipped his switch to coax and opened fire, rotating the turret as the insurgents scrambled for cover. He mowed the last three down.

The Hydra Mosque and Cultural Center were critical RCT–7 objectives. The mosque was on the southeast corner of CATHY and ETHAN and the Cultural Center was across the street on the southwest corner. In addition to being a significant command-and-control node, the Hydra Mosque was also a major staging and re-supply center, as well as a source of sniper and machine gun fire. Brandl expected a tough fight.

Bravo Company was to take the Cultural Center and provide cover to the Charlie Company Marines and the Iraqis while they cordoned off the Hydra Mosque. At sunrise, Omohundro's Third Platoon began the assault on the Cultural Center while First and Second Platoons provided covering fire. As the Marines moved to cross CATHY they were ambushed. Third Platoon was hammered, its Marines pinned down on three sides.

Sergeant Lonny Wells was the first hit. Gunnery Sergeant Ryan Shane rushed into the street to help his wounded comrade. Wells was badly wounded, and the Marines on the north side of CATHY could see his crimson pants and a trail of blood as Shane dragged him across the street. Shane was halfway across the street when he was shot just above the tailbone and fell to the pavement. First and Second Platoon's Marines opened up with everything they had, laying down a massive covering fire, under which Hospital Corpsman Joel Lambotte and a handful of Marines rushed to drag Wells and Shane to the north side of the street. The enemy continued firing on the Marines in the open. Sergeant Kenneth Hudson, Private First Class Samuel Crist, and Lambotte were all hit trying to retrieve their wounded comrades. Captain Steve Kahn, the Weapons Company Commander, got on the radio and called for a casevac.

Meyers, Klingensmith, and their wingmen rushed into the fight to help the embattled infantry. Meyers turned right on CATHY and Lieutenant Klingensmith turned left. With their four tanks they set up a 180-degree cordon at ETHAN and CATHY. Meyers started firing at insurgents as they crossed ETHAN from east to west, and Markley cut down the enemy running across CATHY from north to south.

Meyers ground slowly west and stopped at the next intersection, which was across the street from the Cultural Center. Like so many others, his gunner, Jonathan Ball, had joined the Marines the day after 9/11 and was a veteran of the march to Baghdad in 2003. Now he scanned his turret slowly back and forth, electric motors whining, like a robotic dragon searching for a kill. Ball had only a narrow view through his high-tech gunner's sight, so he had to continually scan from side to side. During one of his slow sweeps he noticed an RPG team sneaking north up a narrow alley. They were rushing from one clump of bushes to the next, hoping to avoid detection by the metal giant. Ball stopped his turret; the dragon had found its next prey. The insurgents in the alley jumped into the street in an effort to get in their shot before the menacing monster in the intersection could fire, but Ball was too fast for the enemy. He sprayed the RPG team with 7.62 rounds, cutting them all down. When he was confident they were no longer a threat, he returned to continuously sweeping the giant turret, searching for his next target.

Neutron, the Navy SEAL sniper team attached to Omohundro's company, was moving toward the Cultural Center when its corpsman was shot in torso. He lay on the ground with a sucking chest wound as the SEALs called for a casevac. Showing a keen presence of mind, the corpsman bandaged his own wound.

Navy Commander Dr. Richard Jadick, a former Marine, had volunteered to deploy to Iraq with 1/8 as the Battalion Surgeon. He left Camp Lejeune only days after the birth of his first child. Jadick was the first to get the SEAL casevac call. When he heard that the corpsman had been wounded, he jumped in a HMMWV and raced into the city, leaving Dr. Carlos Kennedy to run the Battalion's Aid Station.

The wounded corpsman was stable by the time Jadick and his team reached him. They loaded the wounded sailor onto a M113[8] ambulance and headed north. On the way back to the BAS, however, Jadick received an urgent call for another casevac: Bravo Company was caught in the ambush near the Cultural Center. Major Kevin Trimble got on the radio.

"Doc! Doc! Bravo Company is getting hit hard down at the Cultural Center. They have casualties!"

Jadick made the split-second decision to take his existing casualty to the Cultural Center so he could tend to the newly wounded Marines, too. He ordered the driver to turn around and they all headed for the fight.[9]

Jadick's ambulance pulled up next to Wells, Shane, Crist and Hudson on the north side of CATHY—right in the middle of the fight. Jadick spotted the wounded Marines lying in the street once the ramp dropped. Lambotte was kneeling, working on Wells. An RPG whizzed over the top of the tracked ambulance and another exploded in the street. Jadick froze for what seemed like an eternity as he watched two Marines in the street take down two insurgents trying to shoot into the back of his ambulance.

---

8   The M113 is a Vietnam-era, tracked, armored personnel carrier which is still used today by the US Army in several different support roles, one of which is as an armored ambulance.

9   Richard Jadick with Thomas Hayden, *On Call in Hell.*

Jadick's mind raced. "This is where I am supposed to be," he thought to himself. "I need to take the next step." His rational side held him back, but the doctor and Marine in him prodded him forward. "You can't fail," he told himself as he jumped from the vehicle.[10]

Jadick made a quick assessment of the wounded and turned to work first on Lonny Wells. Wells had been hit in the groin just below his protective armor, and the bullet had torn through his femoral artery. He was bleeding out. Jadick tried but couldn't stop the blood flow. Bullets flew overhead as Jadick did his best to help Wells, packing his wound and applying pressure until he died in the street.

Within minutes, another Marine was brought to Jadick. Pfc Paul Volpe had been shot in the exact same place, even the same side. "Doc, I think Volpe is dead," someone told Jadick.

"How long?" Jadick inquired.

"No more than three minutes. We scooped him up and brought him right here," a voice replied.

Volpe was bleeding profusely from his groin. Jadick reached into the gaping wound with both of his hands, grabbed a handful of tissue, and squeezed as hard as he could as he ordered fluids started. It worked. Within a short time he felt a pulse, and Volpe's eyes fluttered. He had enough red blood cells to get him back to Bravo Surgical. This Marine would live.

Jadick wondered, "Would Lonny Wells have lived if I had been there a minute earlier, or if I had been more aggressive?" He knew that he had to be closer to the fight if he wanted to save Marines' lives.[11]

While Omohundro's Marines were fighting on the west side of ETHAN, Bethea occupied the last covered and concealed position on a roof across the street from the Hydra Mosque. Lieutenant Klingensmith's tank section was already out in front of the infantrymen on CATHY. Bethea ordered Klingensmith's tank section to blow several "mouse" holes in the north and west walls of the mosque, then move east to take up a blocking position on CATHY. Bethea started the attack by having one of his platoons lay down a

10 Dr. Richard Jadick telephone interview, 07/09/08.

11 *Ibid.*

smoke screen from the roof, after which Bethea's attached Iraqi soldiers charged across CATHY to occupy the mosque, with the Marines following them inside. Bethea and Omohundro secured the entire facility by 1300.

Brandl moved to the Hydra Mosque to visit his Marines that afternoon. Worried about a counterattack, he set his defenses. Colonel Tucker showed up while Brandl was with Bravo Company. Tucker instructed him to press the attack, and asked if he could move up his assault on the Government Center to early the next morning. Captain Cunningham with Alpha Company was north of the berm, waiting for orders to attack; all Brandl needed was the green light. Brandl told his boss that it would not be a problem.

Pushing South

East of Brandl's Marines, Ramos' battalion moved forward with Bravo and Charlie Companies abreast and Lieutenant Lee's tanks in the lead. They pushed toward the Mujareen Mosque, just north of Dave's Field. Charlie Company moved south through a residential neighborhood for less than a kilometer before reaching the mosque. The Marines pushed rapidly forward, bypassing all of the houses in the neighborhood. Charlie Company's mission was to get to the next objective as quickly as possible: Ramos was conducting a penetration to MICHIGAN, and he would worry about clearing the buildings later. By the time Tennant and Lee reached the Mujareen Mosque, it was empty. Lee's driver pushed in the gate and Tennant's Iraqis charged inside.

Lee and Ducasse ended up in a junkyard just north of Dave's Field. As soon as the tankers arrived, they could see enemy snipers in the minarets of the Blue Mosque only 500 meters to the southwest. Lee sat in the northeast corner of Dave's Field all day. He had a clear field of fire all the way down to MICHIGAN. Newell's attack in the east was forcing the survivors west toward Lee. None of the fleeing insurgents made it across the open field; Ducasse and Lee mowed them all down.

With Lee in the field, Tennant's Charlie Company was directed to hold the Mujareen Mosque. Alpha Company's Marines passed through Tennant's lines and attacked south to MICHIGAN to continue Ramos' penetration to the center of the city. They reached MICHIGAN before nightfall. Once Ramos went firm, Charlie Company sat tight at the Mujareen Mosque and started sending out patrols. Juarez' Marines in their LAVs and gun trucks shifted to performing route security along MICHIGAN and ETHAN, conducting continuous around-the-clock patrols along the two major arteries in and out of the city. Lieutenant Lee and his wingman returned to their re-supply point and waited for their next assignment.

Jim Rainey had been pounding Jolan Park (OBJ PENNSYLVANIA) the entire night. He had pushed AC-130s to the park every chance he got, and he used his 120mm mortars when Basher wasn't available. At sunrise, the enemy responded with their own mortar fire. They used the large water tower in Jolan Park as a reference point and walked their rounds in on Captain Twaddell's vehicles. They also sent teams into the street. "There were several folks that tried to go stand out in the middle of the street with an AK-47 and face down a Bradley," remembered the captain. "It ended badly for them."[12] They offered little real resistance to Twaddell's attack.

By the time Twaddell rolled into Jolan Park that morning, the enemy had had enough. Twaddell swept through OBJ PENNSYLVANIA in a mounted attack. His troopers drove to the southern boundary, dismounted, and cleared on foot, from south to north. All they found were streets littered with rubble and shattered buildings surrounding the city's amusement park—complete with a Ferris wheel and merry-go-round. The enemy had fled. OBJ PENNSYLVANIA was secure by noon.

For the rest of the afternoon, C/3-8 held along HENRY and A/2-7 held at Jolan Park. Rainey had to do two things: position C/3-8 to make a turn west, and leverage all of his fires. By now the enemy's plan was all jacked up, and he was trying to reposition, so Rainey wanted to get his UAVs up to disrupt him further by shooting fires and dropping bombs on him as he fell back. Rainey decided to pound OBJ VIRGINIA just as he had pounded Jolan Park, and by doing so, cripple the enemy before rolling his battalion into the fight again.

---

12 CPT Edward Twaddell's interview with Matt Matthews, Combat Studies Institute, 2/28/06.

Buhl's and Malay's Marines swept behind Rainey's tanks and Bradleys, clearing every building in the Jolan District's tangled alleys. Some of the alleys were so narrow that even a HMMWV couldn't pass through. On the 9th, the Marines encountered only sporadic resistance, mostly from insurgents who had been trapped by Rainey's lightning advance.

The grunts were laden with body armor, helmets, grenades, ammunition, and breaching equipment, while the enemy fighters were largely barefoot and agile—able to easily outrun their pursuers. Nonetheless, Malay's and Buhl's Marines pushed relentlessly forward, with Bodisch's tanks in the lead on the wider streets. Most of the insurgents scampered away to the south as the Marines approached, but occasionally some stood and fought, usually from a single building. Mindful of booby traps and car bombs, the Marines stopped frequently, waiting for one of Bodisch's tanks to destroy any vehicle they found. As a result, their advance was painfully slow, moving about 200 meters every four hours.

The Darkhorse rifle companies had their hands full in the Jolan District. Clearing each building in the initial push was time-consuming and manpower-intensive. Lieutenant Colonel Malay ordered Major Todd Desgrosseilliers' Task Force Bruno to start the detailed back-clearing. Mortarmen, clerks, and comm techs grabbed their rifles and volunteered to help Desgrosseilliers clear behind the assaulting infantry companies. Desgrosseilliers drew his men and vehicles from the battalion's 81mm mortar platoon. He commandeered gun trucks from CAAT, AMTRACs from the AAV Platoon, and a D9 bulldozer and Marines from two platoons of general support engineers. Task Force Bruno was like a pickup football team.

Later, this ad hoc approach would settle into a predictable pattern. Each morning Marines would volunteer to go into the city to help in the clearing of a stretch of buildings. Usually, Desgrosseilliers would muster about forty Marines for the task. They entered every building, searched every room, catalogued every weapons cache, and collected every weapon. They gathered up massive amounts of sensitive documents. And they cleared away rubble and enemy dead.

Meanwhile, around noon, Timothy Jent of 3/1 reoriented his Marines to the west and crossed behind 2-7 and ahead of 3/5 to attack toward the Euphrates River. Jent's thrust became the division's main effort and would remain the main effort until they reached the southern edge of the city. Jent's Marines swept through the shops just north of Jolan Park, then headed for the

Kabir Mosque on the bank of the Euphrates. Every storefront was filled with weapons and ammunition; there was so much ordnance it took the Marines two days to clear it out.

Once Buhl did a battle takeover from Rainey's troopers at Jolan Park and his Marines became the main effort, he really brought the combined arms strength of the MAGTF to the forefront of the battle. Now he owned the battle space in front of his Marines; now he could use indirect fire. In the following days he would expend 5,700 81mm mortar rounds. He would also fire Rainey's 120mm mortars nearly dry, depleting 2-7's supply of ammo every day.

The day had been relatively quiet for McNulty's Kilo 3/5, who watched as Buhl's men passed in front of them. McNulty's Marines spent all day clearing empty houses. They went firm for the night just south of BETH, close to a neighborhood mosque with a green metal roof. By sunset, Bitanga's Lima Company was moving south again as McNulty and Chontosh came on line with his unit. Finally, Bitanga's Marines pushed through the Palm Grove and cleared the buildings the enemy had been holding all day.

OBJ VIRGINIA was a school just south of PL ELIZABETH in what was called the "Pizza Slice." The school was directly in Rainey's planned path of advance. One of Rainey's objectives was to secure the bridges at ELIZABETH and FRAN. Rainey had been pounding VIRGINIA all afternoon in preparation for his attack, and he expected a difficult fight to get to the bridges.

At dusk, Captain Glass turned west with his C/3-8 tanks and attacked. His soldiers had no trouble taking the objective, but as soon as he arrived he was counter-attacked from an adjacent mosque and cemetery. The mosque commanded a view of several avenues of approach and was occupied by at least fifty enemy fighters firing heavy machine guns and anti-tank weapons. The barrage pinned down Glass' infantry.

Rainey jumped on the radio to call for indirect fire support, but was stymied because the mosque was on the protected target list. Even though Rainey's men were being fired upon from the mosque and the rules of engagement clearly allowed Rainey to order his troops to return fire, everyone was sensitive to the fact that they would be firing on a mosque. The

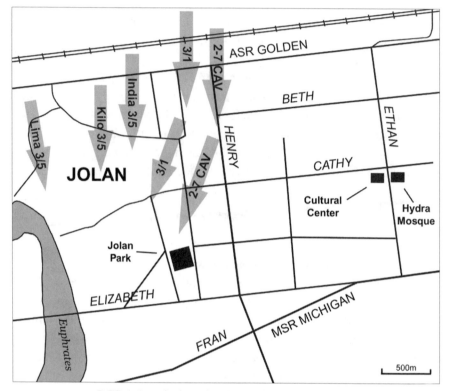

RCT-1 Attacks into the Heart of the Jolan District

artillerymen wanted to get permission to fire, just to be safe. So Rainey spent the next hour talking with several different headquarters in an effort to set up the mission he knew needed to be performed. It wasn't that the guys in the rear didn't want him to shoot; it was just that he had to explain repeatedly, to everyone up the chain of command, that his men were under fire from the mosque. Each headquarters passed Rainey to the next level. Meanwhile, Glass held his ground, returning fire with his Bradleys and tanks, but until the enemy fire could be silenced his dismounts couldn't finish clearing VIRGINIA.

Fortunately, Lieutenant Colonel Ron Lewis of the 1-227th Aviation Regiment and his wingman, Chief Warrant Officer 4 Steven Kilgore, were airborne north of Fallujah in their Apache helicopters listening to Rainey's radio chatter. Lewis and Rainey were longtime friends.

The Apache pilot piped in, "Ghost 6, this is Attack 6."

"Hey, Attack 6," Rainey responded. Frustrated with the bureaucracy, Rainey made a command decision. "I got this problem with this mosque. Can you get into a support-by-fire position?" he asked.[13]

Lewis was almost out of fuel, but he moved in to help his friend anyway. First he had to spend some of his precious fuel to ensure he was firing on the right building, but after that Attack 6 launched a pair of Hellfire missiles into the top floors of the mosque and two more into the first floor, completely destroying the structure and its occupants.

Glass' dismounted troops swept through the remaining western edge of the objective, securing VIRGINIA by 2300.

Glasses men were driving to secure VIRGINIA when the nightly air show resumed. The air cover was devastating. If the enemy tried to move to set up a defense against the advancing Marines, they were mowed down by Basher and Slasher, who could see every move from high above. The soldiers and Marines on the ground were reassured all night long when they heard the steady stream of thump, thump, thump. Colonel Shupp had his Scan Eagle UAV up, and the regiment's fire team, back in Camp Fallujah, was watching via the UAVs and calling fire missions on enemy movements in the city. Shupp and Tucker had a blanket of fire around their regiments to keep them safe in the city.

Charge to the Government Center

Brandl's 1/8 Marines, meanwhile, were preparing for their planned pre-dawn armored penetration into the city. After midnight, Bethea's Charlie Company spread out north along ETHAN to establish a picket line for the incursion by Cunningham's Alpha Company. All of Alpha Company waited in their AMTRACS on Sichir Road for the order to attack.

Second Lieutenant Elliot Ackerman, Cunningham's First Platoon commander, sat in his troop commander's seat wondering if he would be able to bring his forty-six Marines safely through the coming fight. Would he be up to the task? Commanding a Marine infantry platoon is one of the

---

13 COL James Rainey telephone interview, 11/07/07.

toughest jobs in the world. College graduates in their early twenties are asked to lead even younger privates and lance corporals into battle. It would not be long before the enemy was firing at his Marines. Ackerman knew how fierce the upcoming street-to-street fight would be, and he worried whether he had done enough to prepare his men for the inevitable carnage.

With parched mouths, fluttering stomachs, and pounding hearts, the young Marines could taste and feel their own mortality. Each wondered, in his own unique way, whether he would survive the coming fight. All of them pondered whether they would falter or live up to the example of the Marines who came before them. The night was as dark and still as death itself. Some prayed while others cracked jokes. Mostly they waited in silence in the darkened troop compartments.

At 0400 on November 10, after thirty-two hours of watching and waiting, Cunningham's voice crackled on the company radio net. "All Avenger stations, this is Avenger 6. We are Oscar Mike."[14] Meyers and Markley led the mechanized team in their two tanks, with Cunningham riding in the lead track. Eighteen armored vehicles passed under the railroad tracks and raced down ETHAN into the city. Cunningham's orders were to get to the Government Center on MICHIGAN, take it, and hold it. There would be no building-to-building clearing effort to get there. This was a pedal-to-the-metal penetration deep into the city.

Avenger rumbled down ETHAN past Bravo Company's lines at the Cultural Center. Circling above, Basher led the advance with its IR searchlight. Meyers could clearly see the road in front of him through his night vision system—Basher's illumination had turned night into day for the Marines. The armored column drove south on ETHAN, west on CATHY, and left at the giant water tower. The back wall of the Government Center complex was straight ahead.

Task Force Avenger reached the Government Center before dawn. Cunningham did not want to use the existing gates, so he had Meyers and Markley create new entrances. Sergeant Ball blew a hole in the back wall and Meyers' tank thundered into the Government Center. Cunningham's Marines roared through in their AAVs, dismounted, and began clearing the buildings in a counter-clockwise sweep. To the Marines' surprise, the enemy had abandoned the compound.

---

14 Michael Blanding, "The Opposite of Fear," *Tufts Magazine*, Spring 2007.

The Government Center

Alpha Company's Marines spread out. One platoon went west, another east, and the third platoon manned the northern wall. Cunningham knew they had passed lots of bad guys in their race to the Government Center so, in effect, they were surrounded. He needed to set a 360-degree defense.

As the sun rose, Cunningham's Marines moved south through the western buildings of the Government Center complex before sweeping east through the buildings facing MICHIGAN. When they reached the building next to a set of reviewing stands and parade ground, all hell broke loose. The enemy attacked from the south, east, and west with mortars, RPGs, machine guns, and sniper fire. Cunningham called for his tanks and moved to the roof of the tallest building on the grounds to run the fight. That structure was a six-story high-rise on the western side of the Government Complex, a perfect vantage point for Cunningham and his fire-support team.

As Task Force Blue Diamond pushed south block-by-block, the enemy fighters were faced with a dilemma: if they revealed their positions they would be destroyed; if they went out in the open with a weapon or moved outside in large groups, they would be immediately detected by bicycle-sized UAVs buzzing overhead or by their larger, unseen cousins. They couldn't even use the dark of night for cover because Apache helicopters patrolled at the edge of the city and AC-130 gunships prowled overhead like eagles hunting their prey. Anyone wandering the streets with a gun could expect to be cut down; Basher's gunners didn't miss.

If the enemy waited for the Marines to approach, or if they fired on the Marines when they came into view, artillery and mortars quickly responded—usually bringing the building crashing down around them. Then there were American snipers, who silently inflicted instant death.

If instead the insurgents remained inside and waited for the Marines and soldiers to get closer before they fired, they learned quickly what it was like in Hell: 60mm mortar shells raining down on their heads, M1 tanks firing at point-blank range, .50-cal. and 7.62mm machine guns spraying their position, and a vigorous pounding with 40mm grenades, AT4 rockets, and Javelin missiles. If they waited even longer, until the Marines were on their doorstep, the Devil Dogs would swarm their position and not back off until everyone in the house was dead. The insurgents' only choices were to surrender or hunker down in the hope that they would be bypassed.

In RCT-7's area, pockets of insurgents remained entrenched in the Askari District. American tanks and troops had bypassed those insurgents hiding in buildings. They were now isolated, but far from defeated. As they hid and hoped they would not be discovered, their comrades in the south were frantically preparing a defense in depth in an effort to stand and fight all along MICHIGAN.

Chapter 9

Semper Fi! And Happy Birthday

"On November 10, 1775, a Corps of Marines was created by a resolution of the
Continental Congress. Since that date many thousands of men have borne
the name Marine. In memory of them it is fitting that we who are
Marines should commemorate the birthday of our Corps by calling
to mind the glories of its long and illustrious history. . ."

— MajGen John A. Lejeune, USMC, November 1, 1921

Wednesday, November 10, 2004: D+3

The United States Marine Corps' 229th birthday was a sunny, blue-sky day in Fallujah, but the soldiers, sailors, airmen, and Marines of Task Force Blue Diamond would have little opportunity to celebrate on this day of intense combat. As Kilo Company, 3/5 prepared for the coming fight through the Jolan, Captain Drew McNulty went on his Human Exploitation Team's loudspeaker to read the birthday messages of General Lejeune and the Commandant. McNulty's voice echoed through the assembly area in the early morning light. After reading the birthday messages, he concluded with these words: "Slow is smooth and smooth is fast. Today, I expect the enemy to stand and fight. Kill him and kill him twice. HooRah, Semper Fi, and happy birthday."[1]

---

1 Capt Andrew McNulty, USMC. ABC news footage taken by Geoffrey Thorpe-Willett.

Lieutenant Colonel Rainey wanted to change his style on the tenth. He had been attacking under the cover of darkness for the last two nights, so he figured a change of pace would throw the enemy off their game. Rainey knew the enemy was choosing to fight only during the day, and he surmised that they would be up and ready to fight at first light.

Like an experienced quarterback running a draw play, Rainey waited thirty minutes past sunrise to launch his next attack. At 0630, Twaddell's A/2-7 soldiers attacked out of Jolan Park. They rolled in their tanks and Bradleys south past Captain Glass' soldiers at OBJ VIRGINIA and turned right onto Fallujah's main thoroughfare, Highway 10—MICHIGAN. Alpha Company fought its way along MICHIGAN for a half-mile, taking fire from the south side of the street. Twaddell's tankers and Bradley gunners sprayed each of the enemy positions in the buildings to their left as they slowly drove toward the Highway 10 Bridge. When they reached the structure, OBJ KENTUCKY, and found fewer than a dozen enemy fighters, they quickly dispatched these guards and secured the bridge by 0900.

Rainey had warned Twaddell to stay off the bridge. He knew that the enemy would like nothing better than to drop a couple of tanks and Bradleys into the river. That would have been a great victory for them. So Twaddell stayed on the eastern bank. It was lucky that he did. The enemy had placed a string of IEDs nearly the entire length of the bridge, paving them over with a fresh layer of asphalt. EOD teams found the wires later and defused the threat. Was there an insurgent waiting to take the bridge down? If there was, he must have been extremely disappointed that Twaddell's men never set foot on the structure.

Instead, Alpha Company turned north and moved to secure OBJ OHIO, better known as the Blackwater Bridge. The expected fight there failed to materialize because no resistance was encountered during their short drive north, and the bridge itself had been abandoned. The icon of the insurgency—the bridge where the Blackwater contractors had been burned and hung for the entire world to see—was now in American hands, with Task Force Wolfpack's Marines on the west bank and Rainey's Ghost Troopers on the east bank. Twaddell set up a perimeter and remained at OHIO and KENTUCKY for the rest of the day.

At 0800, a mortar round screamed into Bravo 1/23's command post at Sheikh Ghazi's multi-million dollar mansion on the western shore of the Shark's Fin. The projectile exploded in the courtyard and took out the Company's FiST team, severely wounding four Marines. Aviation commanders had restricted flights over the peninsula because there was a real hazard of rocket attacks on allied helicopters. When Major Wittnam heard the call for a casevac, he knew that his boats could get the wounded Marines to medical attention much faster than if they were driven overland.

Wittnam immediately got on the radio, volunteered for the casevac, and ordered two of his boats to the Sheikh's complex. The boats sped upriver less than half mile from their blocking positions and picked up the wounded Marines. Hospital Corpsman Juan Rubio took charge of the injured men, loaded them aboard his boat, and started IVs. Parrello gunned his engines and raced farther upriver at full throttle, with Major Wittnam following in the second boat.

Two and one-half miles west of the Shark's Fin, the rapidly moving boats sped toward a railroad bridge to continue west toward the nearest Shock Trauma Platoon at Habbaniyah. As they raced under the bridge, the Marines spotted military-aged men milling about along the banks of the river. Some of the insurgents took potshots at the passing boats. Both Rubio and Parrello thought they were going to have to fight through this on their way back, but first they had to get their wounded charges to medical attention. They were at the ramp in Habbaniyah in less than thirty minutes.

Wittnam needed to report the enemy presence along the riverbank, so he told his Platoon commander, Lieutenant Andrew Thomas, to take the two boats back to the Shark's Fin while he returned to the Company's HQ to contact the commanders at Division. "I'll come back later tonight," he told Thomas as he pulled away from the ramp.[2]

Sure enough, the boats came under heavy machine gun and RPG fire as they approached the railroad bridge on the return trip. The enemy had established ambush positions along an 800-meter stretch of the river just west of the bridge. Parrello and the other driver slammed their throttles to full speed and the boats' gunners returned fire as they ran the gauntlet. Adrenalin pumped through Parrello's body as he drove through the incoming barrage. His heart pounded so fast and hard that he could hear his

---

2   Maj Dan Wittnam telephone interview, 10/08/07.

heartbeat. Once safely through the hot zone, Parrello slowed his boat and they cruised back to their positions near the Shark's Fin. The Marines of the Small Craft Company would soon return to the railroad bridge to clear that hornet's nest.

Malay's Marines cleared every building in their path. They entered every room, tilted beds up against walls, and opened every cupboard. The methodical process uncovered massive weapons stockpiles: rooms stacked to the rafters with pallets of 155mm artillery rounds, 122mm missiles, 82mm mortar rounds, and 57mm rockets. Al Qaeda had set up a factory for VBIEDs. It had a warehouse full of explosives, an assembly line, and computers to download instructions on building and connecting detonators. There was a separate packaging area and even a small classroom. The Marines found a distribution area and a planning room with network and targeting information. "These guys were not the run-of-the-mill chumps," concluded Colonel Malay.[3] They even found a torture chamber, complete with a Jihadi flag and a plastic chair.

Malay's Marines moved slowly and deliberately through the tangled maze of alleys in the Jolan District. They covered the northeastern corner of Fallujah like a bottle of spilled ink on a white tablecloth: nothing was missed. Chontosh pushed east toward HENRY, then south while Bitanga moved his Marines through the buildings along the river and McNulty's Marines pushed forward between the two.

Corpsman UP!

In 1/3's area, Charlie Company had been taking sniper fire from nearby buildings so Captain Tennant sent his Second Platoon out to clear the row of houses next to the Mujareen Mosque. It wasn't long before his Marines were calling for help: they had run into thirty insurgents barricaded in a group of houses with barred windows.

---

3 Col Patrick Malay telephone Interview, 11/4/07.

Tennant's Marines had rushed into the first house and cleared the first floor. Lance Corporal Aaron Pickering was the first up the stairs. When he stepped into view, the insurgents opened up with a machine gun. Pickering took most of the gunfire and was killed instantly. The four Marines behind Pickering were also hit. As they tumbled down the stairs, Corporal Kane sprayed 5.56 rounds up at the machine gunner. Everyone managed to scramble out of the line of fire under this covering barrage.

Across the street, when Corporal David Willis heard the radio call for help he grabbed his squad and headed over. Willis' corpsman, HM3 Julian Woods, said, "I wanna come with you."[4] Willis responded by telling Woods that all of Second Platoon was over there, and it had its own corpsmen.

"I'm coming whether you want me to or not," Woods replied.

"Okay, roger that," Willis relented. "Just stay behind me."

Willis, Woods, and his squad reached the target house just as an AMTRAC was pushing over the courtyard wall. A fire team jumped over what was left of the barrier and, before Willis could say anything, Woods was following the other Marines into the courtyard. Willis followed on the corpsman's heels. The Marines in the fire team stacked at the front door.

As he crossed the courtyard, Woods spotted the wounded Marines through the living room window, hunkered down inside the house waiting for assistance. Woods never broke stride. He ran right through the front door to get to the wounded Marines. Insurgents on the second floor were waiting for him and opened fire just as he hit the threshold. One bullet pierced his helmet and hit him in the top of the head, killing him instantly.

One of the Marines stacked at the front door helped Willis drag Woods out of the house. Willis continued dragging the body backward across the courtyard, unaware that he was dead. When he hit the remaining knee-high wall, Willis tumbled backward into the street, pulling Willis over with him. Willis was covered in so much blood and gore that his squad thought that both he and Woods were dead—until Willis rose to his feet.

The combined fire of the Marine SAW gunner at the foot of the stairs and the fire team at the front door suppressed the enemy machine gunner long enough for all of the Marines to be pulled from the house. Once the place was clear, Captain Tennant fired rockets into the house and brought a D9 up to knock a corner off the building. The Marines killed the remaining

---

4   Cpl David Willis telephone interview, 2/21/08.

and now fully exposed holdouts. The last insurgent continued to fire on the bulldozer's armored cab, startling but not injuring the driver, who raised the giant blade and dropped it on the last living insurgent, ending the siege of the house with a sickening thud. Once the enemy had been silenced, the Marines moved in and retrieved Pickering's body.

The Fight Along MICHIGAN

In the center of Fallujah, meanwhile, the enemy woke up to find that 1st Battalion, 8th Marines' Avenger Company had occupied the Government Center during the night. Insurgents started firing on the Marines around 0730. Cunningham's Marines returned the fire from every building that faced south. Enemy snipers and machine gunners continued, escalating the action. Meyers' tanks knocked down a wall and Markley and Meyers pulled their tanks in between the parade ground bleachers, next to the buildings where Cunningham's Marines were taking fire. There, they began shooting across MICHIGAN into a mosque and hotel on the far side of the main east-west thoroughfare.

Alpha Company's infantrymen were involved in a sharp 150-meter gunfight. Cunningham and his headquarters team fought from atop the tallest building in the complex. The six-story structure provided a great vantage point from which to call in artillery. First Lieutenant Dan Malcom, Avenger's Weapons Platoon Commander and FiST, was a young studious graduate of the Citadel and a veteran of 1/8's first deployment to Iraq. Malcom called in 81mm mortar fire while the FAC called for close air support to suppress the insurgents in the tall buildings on the south side of MSR MICHIGAN.

There was only a foot-and-a-half ledge on the roof, too little cover to protect Cunningham and his Marines, so when snipers started firing on the command group from a nearby minaret, Cunningham ordered his men off the roof to the safety of the top floor. There, however, visibility was severely restricted.

Meyers and Markley were pounding the enemy from the protected positions among the concrete bleachers. The insurgents fired back from the mosque and charged out in groups of two or three onto MICHIGAN with AKs blasting and RPGs leveled for a shot. Most of them were quickly mowed down by the tankers' machine gun fire. One determined insurgent ran to flank Meyers' tank on his right, hoisted his RPG, and squeezed the trigger. The rocket whooshed toward Panzer 6 and exploded against the side of the tank, rocking the entire vehicle off the ground a couple of inches. The anti- armor projectile penetrated the hull, narrowly missing the fuel cells. Fortunately, none of Meyers' crew was injured and everyone kept fighting; they would worry about the damage later.

After checking to make sure he hadn't been wounded, Gunner Ball returned to scanning for targets, his turret whining like a vacuum cleaner as it rotated from side to side.When he caught a glimpse of the tip of an RPG at the corner of the building next to the mosque, he notified Meyers and got the order to use a main gun round. Ball fired at the corner and watched the High Explosive, Anti-Tank (HEAT) round blow away the side of the building. Bodies flew when the round exploded. Meyers and Markley continued to fight from their protected positions until they were called down to the "Pizza Slice" to help Cunningham's Marines get across MICHIGAN.

From his sixth-floor window in the high-rise building, Dan Malcom itched for a 360-degree view of the battlefield and desperately wanted to go back up to the roof. He was stepping from the stairwell when he took a sniper round in his armpit just above his Small Arms Protective Insert (SAPI) plate.[5] The bullet pierced his heart but did not penetrate his front SAPI plate. Malcom fell back into the stairwell onto Cunningham. Malcom's forward artillery observer reached down and took the maps from his body and continued the fight while several men rushed to his aid. A Navy SEAL corpsman worked to save Malcom's life. "Stay with me! Stay with me!" he pleaded as several Marines carefully moved Malcom down the stairs. Just as Cunningham turned to go back down, he saw the deadly bullet resting on one of the steps. He picked it up and saved it so that it could be sent back to the Citadel.

On November 10, Colonel Shupp hooked his regiment to the west. Third Battalion, First Marines had already passed behind 2-7 and ahead of 3/5 to turn toward the river. At 0800, Captain Jent had attacked behind Twaddell through the marketplace at the center of the old city, driving toward the Al

---

5   The ceramic plate is able to stop up to three 7.62mm rifle bullets with a muzzle velocity of up to 2,750 ft/s. The plate is backed with a shield that is 40% stronger than Kevlar.

Kabir Mosque. The attack was largely uneventful. By mid-afternoon, Jent's Marines had rolled through the mosque and moved south to MICHIGAN. The marketplace, on the other hand, was one giant weapons cache: almost every shop was filled with weapons and ammunition of all sorts and sizes. Malay slowed his Marines to let 3/1 pass in front of them. Captain Brian Heatherman's Lima Company moved to the Euphrates River behind Jent and secured the Brooklyn Bridge so that Rainey's tanks could move on.

Malay's Marines were now encountering a belt of mutually supporting in-depth defensive positions. The enemy had interlocking fields of fire, casualty collection points, and casualty evacuation routes. They had sophisticated communications, including cell phones and Norwegian squad radios. Some of the insurgents even had body armor. They also had excellent weapons—cleaned, maintained and zeroed—including mortars. Many of their tactics had been developed and battle tested in Grozny.[6]

One such tactic was for an insurgent to shoot at the Marines with an AK. When the Marines moved to the sound of the gunfire, they were struck with machine gun and/or sniper fire. The enemy also tried to pick off key Marines—officers, radio operators, and even corpsmen. If the Marines sent vehicles in, they were engaged by RPG teams. This was not a disorganized band of thugs with AKs. These men were sophisticated and tenacious with an ambush mentality. Still, they were no match for Marines.

As Bitanga cleared the houses along the river, McNulty waited for the 3/1 Marines to pass in front of him. Chontosh continued clearing neighborhoods just west of HENRY. Toward the end of the day, India Company took a house that it would use as living quarters and a base for the next several days. Once inside, Chontosh's men started taking sniper fire from a school across the street. They kept watch on the school all night and put together a plan for clearing it the next day.

Commanders on the Battlefield

Natonski preferred face-to-face conversations over talking on the radio, so he drove into the city every day. "All right, Mike," he would begin when he reached Colonel Shupp, "where are we going?" The general always

---

6   Chechen rebels fought a bloody street battle for control of their capital city in 2000 against the Russian Army. Some of these rebels ended up in the 2004 fight in Fallujah.

wanted to go to the most forward position. On several occasions, Army officers would spot the high ranking commander and ask, "What the hell is going on?" Army colonels and generals rarely visited troops in the field and especially troops on the front lines during active combat operations, but Natonski, Shupp, and all the other senior Marines led from the front. General Natonski, Shupp confirmed, "was fearless."[7]

Lieutenant Colonel Rainey was in a mosque courtyard on HENRY, where enemy snipers were shooting at his soldiers from protected positions. Rainey was being prudent, standing behind his Bradley. When he looked down the street, he exlaimed, "Holy shit! Who are these guys?"[8] Walking down the center of the street was a group of Marines, antennas sticking twelve feet up in the air. Colonel Shupp was one of them. Rainey walked out to meet him. When he looked farther up the street he saw another group walking down HENRY. To his surprise, in the center of this second group was General Natonski himself.

Rainey, Shupp, and Natonski discussed the attack south of MICHIGAN. The original plan was for RCT–7 to cross MICHIGAN and then swing southwest, but RCT–1 had gotten to MICHIGAN much faster than anticipated, and RCT-7 had met more resistance than expected. Natonski considered moving Rainey's entire battalion east of HENRY to help Colonel Tucker on the eastern side of the city, but Rainey liked working with Colonel Shupp and First Marines and wasn't keen on that idea. Everyone knew that it was the wrong course of action to suspend the advance, to shift forces around, or to wait for Tucker to be ready to continue the attack. The enemy had been knocked back on their heels. It was time to press the attack and deliver the crushing blow to the remaining insurgents.

And so here was Natonski, standing in the middle of the fight polling his commanders before he made the decision to move forward. All the while, an enemy sniper in a nearby minaret was drawing beads on and firing at the soldiers and Marines. The Marines returned fire, knocking tiles off the mosque around the group of commanders. Natonski, Rainey, and Shupp seemed not to notice, standing in deep discussion in the mosque courtyard with insurgent bodies piled up all around them.

---

7 Col Michael Shupp telephone interview 9/3/07.

8 Col James Rainey telephone interview, 11/08/07.

Delaying the attack would give the enemy an opportunity to regroup, while continuing the assault would keep the enemy off-balance. Natonski turned to Rainey and asked, "Jim, what do you think if I pushed you over to the other side, into the 7th Marine area, and you augment them?"

"Hey, Garry Owen![9] Rainey responded. "It would take me about twenty-four hours . . . would be kind of hard."[10]

Natonski made his decision on the spot: both of his regiments would push forward straight across MICHIGAN, proceeding online with each other to the southern edge of the city. It was evident to everyone that the north side of the city was still crawling with pockets of enemy fighters. Shupp and Tucker would each leave one battalion behind to continue clearing operations: Malay's Marines would back-clear the Jolan, while Ramos' Marines remained north of MICHIGAN to clear the eastern neighborhoods. L'Etiole already had a branch plan in place; all that was needed was for Natonski to issue the order.

Once his war council with Rainey and Shupp ended, Natonski left to visit Colonel Tucker at the Government Center. The general had already decided that RCT–7 would not sweep south and west toward the Euphrates River as originally planned. He talked with Tucker about his readiness to execute the original plan, and Tucker told his boss that all of his battalions were receiving attacks from the north. He needed more time to deal with the bypassed threats before he could move south across MICHIGAN. Natonski understood and informed Tucker that he was going to order the execution of L'Etiole's branch plan: Tucker would leave one battalion in the north to deal with the back-clearing, and prepare to drive straight south with his other two battalions. Newell would continue hugging the eastern edge of the city and attack into the Industrial District, while Lieutenant Colonel Brandl's Marines would continue their push south into the heart of the city. PL HENRY would remain the regimental boundary. The push south would kick off at 1900—nightfall—on November 11, 2004.

---

9 "Garry Owen," an old Irish drinking song, has been a part of 7th Cavalry Regiment tradition ever since the days of George Custer. The words *Garry Owen* are part of the regimental crest, and the phrase has been used as a battle cry and salutation within the regiment for many years.

10 LtGen Richard Natonski telephone interview, 3/11/08.

Tucker had handed out MRE pound cakes and cards with the Commandant's birthday message to all his squad leaders. They were to read the birthday message to their Marines and slice the birthday cakes in the time-honored ceremony—when there was a break in the fighting. As a final ceremonial touch, Tucker asked his commanders to try to play the Marine Hymn at some point during the day.[11]

After Natonski left the Government Center late that afternoon, Tucker and Brandl were standing around during a lull in the fighting. Brandl turned to his boss and suggested, "Maybe we should play the Marine Hymn now." When Tucker agreed, he called over to the Army psyops team and told them to play the Hymn over their loudspeakers.

As soon as the music started, every enemy fighter within earshot opened fire. They were either incensed at the brazen taunt, or they anticipated that the music heralded an attack. The hymn triggered a loss of discipline within the ranks of the insurgents, who began to show themselves as they fired on

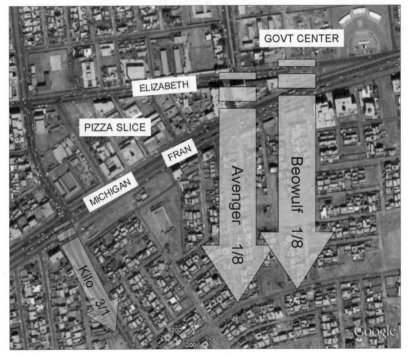

The Attack Across Michigan

11 Col Craig Tucker telephone interview, 01/10/08.

the Marines. With deadly precision, the Marines cut down the exposed fighters as if they were shooting pop-up targets at a carnival shooting gallery. The spontaneous battle raged until the final note, when, as if on cue, the enemy quit firing. Brandl turned to Tucker and said, "That worked pretty well. Let's play it again."[12]

Deadly Enemy Stronghold

3/5 had nearly finished its second, long day of clearing. Only a few more buildings remained, and then Kilo Company could rest. Second Lieutenant Colin Browning's Third Platoon Marines moved into a single house to prepare for the push through the final few structures. Suddenly, McNulty's Marines encountered two enemy positions a block apart.

Sergeant Jeffrey Kirk, a 24-year-old Louisiana native, was Browning's First Squad Leader. Kirk had been a high school honor student who loved poetry. Staff Sergeant Kenneth A. Distelhorst, who had wanted to be a Marine for as long as he could remember, led Second Squad. Both were model Marine NCOs, dedicated to the Corps and their Marines. Both had been handpicked by Lieutenant Colonel Malay to lead their squads.

Kirk and Distelhorst decided that they needed to check out the next house before they moved their squads out of their current stronghold. Kirk took off out the door and down the narrow alleyway. The Marines' squad radios weren't working well and Distelhorst wanted to keep an eye on his friend, so he followed him out the door with one of his team leaders, Corporal William Silcox, Jr., to watch where Kirk was going.

Kirk stopped at a locked gate, and by the time Distelhorst and Silcox caught up with him, he was trying to kick it in. The gate didn't budge, so they started pounding at it with a sledgehammer. After several swings the lock gave way to their abuse and the gate swung open.

The three Marines decided to clear the house on their own. Kirk took point as the three entered the courtyard and pushed toward the front door. Distelhorst looked over and spotted an unmanned RPK machine gun aimed toward the front door.

---

12 Col Craig Tucker telephone interview, 1/10/08.

"Be careful. The door could be booby-trapped," Distelhorst cautioned Kirk as he backed away. Kirk continued to test the doorknob.[13]

With Kirk, Distelhorst, and Silcox at their doorstep, one of the insurgents lobbed a German pineapple grenade into the courtyard. Distelhorst never saw it as it rolled between his legs. Kirk was the first to see the grenade.

"Sergeant D, grenade!" Kirk yelled as he hugged the wall.

Distelhorst looked down, saw the grenade at his feet, and tried to sprint away. He was only able to take a step or two before the grenade exploded, sending a quarter-sized piece of shrapnel through Distelhorst's foot and peppering his legs with pieces of flying debris. Somehow, Distelhorst's left index finger was also split open in the explosion, but in the chaos of the fight he didn't even realize he had been hit at all. He continued running out of the courtyard into the street.

Just as Kirk's fight was beginning, three close friends, Private First Class Chris Adlesperger, Lance Corporal Erick Hodges, and Corporal Ryan Sunnerville, reached a corner house only one block east of Kirk. Together, they entered their umpteenth courtyard of the day. Right behind them at the gate to the street were Lance Corporals Alston Hays and John Aylmer and Corporal Jeremy Baker. Adlesperger moved to the right and kicked in the first door. Hodges and Sunnerville were heading for the second door across the courtyard when a hail of machine gun fire opened on them from inside the building.

The enemy had been lying in wait for the Marines. One had positioned himself so that he could shoot out into the courtyard through a small hole in the wall. His first burst of fire cut down Hodges. Inside the courtyard, Navy Corpsman Alonso Rogero and Sunnerville were also hit, Rogero in the stomach and Sunnerville in the leg.

The Marines exchanged fire, not yet realizing that they were facing eleven insurgents barricaded less than twenty feet away. Adlesperger rushed to help Rogero and Sunnerville, firing as he moved toward the hidden machine gun position. All three made it into an outside alcove, out of the enemy's line of fire.

Aylmer and Hays had just started into the courtyard when the enemy machine gunner opened fire. They hugged the left wall and backed out into

---

13 SSgt Kenneth Distelhorst telephone interview, 03/18/08.

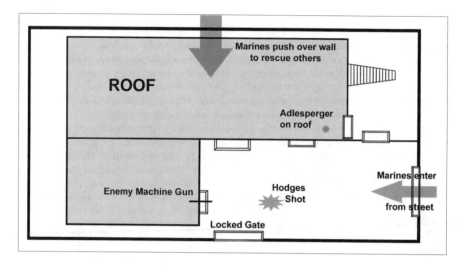

the street. Aylmer grabbed Hays. "Hang on," he told Hays, "just chill right here until we know what's going on."[14]

Corporal Baker could see Adlesperger, Sunnerville, and Rogero huddled just inside the courtyard gate. He waited for the machine gun to stop firing, then rushed through the gate. Hays crossed the line of fire behind Baker and entered an adjacent courtyard, leaving Aylmer at the corner of the house. Inside the courtyard, Baker noticed a stairway in their alcove leading to the roof. He stood at the door covering the courtyard and sent Adlesperger up it.

The Darkhorse Marines had walked into a Chechnya-type ambush. The enemy plan was to surprise Marines as they entered the courtyards, then kill more Marines as they rushed to their aid. In this instance, another enemy machine gunner waited patiently on an adjoining rooftop farther down the alley. With the courtyard now empty, the Muj gunner inside the house continued firing into Hodges' lifeless body.

Meanwhile, a block away, Distelhorst had reached the street after running from the exploding grenade, looked back into his courtyard, and saw that Silcox was down. Distelhorst knew he had to go back in to get him. "Silcox! Silcox!" he yelled into the courtyard. There was no reply.[15]

14 LCpl John Aylmer telephone interview, 07/08/08.

15 SSgt Kenneth Distelhorst telephone interview, 03/18/08.

As Kirk made his way back into the street to start rallying his Marines for an assault on the stronghold, Distelhorst rushed to his team leader's side in the courtyard. Silcox was pale white and had a large hole in his side. He was in dire need of medical attention. Before that could happen, Distelhorst had to get him out of the line of fire.

Without advance warning, an insurgent popped out and sprayed his RPK machine gun at the two wounded Marines. Distelhorst dove for the only nearby cover and snuggled his body in next to Silcox. Fortunately, the enemy fighter fired wildly and missed before darting back into the house. "Dude, you gotta get up or we're gonna die," Distelhorst pleaded to Silcox.

Distelhorst rolled on top of Silcox and then stood, pulling the young Marine to his feet with him. While Silcox was staggering toward the courtyard gate, Distelhorst turned and emptied his M16 into the doorway to give them some extra time to escape. When he turned back to help Silcox out of the kill zone, the Muj machine gunner appeared in the doorway again and let loose with another short burst. This time one of the bullets tore into Silcox's leg, knocking him to the ground.

Meanwhile, Adlesperger had cleared the stairway, checked the roof, and raced back to Baker and the others. "The roof is clear," he told them.[16] Baker and Adlesperger helped Sunnerville and Rogero to their feet and up the stairs—and none too soon. After tossing several grenades into the courtyard, the enemy went on the attack. Several enemy fighters rushed the stairwell, but Adlesperger cut them down as they rounded the corner in the alcove.

Lieutenant Cragholm was just north of the house. When the shooting started he had to make a decision: attack or take cover. Without hesitation he pulled a grenade from his vest and started around the corner into the open. Lance Corporal Steven Fernandez placed his hand on Cragholm's shoulder. "Sir! No," the corporal cautioned.[17]

Cragholm shrugged the corporal's hand from his shoulder and moved forward. Fernandez grabbed Cragholm, spun him around. "Dude! NO!" He shouted the words into his platoon commander's face just as dozens of machine gun rounds peppered the wall just outside the courtyard. If Cragholm had moved into the open, he would have been killed. Cragholm stopped, took a deep breath, and immediately calmed. "Slow is smooth and

16 Cpl Jeremy Baker telephone interview, 06/22/08.

17 Capt Michael Cragholm telephone interview, 03/01/08.

smooth is fast." From that point forward, he became a warrior—not an excited, green lieutenant.

Aylmer was in the second machine gunner's line of fire. Bullets hit all around him and one punctured his pant leg, but miraculously, none of the rounds found their target. He waited for the gunner to stop to reload, then sprinted north in Hays' footsteps into the adjacent courtyard.

Cragholm began positioning his men to support Adlesperger and his wounded comrades. Corporal Terrence van Doorn's Third Squad rushed to the adjacent rooftop, but found a brick wall separating them from the trapped Marines. Together, they pushed on the wall and toppled it over. The enemy machine gunners were holding Kilo Company at bay, and the Marines couldn't get at the barricaded enemy fighters. Compounding the problem was that they couldn't call in artillery or close air support while Adlesperger, Rogero, and Sunnerville were on the roof.

Inside, two more insurgents charged into the courtyard. Adlesperger greeted them with a fragmentation grenade. One tried to run up the stairs to avoid the explosion while the other ran into the street. Adlesperger shot the first man and a dozen Marines sprayed the other as soon as he stepped into the street. Three more insurgents charged out of the house into the courtyard, with one attempting to reach Hodges' SAW. Adlesperger killed all three from his perch above.

Several houses down, Distelhorst pulled Silcox through the gate into the street. It wasn't until a SEAL team corpsman pushed Distelhorst to the ground and started bandaging his wounds that he realized he had been hit.

As this action was unfolding, Sergeant Kirk organized a group of Marines from multiple squads to assault the house. He took point and led his men across the open courtyard, but enemy grenades and machine gun fire forced them back into the street. Kirk regrouped and attacked the building a second time, but couldn't find a spot to get a clean shot at the machine gunners without exposing himself. During this assault Kirk was shot in the butt, but he continued fighting, tossing his grenades through the windows.

The firing was so intense that the Marines were forced to fall back a second time, but not before Kirk took out one of the machine gunners with a rifle shot. Back in the street, Kirk refused medical attention and rallied his Marines one last time. He led the Marines back into the courtyard for a third assault on the enemy position. This time Kirk was able to overwhelm the remaining insurgents; this time he cleared the entire building, all the way to the roof.

McNulty was in the street between Kirk's and Hodges' houses. He had the company's FiST team and his CAAT vehicles with him when the fighting broke out. He could hear the machine gun fire and his Marines yelling, but he couldn't figure out where the fight was developing. Gunshots rang out on his right as Kirk made his repeated charges toward the entrenched enemy machine gunners, and shots seemingly echoed on his left as Adlesperger fought to protect his friends. An AMTRAC was parked just ahead of the CAAT vehicle. McNulty quickly ordered the up-gunner to open fire. The Marine opened fire on Adlesperger's house at point blank range with his .50-caliber machine gun, chipping away large chunks of the building with each round.[18]

McNulty rushed across the street with his First Sergeant, Steve Knox, and some of Taylor's SEALs to get a better view of the fight. They rushed a building that was catty-corner to Adlesperger's house, quickly cleared the rooms, and ran to the roof.

Throughout, Baker repeatedly called his company commander to tell him that Hodges was trapped in the courtyard, but to McNulty the messages sounded like "Hajis in the courtyard."

By now, Corporal van Doorn and his squad had reached Baker, Adlesperger, Sunnerville, and Rogero. Together, they all climbed onto their roof and then rushed the wounded back down to a waiting casevac vehicle.

As McNulty positioned himself to command the assault, nearly all of Kilo Company was moving in on Hodges' house. Once McNulty understood the situation, he moved back down into the street and crossed over to the south wall of the courtyard. There, he ordered the AMTRAC to push in the blue courtyard gate. The moment the track backed away from the crumpled entrance, McNulty pitched two grenades into the courtyard.

By now Adlesperger, Baker, and van Doorn's squad was back down on the street. It was not until this moment that Baker, his face bloody, could report to his company commander that "Hodges is in the courtyard." Adlesperger, whose face was also bloodied by shrapnel and his blouse riddled with bullet holes, refused to be casevaced until Hodges' body was recovered.

McNulty understood and ordered his Marines into the courtyard. Adlesperger led the three-man stack through the collapsed courtyard wall,

---

18 Maj Andrew McNulty telephone interview, 01/23/08.

with Baker and McNulty following him. When McNulty entered the courtyard he noticed a wounded insurgent reaching for his weapon. McNulty shot him, killing this last holdout.

With the courtyard clear of enemy fighters, Adlesperger and Baker looked around for Hodges. When they finally found their friend buried in the rubble of the collapsed wall, they cleared the debris and removed his body. McNulty ordered the house completely demolished.

It turned out, Adlesperger, Hodges, and Sunnerville had stumbled upon an enemy command center. By the time Darkhorse's fight was over, the Marines had killed fifty enemy fighters in that small area. From that point forward, the enemy would fight to the death with a fatal fanaticism.

Re-Positioning Forward

After dark Brandl moved his mobile battalion command post to the Government Center, where he set up alongside Avenger's headquarters team in the high-rise building where Lieutenant Malcom had been killed.

After Dr. Jadick's experiences at the Cultural Center with the arterial wounds suffered by Wells and Nolte, he knew he needed to be as close to the fight as possible. In combat, the Golden "Hour" concept is a myth; Jadick had watched Wells bleed to death in minutes. He knew that he had to get to the casualties as quickly as possible. Jadick left Kennedy at the Battalion Aid Station, loaded up two M113 ambulances, and with a small party headed to the Government Center with Brandl's H&S Company to set up a forward mini-BAS.

At 2100, Captain Bethea moved his force recon Marines to the roof of the Cultural Center, and at 2200 he started his attack against the Blue Mosque. He led with his tanks, which blew holes in the mosque compound walls so that his Iraqi soldiers could move in to clear the facility. The entire compound was secure by 0300. Bethea now had his company spread out in three platoon positions: one held the Blue Mosque, another remained at the Hydra Mosque and Cultural Center, and the third manned a strongpoint between BETH and CATHY on Route ETHAN.

When Dr. Jadick arrived at the Government Center, he found a suitable building on the west side of the complex, just north of Brandl's CP. Under these circumstances, the spot was as good as could be expected. There was access to the main road, parking for his vehicles, and a drive-up "Emergency Room" entrance. It also provided some cover for the medical staff.

Chapter 10

Face-to-Face and Hand-to-Hand

"No man is fit to command another that cannot command himself."

— William Penn

Bellavia's Battle

Sean Sims' infantry had been back-clearing in the Askari District all day. They found several weapons caches, but not a single live insurgent. Just after sunset they got involved in a short scuffle—with some of Ramos' Marines. Fortunately, no one was hurt in the friendly-fire incident, and the Marines and soldiers went back to clearing their own sectors, this time with a little more care.

It had been a long day for Staff Sergeant David Bellavia and his squad. They had been fighting since their entry into the city, so they took some time to rest. As midnight approached, they moved out again and came upon a house that had been left untouched by the bombing and artillery missions. And it was a pretty nice place, complete with a nine-foot wall surrounding its courtyard. Bellavia and his men filed through the open gate to find a beautifully landscaped garden and columns marking the entry. The house was well built, with a sturdy, ornate door.

Sergeant Fitts moved his squad to the door while Bellavia and his men peered in through the living room window. All was quiet inside the mansion.

Bellavia's men spread out in the courtyard and waited for orders, thankful for a couple more minutes of rest while Fitts' squad cleared the empty house. The front door was unlocked, so the soldiers let themselves in. Bellavia stayed outside to watch through the living room window for enemy movement ahead of the advancing soldiers.

A moment later, Specialist Lance Ohle and Misa appeared in the living room. Ohle moved to the far side of the living room and cracked opened a door. The room erupted in gunfire. Red tracers screamed past Ohle, who stood his ground and fired a burst from his SAW into the darkened room. Misa grabbed Ohle and pulled him out of the line of fire while Bellavia ran into the house to help. When he entered the foyer, there was another explosion of gunfire in the entry. Bullets shattered the ornate chandelier hanging from the ceiling. Bellavia hugged the wall separating the foyer from the living room.

Ohle and Misa were now trapped, hunkered down on the opposite side of the doorway, and many of Fitts' men were similarly trapped, pinned down on another wall. Ohle had opened a door to a fortified stairwell, giving the enemy a clear field of fire on the Marines' only exit. They were all trapped in the living room.

There was another door from the stairwell to the foyer. It, too, was open, providing the enemy with another field of fire. Bellavia crouched and moved to the foyer's stairwell door. When he peeked around the door frame his night vision goggles revealed two men hiding behind two concrete Jersey barriers. "How in the hell did they get those barriers in there?" Bellavia asked himself as he tried to figure out what to do next.

The enemy had built a bunker smack-damn in the middle of the upscale house. One insurgent was manning a Russian-made, belt-fed, PKM machine gun, and the other stood security with two AK-47s. They opened fire again, filling the living room with bullets and tearing away at the wall protecting Fitts' men. A third insurgent opened fire from the kitchen window. The platoon's machine gunner responded with a barrage from his 240.

When the firing subsided, Bellavia yelled for help. "Get me a SAW, I need a SAW!"

One of the soldiers in the living room tossed his Squad Automatic Weapon (SAW) to Bellavia. "Sarge, it's loaded with 200 in the drum."

"Sweet," Bellavia replied. "On me," Bellavia announced to the soldiers in the living room. "Pull out. Australian Peel[1] and pull out. On me."[2]

The barricaded insurgents continued to fire, wounding two soldiers. More would be hit if Bellavia didn't act soon. He slowly moved along the wall into the living room toward the bunker door, then lunged ahead. A few quick strides carried him to the center of the living room's stairwell doorway, where he opened fire with his SAW, squeezing the trigger tightly and holding it down for all he was worth. The insurgents shot back, their bullets splintering the doorway but missing Bellavia, who sidestepped into the stairwell and continued firing. His SAW went cyclic[3], spitting bullets out as fast as the weapon could expel them. Fitts' men peeled off and out of the living room. Bellavia continued to fire his SAW, spewing flames and bullets at 725 a minute. Both insurgents dove for cover, and when Bellavia's bolt clanked back, the weapon out of ammunition, he dashed for the door and sprinted out of the house.

Any ordinary soldier would have been happy to be alive and elated that he had saved the lives of most of his platoon. But Bellavia felt like a coward: he hadn't finished the job. Instead, he had run out and the insurgents were still barricaded in their stairwell bunker. Bellavia would never be able to live with himself if another soldier was killed or wounded trying to get to those guys. He had to finish the job.

Bellavia wasn't stupid, though, so he called a Bradley up to help. Unfortunately, the nine-foot wall didn't allow the crew to depress their gun to hit the first floor, but the gunner was able to spray the second story with Bushmaster cannon fire while Bellavia tried to frag the house. The grenades and 25mm HE shells had no visible effect. The only way to get those guys was with another assault on the house.

"Bravo Team, on me!" Shouted Bellavia.

---

1   The Australian Peel is a tactic used for withdrawal from an engagement. The first man in the line fires a burst from his weapon and then retreats while the second man in line opens fire. The third man continues firing while the second man retreats. This "peel" is continued until the last man has broken contact.

2   Bellavia, *House to House*, p. 212.

3   Shooting a weapon at its fastest rate of fire.

Specialists Tristen Maxfield and Ohle rallied at Bellavia's side. "We're going back in," he told them. Staff Sergeant Scott Lawson ran up and asked, "What are you doing?"

"We're going back in."

Lawson tightened his grip on his 9mm pistol. "I'm not going to let you go in there alone."

"You're fucking coming?" Bellavia asked incredulously.

"Absofuckinlutely,"[4] Lawson replied.

The four men moved to the front gate and stacked along the nine-foot wall. Bellavia gave the group one last speech. "If we take fire and somebody goes down, no one render aid," he cautioned. "I don't care if I'm hit and screaming to Jesus—leave me. Do not look down, do not look back. Continue to move forward and shoot. Kill the threat, or we will all go down."[5]

Ohle, Maxfield, and Bellavia formed into a three-man wedge and charged through the garden and up to the front door, with Lawson following close behind. They had taken the insurgents by surprise; not a single shot was fired. Bellavia signaled Ohle and Maxfield to the right and left to cover each front corner of the outside of the house. Lawson moved up next to the kitchen window with his 9mm pistol. If the machine gunner inside tried anything, Lawson was waiting to nail him.

Bellavia entered the house alone. He moved into the living room, then into the stairwell. He had surprised the insurgents again. A single shot from Bellavia's M16 hit the AK-carrying insurgent in the chest. Bellavia turned and watched the other man flee. He fired two shots in rapid succession as the man dashed for the door to the kitchen. Bellavia was moving toward the kitchen when he heard footsteps at the top of the stairs: insurgents were in front and in back of him. Deciding to take the high ground first, he quietly started up the stairs but the insurgent who fled to the kitchen reentered. Bellavia put four bullets into him, and turned back to the stairs. He figured that by now his M16 had to be nearly empty, so he slammed a fully loaded magazine into his rifle.

---

4   Bellavia, *House to House*, pp. 230-231.

5   *Ibid.*, p. 234.

Footfalls at the top of the stairs alerted Bellavia that someone was coming, so he ducked into a downstairs bedroom and waited. The footsteps overhead grew louder. The insurgent was coming down the stairs: he was hunting Bellavia. The sergeant crouched in the shadows of a small alcove in the darkened bedroom, waiting to turn the tables on his stalker. A silhouette appeared in the doorway and AK rounds filled the room. If Bellavia had not been crouching in the small alcove, he would almost surely have been hit. Instead, the unwounded soldier opened fire, hitting the Muj in the doorway with round after round. The insurgent dropped to the floor.

There was not time to feel any relief, because seconds later a tracer round slammed into the wall only inches from Bellavia's head. He froze. Someone else was in the bedroom with him.

In the nearly pitch-black room, Bellavia turned hunter and sought out his unseen assailant. He could barely make out his surroundings, but he could see another small alcove, a mattress in the center of the room, and an armoire on the wall—but no enemy fighter. Just as he reached the center of the room, the armoire doors flew open and out jumped a bandoleered insurgent. He stumbled out into the bedroom, close enough to touch Bellavia, and the armoire came crashing down behind him. Bellavia stepped back as the large wooden cupboard hit the floor between the two men. The insurgent opened fire first, wildly spraying the room and hitting Bellavia in the elbow. The sergeant aimed and fired his M16, hitting his enemy in the leg, but the man darted out the door and up the stairs.

Bellavia was now alone in the darkened bedroom, but another insurgent in the house rushed to cover the door. He was trapped. Waiting just outside the door, the jihadist taunted Bellavia in broken English: "I will cut off your head,"[6] he told his hated American enemy.

And then the fanatic fighter intent on a beheading made a mistake. He peeked around the door jamb, unaware that Bellavia had NVGs. When he spotted the insurgent's silhouette, he squeezed off a single round and watched as the man's shoulder exploded and he fell screaming into the doorway. Bellavia pumped some more rounds into his opponent.

Bellavia ducked behind the armoire to take stock of his situation. He could hear the moans of another wounded insurgent. Had he done enough damage to proudly walk out of the house and back to his men? Had he done

6 *Ibid.*, p. 253.

enough to return home to his family with honor? Then he remembered Sergeant Major Faulkenburg, the first man of Task Force 2-2 to be killed, and resolved, "I am not leaving this house, not until this is finished."[7]

Bellavia stood and slowly headed toward the bedroom door. Both bodies were gone, and there was a bloody trail leading into the kitchen. He decided to go after the insurgent still waiting upstairs, and stepped through the doorway. As he turned to head up the steps, he pulled the magazine from his rifle and replaced it with his last fully-loaded clip.

Bellavia climbed the risers one by one, every few seconds glancing back at the stairwell door; he didn't want to be surprised by the two men he had already shot or by a third insurgent. Bellavia listened for his bandoleered opponent, but could only hear his own heart pounding. He climbed another step, listening, watching. Now, only two stairs from the landing, Bellavia took another step and slipped in a large pool of blood, falling backward. As he reached to keep himself from cartwheeling all the way down the stairs, the waiting insurgent on the landing fired from just three feet away. If Bellavia had not slipped in the blood, he would have been shot in the head.

Bellavia fired a wild shot and missed, and the Muj fighter turned and ran up the second flight of stairs. Bellavia followed his prey, pausing at the top of the steps to look down the darkened hall. One door led to a rooftop balcony, and another to an upstairs bedroom.

Bellavia pulled the pin from his only grenade and inched along the hallway wall toward the bedroom door. When he reached the door, he opened his hand and the grenade's spoon popped free. Bellavia counted "One . . . Two . . . Three . . ." and then hurled the grenade into the bedroom, where it hit the insurgent in the head. The grenade fell to the floor and Bellavia ducked behind the hallway wall for cover.

Boom!

Bellavia charged in, weapon at the ready and spotted the insurgent lying in the middle of the room. Bellavia lifted his weapon—and paused. The smell of propane gas filled the room. He froze. Propane tanks were lining an entire wall of the bedroom. Bellavia was standing in the middle of an Improvised Explosive Device. The entire room was a bomb. He couldn't risk firing his weapon.

---

7   *Ibid.*, p. 254.

Instead, he slammed his barrel into his opponent's head. The insurgent countered, swinging his AK-47 into Bellavia's jaw, breaking a tooth before backhanding Bellavia in the face with the stock of his AK. Bellavia reared back to swing his rifle at the insurgent, but the guy kicked him in the groin before he could do so. The pain was agonizing, and Bellavia dropped his rifle. The fight degenerated into a hand-to-hand struggle to the death. After what seemed like an eternity of fighting, Bellavia managed to unclip his Gerber knife from his belt and thrust it into the insurgent's collarbone. He left the dead man on the floor.

Bellavia picked up his rifle and went in search of the last remaining enemy fighter, whom he found on the balcony. The last shots from his M16 tore into the jihadist, knocking him off the roof.

The fight was finally over.

After several minutes of anxious waiting, the thud in the courtyard announced to Bellavia's men that he had made it to the roof. The soldiers charged into the house to find the path of carnage their sergeant had left in his wake. Staff Sergeant David Bellavia had single-handedly cleared the entire building.

IED

A Task Force Wolfpack CSSC[8] convoy had struck an IED on the 8th of November, and two Marines, Staff Sergeant David Ries, and Lance Corporal Thomas Zapp, were killed in the explosion. On the 9th, an ambulance hit another IED on the Shark's Fin. Dinauer's battalion surgeon nearly lost his foot, and one of his corpsman had his leg blown off. The supply route along ASR BOSTON was laced with radio-controlled IEDs. There was also high ground south of BOSTON, which made it an excellent spot for ambushes.

Because of the dangers along BOSTON, on the night of November 10-11 Captain Matthew Good decided he would try to move his Task Force Wolfpack vehicle supply convoy of fifteen to twenty 7-ton trucks, HMMWVs, logistic LAVs, and bulk re-fuelers, onto the Shark's Fin from TQ along MSR MICHIGAN. Dan Wittnam asked Good if he could hitch a ride back to his boats. Good agreed, and Wittnam hopped into the back of the lead 7-ton truck. Good sent two Cobra helicopters down the route to make

---

8 Combined Service Support Company.

sure it was clear. Both pilots raced above the road up and back, twice, and reported to Good that the route was clear. Good ordered the convoy forward in the dark of night at 40 mph.

MSR MICHIGAN crosses a large, freeway-style four-lane bridge that rises over the only railroad tracks in the area one mile west of the railroad bridge where Rubio and Parrello had been ambushed earlier in the day. As the convoy approached the overpass, one of the Cobra pilots noticed something in the road at the western base of the bridge, and reported that information to Good.[9]

The enemy had piled a berm of earth across all four lanes and buried an IED in it. The pilot's report came too late for the lead vehicle, which slammed into the mound of dirt. The watching enemy detonated the IED and the berm exploded. The 7-ton truck disappeared in the dust and debris, falling off the raised embankment. Captain Good watched in horror as the truck vanished. Down below it landed on its left side, spilling the Marines in the back out onto the ground.

Major Wittnam had visions of his fight in Nasiriyah. As he tried to regain his senses, enemy fire erupted around him. He rallied the Marines, who had been tossed in every direction. They quickly checked for injuries. Sadly, the truck driver, Lance Corporal Justin Reppuhn, had been killed when the truck rolled over, but everyone else survived the crash with only a few minor injuries.[10]

The Marines from the truck began to return fire and the two Cobras swooped in and attacked the insurgents. It would be hours before Good could calm the shooting, recover his wounded and Reppuhn's body, clean up the wreck, and move on. He never did recover the 7-ton; they had to blow it in place.

Crossing MICHIGAN

Captain Cunningham's Marines continued to control the Government Center and the east-west artery to their south, MSR MICHIGAN. They had been fighting insurgents on three sides for most of the day. The heaviest

---

9 Maj Mathew Good telephone interview, 10/29/07.

10 Maj Dan Wittnam telephone interview, 10/08/07.

fighting was with the insurgents who had infested the buildings on the south side of MICHIGAN. Cunningham knew he would have to move Marines south of MICHIGAN to completely control the thoroughfare. After speaking with his boss, Gary Brandl, Cunningham planned to push his First Platoon south in the middle of the night of November 10-11. Lieutenant Ackerman would grab a foothold on the Pizza Slice to support the entire company's move the next day.[11]

Ackerman preceded his move with another AC-130 strike. Basher zeroed in on a large building on the Pizza Slice and started pounding the structure with 40mm and 105mm rounds to "soften up" Ackerman's target. By the time they were finished, they had turned the building into nothing more than a pile of shattered glass, disfigured metal bars, and chunks of concrete.

When Ackerman's Marines slipped out of the Government Center during the night and silently crossed ELIZABETH into the Pizza Slice, they arrived at their destination only to find an indefensible pile of rubble. Ackerman had a decision to make: return to the Government Center, or find another foothold south of MICHIGAN. He opted to go forward.

First Platoon's Marines crossed the four-lane, divided main road. Before dawn they set up their position in a block-long, multi-story building that housed a butcher shop. Because it smelled like dead chickens and rotting swine entrails, the Marines dubbed it "the Candy Store."[12] Despite the stench, the building was a good choice. It had few adjacent structures and open fields of fire, it faced MICHIGAN on its north side, and there were empty lots to its east, west, and south. Ackerman set security, and his platoon settled in for the rest of the night.

The enemy was reeling from the massive assault all along the northern edge of the city. Survivors of the onslaught were fighting a delaying action, most falling back to positions south of MSR MICHIGAN, the main east-west thoroughfare. All of Natonski's battalions spent the night making preparations for their push across Highway 10 and attack into the southern

11 Maj Aaron Cunningham telephone interview, 07/09/08.

12 Michael Blanding, "The Opposite of Fear," *Tufts Magazine* (Spring 2007).

part of the city. November 11 would be the worst day: the enemy would stand and fight.

The morning light exposed dozens of insurgents to Ackerman's south. They were in the open, preparing their gear and staging for a second day of fighting with the Marines in the Government Center. Ackerman quietly passed the word, and when his Marines were ready he commanded them to open fire. They took the insurgents completely by surprise. Many were killed, and those who were not scattered for cover.

But the enemy regrouped and moved to surround Ackerman's Marines (First Platoon), upon which they focused there attention. They struck back with a vengeance, attacking the Candy Store with machine guns, supported by sniper fire from every direction.

The fight had been raging for some time when a single sniper round smashed through one of the windows and hit Ackerman's platoon sergeant, Michael Cauthon, right in his helmet. The impact did not penetrate the Kevlar, but it did knock him unconscious. A second round followed, ricocheted, and hit Lance Corporal Matthew Brown in the leg, severing his femoral artery. Ackerman immediately called for a casevac.

Captain Cunningham dispatched one of his AMTRACs with his First Sergeant to retrieve the wounded Marines, and alerted his other platoons to prepare to cross the road to reinforce Ackerman. But as the track moved out onto ELIZABETH in front of the Government Center, it was hit by an RPG. The grenade hit the left rear of the track in the water-jet exhaust used for maneuvering the vehicle in the water. The round passed through the vehicle's fuel tank and exploded, spewing burning fuel all over the troop compartment.

First Sergeant Derek Fry ordered everyone out, and then climbed up on top of the track. "Hey, Gunny," Fry said, "your track is on fire."[13]

Gunny Ramirez turned and saw the flames. "Oh shit!" he exclaimed. He immediately ordered the driver to stop the track. The vehicle skidded to a stop and the Marines bailed. They forced open a gate to the Government Center and ran to the cover of the nearest building.

Cunningham got on the radio and ordered CAAT gun trucks to take over the disabled track's casevac mission. The armored HMMWVs raced toward the Candy Store to get to Ackerman's wounded Marines. Ackerman popped

13 SgtMaj Derek Fry telephone interview, 7/29/08.

a smoke in the street and then ran out while under fire to flag down the trucks. Seven Marines, including Brown and Cauthon, were loaded into the gun truck and rushed to much-needed medical attention. Fortunately, Dr. Jadick's mini-BAS was only minutes away in the Government Center. They got Brown to Jadick just in time to save his life. If they had needed to transport him out of the city, he would have bled out.

Meyers and his XO, Markley, were refueling outside the city when Fry's track was hit. Meyers heard all of the chaos on the radio and called to his XO, "We need to get into the city, right now!"[14]

Meyers and his wingman raced south to MICHIGAN, where they maneuvered their tanks into the street and Meyers positioned his between the crippled vehicle and the enemy's guns. Meyers absorbed all of the enemy fire broadside, as the Marines worked as fast as possible to clear the burning AMTRAC.

Cunningham's Marines were in the middle of an intense firefight. He had a platoon pinned down south of MICHIGAN with critical casualties, and his effort to evacuate the wounded had just turned into another emergency. Up to his eyeballs in shit, Cunningham was contemplating his next move when Lieutenant Lee and his wingman, Sergeant Ducasse, arrived. RPGs were hitting the side of the building, and Cunningham's Marines were firing everything they had to cover the burning track and suppress the enemy's fire. Lee walked up to Cunningham and tried to introduce himself to his new company commander.

"Are you the tank TWO commander?"[15] Cunningham asked.

"Yes, sir."

"Fine. Get on the net. Talk to Ackerman. That's your job. GO!"

Lee rushed back to his tank and thundered out onto MICHIGAN in search of Ackerman and his embattled platoon.

14 Maj Chris Meyers telephone interview, 5/1/08.

15 Lt. Jeffery Lee telephone interview, 7/10/08.

Chapter 11

MSR MICHIGAN

"When you're in the shit, it's not about America, your mom or apple pie—
it's about the Marine or sailor next to you."

— SgtMaj Derek Fry, USMC, 7/29/08

With the new plan, Colonel Shupp told Lieutenant Colonel Malay that his Marines would be staying in the Jolan District, north of MICHIGAN. Shupp wanted Malay to rid the northwest quadrant of the city of every single insurgent. The Darkhorse Marines continued their squeegee clearing.

Brian Chontosh's India Company Marines continued to push east and south to a point only one block west of HENRY. On that last block there was a school directly to their east. They couldn't attack in that direction because Chris Brooke's men were just ahead on HENRY, along with their Iraqi soldiers. Instead, Chontosh moved his Company north and slid his 1st and 3rd Platoons toward HENRY, where his Marines attacked south, online.

They immediately ran into a pocket of jihadis. Lance Corporal Klayton South was shot in the face as he entered one of the first houses with four other Marines. Two of the Marines managed to dive for cover behind a flight of stairs, but the remaining two were hit by enemy fire coming from one of the downstairs rooms. Sergeant Michael Meisenhalder was in the house next door when he heard the shooting. He immediately left his house and rushed to the sound of the gunfire.[1]

Meisenhalder, the Platoon Scout, surveyed the scene: two Marines had reached safety in the stairwell, but three Marines lay wounded on the floor. An open door led to an interior room, and Meisenhalder focused his attention on it. He laid down a covering fire into the adjacent room as a corpsman dragged South to safety. As Meisenhalder moved toward the open door, a barrage of tracer rounds flashed through it, the bullets passing so close he could feel their heat on his face. Miraculously, none found their target.

Meisenhalder jumped back out of the line of fire and pitched a grenade into the room. By now, Captain Chontosh and Lance Corporal David Jelinek were at Meisenhalder's side. They, too, tossed several more grenades into the room and then charged in after they exploded. Somehow, the insurgent was still alive and shooting. Chontosh put two rounds into him and Meisenhalder shot him in the head, ending the short standoff.

With enemy fighters in buildings all along the block, Second Lieutenant James P. "JP" Blecksmith, Chontosh's Third Platoon commander, took to the roof to get a better view of the area. Blecksmith, physically imposing at 6'3", had been a football star at the Naval Academy. He was also smart, with an incredible sense of humor. JP hadn't been on the roof long when an enemy sniper in a white man-dress fired a single shot from across the street. The bullet missed Blecksmith's SAPI plate, passed through his Kevlar vest, and killed him instantly.

The radio call went out immediately: "Blecksmith's down."

Marines rushed to his aid but he was already gone. The loss of Blecksmith stopped India Company's attack in its tracks. Blecksmith's Marines hadn't even finished clearing the first block when Captain Chontosh ordered his men to fall back, then pounded the buildings with repeated air strikes. Before nightfall he moved his men farther back to the west to prepare to try again the next day.

Meanwhile, Back on the Shark's Fin

Ever since the opening moments of the operation, a West Coast Marine attack helicopter squadron, HMLA-169, had been making gun and rocket

---

1   Sgt Michael Meisenhalder telephone interview, 03/03/08.

runs in support of the attack into the northwest corner of the city. On the morning of the 11th of November, one of its Cobras ventured too close to the river and was shot down over the Shark's Fin.

Major Kassner was headed for the Fallujah Hospital compound when he got word of the helicopter crash. He immediately diverted his three-vehicle patrol to a grassy field north of the intersection of MSR BOSTON and MSR MICHIGAN. Kassner's Marines jumped from their vehicles and spread out across the field to secure a landing zone for a medevac. Captain Victor Pirak's C/1-9 soldiers secured the crash site and got the pilots out of the aircraft. One of the Marine aviators walked away from the crash, but the other was seriously injured. Pirak's men rushed the wounded Marine to the hastily secured LZ as Kassner called in the medevac and marked the LZ with smoke.[2]

Kassner helped three or four other soldiers and Marines carry Captain John Towle into the waiting casevac bird. Once the helicopter had lifted off, Kassner and his men jumped back into their vehicles and continued their journey to the Fallujah hospital to check on Captain Collier. Collier and his Iraqi Intervention Force soldiers had been providing security at the hospital compound since the beginning of the operation. Kassner visited frequently to check on them.

By the time Kassner arrived at the hospital it was after noon. An Iraqi government delegation, including the Iraqi Minister of Health, was conducting an independent assessment of the ability of the facility and staff to provide medical care to the civilian population. Kassner hadn't been there long when the enemy attacked with several volleys of rockets.

As with most of their attacks, the enemy was relying on volume rather than accuracy of fire. Some of the rockets screamed past the hospital and exploded behind the compound, some hit to the left of the hospital, and some in front. Kassner's immediate concern was for the Iraqi VIPs inside. He and Lance Corporal Hutchinson raced out into the courtyard to try to get one of Pirak's Bradley Fighting Vehicles that was dug in along the bank of the river several hundred meters away. The major wanted to load the Iraqi officials into the Bradley and evacuate them as quickly as possible.

As they were heading for the radios in their vehicle, the eighth or ninth rocket slammed into the hospital, blowing the glass out of the entrance. The deafening explosion knocked Kassner to the ground. He promptly stood up, ears ringing, and ran back into the hospital all the while thinking that the hospital had suffered a direct hit.

As it turned out, the rocket had missed the entrance and exploded on the roof; no one inside had been injured. When Kassner entered the lobby, one of the Iraqis standing in the hospital shouted at him, ran over, and pointed at his arm: Kassner's right hand was bleeding profusely, and his right sleeve was soaked in blood. Shrapnel from the rocket had ripped into his hand and arm.

Once Kassner realized that everyone in the hospital was safe, he turned to run back to his vehicle. His main concern now was to get the civilians out of the hospital compound before another rocket found them—and he had to find the source of the rocket fire. These tasks seemed much more important to him than taking care of his wound. One of the men traveling with the Iraqi Minister of Health had noticed Kassner's wound and followed him to his vehicle. While Kassner was talking on the radio, the guy took some bandages out of Kassner's first aid kit and started wrapping up his hand and arm.

Kassner's focus—everyone's focus—was to neutralize the enemy targeting them and to get the folks out who needed to leave. Kassner called in the Bradleys, loaded up the half-dozen VIPs, and had them driven away from the heart of the enemy's rocket barrage. Ignoring proper medical treatment, Kassner simply returned to the battalion command post.

Preparing to Attack the Southern Half of the City

As soldiers and Marines were preparing to pour south across MICHIGAN, General Natonski and Lieutenant Colonel Bristol paid another visit to Colonel Tucker at the Government Center. Natonski decided he wanted to visit Captain Bethea's Marines before they pushed south. There was a large open field between Brandl's command post and Charlie Company. Natonski set off across the muddy field, followed by Bristol, Tucker, L'Etiole, and his security detachment. "Next thing I know," remembered L'Etiolee, "everybody is shooting at us"[3] from the three large buildings and a minaret south of MICHIGAN. Any number of windows

---

3   LtCol Joe L'Etiole telephone interview, 10/27/07.

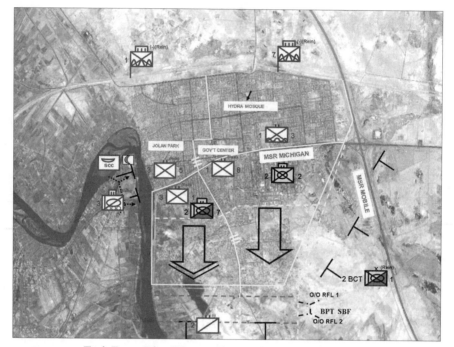

Task Force Blue Diamond's Attack South of Michigan

Graphics from LtGen Richard F. Natonski's
PowerPoint presentation and are used with his permission

could have shielded the snipers. The Marines were an enticing target: Bristol is even taller than Natonski, who stands 6' 3." About halfway across, a bullet impacted between Natonski and Bristol, who was trailing his commanding general. "I didn't even know that a bullet had hit right behind me when I made a quick pivot to go talk to some Marines," recalled Natonski.[4]

When the senior leaders reached the far side of the field and hit the door, a loud OOH-RAH greeted them. The Marines inside had been watching their commanding general's perilous sprint across the field, and cheered as if their favorite running back had just scored a touchdown.

---

4 LtGen Richard Natonski telephone interview, 3/11/08.

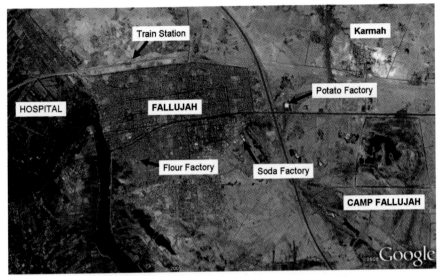

A satellite view of Fullujah, the Euphrates River, and the
surrounding road network and terrain. *Google*

Planning the attack (L to R): Col Craig Tucker (hands on hips); Col Gary Patton (with
pointer); Col Lee Miller (forearm on Knee); BGen Joseph Dunford (standing to
Natonski's right); MajGen Richard Natonski (hand to chin); and Col Mike Shupp
(hand extended toward map). *USMC*

MajGen Richard Natonski and LtGen John Sattler. *USMC*

Task Force 2-7 Cavalry's TOC. *CPT Michael Erwin, USA*

AC-130 Spectre Gunship. *USAF*

Apache AH-64 Helicopter over Fallujah. *Dan McClinton*

D9 Bulldozer. *Maj Rob Bodisch*

L to R standing: LCpl Ryan Sunnerville (WIA); LCpl Adam Rouse (WIA); LCpl Chris Adlesperger (KIA); Sgt Eric Copsetta (WIA); Cpl Jeremy Baker (WIA); HN Alonso Rogero (WIA). L to R kneeling: LCpl Erick Hodges (KIA); LCpl John Alymer (WIA); Sitting on top of tank: Sgt Borel. Sitting on back of turret: LCpl Betancourt. *Author*

LtCol Patrick Malay. *Maj Eduardo Bitanga*

Marine Tanks in attack positions, north of Fallujah. *Lt. Jeffery Lee*

Bradley Fighting Vehicle north of Fallujah. *CPT Mike Erwin*

Lima Company, 3/5 north of the Apartment Complex. *Maj Ed Bitanga*

Entering Fallujah. *Maj Rob Bodisch*

"Brooklyn Bridge." *LtCol Ken Kassner*

Gunny Sergeant Nicholas Popaditch, who was severely wounded by an RPG during the first battle of Fallujah in April 2004.

Nick Popaditch

LCpl Brian Parrello

Shirley Parrello

Hospital Corpsman 3 Juan Rubio. *Juan Rubio*

Maj Todd Desgrosseilliers

Maj Ed Bitanga

LTC Jim Rainey. *CPT Mike Erwin*

Capt Rob Bodisch. *Bodisch*

On the Point of the spear in the Jolan District. *Maj Rob Bodisch*

3/1 in the Jolan District. *Maj Rob Bodisch*

Lima Company, 3/5 inside Fallujah. *Maj Ed Bitanga*

Collecting RPGs. *Maj Ed Bitanga*

Clearing a building, one floor at a time. *Getty Images*

Tanks in the narrow Jolan streets. *Maj Rob Bodisch*

Calling an audible: MajGen Natonski traces new plan in the dirt for LtGen Sattler. *USMC*

Top: Burned AMTRAC outside the Government Center. *Maj Aaron Cunningham*;
Middle: The result when you shoot at an M1 tank from inside a building. *CPT Mike Erwin*;
Bottom: The Blackwater Bridge. *Maj Ed Bitanga*

The Blue Mosque. *Maj Rob Bodisch*

1/8 in the Garbage Field. *Maj Aaron Cunningham*

Second Lieutenant Jeffery Lee. *Lt Jeffery Lee*

Blue1 (2nd Lt. Jeffery Lee) in Queens. *Lt Jeffery Lee*

Lieutenant Colonel Peter Newell attacked south with his mechanized task force to conduct another rapid penetration into the Industrial District. The enemy was different in this sector of Fallujah. These fighters appeared to be all foreigners, and they had more military experience and discipline than the irregular Iraqi insurgents. Someone with some tactical sense had tried to establish a defense on the northeastern corner of the industrial area. The defenses were what one would expect of a dug-in Soviet motorized rifle company: there were communication trenches, bunkers, engagement areas, and minefields protecting the flanks. The enemy had tunneled under the buildings.

Newell used a combination of high explosives and white phosphorous smoke rounds to get the enemy up and out of their bunkered positions. In an urban environment, a high-explosive artillery round exploding across the street, or even in the building next door, did little more than stun the enemy. After the initial shock, most of the enemy fighters remained unscathed. But when the Americans mixed in smoke, the enemy became emotionally stunned: they couldn't see, they couldn't hear, they couldn't breathe, and they didn't know which way to turn.

A/2-2 and A/2-63 moved forward, side by side, clearing the area. South of MICHIGAN the landscape really changed. Here, the area was filled with factories, junkyards, repair shops, and warehouses. Newell's mechanized juggernaut pushed a mile into the Industrial District before stopping at 2000 along PL HEATHER. The enemy's defense, though reasonably well organized, was simply no match for Newell's artillery, tanks, and Bradleys. The lieutenant colonel wanted to fight his way all the way to ISABEL, but he was ordered to halt to give Colonel Formica time to move his southern cordon back out of Newell's line of fire.

1/8's Attack Across MICHIGAN: Tanks lead the Charge

Lieutenant Colonel Brandl ordered two of his companies to cross MICHIGAN. He pressed the attack south, with Bravo and Charlie companies abreast just west of Newell's soldiers. Read Omohundro's Marines would fight their way south on Cunningham's left shoulder, while Bethea's Marines were held in reserve at the Government Center. Pushing directly south from the Government Center, RCT-7 left an entire neighborhood south of MICHIGAN and east of HENRY untouched by either regiment.

Attack Across MICHIGAN, November 11, 2004

As Cunningham was preparing to push the rest of his company across the open, four-lane, divided road at 1500, a Marine approached First Sergeant Fry. Fry's track was still smoking in the street from the earlier RPG hit. "First Sergeant, we got you a new track."

"Fuck you," he snapped, "I'm walking."[5]

Fry might have preferred to hoof it, but Cunningham was concerned about taking his company across that large open, and dangerous area in broad daylight. It had been easy to fight from behind walls, but now the Marines would be completely exposed as they attacked across MICHIGAN. Their only protection would be the amount of fire they could lay down.

5 SgtMaj Derek Fry telephone interview, 7/29/08.

Cunningham ordered Meyers to move his tanks back out onto MICHIGAN, and he ordered his entire CAAT Platoon to lay down a barrage of rockets and machine gun fire. Weapons Platoon created enough chaos that Cunningham's Marines were able to charge on foot across MICHIGAN without taking a single casualty. Once on the far side of the wide thoroughfare, the Marines swarmed into the alleys around the Candy Store, where Ackerman's platoon was still trapped.

Because the enemy still covered the only door in or out of the former butcher shop, Cunningham had his engineers blow a hole in the back of the building. First Platoon's Marines charged through the shattered wall to join the rest of the company. Together, they all pushed south, with Meyers' and Lee's tanks in the lead.

Lee, Ducasse, Meyers, and Markley led Cunningham's Marines down several small alleyways. Lee pulled into one of the narrow alleys just west of the Candy Store, and before Sergeant Ducasse could pull in behind him, an AMTRAC, minus 1stSgt Fry, followed Lee's tank between the buildings. One of Alpha Company's squad leaders, Sergeant William Leo, and Staff Sergeant Ricardo Sebastian, followed Lee into the alley. Lee made a small S-turn about fifty meters from MICHIGAN.

The enemy opened fire from the side streets and every window in sight. They had set up a complex ambush and had been waiting for the Marines to approach. Lee's tank acted like a bullet magnet: every insurgent in every window zeroed in on it. Luckily, the RPG rounds bounced off the M1 and the enemy's small-arms fire harmlessly pinged off its thick skin. Sebastian took cover at the corner of a nearby building, while Leo ducked behind Lee's tank.

Leo picked up the "grunt phone"[6] and yelled into it, "Destroy everything from 9 o'clock to 3 o'clock."

Cunningham's infantry were pinned down in the small alleys. They were fighting in such close quarters that Lee barely had room to traverse his turret. He needed Ducasse, his wingman, to protect his flanks, but Ducasse could not get in behind his boss because the AMTRAC blocked his path. Around the corner behind Lee, Captain Cunningham was on the ground

---

6   Marine tanks still have a handset mounted on the back of their tanks so that the infantry can easily communicate with the tankers inside. It is affectionately known as the "grunt phone."

trying to get the track to back up in the narrow alley while Lee fired as fast as he could. Corporal Rios slewed his turret as far as he could to the left, found a target, and let loose with his main gun. While his loader, Lance Corporal Matthew Sevald, slammed another round into the main gun, Rios rotated the turret slowly to the right, spraying coax gunfire. Lee continued to fire his .50- caliber machine gun.

As soon as Sevald finished reloading, he yelled "Ready!" Rios stopped the turret and aimed the main gun.

BOOM!

Another 120mm shell slammed into the nearby buildings. Rios resumed slewing and spraying 7.62 bullets while Sevald reloaded again. By now, Leo had returned to the corner of the building with Sebastian. He took a knee and fired at the muzzle flashes ahead. Sebastian stood above Leo and also fired. An insurgent jumped out into "Haji Alley" and fired an RPG at Lee's tank; Sebastian answered with a SMAW.[7] Leo and Sebastian continued firing until they were nearly out of ammunition, knowing they were providing Lee's only security.

When a bullet snapped past Sebastian's head, he pulled back around the corner for a second. "That would have really hurt," he thought. Had the bullet found its target, it would have done more than just hurt.[8]

Nearly out of ammo, Sebastian sprinted north, leaving Leo at the corner of the building. He ran up to Captain Cunningham and Lieutenant Barnes and grabbed all of their magazines, stuffed them in his pockets, and ran back to rejoin Leo.

Lee's tankers continued fighting for about an hour, slewing, shooting, and reloading, firing thirty main-gun rounds, 8,000 7.62 shells, and 4,000 .50-caliber rounds. By this time, Lee was also running low on ammunition. Fortunately, he had stored extra boxes of ammo on top of his tank; all he had to do was reach out of his hatch and grab the boxes. When he popped his head out of the turret, he immediately spotted a sniper in a building just to his right—and the sniper was aiming directly at him! Before Lee could act the insurgent pulled his trigger and a burning sensation ripped through his

---

7   The Shoulder-Launched Multipurpose Assault Weapon is a man-portable, reusable rocket launcher. Several different types of munitions are available for use in the 83mm launcher: anti-armor, HE and thermobaric.

8   GySgt Ricardo Sebastian telephone interview, 07/24/08.

biceps. To Lee, it felt as if his arm were on fire or melting off. Refusing to button up without what he needed, he remained exposed, grabbed the ammo, and dragged it down into the turret.

As Rios focused on Lee's wound, Sevald took the ammo and started reloading, and also worked to replace his machine gun's hot, carbon-fouled barrel. Rios rummaged inside the turret for anything he could find to stop the bleeding. He ended up grabbing a roll of duct tape and wrapping it tightly around Lee's wound while the injured commander got on the radio to speak to his wingman.

"I need you in front of me—NOW!" Lee ordered. "I don't care how you do it, but you better be in front of me in thirty seconds, or you're fired."[9]

Ducasse got the message. His driver gunned his engine, smashed through a wall, plowed the giant tank between two buildings, knocked the corner off a house, thundered through another wall and, with guns blazing, exploded into the alley. He was in front of Lee's tank in less than ten seconds.

With double the firepower, both tanks sprayed the enemy positions with main gun and machine gun rounds. As Lee and Ducasse slowly pushed twenty feet forward, Cunningham's Marines rushed into the first building. Once that was cleared, Barnes' Marines jumped to the next rooftop, and Lee and Ducasse pushed forward another twenty feet, with Leo and Sebastian following on the ground.

First Sergeant Fry joined his Marines in the ground attack. A young corporal looked up. "First Sergeant, what are you doing here?"

"I'm shooting motherfuckers like you," Fry gruffly replied. "Shut up and keep shooting."[10]

As the battle raged, Gunny Ramirez filled his AMTRAC with eleven casualties and raced back to Dr. Jadick's mini-BAS at the Government Center. He delivered his load of wounded Marines, loaded up with water and ammunition, and returned to the fight.

In the BAS HM1, Brian Zimmerman kept everyone calm in an exceedingly tense atmosphere. He was a funny guy. Jadick would scream at his men, and Zimmerman would come around and pick them up with his

---

9 Capt. Jeffery Lee telephone interview, 7/10/08.

10 SgtMaj Derek Fry telephone interview, 07/29/08.

kind words and lighthearted attitude. Zimmerman really made the mini-BAS work.

Just west of Lee and Ducasse, Markley's alley was full of hundreds of low-hanging wires. As he pushed slowly forward, his gun barrel snagged the wires, dragging them down to the base of his turret. Before long, Markley had snagged so many that his tank started pulling up telephone poles and dragging them through the street. The wires jammed between his hull and turret like fishing line in a tangled reel. It would take the tank leader, Frank Herbert, and his maintenance Marines all night to pull the turret and remove the fouled wires.

Farther east, Captain Juarez had ordered his First Platoon Commander, Lieutenant Paul Webber, to move west and link up with Omohundro. Webber moved out with his platoon of LAV-25s[11] to link up with 1/8, rolling west on MICHIGAN in his three vehicles. When they reached the intersection with ETHAN, his Marines came under sporadic fire from the south. Webber stopped to return fire, dismounted his scouts, and reported the contact. The enemy was firing from buildings hundreds of meters south of MICHIGAN. Webber felt good about his position; it would be nearly impossible for an enemy RPG to hit his vehicle from such a long distance, yet his 25mm gunner could direct accurate fire more than a kilometer downrange.[12]

Webber held his LAV in position on MICHIGAN, firing at the enemy while Sergeant Rhyne Spencer and the scouts fanned out to provide security for Webber's vehicle. They continued to cut down insurgents, but the enemy kept advancing. Gun toting, black-clad muj and RPG teams dodged between buildings for more than an hour, getting closer to Webber's vehicle with every bound. Omohundro's Marines were attacking south, just to Webber's west, and the enemy fighters were squirting over onto ETHAN in an effort to get behind the Bravo Company Marines. As the enemy moved north through the buildings along ETHAN, Webber's fight started to escalate.

11 The LAV-25 is a variant of the Light Armored Vehicle, carrying a 25mm Bushmaster cannon in a tank-like turret.

12 Capt Paul Webber telephone interview, 11/10/09.

It is not good for armored vehicles to linger too long in one position. When they do, enemy RPG teams often work their way in close enough to get off a shot. And that is exactly what happened to Webber's LAV, which took a direct hit from an RPG. The explosion rocked the 12-ton vehicle and blew a tire. Certain his driver had been hit, Webber reached over and opened the hatch, but found him unharmed. He ordered his driver to back out of the line of fire. With the enemy firing from protected positions inside the buildings along ETHAN, Webber decided to go on the attack. He pushed his three LAVs 500 meters down ETHAN, along with his twenty dismounted scouts.

As soon as Sergeant Kenneth Andrews' scouts hit the street, they started taking heavy fire from the front and the buildings on their right flank. They had unwittingly moved into an L-shaped ambush. Lance Corporal George Armendariz was shot in the legs and went down in the open. Several Marines rushed to his side and dragged him out of the line of fire, but ended up pinned down by an insurgent machine gun.

Lieutenant Webber and his gunner, Lance Corporal Kyle Burns, continued to fire. Webber had handpicked Burns to be his gunner. As Platoon Commander, Webber needed the best gunner he could find—someone who could work with little direction—and Burns was that Marine. Burns and Webber spent many an hour cooped up together in their small turret, and knew each other well. They were as tight as a Marine officer and enlisted man could be. Webber was spraying the enemy with his turret-mounted 240 while Burns was pounding them with the 25mm cannon, trying to relieve the pressure on the embattled scouts. Then, at the worst possible moment, Burns' Bushmaster went down. He struggled to get the gun back up, breaking it down and reassembling it several times, but a critical screw had vibrated loose, and Burns could not get the weapon to operate. Instead, he popped out of his gunner's hatch to relieve Webber on the 240. Just as Burns exposed himself an RPG exploded in front of their vehicle. The rocket's fins spun and hit Burns in the side, dropping him into the turret with a mortal wound. Webber retreated to get Burns medical attention.

The Marine scouts were still pinned down. They couldn't move forward, and they certainly couldn't make it back to the safety of their vehicles without being mowed down in the street. Staff Sergeant Theodore S. Holder II and his wingman, Sergeant Andrews, raced forward in 1st Platoon's two other LAVs. Holder positioned his vehicle between the enemy machine gun and the stranded Marines on the ground, engaging the insurgents who were firing from windows only twenty-five meters away. Exposed from the chest up, Holder continued firing his 240 machine gun while directing Lance Corporal Adam Solis' 25mm Bushmaster cannon fire. The enemy quickly turned their attention to Holder and a burst of gunfire struck his vehicle. A wounded Holder dropped into the turret.

"Hey, Staff Sergeant, are you okay?" Solis asked.[13]

"Whatever that was, it really hurt," Holder replied. "I'm fine," he added, and stood to resume firing. He continued shooting long enough for the besieged Marines to retreat with Armendariz, their wounded friend, who was whisked to a corpsman in the logistics LAV being used for the casevac. Holder's brave actions cost him his life when another machine gun burst sprayed his turret.

The enemy continued pressing their attack. When the dying Burns slumped next to Webber, a wave of emotion swept over him and he began to lose control. Captain Gil Juarez could hear the grief, the apprehension, and the excitement in his voice—all enemies of command. In the calmest tone he could muster, Juarez told Webber, "Red 1, get it together. We need you."[14]

Webber took a deep breath and remembered who he was—a Marine platoon commander. He could not let his men down. He had to lead them out of this, and he couldn't do that if he wasn't calm and thinking straight. He had to get a grip, and he knew he owed that to his men, to the Corps, and to himself.

The enemy had pushed even closer to MICHIGAN, and were now hitting Webber's platoon with small-arms fire. Pulling himself together, Webber rallied his men. He yelled to the Marines in the logistics LAV to provide covering fire while he helped load the wounded. With his leg bandaged and still bleeding, Armendariz grabbed a SAW, stood in the vehicle, and began spraying the enemy with 5.56 rounds while everyone mounted back up. Armendariz' covering fire was just enough to allow the rest of the platoon to disengage.

---

13 Sheeler, Jim. "Remembering the Brave." *Rocky Mountain News*, July 22, 2006.

14 Maj Gilbert Juarez telephone interview, 02/21/08.

The Fighting Spreads

For the rest of the day, Cunningham and Omohundro fought their way south with their infantry companies. By the time they went firm at PL BLUE, they were sweaty and exhausted. The enemy had been fighting Brandl's Marines in a running street fight all day. They would fight until they were overwhelmed, and then fall back and repeat the process. They conducted a defense-in-depth, retreating but never giving up. The Marines went through all of their ammunition several times. Cunningham's men had been going ever since they mounted up in their tracks nearly thirty-six hours earlier. Having fought so many insurgents on so many streets, the Marines' days were melting into their nights.

They fought until after sunset, as the daylight ebbed away with the enemy fire. The Americans owned the night with their thermal sights, night-vision goggles, and AC-130s flying overhead. As soon as the sun went down, Basher checked in and began working the area south of Cunningham's position, giving the Marines of 1/8 a much-needed chance to get some rest. Marines nodded off to sleep under the comforting BURRRRR, bump, bump, bump in the night sky. The tankers went north to refuel, rearm, swap out Markley's tank, and get medical attention for Lee.

Cunningham's Marines rested under the protective umbrella of the AC-130s. But not for long.

The fighting extended well beyond Fallujah's bloody urban jungle. While Jim Rainey's 2-7 troopers, Peter Newell's soldiers, and Gary Brandl Marines were attacking across MICHIGAN, soldiers, sailors, airmen, and Marines were fighting the battle throughout Anbar and North Babil provinces. Dan Wittnam and his Marines ranged the Euphrates River and engaged in several heavy firefights. Myles Miyamasu and his soldiers were moving on the roads northwest of the city, and Colonel Formica's Black Jack Brigade continued to isolate the battlefield in the south and east. Mike Ramos' Marines were patrolling from firm bases in the northeast section of the city, and Pat Malay's Marines were clearing every room in every building in the northwest. By now Task Force Bruno had grown to 250-300 Marines.

Now that RCT-7 controlled MSR MICHIGAN, Colonel Tucker shifted his rear area to the Potato Factory, just east of the Cloverleaf, so that he could dramatically shorten his casualty evacuation and supply route. Now the wounded could be raced due east to Bravo Surgical at Camp Fallujah, instead of having to be driven north to MSR MOBILE before heading back south and east to Camp Fallujah. Wounded Marines could now get into surgery in one-third the time it had taken before.

Friday, November 12, 2004 – D+5: Eavesdropping

Sometime between midnight and 0100 on November 12, Cunningham received a new fragmentary order to push south again.[15] That night, he pushed his Marines south. Cunningham knew he was bypassing bad guys and that eventually he would have to back-clear, but right now his orders were to move south as fast as he could.

An intercepted cell phone conversation between two jihadists informed the Marines that the enemy had finally realized it was impossible to stand and fight in the streets.

A: "Where is the shooting?"

B: "Everywhere! In every area."

A: "What is it, artillery?"

B: "Artillery, mortars, tanks—everywhere."

A: "Where are you?"

B: "By the flour mill."

A: "Are they attacking the flour mill?"

B: "Yes, and they are attacking us too. The artillery is destroying us. All of Fallujah is in ruins. Not a house is left standing. What can stand? The tanks come down every street with artillery falling ahead of them."

A: "Get out of there."

B: "Where? How? If I go in the streets, I get shot. If I stay inside, I get shelled. And let's not forget the mortars and the aircraft and the snipers!"

A: "But . . . they said the Americans have withdrawn!"

B: "The Americans are everywhere."

---

15 Fragmentary Order or FRAGO, used to send timely changes of existing orders to subordinate and supporting commanders.

A: "They said Nazal was still safe . . ."

B: "Nazal is a war zone."

A: "Try to make it somewhere . . ."

B: "Even if I go in the yard, I will be attacked."

A: "What about Shuhada?"

B: "Just bombing there, they have not entered yet."

A: "Listen, on the streets, it's just tanks, right? Nobody on foot . . ."

B: "Yes. But you see, a tank is roughly as big as a house. . . . You can hit it with a rocket and it doesn't blow up."

A: "What about Jolan?"

B: "War zone."

A: "They said Mujahedeen reinforcements were arriving."

B: "Well, they haven't arrived yet. There are still Mujahedeen in Askari, only because they regrouped there from Souq[16] and crossed over the new road. Fallujah is finished. It is the attack of all attacks."[17]

Cunningham's Alpha Company, 1/8 occupied a group of houses to bed down for a few hours of rest before the sun came up. There was still a block of houses that hadn't been cleared to their west, leaving a 150-meter gap between Tucker's regiment and the regimental boundary along HENRY. Brandl had not yet linked up with Buhl.

Cunningham had picked a perfect spot to defend. As the Marines moved south the dense urban environment had opened up some; there was an increasing mixture of rows of houses and undeveloped sections of the neighborhood, and there was a large open field facing south of Alpha Company's position, giving his Marines a clear field of fire. As as result, at dawn on the 12th, the enemy started coming at Cunningham's Marines, and the Marines cut them down with amazing ease—pounding them with 81mm mortars, machine gun, and small arms fire. Avenger spent most of the morning repelling the counterattack.

16 Souq – the marketplace.

17 Intercepted enemy conversation as detailed in Kenneth W. Estes, LtCol USMC(ret), "U.S. Marine Corps Operations in Iraq, 2003-2006," History Division, USMC, Washington D.C., 2008

Another Hero Goes Down

As the dark of night was giving way to morning twilight, Lieutenant Colonel Newell and his soldiers were getting ready for another day of fighting. Several vehicles had pulled into a big square between PL ISABEL and PL JENNA, with buildings on all four sides. The battalion was attacking from north to south, and Newell's rear elements were parked in the open area. There were some tanks, a few Bradleys, a couple M113s, an M88 tank retriever, and several HMMWVs, all parked around the square. As the soldiers prepared to move out, enemy insurgents were moving into positions around Newell's vehicles.

Twenty-eight year old Lieutenant Edward Iwan, A/2-2's XO, had just dropped off some reporters who were there to report on the night's intelligence find (a series of enemy tunnels). Iwan had backed his track up close to the building and dropped his ramp. The reporters climbed out of the back of the armored vehicle and headed into the building. One of the reporters waved thanks to him. As the reporter turned away to follow the others, an RPG flashed out of an alleyway and whooshed toward Iwan, who was standing in his commander's hatch atop his Bradley's turret. The projectile slammed into his stomach.

"I'm hit," Iwan exclaimed as he slumped down in the turret.

Staff Sergeant Albert Harris, Alpha Company's senior medic, was riding in the back of Iwan's Bradley with the company's communications specialist, Specialist Batiste. Harris heard a thump on the turret and a muffled explosion and saw a bright flash through the turret door, followed by sparks and a cloud of smoke.

A moment later, all Hell broke loose outside the track. Three more RPGs screamed through the square, skipping along the ground and hitting nearby walls. The fifth RPG hit one of Newell's tanks, setting its smoke grenade launcher ablaze. Small-arms fire erupted all around the square. Newell's soldiers were instantly involved in a 360-degree firefight.

Alpha Company's commander, Captain Sean Sims, couldn't see Iwan's Bradley. "Terminator 5, this is Terminator 6," Sims tried to radio Iwan. No answer. "Terminator 5!"

Sims needed to know what was happening. Why wasn't Iwan answering? A little irritated, he tried again. "TERMINATOR 5!"

Iwan's gunner, Specialist Colley, finally answered. "The XO is dead."

When Sergeant Wes Smith, in the M113 ambulance, heard Colley's answer, he shouted to his driver, "We need to get up there—now!" They pushed forward to Iwan's Bradley. Alpha Company's First Sergeant, Peter Smith, also raced his M113 across the open area to Iwan's aid. Everyone in sight was rushing to the stricken vehicle.

Inside, Harris and Batiste pulled Iwan down from the turret into the back of the Bradley. "Drop the ramp!" Harris ordered the driver. The ramp clanked down and Harris and Batiste pulled Iwan outside. Harris quickly assessed Iwan: he still had a pulse, but he was unconscious and the fins of the RPG were sticking out of a massive wound in his abdomen. Harris was evaluating Iwan when Lieutenant Colonel Newell ran up, bent down, and felt Iwan's neck, checking for a pulse. "He's still breathing."[18]

Sergeant Wes Smith pulled up with the M113 ambulance and his driver backed up so that the vehicle and Iwan's Bradley were parked ramp-to-ramp. As Harris wrapped Iwan's torso in a field dressing, he yelled to Smith to bring a litter. They needed to get Iwan to the aid station as quickly as possible. As soon as Smith returned with the stretcher, they loaded Iwan into the ambulance. All the while, enemy rounds were kicking up puffs of dust at their feet. It was a miracle that no one else was wounded by the heavy small-arms fire. First Sergeant Smith returned to his M113 and the two vehicles raced toward the Forward Aid Station northeast of the city.

Wes Smith was with Lieutenant Iwan. There wasn't much he could do in the back of the ambulance except try to keep him alive long enough to get to a surgeon. Smith kept his hand on Iwan's shoulder in an effort to monitor him. He still had a pulse, albeit a weak one, and was barely breathing. Smith kept screaming at him, "We're getting you to the aid station. You're going to be okay!"

At the same time, Smith was trying to call ahead on the radio. Half yelling, half crying, and scared to death, he finally got through to the aid station. "We have a serious abdominal injury, due to an RPG, coming in." Smith didn't even think to tell them that it was Ed Iwan. To Smith, the ride seemed to take forever. In reality, they pulled up at the aid station in less than ten minutes.

Captain Greg McCrum, Dr. Lisa Dewitt's Physician's Assistant (PA), met the 113 ambulance. McCrum's job was to triage the patients. Dewitt,

---

18 COL Peter Newell telephone interview, 10/29/07.

2-2's Battalion Surgeon, was waiting at the portable treatment table twenty feet away. Lisa watched Wes Smith turn his patient over to McCrum and his team. His job finished, Smith fell down on his knees and put both hands on his helmet. Lisa knew that this would be bad, but she still didn't know the identity of her casualty.

McCrum and the other medics laid the wounded soldier in front of Dr. Dewitt, who was standing at his head. She looked at her patient and thought he must be dead, but as she lifted his jaw to intubate him, he gasped for air. Dewitt quickly inserted the tube to secure his airway and began barking out orders for medication. At her side, the team worked to insert IVs, start fluids, and administer the medications.[19]

"Who is this?" Lisa asked Greg McCrum. Lisa knew most everyone in the battalion.

"It's Lieutenant Iwan," Greg replied.

Lisa's heart sank. Ed Iwan was a great guy, loved by his men, his peers and his superiors alike. McCrum pulled her out of the moment. "Lisa, Lisa, you gotta look at this!"

Dewitt had been so focused on the initial treatment and intubation of Lieutenant Iwan that she had not examined his wound. She looked down at his belly and saw that his entire abdominal-pelvic cavity was open, with the RPG fins sticking out. McCrum called over the explosive ordnance disposal guys. Only the fins of the RPG remained; the warhead was gone.

"How do I dress this wound?" Greg asked Lisa.

"Just throw abdominal dressings around it. Leave the RPG portion in place and wrap around it," Lisa ordered. It was hard to wrap the bandages around such a severe wound, but within minutes Iwan's airway had been secured, IVs had been started, meds had been administered to insure he was not in pain, and his wound had been dressed, albeit haphazardly. Iwan was ready for transport.

The medics rushed Iwan to a nearby Field Litter Ambulance (FLA) and Lisa jumped in with her patient. The driver floored the accelerator and didn't lift his foot until he arrived at Bravo Surgical. In the back, Lisa struggled to keep Iwan in his litter. In their rush, they had strapped down only his legs, and not his upper torso. The off-road journey was bouncing them around inside, the IV bags were swinging back and forth, and Lisa was getting

---

19 MAJ (Dr.) Lisa DeWitt telephone interview, December 22, 2007.

thrown around. She held Iwan's chest down with one hand while with the other she "bagged" him with an Ambu bag and oxygen.

"Did you call ahead?" Lisa shouted up to the driver and his companion who was manning the radio.

Lisa bent over trying to listen to Iwan's lungs. It was so noisy in the back of the FLA that she couldn't hear a thing.

"How much farther?" she shouted to the driver.

Like Wes Smith, Lisa had all she could do to keep Iwan in his stretcher and breathing. Since there wasn't much she could do medically, she prayed instead.

Finally, after about fifteen minutes, they rolled up in front of Bravo Surgical. The doors of the ambulance opened and a team of stretcher bearers whisked Iwan into the resuscitation bed. Dr. Dewitt was at his side the entire time, rhythmically squeezing the Ambu bag.

"I'm Doctor Dewitt," Lisa announced to the emergency room staff. "Who is the doctor here?"

"She's coming," one of the team replied.

The answer infuriated Lisa, but before she could erupt a very competent ER nurse started hooking Iwan up and asking her for a report. Lisa spouted out her patient's status in her rapid ER fashion. The first doctor showed up, followed by the ER doctor and a surgeon. They were all their in scrubs, they were all clean, and they all smelled good. Lisa was filthy. She had been living in the field for days and she was in full kit and sweating. She had just laid her soldier down on the table.

The surgeon examined Iwan and said, "We know that with an injury like this, he is not going to survive. Do you mind if we call it?"

"Does he have a pulse?" Lisa asked. She knew that in her ER experience in the civilian world, they would never give up on a patient who had a pulse. A nurse checked Iwan's wrist. "No pulse," she reported.

"Check his groin and neck?" Lisa appealed.

The ER doctor checked Iwan with an ultrasound unit and announced to the room, "He's got cardiac activity." They rushed him into the operating room, and Ed Iwan somehow survived thirty minutes of surgery.

And then he died. Another American hero whose life was snuffed out too early.

Chapter 12

More Heroes

"When a man gives you his word, it's set in stone.
When a Marine gives you his word, it's set in blood."

— HM2 Juan Rubio, USN, 12/6/07

The Fighting Intensifies

After the morning courtyard attack, Lieutenant Colonel Newell gave the order to move everyone back to Phase Line ISABEL, and then called in artillery and air strikes to clear the buildings around the ambush site. Jim Rainey's Cougar tanks had been pushing south down HENRY all night, bounding from one phase line to the next. Twaddell's Bradleys followed Pete Glass's tanks, leaving two armored vehicles at each major intersection. By dawn, Twaddell was spread out a mile and a half along HENRY, from DONNA to ISABEL. And once again, as soon as the sun came up, the enemy attacked.

Twaddell and Glass started taking intense RPG and mortar fire. Glass' tankers were beginning to run low on fuel, so Twaddell took the lead while Glass returned with half of his company to refuel and rearm. Instead of just sitting there "eating mortars,"[1] Twaddell recalled, he pressed the attack.

1 CSI Interview with CPT Edward Twaddell, 2/28/06, p. 9.

As his Bradleys ground west along ISABEL toward ISAAC, Twaddell was busy in the turret of his track commanding a company-plus attack. The captain was on the radio with his platoon leaders and his boss; he was constantly checking his map and trying to maintain situational awareness; and he was busy maneuvering his vehicles away from the mortar barrage.

As he glanced down at his map around 0900, Twaddell saw a bright flash between his knees. As he would soon learn, an insurgent had jumped from cover as Twaddell's vehicle passed and fired at it with an RPG, which punched through the lightly armored ramp and screamed through the troop compartment, filling the inside of the vehicle with smoke. The projectile hit Sergeant Brian Newman first, tearing off his left arm, after which the deadly dart passed through the interpreter, "Izzy," killing him instantly.

Once the grenade whizzed through the troop compartment, it blew through the front of the track. "The penetrator passed through the turret shield, into the ammo ready box and detonated a couple of rounds," recalled Twaddell.[2] The lethal round must have been some kind of Explosively Formed Penetrator (EFP). The through-and-through hit killed one Iraqi and severely wounded another soldier, yet left only a tiny hole the size of Twaddell's thumb in his back ramp.

It had been nearly twenty-four hours since Major Kassner had been wounded in the rocket attack on the Fallujah Hospital, yet he still refused medical attention. When Lieutenant Colonel Dinauer found out, he ordered his XO to return to the Surgical Shock Trauma Platoon at TQ.

Kassner reluctantly complied and hitched a ride back to TQ. After he was evaluated and his wounds had been properly dressed, he asked his nurse, "Have you received any pilots recently?"[3]

"Yes, I think we did," she replied.

Kassner said, "I'd like to see him."

"I think he's in another ward."

2 *Ibid.*

3 LtCol Kenneth Kassner telephone interview, 11/04/07.

The nurse helped Kassner, grabbing his IV bags and whatever else was plugged into him. Together, they walked over to the tent where Captain John Towle was supposed to be, but his bed was empty.

"Where is this Marine?" Kassner's nurse asked the nurse on the ward.

"An ambulance just took him. They're medevacing him," the ward nurse replied.

Kassner looked at his nurse. "I'd like to try to find him."

The two raced out to the parking area and found the ambulance. Kassner climbed in the back with his IVs and found the wounded, sedated, and heavily bandaged Cobra pilot. When Kassner confirmed this was his man, he began asking him questions. Because his ears were still ringing from the rocket attack, he had no way to know he was shouting.

"WHAT'S YOUR NAME?" Kassner asked.

"Gorby," the pilot answered.

"IS THAT YOUR NAME?"

"It's my call sign."

"I JUST WANTED TO SEE HOW YOU ARE DOING."

"Who are you?" the wounded Marine aviator asked.

"MY MARINES AND I CARRIED YOU TO THE HELICOPTER."

Captain John Towle leaned over and grabbed Kassner's hand. "Thank you."

"TAKE CARE," Kassner added, and climbed out of the ambulance.

Back at MICHIGAN, meanwhile, Willie Buhl's Marines prepared to move south behind Jim Rainey's tanks and Bradleys to clear the southern half of the city. Captain Timothy Jent's Kilo Company attacked down HENRY. When Jent's First Platoon turned south onto HENRY, the daylight revealed a string of five 155mm artillery shells strung out down the middle of the road. Lieutenant Adam Mathes, the First Platoon commander, halted the attack, with the rest of Jent's Company grinding to a stop behind him.

At the head of the attack, Mathes called for an EOD team to deal with the daisy-chained IED. They had only been stopped a short time when enemy 82mm mortar rounds started landing all around them. A Marine was hit and a Corpsman nearly lost his arm to a large chunk of shrapnel. A Navy SEAL sniper team, riding near the front of the column, jumped from their vehicles and raced to the wounded men's aid—just as the next round came screaming in. The explosion that followed wounded nearly all of the SEALs.

Lieutenant Mathes was facing a complex situation: he had a wired explosive device in the street ahead that could take out his entire platoon, and perhaps most of the company; mortar rounds were already landing on his position and had caused multiple casualties; and, to make matters worse, the enemy had opened up with small-arms fire.

RPG teams were another threat, and they appeared quickly, hitting Bodisch's tank at the intersection with three rounds. Mathes had a real fight on his hands, and Jent's entire company was stalled. The enemy was shrewdly exploiting the 500-meter seam between Brandl and Buhl's Marines.

Colonel Shupp, who was waiting impatiently for a report on Buhl's attack south, finally decided to go forward again. Shupp ran to the roof of a Russian-style apartment building that faced MICHIGAN to get a view of the situation. Brandl's infantry was stalled, but Jent finally got the IED defused. Still, he continued to take fire from the east side of HENRY as he pressed forward with his Second Platoon.

Bodisch kept his turret oriented to the left across HENRY, the regimental boundary. All of Bodisch's fire was going to the east. Not knowing that Brandl's Marines were involved in a fight of their own blocks away, Bodisch kept asking about the Marines on his left: "Is our left flank protected?"[4] He could see the enemy running alongside his advance. They were moving to every intersection and popping off RPGs. Lieutenant Smithley, Bodisch's XO and wingman, was second in line behind his company commander's tank on HENRY. He watched as RPG teams fired on his boss, then he cut them down with his 240. Team after team met the same fate: they would jump out to launch on Bodisch's tank, and a few seconds later take dozens of 240 rounds.

During the day's fighting, Corporal Robert J. Mitchell, Jr., a squad leader in 3rd Platoon, Kilo Company, 3/1, was shot through the triceps. The corpsmen wanted to casevac him, but he insisted on staying in the city with his Marines. Because the injury was not life-threatening, they bandaged his through-and-through wound and let him return to his squad.

---

4 Maj Robert Bodisch telephone interview, 01/07/08.

By day's end, Jent's Marines had reached a compound of buildings at the intersection of HENRY and ISABEL that could only be described as a palace—a walled compound that took up an entire city block and included two large three-story homes. The buildings in the compound were the dominating structures in a neighborhood of smaller, one- and two-story houses. Jent's Kilo Company occupied this palace and went firm for the night.

At sunset, Brandl's Alpha and Bravo companies were on the move again, pushing south to HEATHER. Omohundro's Marines sustained more casualties as they cleared houses. One of his men, Corporal Nathan R. Anderson, was killed by insurgents disguised in Iraqi National Guard "Chocolate Chip" uniforms.

Just after midnight, Corporal Jacob Knospler, one of Omohundro's squad leaders, led his Marines into a house in search of a safe place to catch a few hours of rest. They moved cautiously inside, tossing grenades into the darkened first-floor rooms before moving to the stairs to clear the second floor. Knospler took the point, climbing the stairs in the dark.

Without warning, an insurgent lobbed a grenade down the stairwell that hit Knospler in the face and exploded. Two more grenades bounced down the stairs past Knospler and detonated, peppering six more Marines with shrapnel. In shock, Knospler stumbled back down the stairs, staggered out of the house, and collapsed in the street badly wounded.

Bravo Company corpsmen whisked Knospler into a vehicle and raced him back to Jadick's mini-BAS at the Government Center. By the time he arrived, he was drowning in his own blood. Jadick rushed to the wounded Marine and found him unconscious and not breathing. His lower face had been blown away, including his teeth, his tongue, and his entire jaw.

Jadick suctioned his airway with a stainless-steel turkey baster and, astonishingly, Knospler gasped for air and sat up—awake. Jadick pushed as much morphine as he thought Knospler could tolerate and told him, "We're going to ride back together."[5]

---

5   Jadick, *On Call in Hell*, p. 193.

Jadick and his corpsmen bandaged Knospler's face as best they could—surprisingly, he was not bleeding too heavily—but Jadick was still worried about his airway, which could swell shut at any moment.

Miraculously, Knospler turned out to be a walking wounded. Jadick and an Army medic, Specialist Kristine Knight, helped Knospler to her waiting M113 armored ambulance. Knight was one of a handful of women attached to an ambulance company from the North Carolina National Guard. Jadick had "borrowed" her ambulance when he opened the mini-BAS, and Knight was one of the few women working at the front lines inside the city. She had been ferrying wounded all day, but this was the worst injury she had encountered.

Knight sat at Knospler's and Jadick's feet inside the darkened ambulance, ready to intubate her patient, if needed. Jadick held Knospler's head so that fluids would not flow into his airway, and worked for the entire thirty-minute trip back to Bravo Surgical to keep the young Marine from reaching up to touch his face. Knospler couldn't talk, so he knew something was wrong; Jadick just tried to keep him from realizing how bad it really was.

"It's going to be OK," Knight kept telling Knospler, as she prayed harder than she has ever prayed in her life. "You're going to be OK."[6]

Knight's ambulance rolled up to Bravo Surgical, where the waiting stretcher bearers whisked Knospler into the trauma room. The ER physician and surgeons rushed him into surgery to start repairing his mangled face. Hours later Knospler emerged from surgery—alive.

Saturday, November 13, 2004 – D+6: Junkyard Dogs

The enemy was now fully aware this fight was nothing like the first battle for Fallujah, so they did one of the few things they could do: they went to ground. Instead of fighting in the open they set Chechnyan ambushes, turned more bedrooms into bunkers, and even hid behind mattresses and inside bureaus waiting for some lance corporal to appear in the doorway.

Newell's soldiers continued pushing south into a flat open space filled with industrial waste. The ground was covered with mountains of trash, piles of metal filings, and dozens of junk cars. The area was nearly impassable.

6 Christine Knight telephone interview, 05/20/09.

South of the junkyard was another residential area. The Shuhada District was erected without any sense of organization, a hodge-podge of a 1,000 haphazardly placed buildings. This is where Al Qaeda had set up house. They had forced all of the civilians from the neighborhood and emptied the structures. They controlled access in and out of the district, and they expanded their defenses into the industrial area. Shuhada was a well defended stronghold.

By the morning of November 13, Task Force 2-2 had pushed through the junkyard. Newell was shifting units in preparation for clearing Al Qaeda's Shuhada stronghold. At 1030, Captain Sean Sims pulled up in search of a rooftop OP to utilize for the push south. Compared to the last few days, it was a relatively quiet morning. Some of Sims' soldiers pointed out a building that First Platoon had occupied the night before. From the ground it looked as if the roof would provide a commanding view, so Sims decided to investigate.

"Sir, do you want me to send a squad with you?"[7] Lieutenant Meno asked his boss.

"No, it's OK," Sims replied. "I'll be fine."

"Are you sure?"

"I have my guys. I'll be fine."

Sims never went anywhere without Corporal Travis Barreto and Specialist Joseph Seyford. They were "his guys," his personal security detachment. Air Force Staff Sergeant Greg Overbay, Alpha Company's Joint Tactical Air Controller (JTAC), and Sergeant Sean O'Brien, Captain Cobb's forward observer, were also moving around with Sims.

Before they entered the building, Sims sent Barreto up an outside wall to the roof. Once atop the building, Barreto found a stairwell leading back down. He covered the stairs, making sure no one came up or went down. Sims, Overbay, Seyford, and O'Brien entered the front door of the building, with Sims, Overbay and O'Brien carrying M16s, and Seyford his SAW. Once in the hallway, Seyford peeled off the stack to check the first room on the right while Sims and Overbay moved deeper into the house.

When Seyford stepped into the room, two insurgents hiding under a blanket jumped up and started firing their AKs. Seyford returned fire and O'Brien quickly backed out of the house. The room filled with flying bullets,

7   History Channel FIREFIGHT!

passing each other in midair. All three men were tangled in an eight-foot gunfight. Seyford, who was struck in the left shoulder, shot down both insurgents. The enemy fighters tried to get back up, but the wounded American butted both of them with his SAW, then turned to get the hell out of the room. In a dying effort, one of the men lifted his rifle and shot one last time, hitting Seyford in the left leg. He half-crawled, half-dragged himself down the hallway yelling, "Barreto! Barreto!"

Manning the roof, Barreto heard the gunfire but held his position until he heard Seyford's call for help. Instead of running down the stairs, he jumped from the roof and rushed to the front door, where he found Seyford struggling to make it to safety. Overbay was already out of the house. He, too, had been shot. Barreto grabbed Seyford and dragged him into a small alley.

With Seyford safe, Barreto went in search of his captain. He stopped at the front door and called out, "Captain Sims!" He was just starting to call out a second time when a grenade rolled out of the door. Barreto dove for cover just a moment before it exploded. Unscathed, Barreto returned to the doorway.

"CAPTAIN SIMMS!"

Still there was no reply. By now a squad from First Platoon had showed up and stacked itself at the door. The remaining insurgent rolled out another grenade to cover his escape, scattering the squad.

BOOM!

The squad regrouped and rushed into the house shouting, "Captain Sims? Captain Sims!" They found him in the back room, dead on the floor. In less than twenty four hours, Alpha Company, 2-2 Infantry had lost both its Company Commander and its XO. The losses of their admired leaders devastated the men of Alpha Company.

Devastated or not, there was still work to be done. Task Force 2-2 pushed south through the Shuhada District to the southern edge of the city. They consolidated, brought in Iraqi Intervention Forces, turned around, and went back up to the industrial area to systematically clear every building.

A Different Battle

As noted earlier, the enemy fighters holding the southern part of Fallujah were composed of large numbers of foreigners from Syria, Saudi Arabia, and a dozen other countries. The terrain was different too, with many more detached houses and deliberate fortifications. Some of the houses were rigged with explosives, and many rooms were filled with mattresses and other items to protect their defenders. Fortunately, many of the enemy's positions were oriented to the south or west toward the Euphrates River.

Buhl's Marines were more cautious entering these homes. If they suspected that enemy fighters were holed up inside, they blew in the front door with HE, then fired a thermobaric[8] charge in to drop all the floors. It wasn't long before The Thundering Third ran out of SMAW thermobaric rockets. In an urban fight, you can never have enough rockets and grenades. They are like hamburgers and beer at a Marine picnic: consumption is always proportionate to availability.

Buhl's India Company lost a Marine to a suicide bomber on the 13th as it was sweeping toward a mosque with a blue and white minaret. The bomber rushed out of one of the nearby houses toward the Marines, who opened fire and filled him with 5.56 rounds. Somehow the fanatic jihadist managed to stagger forward and detonate his explosive-filled vest. The explosion blew the bomber to pieces and killed Lance Corporal Justin D. McLeese.

The mosque had been a gathering point for insurgents in southern Fallujah. The structure was heavily guarded, and the enemy had set supporting machine gun positions in nearby houses. They fought stubbornly to protect one of their last strongholds in the city. When the American forces first rolled down HENRY, the enemy had fired RPGs at Pete Glass' tanks from the mosque compound and its minarets. Kilo Company had cleared the mosque on the 12th and found a cache of mortars and RPGs inside. By the 13th, the mosque had changed hands more than once. Each time the Marines thought they had cleared the stronghold, enemy fighters returned to occupy it.

When India Company's Marines re-entered the mosque on the 13th, they found dead and wounded insurgents from the previous fighting. The Marines ordered the injured to show their hands and remain still, but one of the insurgents refused to comply, pretending he was dead.

"This guy's not dead," a Marine blurted out. "He's faking."

---

8 Thermobaric munitions have been used by many nations of the world and are quite effective in an urban environment. Thermobaric weapons provide massed heat and pressure effects at a single point in time that cannot be reproduced by conventional weapons without massive collateral destruction.

After days of fighting and surviving booby-trapped bodies and houses, the Marines were in no mood to take chances. They had already encountered enemy fighters feigning surrender, and others disguised in Iraqi National Guard uniforms. They had seen their friends die at the hands of suicide bombers. They were not going to fall for any further jihadi treachery.

A young Marine who had been wounded the day before, but had remained with his squad, moved forward to take a look. The insurgent was still playing possum and ignoring their commands. When he moved slightly again, the Marine shot him in the head.

"He's dead now," he announced.

Kevin Sites, a freelance NBC correspondent, and his camera man had followed the Marines into the mosque and captured the entire incident on film. He showed it to Colonel Shupp and Lieutenant Colonel Buhl when he returned to the train station. Shupp immediately reported the incident to Division. The Marines authorized the release of the news footage, and within hours it was available on every television and computer in the world. The young Marine was removed from the battlefield pending a complete investigation of the incident. He was returned to duty when it was later determined that he had followed the established rules of engagement. For now, however, the enemy had their first media victory.

Unlike the Americans, the enemy had no rules of engagement. They fought from mosques, minarets, hospitals, and homes. They used tunnels, spider holes, and underground complexes. They routinely feigned surrender or injury. They used women and children as shields. They booby-trapped the dead and fought to the death from fortified positions. Natonski's young soldiers and Marines, however, were held to a higher standard. In today's world of instant communication, satellite television links, and the internet, nearly every action is scrutinized by the entire world. Enlisted soldiers and Marines could lose the battle in the media with one moment of poor judgment. Operation Iraqi Freedom produced the "strategic corporal." Despite this, explained one battalion commander, the young American "corporals and sergeants out-fought the bad guys and left them lying dead in the streets."[9]

9   Col Patrick Malay telephone interview, 11/4/07.

Cunningham's Marines had finally reached HENRY. Gary Brandl was traveling with Alpha Company when they reached the regimental boundary. Bravo Company, on the left, had already linked up with Newell's soldiers. The built-up areas of the city had narrowed to a mile-and-a-half corridor south of the garbage fields, bringing Natonski's battalions closer together. Cunningham's men ran into dozens of entrenched fighters, many of whom were squirting over to the west side of HENRY.

Brandl got on the radio to his boss, Colonel Tucker. "We really need to coordinate with Willie's guys," he told Tucker. "They're pressing and we're pressing. We kind of need to link up and press together."[10]

Tucker agreed and coordinated with Shupp to push to the edge of the city in a coordinated attack. Brandl and Buhl's Marines would finally link up just outside the southern mosque. Cunningham moved his Marines south across the garbage field to come online with 3/1, closing the seam between the two regiments.

RCT-1 and RCT-7 fought the rest of the way to the edge of the city side by side.

10 Col Gareth Brandl telephone interview, 11/20/07.

Chapter 13

Houses from Hell

"Marines are trained to always attack."[1]

— 1stSgt Bradley Kasal, USMC

Bullets Rain Through a Skylight

While 1/8's Marines were closing with 3/1 near PL JENNA, Jent's Kilo Company drew the morning's house-clearing patrol north of the palace. Third Platoon pushed off first while Second Platoon stayed in the palace as the Quick Reaction Force. The morning was eerily quiet. After four days and nights of steady fighting, the empty streets were a welcome sight.

The quiet streets gave the exhausted Marines a false sense of security. The long days and nights of combat had dulled their senses and their razor-sharp edge; they were running on adrenalin. As a result, the morning's clearing was routine—perhaps a little too routine. They entered houses and cleared rooms more casually than they would have done a day or two earlier.

The morning's clearing was nearly complete and only one house remained on the block, a modest light yellow single-story dwelling on the

---

1 Nathaniel R. Helms, *My Men are My Heroes*, p.13.

corner with the typical gated courtyard and a short wall surrounding a rooftop balcony.

As Sergeant Christopher Pruitt, Third Platoon's Guide, Corporal Ryan Weemer, and Lance Corporal Cory Carlisle approached this last house, each had a feeling the enemy was nearby, but the streets remained quiet. Pruitt led the three Marines around to the back of the house, where they found a single locked metal door. Pruitt, Weemer, and Carlisle continued around the house, whose windows were covered with metal gratings. They continued circling until they got back to the open gate at the front of the house.

Weemer took point with his 9mm pistol and the three Marines moved into the courtyard. They checked the outhouse just inside the gate and found fresh human waste on the floor; someone had used this facility recently. The three Marines stacked at the front door and Weemer entered first. A dazed insurgent was waiting just inside. All three Marines opened fire, dropping the surprised man before he could lift his weapon.

Weemer, Carlisle, and Pruitt rushed into the darkened foyer. Two full-length swinging doors led to the next room. Carlisle pushed the doors open and Pruitt rushed into the center of the house, with Weemer following. A large bearded man stood in the shadows. When he saw Pruitt he opened fire, spraying the interior room with AK fire, hitting Pruitt in the wrist and leg. Weemer emptied his 9mm into the man, and both Marines retreated back to the foyer.

Pruitt, his wrist shattered and his leg bleeding, decided to return to the street to get help. He was exiting the house when he was knocked to the ground by a tremendous blow to his back. The short wall on the roof sheltered an insurgent fighter, who had shot Pruitt from behind. Luckily, his SAPI plate saved his life. Before the sniper could shoot again, Pruitt jumped to his feet and stumbled into the street.

Lucian Read, a freelance news photographer, was talking with the Marines in the gun truck when shots, dozens of them, shattered the conversation. "What the fuck is that?" Read exclaimed before jumping from the vehicle and sprinting around the corner toward the gunfight.[2]

More Marines were moving to the sound of the gunfire. Brad Kasal, Weapons Company's First Sergeant, was walking alongside one of his CAAT vehicles with Corporal Mitchell, Staff Sergeant Jon Chandler,

---

2 Lucian Read telephone interview, 03/25/08, and personal written eyewitness account.

Private First Class Alexander Nicoll, and Lance Corporal Samuel Severtsgard. When the shots rang out, all five men rushed toward the target house.

Covered in blood, Pruitt staggered out of the front gate into the street, his hand a mangled piece of meat. Kasal hustled Pruitt between two buildings. "Come over here and sit down," Kasal gently ordered. Mitchell, who had been wounded the day before, rushed to Kasal's side and together they tended to Pruitt, Mitchell bandaging his leg and Kasal attending to his hand.

As they worked on him, Pruitt explained the situation inside the house, including the fact that Marines wre still inside. Mitchell got on his radio and reported to Lieutenant Jesse Grapes: "We are in contact. We have wounded."

After Pruitt exited the house, Weemer left Carlisle in the foyer and he too ran for help. Just as he reached the courtyard, Severtsgard, Corporal Jose Sanchez, and Chandler were rushing through the gate. All four Marines charged into the front room where Carlisle still guarded the swinging doors. Shell casings covered the floor along with two discarded pistol clips. A bespectacled insurgent lay dead in the corner with several gunshot wounds to the head. The five Marines stacked and prepared to assault the house again.

Severtsgard cracked the saloon door to the room in the center of the house. It was a large, open space with stairs on the left leading up two walls to a rooftop balcony. The center of the room was dominated by a large skylight. Severtsgard lobbed a grenade into the room, and Weemer and Carlisle followed the explosion into the center of the house, with Weemer going left and Carlisle going right.

Two insurgents sprayed the large room with AK fire from the skylight above. Weemer was hit in the leg, dove back into the foyer, and staggered out the front door with two rounds lodged in the bone below his right knee. Carlisle also went down but was lying against the far wall inside and bleeding badly. One or more rounds had shattered his leg, and he had a twisting fracture from his hip to his knee. Helpless, Carlisle lay screaming in pain and unable to move.

Staff Sergeant Chandler surveyed the open room from his position at the swinging doors. Three more doors opened onto the large center room: one next to the door leading outside, and two more on the opposite side of the interior room.

Chandler organized the first rescue attempt. He stacked everyone on the wall and they charged in to get Carlisle—Severtsgard and Chandler going right while Sanchez headed straight across the open room to the wounded Marine corporal.

The rescue attempt was dashed by a single grenade dropped through the skylight. The explosion peppered Severtsgard and Chandler with shrapnel, and another long burst of automatic weapon fire hit Chandler in the leg. Severtsgard dragged his platoon sergeant into one of the back rooms on the far side of the house. As the insurgents above focused on Chandler and Severtsgard, Sanchez dragged Carlisle to relative safety in a back bedroom.

Standing in the front room and unsure what was happening, Private Rene Rodriguez shouted, "Corporal Sanchez! Sanchez!"

"I got Carlisle!" Sanchez replied.[3]

Rodriguez and Lance Corporal Michael Vanhove braved the kill zone to rush toward the bedroom. Vanhove was driven back into the foyer by the hail of gunfire, but Rodriguez made it to Carlisle and Sanchez. Because the windows of the house were barred, they were now trapped—unable to go back, unable to get outside. Sanchez did his best to help Carlisle while Rodriguez covered the door.

By now all of Third Platoon had converged on the fight, along with their CAAT support. After talking with Weemer, Grapes ordered his men to surround the house. The Marines swarmed around it and cordoned off the area. Next, Grapes called for Second Platoon, the QRF, and then set out to find a way into the house. What he found were the grated windows and the locked metal kitchen door. There was no easy way into the bunkered structure, and there was no nearby high ground, so the insurgents on the roof were protected by the rooftop patio wall.

While Grapes was assessing the situation and searching for a weak spot in the enemy stronghold, the next wave of Marines mounted another rescue attempt. First Sergeant Kasal, Mitchell, McCowan, and Nicoll rushed into the courtyard and entered the house, Kasal and Nicoll going in first, Mitchell and McCowan following. The foyer floor was covered in blood. The men moved to the door leading to the center room, where Kasal peeked through the swinging doors to get a better understand of what was inside. After a few

---

3   Bing West, "The House From Hell," *Small Unit Actions*, p. 64.

moments, he took a deep breath and moved into the center room to get to his wounded Marines; Nicoll was right on Kasal's heels.

As he moved into the center room, Kasal noticed a dead insurgent lying in the doorway to a small room back in the far right corner—the big guy Weemer had killed in the first gunfight. Kasal grabbed Nicoll and shouted, "Help me clear that room!"[4] The two Marines moved across the open room to the far doorway. Luckily for Kasal and Nicoll, the insurgents hidden above held their fire, waiting for more Marines to enter their kill zone.

Kasal cautiously moved toward the door, scanning as much of the small room as he could before he moved into the doorway. When Kasal and Nicoll reached the far wall, Kasal sidestepped to view more of the room and found an insurgent, close enough to shake his hand, brandishing an AK-47. The enemy combatant raised his weapon and fired. The bullets barely missed Kasal, who took a step back, pressed his muzzle into the guy's chest, and pulled the trigger. The insurgent dropped to the floor. Kasal finished the job with two rounds to the forehead.

On his own, Mitchell had moved across the open room to the bedroom where Carlisle lay bleeding. Mitchell tried to slow the flow of blood, but when he applied a pressure bandage Carlisle screamed in pain and Mitchell could feel bones shifting. He stopped, not wanting to hurt Carlisle any more than he already was.

The enemy upstairs finally decided to open fire again. Kasal heard the gunshots and felt a sledgehammer blow to his lower leg. His legs gave way and he fell to the floor. Nicoll was also hit in the leg, but he didn't go down. Kasal's world turned to slow motion as rounds continued impacting around him. He clawed his way to the doorway, pushed the dead insurgent out of the way, and continued crawling into the small room. Nicoll dove toward the door as another shot rang out. He grimaced and grabbed his stomach, watching as blood flowed out between his fingers. Kasal grabbed Nicoll, rolled him over the top of his own body, and pushed him deeper into the small bathroom. As Kasal was twisting out of the line of fire, another round struck him square in the ass. The shooting stopped as quickly as it had started. Wounded Marines were now trapped in three separate downstairs rooms.

4 Helms, *My Men Are My Heroes*, p. 217.

More Marines rushed into the house, but stopped short at the door to the center room. They stacked along the wall, reached around the door frame, and sprayed the ceiling of the ambush room with bullets. Outside, Sergeant Byron Norwood, part of the CAAT section attached to Grapes' Third Platoon, wanted to use his CAAT vehicles to turn the tide by pumping 40mm grenades onto the roof with his MK-19. First, though, he needed to ensure that he would not be endangering any of his fellow Marines. Norwood raced into the building and crouched in the doorway.

"Where are our guys?"[5] Norwood shouted into the room, not addressing anyone in particular. "Where are the bad guys?"

Not waiting for an answer, he moved to the doorway to see for himself.

As Norwood peered into the house, the room exploded with another hail of insurgent bullets. The rounds hit all around Norwood and kicked up debris on the floor at his feet. In the blink of an eye a single deadly round struck Norwood in the temple. The hammer blow knocked him to the ground, and he was dead before he hit the floor. "Norwood didn't have to go into that house," Colonel Shupp later explained. "He heard that his buddies were hurt inside, so he went in to help them."[6]

The failed effort left another Marine dead and Kasal, Nicoll, Carlisle, and Chandler bleeding and still trapped in the rooms downstairs. Kasal was determined to keep Nicoll alive, and he used all of the dressings they both carried on Nicoll's wounds. He also kept talking to keep Nicoll awake.

The Marines outside needed to get their buddies out before they bled to death, but the insurgents firmly entrenched on the roof were frustrating every effort. The Marines tossed flash-bangs into the room and tried to charge into the house again, but the unfazed insurgents sprayed the room with fire again and forced the Marines to fall back yet again. Direct assaults weren't working; Grapes would have to do something else.

As Second Platoon rolled up with reinforcements from the palace, Kasal was getting weaker by the moment and Nicoll was drifting in and out of consciousness. Still with enough presence of mind to attempt a defense, Kasal lay there, weapon ready, in case an insurgent tried to enter the room. It was not an enemy fighter who made an appearance but a grenade, which

---

5   Lucian Read's personal written eyewitness account.

6   Col. Mike Shupp telephone interview, 9/25/07.

bounced onto the floor and came to rest only three feet from Kasal and Nicoll. Kasal rolled on top of the young wounded Marine to shield him from the inevitable blast.

BOOM!

The concussion pounded the two Marines and sent more shrapnel tearing into Kasal's already battered body.

The grenade explosion worried Mitchell, who knew his first sergeant and Nicoll—the most popular Marine in the company—were trapped in the small room. Worried about their safety, Mitchell sprinted across the center room as bullets rained down from above and another grenade exploded behind him. Somehow he managed to dive into Kasal's bathroom.

Kasal looked up at Mitchell. "We need help," he told him in his matter-of-fact style. "Don't worry about me, just save Nicoll." Both Marines were bleeding badly, but Nicoll was dying.

Mitchell turned his attention to the unconscious Marine, trying as best he could to stem the bleeding. A short time later he got on his squad radio to talk to his platoon commander. He informed Grapes that Nicoll and Kasal were in bad shape, that Carlisle had a badly mangled leg, and that other Marines were with him in the back bedroom. He also described the merciless fire from the skylight above.

Grapes decided to try to get to Mitchell, Kasal and Nicoll by smashing a hole in the concrete wall with a sledgehammer. Large chunks of concrete showered the wounded Marines inside the small room. Mitchell radioed Grapes to stop pounding.

About ths time Nicoll came to, looked up at Mitchell, and out of nowhere said, "Your rifle ain't worth a shit." Mitchell looked down and saw that a bullet hole in the bolt of his rifle had rendered it completely useless.

Meanwhile, Severtsgard had pried the metal kitchen door open just enough to allow him and Chandler to squeeze out to safety. While Severtsgard covered the inner door, other Marines pulled Chandler, screaming in pain, through first. Once Chandler was out, Severtsgard squeezed through, too.

Lopez ran for bolt cutters and started working on the grate over a window in an empty back bedroom. After several minutes he was able to remove the metal covering. Grapes and Private Justin Boswood stripped off most of their gear, handed their weapons to nearby Marines, and then shimmied through the tiny window. Once inside they retrieved their weapons. Grapes dropped to the floor and slid on his back through a pool of blood into the doorway, M16 pointed skyward; Boswood took a knee over his platoon commander, aiming toward the roof.

As Grapes and Boswood positioned themselves, Rodriguez and Vanhove moved to the doorway of their room. Lieutenant John Jacobs was in the foyer, and he ordered one of his SAW gunners to the swinging doors. Outside the front door, Lance Corporals Christopher Marquez and Dan Schaeffer set down their weapons and prepared to rush into the house.

When all were in position, Grapes gave the command and everyone opened up, unleashing a torrent of gunfire toward the balcony from three different directions. The insurgents above dove for cover, unable to return fire. Marquez and Schaeffer sprinted into the house, through the kill zone, and into the small room where three Marines lay bleeding. First they scooped up Kasal and whisked him to safety. The Marines opened fire a second time, and Marquez and Schaeffer ran back to retrieve Nicoll. One last time the Marines fired all they could into the ceiling while Marquez and Schaeffer ran back to rescue Mitchell.

Sanchez, Rodriguez, and Carlisle were still trapped in the back bedroom—but not for long. As Marquez and Schaeffer shuttled back and forth, Marines wrapped a chain around the grating over Carlisle's window and, using a HMMWV, ripped away the entire window, metal grating and all like a Wild West prison break. Sanchez and Rodriguez carefully handed Carlisle, who was now unconscious, out the window and then climbed out themselves.

Now there were only two men left inside: Boswood and Grapes. Grapes gave a fourth, and final, command for all of the Marines to open fire and the two Marines ran for it across the killing field.

Corpsmen started working on Kasal as soon as he was in the street. He had more than forty shrapnel wounds and had been shot seven times. Kasal had also lost more than half of his blood, but he was still conscious and still clinging to his 9mm pistol. Miraculously, Nicoll was also alive, though just barely. Mitchell had been seriously wounded too, peppered with grenade fragments as he ran to rescue Kasal. In all, eleven Marines were wounded in the fight, many seriously, and Norwood had been killed.

Once all of the Marines were out of the house, Jacobs ordered it demolished. Gonzo, the company's "mad bomber," had learned that C-4 worked much better when used in conjunction with the homeowner's propane tanks. Gonzalez piled his twenty-pound satchel charge next to the propane tanks in the kitchen. Meanwhile, Lucian Read and Gonzo screamed at each other to provide the illusion that all the Marines were still in the house. When the charge was ready, Gonzo ignited the satchel fuse and the two men ran for cover across the street. The explosion raised a giant cloud of dust and debris high into the air. As the dust settled, the Marines and Read saw that the building and even the outer courtyard wall had been reduced to a pile of smoking rubble.

They also spotted a single insurgent lying dead, half buried in the debris. Read limped over to get a picture, and as he was framing his shot he noticed movement in the corner of his eye: a second insurgent was pinned in the rubble, alive but buried up to his rib cage. Only eight feet apart, Read and the insurgent's eyes locked in a deadly stare. And then Read saw the dying insurgent's outstretched hand.

"GRENADE!"[7] screamed the photographer, and all of the Marines scattered for cover.

Read and the Marines around him somehow managed to elude the grenade's shrapnel. A dozen rifles turned on the trapped enemy fighter and as many shots rang out before the reverberation of the explosion had subsided. The final Hell House insurgent was now dead. Jesse Grapes, whose platoon had suffered so many casualties in this fight, calmly walked up and put a three-round burst into the corpse—just to make sure.

A Texas Shootout

Just a block north on HENRY, A/2-7's First Platoon came under attack around 0900 from a mosque and a complex of houses. Twaddell dismounted his rifle squads to clear the surrounding buildings. During the clearing an insurgent jumped from cover and sprayed one of Twaddell's Bradleys with AK-47 fire. He ran into a house on the east side of HENRY, north of HEATHER.

Staff Sergeant Carlos Santillana's Third Squad rushed the house. Santillana's squad members, most of them from Texas, were incredibly tight and seemed to fight with one brain. With little chatter, they all charged the two-story grey dwelling. Some of Santillana's men rushed in and cleared the building to the left of the target house, while the rest of the squad stacked along the courtyard wall. Sergeant Akram "Abe" Abdelwahab was on point,

---

7 Lucian Read, personal written eyewitness account.

with Specialist Wayne Howard right behind him.[8] Abe was the personification of "an Army of One": he walked and talked like a seven-foot-tall, 300-pound killer, but under his gear he was just a skinny farm boy from Spartanburg, South Carolina.

They threw two grenades over the wall and charged into the courtyard behind the explosions. Abe went straight for the house and charged through the front door into the kitchen. As he rushed in, he spotted two insurgents in the next room back in one corner, and another two under a stairway. Abe was on the far side of the doorway before the enemy could even react. When the two combatants under the stairs started shooting, Howard was in the doorway. Santillana's squad fell back into the courtyard, but Howard and Abe were now pinned down.

Santillana's squad moved on muscle memory, taking up positions at each window in the courtyard, where they all started firing into the house. Specialist Benny Alicea moved to another courtyard door and fired into the darkened room. Suddenly a sniper started shooting at Santillana's soldiers from the house across the street. Specialist Jose Velez, Alicea's good friend and the squad's SAW gunner, spun around and sprayed 5.56 rounds into the sniper's window.

Meanwhile, Abe and Howard were locked in a fight for their lives, picking off insurgents one by one inside the house. Alicea moved with a team around the west end of the building, looking for another entrance. There they stumbled into a dozen insurgents running into the back of the house. Alicea took five of them out with a grenade, but the others rushed inside unharmed. As fast as Abe and Howard shot them, more appeared. Abe and Howard just kept shooting, popping jihadists as they entered the house. They hit more than a dozen Muj fighters, but more kept coming.

The trapped pair started lobbing grenades into the house, and the enemy started throwing their grenades at Abe and Howard. One made it through their door. "GRENADE! Get out, get out!" Abe yelled to Howard. Howard ran out of the house, but Abe stayed behind, unwilling to cross the open doorway. Instead, he tucked in on the wall like a pill bug. The grenade injured him, but Abe's adrenalin was running so high he did not feel his wounds. Instead, he resumed his fighting position at the edge of the doorway

---

8   Flight 33 Productions. "SHOOTOUT! Return to Fallujah." The History Channel.

and continued shooting. He pitched another grenade into the house. His opponent picked it up and tossed it back.

BOOM!

The explosion broke Abe's right leg. His adrenalin still pumping, Abe later recalls feeling no pain, although he was now seriously wounded. He returned to the fight again, and a third grenade landed only inches away.

BOOM!

Shrapnel peppered Abe's leg a second time. Having had enough of this, Abe stumbled to the front door and collapsed, unable to go any farther. Lying on his back, he continued to fire his weapon into the house.

Howard grabbed Abe's flak vest and dragged him outside. As he was pulling Abe to safety, the sniper appeared again in a window in the house across the street and fired. The bullet ripped through Howard's shoulder. He realized something was wrong only when his right arm quit working and he dropped Abe. Not even realizing that he had been shot, Howard grabbed Abe's vest with his other hand and continued dragging him away from the house.

Velez, in his brown-frame "birth-control" glasses, rushed to his two wounded friends. Determined to protect them, he stood over them in the open, rocking away with his SAW and pouring rounds into the building across the street.

Meanwhile, everyone else was trying to reorganize to re-assault the building. Santillana stacked his men at the door again, but as they did so two more grenades bounced outside.

The squad scattered, some dropping to the ground while the the rest ran.

BOOM! . . . BOOM!

"Who's hit?" Santillana yelled. One soldier had been struck in the hip, and Goodwin, the youngest in the squad, had been struck in the leg. Santillana realized that he was outnumbered, so he ordered everyone out of the courtyard. To cover their retreat, he told Velez to spray the target house. With empty drums and shell casings piled up at his feet, Velez turned, reloaded, and lit up the target.

When Velez paused to reload, the window sniper put a bullet through his neck. Velez dropped like a stone and fell dead across Abe's legs. Velez and Alicea had been planning a motorcycle road trip across the western United States once he returned home from Iraq. But now there would be no road trip. There would also be no more SAW gunfire to cover the squad, so Alicea rushed to take Velez' place. He turned his fire on the sniper, lobbing M203 grenades at the house. The determined sniper kept firing, hitting Abe two more times before Alicea managed to get a grenade through the window, finally silencing his friend's killer. Just as Alicea was running out of ammunition, two Bradleys rolled down the street. Alicea directed the gunners to fire into both houses. The remaining insurgents had no stomach for fighting against Bushmaster cannons, and the enemy fire subsided.

Abe and Velez were loaded into the track and rushed to the aid station. Santillana was shattered. He was unharmed, but nearly everyone else in his squad—his family, his band of Texas brothers—had been wounded. Velez—the quiet, determined soldier—was gone.

Santillana wished that it had been him.

Chapter 14

The Three-Block War

"Death is too often the fate of those who are timid."
— Major George (Ron) Christmas

Back Clearing

The Darkhorse Marines continued their room-to-room clearing behind 3/1 in the Jolan and around MICHIGAN, while Buhl's Kilo Company Marines climbed into their vehicles and drove north to GRACE, dismounted, and started another squeegee stroke to clear from the north to the south. Ramos' Marines conducted patrols from firm bases scattered throughout the northeast section of Fallujah. Gary Brandl's Charlie Company pushed south to clear behind Cunningham's and Omohundro's advance. As Bethea's Marines moved south to clear the large buildings across from the Government Center, Colonel Shupp packed up and started moving his regimental command post from the apartment complex to a four-story building in Fallujah's Government complex.

Newell still held the industrial area down through the garbage field. Task Force 2-2 had found VBIED factories, one with a large stockpile of a white powdery substance.[1] Just to be safe, the soldiers called in the

---

1   LTC Peter Newell CSI interview with Matt Matthews, 03/23/06.

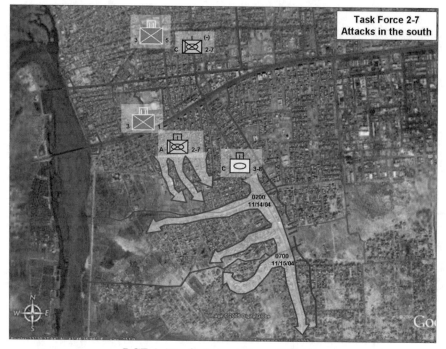

RCT-1 Attacks into southern Fallujah

Graphics provided by Task Force 2-7,
and are reproduced with permission

Division's NBC[2] unit to clean up the potentially hazardous material. They uncovered tunnel networks, weapons caches, fighting positions, and enemy casualty collection points with pre-staged medical supplies. Newell called in a Marine 155mm artillery barrage on one of the larger underground bunker complexes he found deep down south. Some 150 rounds pounded the area in an effort to collapse the bunkers, but the barrage had little effect on the fortifications.

Newell's armored vehicles rolled through the remaining blocks of the southernmost neighborhood on the 14th of November. Little resistance was encountered because by now, the enemy wanted nothing to do with American tanks and Bradley Fighting Vehicles. Instead of fighting, they

---

2 Nuclear, Biological and Chemical.

hunkered down and let Newell's armored vehicles pass them by. Newell pulled his soldiers back to let 1/8 sweep in behind them to clear house-to-house. Omohundro and Cunningham would have to root out the remaining insurgents.[3]

At 2100 on November 13, Lieutenant Colonel Rainey's mission changed. The cavalrymen were ordered to maintain the picket line along HENRY while the Marines continued the fight. He arrayed 2-7 from north to south along HENRY, with C/2-7 in the north, A/2-7 in the middle, and C/3-8 in the south. Rainey's C/3-8 troopers conducted supporting operations ahead of Buhl's infantry by probing west from the regimental boundary a couple blocks ahead of the Marines' movement south. They pushed west until they reached streets so narrow that Glass' tanks had to back out, leaving the remaining areas for Buhl's Marines to clear.

Sunday, November 14, 2004 – D+7: Action on the River

Wittnam and his Marines continued ranging the Euphrates River in their small craft. As the only corpsman deployed to Fallujah with the boat company, Juan Rubio made nearly every patrol. On November 14, the Small Craft Company returned to the railroad bridge where it had been ambushed days earlier. This time the boats were loaded with a ground combat element, and Wittnam's Marines were looking for a fight. A platoon-sized element of twenty-five insurgents was dug in along the river just west of the bridge. Just as before, the enemy opened fire as the boats approached.

Its not clear what the insurgents expected, but what happened next was likely an option they failed to consider. Instead of running the gauntlet up the river, Iversen and Vasey turned their boats toward the shore and sped toward the center of the insurgent position at forty knots. As they did so, the rest of Wittnam's boats sprayed machine gun fire from the middle of the river to cover the approach. Bow guns blazing, the two boats drove onto the bank at full speed, plowing into the enemy's foxholes. Firing deadly bursts, Marines poured from the boats within arms-reach of the stunned insurgents. Some of the enemy panicked and ran, while others stood and fought. Within seconds the Marines on the ground were immersed in a four-foot gunfight.

---

3   Graphics provided by Task Force 2-7.

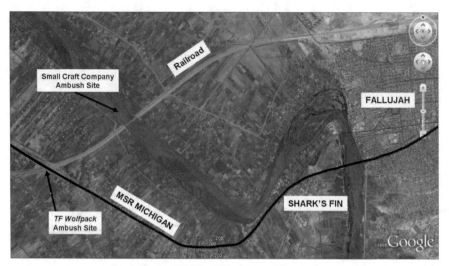

Small Craft Company
Ambush Site

Railroad

FALLUJAH

MSR MICHIGAN

SHARK'S FIN

TF Wolfpack
Ambush Site

Task Force Wolfpack's Area of Operations

Wittnam's infantry quickly overcame the enemy, spread out, and began methodically chasing down the panicked insurgents.

More enemy fighters tried to cross the railroad bridge with RPGs and AKs to reinforce their embattled friends, but Cobra helicopters swept in and attacked them on the bridge. Major Kevin Badger, who commanded the 1-5 CAV's ground component in the area, moved a patrol down to the bridge area in support of the Small Craft Company. The soldiers and Marines fought for about ninety minutes, attacking from the front, rear, and above. Finally, running low on ammunition, Lieutenant Andrew Thomas ordered his Marines back to the boats, leaving the cleanup up to Major Badger's soldiers.

A Future Sergeant Major Dies as a Lance Corporal

On November 14, the Darkhorse Marines worked their way south behind 3/1. India Company moved south of MICHIGAN along HENRY while Kilo Company stayed north of Route 10. Captain McNulty's Marines ended up searching houses in an upper-class neighborhood filled with three-story structures and landscaped courtyards. Both companies conducted detailed clearing operations, opening every drawer and looking under every bed in every room they encountered.

By midmorning, McNulty's Third Platoon was clearing the block just north of the Martyrs' Cemetery. The graveyard was across the street from the mosque that Lieutenant Colonel Lewis had obliterated four nights earlier in Task Force 2-7's fight to take Objective VIRGINIA. Lance Corporal George Payton led his squad up the stairs inside one of the expensive houses. Payton wanted nothing more than to lead Marines, and dreamed of one day becoming a sergeant major. His team set security on the second floor landing.

Payton moved to clear the first upstairs room. When he opened the door he was greeted by a burst of machine gun fire. The bullets ripped through his left leg like a buzz saw, nearly severing it. He fell to the floor, but continued to fire on the enemy until a grenade explosion completely severed his leg near his pelvis.

Lance Corporal Kip Yeager—the grandson of the famous Air Force test pilot Chuck Yeager (the first human to fly faster than the speed of sound)—emptied his M16 magazine into the doorway before dropping to pull Payton out of the line of fire. Lance Corporal Mason Fisher lobbed a grenade in through the door to buy some time while the Marines worked frantically to stop Payton's bleeding.

An insurgent inside the room picked up Fisher's grenade and tossed it back out the door. Fisher caught it on the second bounce and lobbed it back into the room. Yeager waited for the explosion, then emptied another M16 magazine into the room. "If there was anyone in the world you would want in a firefight, it would be Yeager,"[4] remembered the corporal's squad leader. The dust from the explosion had not yet fully settled when Yeager and Lance Corporal Phillip Miska charged into the room. Sergeant Distelhorst's replacement as Squad Leader, Sergeant Martin Gonzalez, followed the fire team into the room. Two insurgents were dead on the floor, but another jumped out of a cupboard. Gonzalez shot him before he could raise his rifle. When a fourth insurgent was found fumbling with an RPG behind the bedroom door, Yeager dispatched him with his bayonet.

Payton was still alive, but only because the corpsmen managed to get a tourniquet onto what was left of his leg. They carried him downstairs into a waiting casevac vehicle and rushed him to Bravo Surgical. This was Kilo Company's second major casualty, the first since Hodges had been killed.

---

4   SSgt Kenneth Distelhorst (Yeager's squad leader) telephone interview, 3/18/08.

They had been clearing buildings for a week, and had already cleared 1,000 rooms. Sergeant Jason Arellano worried that his squad members might be losing their edge. He pulled them all together and warned, "You can't get complacent. Payton lost his leg today."[5] Lance Corporal George Payton lost more than his limb. He fought for his life, but died four days later from his wounds.

Darkhorse Reaches a Limit

Chontosh's India Company Marines crossed south of MICHIGAN and swept through the houses on the west side of HENRY toward GRACE. The blocks were long, running 400 meters without a cross street. A/2-7 had swept down these streets on the 11th, but they had not cleared the buildings. As a result, Chontosh's Marines cleared all day, and by mid-afternoon were only a few houses away from GRACE.[6]

When First Platoon's Marines (on India Company's far eastern flank) entered the last houses on their block, a waiting insurgent shot and killed Lance Corporal Antoine Smith. The only child of a single mother, the easygoing and friendly Smith was well liked by the Marines in his platoon. Incensed by his death, his friends went in with grenades and killed every insurgent in the house. Chontosh ordered First Platoon to back up, moved over to HENRY, and flagged down some of Jim Rainey's tanks. The tankers pounded the house and the buildings next door until they were out of ammunition.

When the tankers were finished, Chontosh ordered his men back at it. As 2nd Squad moved south again down the street just west of the original fight, they got into a gun battle with jihadists barricaded in houses on their block. Lance Corporal Shane Kielion was killed in the fight. Hospital Corpsman 3rd Class James (Doc) Pell and two other Marines were wounded trying to save his life.

With casualties mounting and darkness setting in, Chontosh pulled his entire company back north and called in an air strike to level the entire

---

5   *Perfect Valor.*

6   Capt Brian Chontosh telephone interview, 12/08/07.

neighborhood. It was later determined that about 150 insurgents were hiding in the buildings; the air strike killed most of them.

This would be the Darkhorse Marines' farthest penetration south. That night, India Company pulled back north of MICHIGAN to help clear the northwest.

Regiments Meet Up

In RCT-7's area east of HENRY, Lieutenant Lee's Blue Platoon M1 tanks led Avenger by successive bounds to HEATHER. The two Marine regiments had finally met along HENRY, with Buhl's Marines on the west side of the road and Brandl's Marines on the east. They cleared houses as they moved, but Willie Buhl was not going to send his Marines into another Hell House. If there was any indication that enemy fighters might be in a house, he simply leveled the building. He was decimating everything in front of him, using artillery and other explosives, firing everything he had to finish the job.

At 1600 on November 14, Colonel Shupp arrived at the infamous Brooklyn Bridge. It had already been swept by EOD and dog teams. "Come on, Marines, let's go across," he urged. "Let's go meet the Wolfpack."[7] Shupp patrolled across the green bridge as if he were a lance corporal, with an M4 slung across his chest and a 9mm and bayonet dangling at his waist. When Shupp, Malay, and Desgrosseilliers reached the center of the bridge, Lieutenant Colonel Dinauer was waiting to welcome them. The commanders greeted each other with handshakes and pats on the back. This bridge had become an icon of the insurgency, signifying defiance of the American occupation. For the Marines, it conjured up images of Mogadishu. It was a huge matter of pride for the Marines when they were able to stand on this bridge unopposed.

The mob that had picked the fight in April had written on the bridge in white paint: "Fallujah—Downfall of the United States and death to the Marines." One of the Marines had already painted a reply in black, block letters:

---

7 Col Michael Shupp personal interview, 09/25/07.

THIS IS FOR THE AMERICANS OF BLACKWATER
MURDERED HERE IN 2004
SEMPER FIDELIS 3/5 DARKHORSE
P.S. Fuck You

When Lieutenant Colonel Malay read the Marine graffiti, he smiled. "Paint over the bottom line," he ordered. "Leave the rest."[8]

By the end of the day, Natonski had backed the diehard foreign fighters into a corner in Queens. The neighborhood that had once been their stronghold was now becoming their coffin. Newell's armor was pushing south along the eastern edge of the city and two Marine infantry battalions were pushing relentlessly forward, building after building. Most of the enemy's defenses had been placed at the edge of the city to stop an attack from the south, so now their own barricades and Colonel Formica's cordon had them trapped. They had nowhere to run, and fewer places to hide by the hour. A group of Syrian insurgents tried to flee the fight by floating on inflated beach balls across the Euphrates River under cover of darkness. None made it to the far side. The Marines dubbed the dead insurgents the "Syrian Beach Ball Team."

Natonski's iron vice was tightening.

Monday, November 15, 2004 – D+8: Tanks and Infantry Gang Up

By the end of November 14, Lee and Cunningham were sitting on the northern end of the garbage field. Lee moved his two tanks out onto HENRY and supported Cunningham's push across the open area to the houses on the other side. Once across the field Cunningham set up his CP in the house across the street from the same mosque where the cameraman had filmed the Marine shooting an insurgent the day before. Cunningham's sector was only 200 meters wide, with a platoon just south of his CP and another just to his east. Bravo Company held another narrow corridor on Cunningham's left.

---

8   US Marine Corps History Division, *Small Unit Actions*, p. 76.

Cunningham decided to infiltrate a platoon during the night of the 14th, just as he had done at the Government Center.[9] Under cover of darkness, he pushed Ackerman's platoon about 100 meters south. When the sun came up on the 15th, Ackerman had a much better view of the enemy than did Cunningham from his CP, and what he observed was another enemy staging area: a bunch of insurgents gathering, forming into five-man teams and preparing rockets and ammunition. They were moving across HENRY into 3/1's area. The enemy fighters thought that they were far enough south to be out of the Marines' view, and had no clue that Ackerman's platoon had moved forward during the night.

Lee pulled up on HENRY just as the sun was coming up, climbed off his tank, and walked inside Cunningham's CP to get his orders. And, just like every other morning in the last week, the enemy attacked Alpha Company. It started with gunfire and rockets from the south. Cunningham's CP was rocketed hard. More insurgents opened fire from the mosque across HENRY. Soon fire was coming from every building across the street.

Cunningham turned to Lee. "See what you can do to silence the attack."[10]

Lee returned to his tank and ordered all four of his platoon's tanks out into the open. They pounded the daylights out of the insurgents, shooting main gun rounds, and 7.62 and .50-caliber machine guns. Meanwhile, Ackerman directed the battalion's 81mm mortars down on the insurgents from his forward position. When the mortar rounds started falling, the enemy soldiers scattered. Ackerman's men opened up and didn't let up for three hours. It was almost like a professional boxer pounding his stunned opponent while he hung on the ropes in the corner; the enemy fighters had nowhere to go, and were unable to defend against the Marines' combined-arms jabs and roundhouses.

Bodisch and Smithley came south on HENRY to lead 3/1's attack down the west side of the road and, for the first time, he linked up with Lee and his wingman on the regimental seam. The tankers couldn't communicate because they were on different radio frequencies, so Bodisch pulled up next to Lee's tank to shout over to him.

9   Maj Aaron Cunningham telephone interview, 07/09/08.

10 Capt Jeffery Lee telephone interview, 07/10/08.

The captain had never seen Marine tanks in such bad shape. Bodisch thought his tanks looked bad—he had holes in his own tank—but Lee's and Ducasse's tanks were really shot up, covered with scorch marks, broken optics, and other general damage. Ducasse's tank, with bent skirts and dinged hull, looked like he had been using it to knock over buildings.

Bodisch yelled over to Lee. "Hey, I'm about to go at Zero-Seven. Are you guys going to attack alongside me?"[11]

"Yeah," Lee replied. "I think we are."

"All right," Bodisch yelled above his tank engine. "I'm going south. I need you to protect my left flank."

But when Bodisch and Captain Clark's India Company, 3/1 started moving south at 0700, Lee stood fast. 1/8 was trying to coordinate with 3/1, but with all the fighting, 1/8 got held up. When Lee started to move online with Bodisch, Ackerman yelled at him to wait because his platoon was still engaged and not yet ready to move. As a result, Bodisch pushed forward without Lee.

Bodisch watched his left flank while his gunner scanned right. Bodisch moved very slowly, with Clark's entire infantry company led by gun trucks and AMTRACs. While standing still back on HENRY, Lee could see insurgents running back and forth across the road, so he started launching main gun rounds in their direction, knocking down Texas barriers at the edge of town. Lee did his best to protect Bodisch's left flank.

As Bodisch moved south, the southernmost berm at the edge of the city came into view. When he looked to his left across HENRY, he spotted a group of thirty hardcore insurgents in a field dressed in running suits and heavily armed with bandoliers of ammo strapped across their chests. They were mingling and chatting because they hadn't heard Bodisch's tank approaching. The captain rolled forward to within 100 feet of the group before the first enemy combatant saw the giant tank approaching. What followed can only be described as a mass scramble to safety. Bodisch grabbed the turret control handle, rotated his turret to the left, and ripped a burst of 7.62. Three insurgents fell under the fire. One of them, nearly cut in half, went down screaming "Allahu Akbar!" Bodisch's XO moved up on his right and together they switched to their main guns, killing many more Mujahedeen in the scattering group.

11 Maj Rob Bodisch telephone interview, 1/7/08.

The mob moved into a building south and east of the Marines. Bodisch tossed his map to his loader, the artillery Forward Observer (FO) from Mike Battery, and told him to place an immediate fire mission on that building. Rainey's 120mm mortars responded in less than a minute. The first adjust round screamed in and hit right on target.

"Fire for effect," the FO called into the radio.

Round after round rained down on the house, completely destroying the building and killing the remaining twelve insurgents in the group.

With the southern edge of the city at their backs, the Al Qaeda fanatics fought ferociously, but they were no match for the Marines and their combined-arms attack. Lee continued fighting while he was waiting for Ackerman to move. He could see Bodisch's tanks and Buhl's infantry engaged on the west side of the road, and he watched enemy grenadiers pop out with RPGs on his side of HENRY in an effort to fire on 3/1's vehicles. Lee opened fire with all of his weapons to stifle the barrage against Captain Bodisch's tanks and 3/1's gun trucks.

Lee finally got the call to push all the way south. He immediately pulled off HENRY into an alley and escorted Ackerman's Marines while they ran the rooftops. After Ackerman's fight, there wasn't a lot of enemy contact, but they did find a lot of arms caches and cleared numerous houses before reaching the southern edge of Fallujah.

By nightfall, the Marines were beyond exhausted. Brandl's and Buhl's infantry had fought their way the entire length of the city in a week of heavy and nearly non-stop fighting. Bodisch's and Meyer's tanks had been in the lead every step of the way. Of the forty-six Marines in Ackerman's First Platoon, more than 50% had been seriously wounded. Remarkably, none had been killed, though all but six of his Marines would go home with Purple Hearts.[12] Buhl's Thundering Third Marines had also taken heavy casualties, losing twenty-three killed and nearly 350 wounded during the fight.

Everyone was elated to see the open area to the south. They had bludgeoned their way through the most dangerous city in Iraq and left many hundreds of enemy fighters dead in their wake. The insurgency inside Fallujah had been defeated. But it had not been completely driven from the city.

---

12 Blanding, Michael. "The Opposite of Fear." *Tufts Magazine*, Boston, Spring 2007.

The Hard Part

"The real story—in terms of skill, discipline, and courage—was in the clearing phase,"[13] Colonel Tucker later explained. Ramos' Alpha Company sent Marines out on patrol, clearing houses in the northeast on the 15th. Sergeant Rafael Peralta, a Mexican-American born in Mexico City, went with them to add another rifleman to one of the squads. Peralta, the Platoon Guide, didn't have to go because he was a facilitator within the platoon and an advisor to the platoon commander. But Peralta wanted to do his part, so on this day he was just another grunt in just another stack, kicking in doors and doing his job.

Peralta's father had been a truck driver in Mexico until he died in an accident. After her husband's death, Peralta's mother moved the family to the United States and raised her children in the San Diego area. Rafael joined the Marine Corps on the day he got his green card, knowing that this would be the best way to help his mother support the family. He loved the Marines and he loved America.

Peralta and his platoon methodically cleared houses along their allotted block. The first three were empty, but when the Marines entered the fourth house and Peralta opened a door leading from the central interior room, all hell broke loose. At least three insurgents opened fire, hitting Peralta several times in the chest. As he fell to the floor, the Marines in the room let loose with their SAWs and M16s. In the confusion of the close-quarter gunfight, one of the Marines accidently shot Peralta in the back of the head.[14]

As the Marines maneuvered into position to get a clean shot at the enemy fighters, a grenade rolled out into the middle of the room and stopped less than a foot away from Peralta. As the Marines scattered for cover, Peralta— in his last dying act—reached out and scooped the grenade under his body. It exploded with a muffled thud.

Stunned, and with some minor shrapnel wounds themselves, the surviving Marines fell back to their rally point down the street. Staff Sergeant Jacob Murdock did a quick head count and came up one short. "Who's missing?" he demanded.

13 Col Craig Tucker telephone interview, 1/10/08.

14 Col Mike Ramos telephone interview, 03/04/08.

"Sergeant Peralta! He's dead! He's fucking dead!" screamed Lance Corporal Adam Morrison. "He's still in there. We have to go back."[15]

The Marines rushed back to the target house, moved inside, killed three insurgents, and retrieved Sergeant Rafael Peralta's body. Had he not pulled the grenade under himself, more than one Marine would have died in that house.

Lieutenant Colonel Buhl's Marines got into a big firefight late in the day in the Queens District. Captain Bodisch was moving from HENRY toward the Euphrates River when he ran into a strongpoint where a couple of Marines had been shot. When Bodisch pulled up he found Buhl standing out in the open; the rest of his Marines were under cover behind a wall.

Buhl had an M79 grenade launcher in his hand, a weapon Bodisch recognized immediately because he had carried one years earlier when he was a reserve enlisted Marine. The M79 grenade launcher is a Vietnam-era weapon with a full wooden stock and a stubby, wide-bore barrel. It is slightly more accurate than its modern-day M203 replacement, which attaches directly to the M16 rifle. Lieutenant Colonel Brennan Byrne's 1/5 Marines had captured the fully functional M79 back in April during Operation Vigilant Resolve.[16] When Buhl's battalion arrived, Byrne gave the grenade launcher to Buhl before 1/5 left Iraq. As a Pfc, Buhl had been trained to use an M79, but that had been so long ago it seemed like another life. Nonetheless, Buhl had it checked out, cleaned, and kept it strapped behind the seat in his HMMWV with an assortment of smoke, flares, and 203 HE rounds—just in case he ever needed it.

Major Christian Griffin, Buhl's Operations Officer, was behind the wall yelling for his boss to get to cover, but the short and stocky colonel stood there with a stogie in his mouth using his M79 to bloop grenades into the target building—until Bodisch showed up. Buhl yelled at Bodisch to get

15 LCpl T. J. Kaemmerer, "A Hero's Sacrifice," *Marine Corps News*, 12/2/04.

16 Col Willard Buhl telephone conversation, 11/09.

inside his tank and, "Soften that building with as many rounds as you can spare."[17]

Bodisch dropped into his turret and called Lieutenant Smithley to also bring his tank online. Together they both opened fire, pounding the strongpoint with six main gun rounds, after which Buhl sent his infantry forward again. When two more Marines were shot in the assault, he pulled them back one more time.

Undaunted, Buhl called for his D9 dozer. The powerful machine lumbered west past Bodisch's tanks and pushed into the building, backed up slowly, and pushed into the building again. Working for several minutes, the driver completely flattened the structure, leaving nothing behind but a pile of concrete rubble. As the bulldozer backed away from the demolished house, a lone insurgent popped out of the wreckage and began firing at the armored cab. The young Marine bulldozer driver paused for a few seconds, turned his giant vehicle toward the insurgent, and raised the blade. The insurgent's AK rounds were pinging harmlessly off the heavy steel when the driver dropped the heavy blade on top of him, flattening him like a pancake.

Wednesday, November 17, 2004 – D+10: Split Level

While conducting house-to-house back-clearing sweeps on the 17th, only a block away from the house where Hodges had been killed, Lance Corporals Jacob Fernandez and William Lenard from Second Platoon, Kilo, 3/5 came under fire from fighters on a second-floor balcony.[18] The Marines dashed into a house across the street from the enemy stronghold and began returning fire, while most of the Marines of Second Platoon rushed to the high ground of adjacent buildings. Fernandez and Lenard had managed to get out of the enemy's line of fire, but they could not return fire effectively from their new position. They returned to the street and threw grenades onto the enemy rooftop. The grenades, coupled with the platoon's barrage of small-arms fire, killed a couple insurgents before they could scramble off the balcony.

---

17 Maj Robert Bodisch telephone interview, 01/07/08.

18 Sgt Jason Arellano telephone interview, 03/10/08.

Lenard rushed into the building with his fire team and headed up the stairs. As he turned the corner at the top the enemy opened fire from less than fifteen feet away. One of the rounds struck Lenard's weapon, knocking it from his hands, while another grazed his left arm before he could jump back out of the line of fire.

Doc G. rushed to Lenard's side on the stairwell to check his wound, but Lenard shrugged him off. "I'm OK," he said as he grabbed Hospital Corpsman Joseph Gagucas' shotgun. Fernandez pressed the attack, throwing two grenades onto the second floor. By now, Jason Arellano had worked his way up the stairs toward the fight. The Marines were closing in on the insurgent when a grenade clanked out onto the second deck's open-air patio.

"Grenade!" Fernandez shouted, and the Marines dove back into the stairwell and waited for the explosion.

Silence.

When the insurgent had tried to pull the safety pin, the ring had detached but the pin had remained in the grenade. Once Fernandez and Arellano realized it was a dud they redoubled their attack, rushing out onto the open patio and firing into the upstairs rooms. Arellano provided covering fire while Fernandez charged into the smoke-filled room.

Fernandez disappeared as soon as he crossed the threshold, but he reappeared almost as quickly as he had vanished. The enemy insurgent had selected a good spot to make his last stand. The room was two or three feet lower than the second-floor landing, so when Fernandez crossed the threshold he fell into the room. The surprised Marine scrambled out as fast as he could.

This time Arellano and Fernandez redirected their fire downward. They could hear someone moving inside, but they still could not see into the room. Arellano didn't know how many rounds he had left, so he fixed his bayonet and together they jumped into the darkened room.

The bold assault finally uncovered their enemy. Fernandez tackled the man as he tried to scurry away, and Arellano stepped over his torso and began bayoneting him. Fernandez pulled out his own bayonet and stabbed him in the side. Arellano continued attacking, just as he had been trained to do. He thrust the blade into his opponent, twisted his rifle, and pulled back to thrust again. The two Marines continued until there was no more movement. The fight was over almost as quickly as it had begun.

Arellano and Fernandez checked the rest of the small room and climbed back out onto the second-floor landing.

Victory? Not Yet...

Once Task Force Blue Diamond cleared the southernmost houses in Fallujah, most everyone in the media believed that the fighting was over. General Metz' I/O threshold had not been exceeded. With the exception of the Marine mosque shooting, the world news media had little to report other than footage of Marines firing at unseen enemy fighters in the distance. When the Iraqi government declared the city secure, the media reported a coalition victory and embedded news crews packed up their gear to leave for their next assignments.

But the fighting was far from over. The Marines of 3/5 would lose more men in the coming weeks than they had in November. For them, the worst was yet to come.

The remaining enemy fighters had dug themselves in deep. Those who were smart enough to evade the initial onslaught had bunkered themselves into heavily-fortified positions. Some kept tourniquets on their arms and legs, ready to be tightened when they were wounded. Others wrapped their torsos, arms, and legs in blankets—more to stay warm than anything else. Many were shot up with adrenalin, lidocaine, and amphetamines. When the Marines ran into those guys, the killing was very close and very quick.

The Marines were repeatedly reminded why the American military had replaced the .38-caliber sidearm with the more powerful .45-caliber handgun. Their 5.56 M16—its rounds designed for small animals, targets of fifty pounds or less—couldn't knock some enemy fighters off their feet. They were simply too light for a large grown man jacked up on drugs. While the M16 can be deadly, many times Marines were forced to empty entire magazines into charging insurgents before they would go down.

Once the Marines reached the southernmost houses in the city and the high-impact fighting was complete, there was no longer a need to maintain the massive attack force. Newell's heavily armored battalion returned to Camp Fallujah on Saturday, November 20, in preparation for its return to Muqdadiyah. Similarly, Rainey was ordered to break contact on the night of the 19th; 2-7 CAV returned to Camp Fallujah on the 20th, and the Battalion was relieved on the 24th, returning to the operational control of the 1st Cavalry Division.[19] Task Force Wolfpack was relieved in place by A Company, 2nd LAR,[20] on the Shark's Fin, and Lieutenant Colonel Dinauer began his movement back west to return to his duties near the Syrian border.

Since Rainey had already left, Newell's soldiers were about to leave, and Colonel Tucker was planning his move back to western Anbar Province, Natonski started rearranging his forces. When Colonel Shupp was told that both Army battalions and 7th Marines would soon be leaving the city, he begin expanding his area of influence in preparation for the large shifting of forces. Ramos' 1st Battalion, 3rd Marines would stay behind and be chopped to Shupp's control. Also, Cajun 1/8 filled the vacuum left by 2-2's departure and moved east into the industrial area. They established a new firm base at the Soda Factory, and Dr. Jadick moved his mini-BAS along with them.

Buhl's Thundering Third strengthened its hold on the southwest quadrant of the city. Malay's Marines prepared to extend their battle space east of HENRY to ETHAN. Lieutenant Colonel Malay knew that once RCT-7 left, his battalion was going to be given responsibility for the entire northern half of the city, so he ordered his Darkhorse Marines to start clearing across HENRY, picking up ever-expanding pieces of the battlefield, and moving east to encompass the city center.

While the big fight was over in the city, there were still deadly days ahead. Natonski, Shupp, and Malay knew that if they didn't destroy the enemy's operational base, Al Qaeda would simply move back in. The city needed to be scrubbed clean. It would be RCT-1's job to remain in Fallujah to police up the enormous amount of stockpiled weapons and explosives. On the 21st of November, Task Force Blue Diamond shifted its focus when it initiated a detailed clearing of the entire city. The Marine commanders realized that they needed to clear every room in every building, and every cache in the city needed to be destroyed. If the caches were not cleared, the past weeks of fighting would have been largely for naught.

19 1st Marines Command Chronology, November 2004.

20 *Ibid.*

As soon as the Darkhorse Marines crossed over into RCT-7's area of operations, they ran into groups of four and five insurgents. McNulty's Kilo Company started in the north and cleared between APRIL and CATHY, from HENRY to ETHAN. There was only one gunfight, but Malay's Marines kept catching the enemy trying to slip around behind them. To Malay's surprise, his men found several large caches of weapons and ammunition. Between Thanksgiving and December 8, the Darkhorse Marines patrolled relentlessly to keep their area clean, all the while training the Iraqi forces to maintain order on their own.

Clearing in the City—And Life—Continue

Ironically, even as Colonel Shupp began setting up Humanitarian Assistance Sites on Thursday, Thanksgiving Day, Gary Brandl's Marines continued to take casualties as they swept back and forth in the southeast section of Fallujah. A pair of 1/8 Marines, Lance Corporal Jeffery Holmes and Corporal Gentian Marku, were killed on the 25th. Brandl lost two more Marines the next day, Lance Corporal Bradley Faircloth and Lance Corporal David Houck. Yet another, Corporal Kirk Bosselmann, fell on the 27th.

The 1/8 Marines were conducting large clearing operations such as Operation Deer Drive. Brandl, the avid hunter, had Alpha and Bravo companies sweep from west to east through the Industrial District and its adjoining neighborhoods, while his Iraqi forces and Charlie Company waited for them in the east. Brandl kept mixing it up so that the enemy never knew from which direction he would attack next. His Marines and Iraqi troops cleared houses and buildings—and then they did it again. It never ceased to amaze Brandl how the remaining insurgents managed to regularly move back into areas he thought he had completely cleared.

On the afternoon of the 25th, Marine tanks were patrolling ahead of Brandl's infantry who were clearing just east of HENRY. Suddenly, some Iraqi Security Force soldiers were shot up, and Lee's and Ducasse's tanks were in the middle of another gunfight. Meyers, who had been clearing with other platoons of Bravo Company, heard the shooting and rushed to the scene.[21]

---

21 Sgt Jonathan Ball telephone interview, 07/15/08.

When Meyers arrived, he learned that a group of insurgents were holed up in a nearby building. Lieutenant Lee was already shooting them up, but one or two guys were still shooting from inside the stronghold. Omohundro called a D9 bulldozer forward, but the D9 driver went to the wrong building and no one could contact him because he didn't have a radio in his vehicle. Meyers climbed out of his tank and ran toward the earthmover to personally tell the driver that he was working the wrong structure. When he reached the D9, he saw bullets ricocheting off the vehicle's armor plate, realized that someone was shooting at him, and turned to sprint back to his tank. The enemy sniper zeroed in on Meyers and fired. The bullet hit his neck protector and exploded into tiny pieces, peppering his arm with a dozen bits of shrapnel. The wound was serious, and Meyers was bleeding profusely.

When Lee saw his company commander hit, he called for a casevac: "Black 6 is down." Marines raced to his aid and helped Meyers to Omohundro's medevac AMTRAC. As the corpsmen bandaged his arm, Meyers told Ducasse where he thought the sniper was hiding. Ducasse climbed back in his tank, rolled down the street, and fired a blast of coax into a tree. Palm fronds flew, and the sniper's corpse fell to the ground.

With the major fighting finished in the city, Dan Wittnam returned to al Asad with his Small Craft Company by the end of November. Wittnam's men were only going to be in al Asad a short time before moving to their next assignment: protecting the Haditha Dam. Rubio, Parrello, and several other Marines decided to take a trip to the exchange before the unit moved to the more austere surroundings at Haditha Dam. They wanted to do some Christmas shopping while they still had access to a store and post office.

Rubio went overboard. Once he bought the gifts for his sons, he realized the package would be large and he didn't have enough money for the postage to mail it home. He needed ten dollars more, so he started asking his Marines if they could lend him a couple bucks. Some pitched in a dollar or two here and there, but he was still short. As they were all walking out of the exchange, Parrello piped up, "Hey Doc, are you still looking for money?"

"Yeah, I'm still a couple of bucks shy."[22]

22 HM2 Juan Rubio telephone interview, 11/15/07.

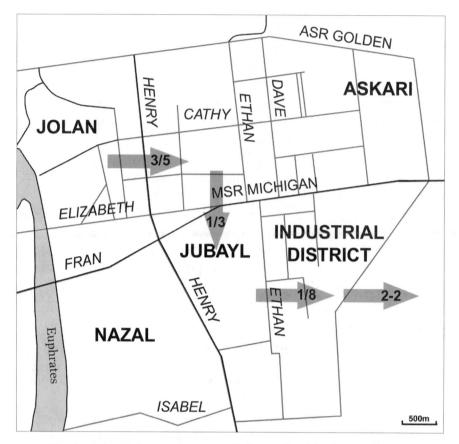

Thanksgiving Unit Reassignments (3-1 remained in the southwest)

"All I have is a twenty," Parrello continued, slapping the bill into Rubio's hand. "Here you go, Merry Christmas," he said before walking away.

Brian Parrello had grown up in these last months. He loved being a Marine, and he was damned good at it. He eagerly accepted each new responsibility, and he was a natural-born leader. As a squad leader, he worked very hard to make sure that his Marines were properly trained. He watched over them like an older brother, and seemed to thrive on the responsibility. Gunny Vinciguerra and Staff Sergeant Iversen knew this young man would go far in the Marine Corps. He had the right stuff.

The Marines wanted to return control of a secure city to the Iraqi people and their fledgling government as quickly as possible. Before the civilians could return, however, all the weapons and explosive caches would have to be cleared, bodies would have to be removed, and more Iraqi forces would have to be brought in to help the people resettle and maintain order. The Marines wanted to put an Iraqi face on the security of Fallujah; the last thing they wanted was to be perceived as an occupying force.

With the enemy inside the city defeated, there was no longer a need for the Black Jack Brigade's cordon in the south. On the 8th of December, Colonel Formica was ordered to return to Baghdad to resume his responsibility as the Multi-National Corps' reserve. RCT-7 started pulling out of Fallujah to relieve the Black Jack Brigade, and RCT-1 began the process of relieving RCT-7 in place. During the transition, 1/3 would be chopped to RCT-1 while Gary Brandl's Marines packed up and left the city. Along with the shifting of American forces, two more Iraqi Battalions arrived in Fallujah: the 8th Battalion, Iraqi Interim Force, and the 16th Battalion, Iraqi Army Forces.

The Marines held their belated Birthday Ball in Camp Fallujah on December 4. General Metz was the guest speaker. General Sattler had arranged to bring in 77,000 bottles of beer from Germany so that each soldier, sailor, airman, and Marine of Task Force Blue Diamond could have a cold beer or two for the celebration. The 4th was also the day of the Army-Navy football game. Metz was a West Point graduate (Class of '71) and Sattler was a graduate of the Naval Academy (Class of '71). This would have been the perfect time for Sattler to yell at the top of his lungs to "Beat Army!" Instead, when Sattler introduced Metz, he said that after the way the Army had fought beside the Marines, he would never be able to shout "Beat Army!" again.[23]

The Marines enjoyed their traditional celebration, with the oldest Marine giving a piece of birthday cake to the youngest Marine. And, of course, they all toasted with their cold bottled beer. Everyone agreed it was the best beer they had ever tasted.

---

23 LtGen John F. Sattler telephone interview, 12/03/07.

Clearing On the Euphrates River—And Death—Continue

On December 5, 2004, Dan Wittnam's Small Craft Company went out again on a sweep along the Euphrates River east of Ramadi with engineers from Colonel Patton's 44th Engineer Battalion, 2nd Infantry Division. After a productive day of clearing caches, the boats turned west to return to Camp Blue Diamond.

During their patrol, the enemy set up a large ambush to attack the soldiers and Marines during their return to their base. They were only seven or eight kilometers from Blue Diamond when the insurgents attacked with RPGs and heavy machine guns. One of the RPGs whizzed across the water and hit the side of Staff Sergeant Iversen's boat.[24] The round pierced the hull and severed the port fuel line, killing the port engine. The starboard engine took a round in its block, making it sputter and cough. Iversen's boat slowed to a crawl. Now that they were sitting ducks in the hot zone, Iversen's crew lit up both sides of the river, allowing the other boats to safely navigate through the ambush.

Four soldiers had been hit. One of them, Private First Class Andrew M. Ward, was bleeding heavily from a shot in the neck and was in urgent need of surgical attention. Iversen called for help, so Vasey pulled his boat alongside and Doc Rubio jumped over to attend to the wounded. Rubio had two of the soldiers bandaged before he learned of the critically wounded Ward lying in the bow of the boat. He rushed to the injured private's side and found him still alert. Soldiers and Marines moved Ward to the stern of the boat and Rubio went to work. He knew that if he didn't stop the bleeding this young soldier would die. The corpsman sliced into Ward's neck, located the damaged artery, and clamped off the bleeding with an IV hose clamp.[25]

Just as he finished, Iversen said, "Doc, we need to move the people off to another boat." Parrello, driving Vasey's boat, had remained alongside.

"What?" Replied Rubio. This was not the time to be moving this soldier.

Rubio didn't know that Iversen's engines were nearly dead and that they were still in the kill zone. He had been so focused on treating the severely wounded soldier that he hadn't noticed the bullets whizzing over his head.

---

24 SSgt Joshua Iversen telephone interview, 10/29/07.

25 HM2 Juan Rubio telephone interview, 11/15/07.

But if Rubio had learned anything in his years with the Marines, it was that when you are told to do something, you don't ask why—you just do it. So the corpsman rallied the soldiers around him to lift Ward. Rubio straddled the two boats, one foot in each one, while bullets zipped past him.

"Oh my God, I cannot believe I'm doing this," he thought.

The soldiers passed Ward to Rubio and Rubio passed Ward to an Army medic in Vasey's boat. As they were moving to Vasey's boat, the Army medic slipped and dropped Ward on the deck, where he started bleeding again. Rubio went back to work to re-secure the clamp.

"Are you good, Doc?" Vasey asked.

"Roger, I'm good."

Parrello gunned his engines. The stern sank, the water jets kicked up large white plumes, and the boat surged forward at fifty knots.

Three ambulances were waiting when they arrived at the boat ramp a few minutes later. Soldiers and Marines rushed to offload Ward on a stretcher. When they hit the water, one of the soldiers panicked and let go of his corner. The always-attentive Rubio jumped into neck-deep water, grabbed the untended corner, shoved it above his head, and helped get Ward to shore. They rushed him into one of the waiting ambulances where a First Class[26] Corpsman blurted, "What are you doing? He's going to die!"

Anger swept through Rubio's body. He got in the guy's face and heatedly spat, "He's alert and he knows where he's at. Get his ass to the Battalion Aid Station." Ward was rushed to a helicopter, which whisked him to surgery.

That night, Lieutenant Thomas came to Rubio, sat down, and told him that Ward had made it back to the hospital and into the operating room, but died while the surgeons were trying to repair his artery.

The next morning, Juan Rubio went to the Battalion Aid Station to confront the First Class Corpsman. "How can I trust my casualties to someone who has already given up?" he asked, though he was not expecting an answer. "I don't want to see you on my medevac team ever again."

With that, Rubio turned and walked out.

---

26 Petty Officer First Class, Hospital Corpsman 1, E6 is equivalent to a Marine Staff Sergeant.

Chapter 15

Behind the Next Door

"The worst fight to be in is the five-foot fight."

— Major Andrew McNulty, USMC, January 23, 2009

Transitions

For the final phase of the fight, Colonel Shupp was left with three Marine battalions supported by several Iraqi units. Shupp was confident in the capabilities of his own two infantry battalions: the Thundering Third had performed superbly since the beginning of the fight, and Darkhorse was a well-disciplined, lethal fighting machine. But the Broncos of 1/3 were still a question mark. Shupp had little knowledge of their training and ability. His Iraqi forces had varying degrees of competency; some had just been handed rifles, while others were professional soldiers.

Shupp's Marines worked hard to introduce the arriving Iraqi forces to the city and to train and equip them to maintain security. They built the Iraqis' confidence by giving them missions they could handle; initial successes led to more complicated missions. Even from this early stage Shupp was working to build the capabilities and confidence of the fledgling Iraqi soldiers and police to enable them to maintain security on their own.

Shupp's next challenge was to assign the right job to the right unit. The Thundering Third had fought hard to gain control of its quadrant and had taken heavy casualties during the fighting, so Shupp left 3/1 in the southwest part of the city.

Lieutenant Colonel Ramos was ordered south of MICHIGAN to begin the relief in place of 1/8; as 1/8 moved out, 1/3 moved in. Brandl's 1st Battalion, 8th Marines were completely out of the city by December 15. They spent a few days resting at Camp Fallujah before returning to the fight in Anbar Province.

As 1/3 moved south, Lieutenant Colonel Malay's 3/5 Marines moved east to take control of the entire northern half of Fallujah, including Ramos' old area of operations north of MICHIGAN. In anticipation of having to assume responsibility of 1/3's area of operations in the north, Darkhorse conducted a leader's reconnaissance into the Askari District on the 8th of December. During the recon, Malay met with Ramos, who guaranteed that there were no enemy fighters remaining in his AO.

Malay and everyone else in the 3/5 chain of command knew Ramos' Marines had not used Malay's squeegee tactics and had not cleared every building. Colonel Tucker's RCT-7 had conducted its operations much differently than RCT-1. They had been objective-oriented, had allowed military-aged men to stay in their area, and had implemented a jobs-for-food program at the Janabi Mosque.[1] Tucker brought the Red Cross into his zone and hired men to help clear away the rubble. The males worked during the day and collected their pay. After RCT-7 left Fallujah, they fought to kill Americans. In contrast, RCT-1 in its sector had moved methodically forward, searched every building, and rounded up and shipped all military-aged men out of the city. Lieutenant Colonel Malay and his officers knew that enemy fighters had not been rounded up in the northeast sector of the city because they had flown their UAVs over the area and observed military-aged men with weapons roaming the streets.

As a result, Malay told Ramos that he did not want to conduct a Relief-in-Place (RIP).[2] Not willing to trust Ramos' information, Malay decided to move into the eastern side of the city prepared for a fight. The Darkhorse Marines would have to re-clear the northeast one last time. By Thursday, December 9, Malay had been given responsibility for the entire northeast urban sector.

---

1 Some enemy fighters were later found to have MREs on their bodies.

2 Col Patrick Malay telephone interview, 11/04/07.

Todd Desgrosseilliers' Task Force Bruno was given the deadly job of searching for caches in 1/3's old sector, while the battalion's Kilo and India companies were ordered to quickly clear the Askari. Ed Bitanga's Lima Company Marines remained in the Jolan District to ensure that no insurgents returned to the city from the west.

All of Malay's Marines expected that they would encounter isolated pockets of stragglers, but no one imagined that the battalion's deadliest days were still to come.

Colonel Shupp decided to monitor his new battalion's movement into the southeastern section of the city from his perch atop the Government Center. He watched for two hours, but was unable to see Ramos' Marines moving east. Shupp told Major Arnold to get his security detachment together so he could visit Ramos' companies. Arnold, Shupp, Gunner Chuck Carleton, Sergeant Major Leardo, and the colonel's small personal security detachment patrolled dismounted across MICHIGAN while their armored HMMWVs followed for support.

If the last few weeks had taught Shupp anything, it was how to find the action. He would approach the advancing Marines from behind, looking for the radio antennae on the highest rooftops where his company commanders had taken the high ground. From that vantage point they could monitor the platoons' movement and provide fire support and command and control. Once Shupp spotted the antennae, he would move to the command post.

But Shupp and Carleton couldn't find 1/3's antennae. "Where are they?" Shupp asked aloud. Arnold worried that he and his commander might be out in front of the Marines, so he ordered his vehicles to move west. Moments later Shupp and his vehicles pulled up in front of a schoolhouse only to find that Ramos' Marines hadn't even kicked off. It was two hours past the planned starting time of the operation, but they hadn't even left their line of departure. As Shupp later described it, "They looked like they were out of Schlitz."[3]

When they finally moved out, Shupp followed with his vehicles and pulled up on one of the first north-south running roads where, to his

<hr />

3 Col Mike Shupp telephone interview, 1/21/08

amazement, he found a 1/3 platoon commander running his Marines in circles. They were moving from hotspot to hotspot, clearing from the bottom up. The men would clear a building in the middle of the block, then abandon it and move to another. The enemy was running between buildings to avoid the Marines. As the infantry charged one house, the enemy would scramble to the next. It was like trying to herd cats: whenever and wherever they pushed, the enemy simply moved elsewhere. Shupp watched the operation for about fifteen minutes before finally ordering Major Arnold to move up and suppress the enemy with his .50-caliber machine guns to give the platoon a chance to get a grip on the situation. Shupp dismounted and, along with his small security detachment, started to clear and hold buildings. When he spotted a hardware store down the street, the colonel sent a few of his scouts to bring back ladders.

When he noticed what was going on, a completely exhausted young lieutenant moved down the street and asked Major Arnold, "Who the hell is clearing buildings?"

"It's the colonel," Arnold replied. "If you would do your job, you wouldn't have to ask."[4]

Colonel Shupp appeared on scene. "You need to be clearing from the top down," he told the harried lieutenant.

"I can't find anything to climb, sir," came the reply

"Use your vehicles," Shupp snapped back. "Drive them up next to the building, climb up on them, and then onto the second deck."

With his new regimental commander's assistance, the young officer got his first real lesson in MOUT warfare.

Thursday to Sunday, December 9-12, 2004 – D+32/35: Routine—and Unpleasant Surprises

Shupp was tutoring the lieutenant when Darkhorse began clearing east of ETHAN to extend its control into the far eastern side of the city. They cleared from south to north, two companies abreast, with Kilo Company on the left. The Marines methodically pushed ahead, with tanks and AAVs in support of the operation.

4 *Ibid.*, 9/25/07.

Sergeant Eric Copsetta's squad moved to enter another courtyard, as they had done a hundred times before. Christopher Adlesperger had been meritoriously promoted to lance corporal for his actions in combat and given responsibility for his own fire team. The teams had been swapping jobs: one would stand in overwatch while the other rushed a courtyard. This time Adlesperger's team would be first in. The new team leader took the lead and moved through the outer gate into the courtyard. Together with Private First Class Gerardo Gonzalez, they moved toward the front door of the house. Lance Corporal John Aylmer peeled off to check an outhouse just inside the gate.[5]

Adlesperger had just reached the front door when barricaded insurgents opened fire with two automatic weapons. He never stood a chance as multiple impacts to his body spun him around, exposing his unprotected side. The enemy kept firing, and more rounds tore into Adlesperger's body between his SAPI plates. Gonzalez was also hit and went down in the courtyard severely wounded. With guns now blazing from several windows, Aylmer dove for cover in the outhouse. Two other Marines managed to crawl back into the street. Aylmer could hear Gonzalez moaning and Adlesperger struggling to take his last breath. Stranded in the outhouse, the corporal thought that he would not survive this day, but he would fight to the last, bringing his SAW up to the ready while he waited for a Muj to appear in the door.

Adlesperger, the company's hero, had seemed indestructible in recent weeks. He had single-handedly taken out a dozen insurgents on the Marine Corps' birthday. He had saved his friends' lives and gone on to lead stack after stack into house after house. Copsetta had yelled at Adlesperger several times over the last few days, "You're a team leader now. Stop leading them from the front of the stack!" "Sperge," however, wouldn't have it any other way. He wanted to be the first in, and now he was lying dead in a Fallujah courtyard—another American who bravely gave his life for the Marines on his left and right.

Having gained the initial upper hand, the enemy started lobbing grenades into the courtyard and over the wall into the street. One landed dangerously close to Aylmer's outhouse, the explosion rattling the cinderblock structure, while others bounced off the parked AMTRAC and

---

5   LCpl John Aylmer telephone interview, 07/08/08.

clanked to the ground between Copsetta, Lance Corporal Luis Martinez, and Lieutenant Cragholm. Cragholm grabbed Martinez and they scurried to get out from between the track and the wall, while Copsetta ran in the other direction.[6]

BOOM!BOOM! The explosions echoed in the street.

Several pieces of shrapnel tore into Martinez while another penetrated Cragholm's backside. Copsetta was also hit, struck by a nickel-sized piece of metal in his jaw. Copsetta turned to Cragholm, his wound grotesquely spurting blood with every word, and blurted, "Holy shit, sir, is my jaw still there?" Shocked by the gruesome wound, Cragholm hesitated a second but then reassured him, "You're fine." Copsetta's injury turned out to be nothing more than a bloody flesh wound.

Within minutes Captain McNulty, First Sergeant Steven Knox, and Gunny Keith Brockmann pulled up. McNulty assumed control while Knox and Brockmann helped with the wounded. The Marines peppered the courtyard with smoke grenades and then charged in to retrieve Aylmer, Adlesperger, and Gonzalez. Once all the Marines were out of the courtyard, McNulty ordered the AMTRAC to hit the stronghold with its .50-caliber machine gun and 40mm grenades while he isolated the house with his infantry. McNulty's Marines surrounded the place, assuming covered positions far enough from the target house to be safe but close enough to maintain their cordon so that the enemy within could not escape. With the perimeter established, McNulty called in air support to drop four 500-lb. Bombs—"danger close"[7]—within sixty meters of his Marines. All four bombs were direct hits, killing the barricaded jihadists.

The day started as just another in a long string of them, on just another block clearing just another courtyard and just another house. But this one was different. The structure contained a well-constructed ambush position manned by seven determined enemy fighters. The fortified house was less than 200 meters from Bravo Company, 1st Battalion, 3rd Marines' former command post. Kilo Company hadn't lost a single Marine since Payton was killed on the 14th of November, and was fortunate not to lose more Marines clearing this house.

---

6 Capt Michael Cragholm telephone interview, 03/01/08.

7 Danger Close—an indication in a call for artillery and naval gunfire support that friendly forces are within 600 meters of the target.

But that did nothing to lessen the loss everyone in the company felt at losing Christopher Adlesperger. Even Lieutenant Colonel Malay was shaken by Adlesperger's death. That night, Malay visited the mortuary affairs unit at Camp Fallujah. He felt compelled to say goodbye to Chris. "He had a touch of greatness," said Malay.[8]

By December 10, Colonel Shupp had completed the transfer of authority from Colonel Tucker. Shupp was now responsible for all of Fallujah. When General Natonski, Shupp, and Malay toured the Janabi Mosque, they were surprised to find an enormous weapons cache. Nearly every room had different types of weapons and ammunition stacked from floor to ceiling, including anti-aircraft guns, rockets, surface-to-air missiles, artillery and mortar shells, and all kinds of small-arms and small-caliber ammunition. There were also RPKs, RPGs, and AKs inside the mosque, and even an ice cream truck crammed full of IEDs parked outside.[9] RCT-7 Marines had earlier reported this area as "green,"[10] but this was one of the largest caches found in the city.

Malay's Marines continued to find caches and encounter enemy strongholds throughout Ramos' former area of responsibility, and they started running into groups of twenty, thirty, and even forty fighters at a time. The Darkhorse Marines redoubled their clearing efforts. There was heavy fighting on Saturday, December 11 and another Marine, Lance Corporal Gregory Rund, of Littleton, Colorado, was killed and eight more were wounded. Twenty-four enemy fighters were killed in the fight. On Sunday, December 12, RCT-1 scouts killed five more insurgents on PL HENRY, and the Thundering Third lost another Marine, Lance Corporal Joshua Dickinson, as a result of enemy fighters squirting over from 1/3's new sector in the south.

---

8   Tom Perry, "His Corps Value Was Bravery," *Los Angeles Times*, October 3, 2006.

9   Col Mike Shupp telephone interview, 1/21/08.

10 Clearing of the city was done by district and color coded: Red – Not cleared, Yellow – cleared by assault troops, but not in detail, Green – All resistance eliminated and enemy supplies captured or destroyed.

Major Desgrosseilliers set up Task Force Bruno's command post in the same schoolhouse that Ramos had used. Desgrosseilliers had a bad feeling that he was being watched, so he ordered his Marines to search the nearby houses.[11] Just before noon on the 12th, one of his patrols encountered an enemy strongpoint in a house they had searched just the day before. Fifteen to twenty enemy fighters had entrenched themselves in the house less than a block from where Adlesperger had been killed. When the Marines entered and started up the stairs, the barricaded insurgents opened fire.

Desgrosseilliers rushed to the fight. One of his men was trapped inside, so he stacked Marines along the outside wall at the front of the house. Just as he reached the wall an enemy grenade bounced on the ground and came to rest at his feet. Without thinking, Desgrosseilliers pushed the two closest

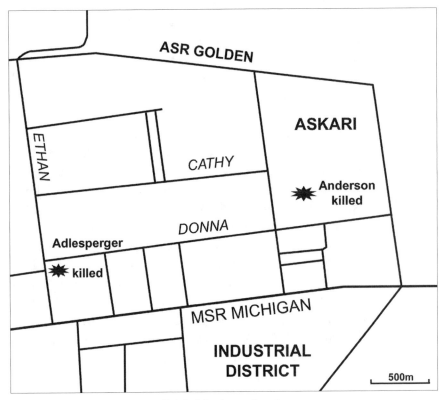

Fallujah: Northeast Quadrant

11 LtCol Todd Desgrosseilliers telephone interview, 12/07/07.

Marines against the wall and tried to shield them with his body just as the wire-wrapped concussion grenade exploded. Pieces of wire ripped into Desgrosseilliers' legs and the shock knocked him senseless. Had the grenade been a frag[12], the odds are that all three Marines would have been killed. The two shielded Marines dragged the stunned major around the corner.

It took a few minutes for Desgrosseilliers to shake off the shock of the explosion and regain his composure. When he did, he moved along the outside wall, shot the lock from an outer door, and the trapped Marine rushed back into the street. Desgrosseilliers rallied his men and set about making sure that no more Americans were in the building. Together, Desgrosseilliers and his Marines moved back inside the house, where they found the enemy pouring down the stairs. The Marines opened fire, riddling the first fighters with bullets. More fanatics lobbed hand grenades to the first floor and followed them, screaming "Allahu Akbar!" Desgrosseilliers and his men cut them down, too, piling bodies at the foot of the stairs.

Once he was certain that no other Marines were trapped, Desgrosseilliers ordered his men to fall back and regroup in the street. With only the enemy left inside, he cordoned off the block and directed heavy machine gun and tank main gun rounds into the stronghold.

When the enemy fled to the roof, Desgrosseilliers and his Marines pressed the attack, moving to the roof of an adjacent house to get at them. They lobbed grenade after grenade onto the enemy's rooftop, balcony, and into the windows. McNulty's Kilo Company moved in to assist Task Force Bruno with his Fire Support Team and a platoon of Marines. Once on scene, Kilo's FiST called in mortar fire to pummel the insurgent positions.

Major Desgrosseilliers had one last surprise for the bad guys holding up inside the barricaded house. With attack aircraft waiting overhead, he ordered all of his Marines to fall back, but to continue to maintain the perimeter. None of Task Force Bruno's Marines would die today. Once the Marines were in safe positions—even though a mere sixty meters from the target—he called in a waiting jet to drop a 500-pound bomb. The direct hit demolished the house and killed everyone inside.

Nine Marines had been wounded, but none had lost their lives.

---

12 Concussion grenades only develop an over pressure while frags, fragmentation devices, are scored so that the explosion throws out multiple pieces of deadly shrapnel.

Deadly Gunfight

With sunset approaching, Captain McNulty ordered his Second and Third Platoon Marines to move north from MICHIGAN into the schoolhouse northeast of the Janabi Hospital along DONNA, where they would go firm for the night. Along with the company's supporting tanks, McNulty and First Platoon moved east from Task Force Bruno's fight to link up with the rest of Kilo Company.

Once they reached the school, Second Lieutenant Colin Browning, Third Platoon's commander, ordered his men back out into a row of houses designated as the 915 Block to get bedding. With winter approaching, the Fallujah nights had turned bitter cold. The houses ran along the northern edge of the Janabi Hospital, sixteen houses long and two houses deep. One of Second Platoon's squads also joined in, taking the northern road and searching each of the sixteen houses that faced north. Third Platoon moved along the southern road, entering each of the sixteen southern-facing homes.

Clearing this last block should have been routine. After all, it was right across the street from RCT-7's former command post. Thirty-two more houses to clear, and then McNulty's Marines could rest for the night. All was quiet for most of the block.

Arellano's men had finished clearing for the day, so they headed for the school. As soon as Arellano arrived, he climbed to the roof with Sergeant Gage Coduto, Corporal Jonathan Herren, and his platoon commander, Second Lieutenant Todd Moulder.[13] As Moulder and the company XO, Lieutenant Diaz, worked to set up defenses at the school, Arellano's squad left the school to join in the search for blankets. Third Squad moved into the houses just south of the school and east of the 915 block hoping to find anything that could help keep them warm during the evening hours. Arellano stayed behind on the school roof with his platoon commander.

Back on the long skinny 915 Block, Arellano's good friend Corporal Jason Clairday led his squad into the eleventh northern house. Sergeant Jeffery Kirk split his 3rd Squad Marines: some entered the eleventh and twelfth southern houses, while others moved to a building in the Janabi Hospital complex across the street to provide overwatch for the foraging Marines.

13 Todd Moulder telephone interview, 03/31/08.

Corporals Ian Stewart and David Cisneros and Lance Corporal Chad Pioske entered the eleventh southern house. Cisneros and Pioske cleared the bottom floor while Stewart went up the stairs to clear the second floor. When Stewart entered an upstairs bedroom, shots rang out: he had encountered the first group of a platoon-sized enemy force. Stewart went down in the open doorway, mortally wounded. He called for help, and when Cisneros and Pioske charged for the stairs to get to their friend, gunfire and grenades rained down on them from a dozen insurgents holed up in the second-floor bedrooms. Cisneros and Pioske fell back, unable to reach Stewart.

Arellano hadn't been at the school for more than five minutes when the gunfire erupted. "That's our Marines in contact!"[14] Arellano exclaimed. He turned and sprinted down the stairs, taking two, three, and four at a time to reach the street, where he could see his squad running west toward the fight. Arellano ran to join them. As he shot past the gun trucks and AMTRACs, he pointed and yelled for them to turn around. More Marines poured out of the school and rushed to the sound of the gunfire.

Sergeant Jeffrey Kirk and Staff Sergeant Melvin Blazer were in the house next door when Stewart was gunned down. Kirk had just returned to duty after having been wounded on November 10. He had given the medical staff such a hard time that they finally relented and let him check out to return to Kilo Company. The sergeant moved outside and started looking for another way to get to the enemy on the second floor. He moved west and found a narrow alley between the stronghold and the next house. He was turning to enter the alley when he was shot in the head. Did Kirk have a premonition that he would not return home when he framed one of his poems and gave it to his mother?

The things my mother taught me.
The important things are always the hardest to do.
Love is not just about making someone happy; it's about what's best for
    them, even if it hurts.
Patience is not a virtue that comes easily.
Joy is found wherever you choose to look for it.
Being a loving and courageous parent is infinitely better than a rich parent.
Never regret a mistake you learn from.

14 Sgt Jason Arellano telephone interview, 3/10/08.

We are the sum of our decisions, sacrifices, principles and accomplishments—make them good ones.

Just as Kirk made his ultimate sacrifice, Arellano reached the house where Stewart was still trapped. Cisneros, Pioske, and others tried repeatedly but in vain to rush back into the building and up the stairs to Stewart's aid. Each time they were met by a hail of gunfire and grenades that forced them to fall back. Marines to Arellano's north were shooting down from their rooftop positions. Arellano, heart pounding, shouted at the top of his lungs, "Where are they at, Clairday?" Clairday pointed downward and continued to fire onto the rooftop and into the alley below.

When the shooting started, Corporal Daniel Williamson moved to the rooftop of the building in the Janabi complex south of the fighting and began firing at the insurgents hidden in their fortified positions. An enemy sniper quickly returned the fire and hit Williamson in the hand. Corporal John Wilson helped Williamson into the rooftop stairwell, but just as he headed through the door he was shot by the same sniper. Corporal Jerome Hutcheson helped both wounded men down the stairs to the street. Two more Kilo Company Marines had been taken out of the fight.

Arellano's team leaders had also moved into a building south of the 915 block. Lance Corporals Jacob Fernandez and William Lenard positioned the squad in overwatch. Once they knew that their Marines were in a secure position, they went looking for their squad leader.

Still not knowing Corporal Stewart's fate, Corporal David Cisneros and Lance Corporal Phillip Miska repeatedly tried to re-enter the building where Stewart was trapped. They kept the enemy pinned for fifteen minutes, preventing them from fleeing or attacking other Marines downstairs. On Cisneros' third attempt, he too was wounded, peppered with shrapnel from one of a dozen enemy grenades.

The enemy fought ferociously, firing automatic weapons and lobbing grenades down the stairs. "Grenade!" yelled Corporal David Hawley, as another hand grenade rained down on the Marines. Hawley turned and pushed two Marines down the stairs. BOOM! The explosion hurled a golf ball-sized chunk of metal into his thigh, knocking him down the stairs. Hawley continued to fire his M16 until his friends dragged him out of the house.

Then Miska noticed an RPG pointed over the half-wall at the top of the stairs. He repeatedly fired at the metal projectile, hoping to detonate the grenade. His volley forced the grenadier to fire without aiming. The grenade missed the Marines in the stairwell, but the explosion knocked them back down the stairs. Undaunted, Miska and the other Marines regrouped and tried once again to fight their way up the stairs.

Private First Class Renaldo Leal repeatedly rushed back into the fight, pulling three wounded Marines to safety. The casualties were mounting; several Marines were now huddled at a casualty collection point, waiting for medical evacuation.

Frustrated by his inability to get to Stewart, Pioske moved to a second-floor patio in the next building, and from his new position obtained a clear shot. He exchanged protracted fire with the enemy, eventually killing five insurgents. All the while Kilo Company Marines were swarming into all of the adjacent buildings, sealing the enemy's fate.

The Kilo Marines continued to attack. Arellano ran out of one courtyard into the street. He quickly moved along the wall in search of the next gate and approached a narrow alley. He saw a Marine lying on the ground, and wondered why there was no corpsman helping him. Then he realized that another hero had fallen: Sergeant Kirk was dead. Arellano would remember this sight for the rest of his life, but there was no time to mourn now; he had to keep his head clear, he had to stay in the fight, he had to keep his other Marines from the same fate, he had to get to the trapped Marine. Arellano jumped over Kirk's body and continued his search for the next gate.

Two doors down to the east, Staff Sergeant Melvin Blazer, Jr., a seasoned, seventeen-year veteran of the Corps, had moved into the next house with a group of Marines; they were trying to find a way across the roof to get to Stewart's house. Blazer headed up the stairs for the roof. When he reached the landing, three insurgents cut him down in a hail of gunfire. Corporal Mason Fischer rushed to the top of the stairwell, protecting Blazer's body, while Lance Corporal William Vorheis ran to Stewart's house for reinforcements.

"Staff Sergeant Blazer's been hit and is trapped on the second deck!" he announced between breaths.

First Sergeant Steve Knox, Leal, and the other Marines rushed to Blazer's aid in the building where Corporal Fisher was holding the enemy at bay. Without pause, Leal charged up the stairs, jumped into the enemy line of fire, and emptied an entire drum of 5.56 from his SAW. Fisher reached underneath the torrent of outgoing lead to drag Blazer's lifeless body out of the line of fire and down the stairs. Leal followed Blazer and Fisher, both of whom somehow emerged unscathed.

By now Captain McNulty, Lieutenant Moulder, and the Kilo Company command group had moved to the second-floor balcony of the house between the houses where Stewart and Blazer had been shot. The enemy insurgents were barricaded on either side of them.[15] Arellano moved to the patio to link up with his platoon commander. Moulder ordered him into the house next door to where Blazer had just been killed. Arellano's mind was racing. He scanned the scene, looking for men from his squad.

Moulder pointed and repeated, "Get into that house!"

Not seeing any of his own squad, Arellano turned and pointed at Marines near him. "You, you, you, and you, come with me," he ordered.[16]

Lieutenant Moulder ordered Sergeant Coduto to clear the building below and to find a way into Stewart's building. Corporal Herren was ordered to return to Stewart's building and secure the ground floor.

While Coduto's squad secured the center building, Sergeant Arellano and his shanghaied squad hurried down the stairs to assault the neighboring house. One of Kilo Company's gun trucks was parked in the street. Arellano checked to make sure that no Marines were inside the house, then ordered the truck gunner to open on the house with 40mm grenades with his MK-19 automatic grenade launcher. Thunk, thunk, thunk, thunk . . . the grenades slammed into the building and exploded in rapid succession—BOOM! BOOM! BOOM! BOOM!

Two simultaneous assaults were now underway: Arellano and his Marines followed the grenades into the courtyard, and Corporal Clairday and his squad moved roof-to-roof, north-to-south to Stewart's house. One after the other, Clairday, Yeager, and Lance Corporals Travis Icard and Hilario Lopez jumped the four-foot gap between the buildings. Once on the roof, Clairday moved to the front of the stack. Simultaneously, Arellano and his newly-formed squad prepared to enter Blazer's house. Arellano charged in and lobbed grenades into the interior rooms. When Clairday, Arellano's close friend, moved to enter the second-floor room, an AK-47 rattled, hitting him in the arms and legs. Lance Corporal Yeager laid down a spray of bullets while Clairday crawled out of the line of fire. He refused medical treatment

---

15 Maj Andrew McNulty telephone interview, 01/23/08.

16 Sgt Jason Arellano telephone interview, 03/10/08.

and returned to the front of the stack. Arellano and another Marine headed toward the bottom of the stairs.

The Marines could now see Corporal Stewart's boots just inside and to the right of the patio door. Yeager tossed two grenades into the house. Clairday and Lopez charged in and moved left while Gonzalez and Icard charged right.[17] Sergeant Gonzalez sprayed the wall lockers with bullets as another Marine retrieved Stewart's body. One of the bullet-riddled cupboard doors swung open and out stumbled an insurgent; Gonzalez instantly cut him down.

On the other side of the house, Clairday led more Marines into the last room. As Clairday, Yeager, and Lopez were assaulting the enemy, Miska and his squad leader charged the stairway one last time. Gunfire rang out and Clairday fell, this time mortally wounded. Lopez jumped into the doorway and began firing while Yeager pulled Clairday's body from harm's way. The enemy opened fire on Lopez at point-blank range, killing him, too.

Once Yeager had retrieved Clairday he and Icard returned to the fight, attacking the enemy's last stronghold. Yeager killed another Muj, but more remained. When Icard and Yeager fired into the door jamb, the insurgents responded by lobbing a grenade onto the landing. Yeager and Icard tried to melt into the walls, hoping to protect themselves from the impending blast, but the grenade failed to explode. Yeager, Miska and Icard resumed their attack and didn't let up until the final two insurgents were dead.

Meanwhile, two houses down, Arellano moved toward the stairwell on which Melvin Blazer, husband and father of two, had just been mortally wounded. With his M16 pointed upward, Arellano began climbing the first flight of stairs backwards, keeping his weapon trained on the second floor. Another Marine followed and threw a grenade upstairs. As soon as it went off, Arellano and the trailing Marine charged up the remaining steps. They quickly moved past the room into which Leal had emptied his SAW and headed straight toward the adjacent bedroom.

Smoke from the previous grenades filled the house. Enemy rounds were chipping at the walls all around them. Like Gonzalez, Arellano shot at areas where the insurgents could be hiding as he charged into the bedroom. His bullets ripped into each corner, through a bed, and splintered a row of standup wooden dressers.

---

17 : LCpl Travis Icard telephone interview, 07/24/08.

"Clear left! Clear right! Room clear! Nada!" Arellano shouted.

He returned to the bedroom door and grabbed a grenade to throw into the room the two men had just run past. A group of Marines was stacked on the stairs waiting to charge onto the second floor, so he shouted to them that he was about to frag the room. But they had their own plan, and one of the Marines broke from the stack on the stairs and ran toward Arellano. Grenade in hand, pin pulled, Arellano made way for the Marine charging toward his room.

The Marine who rushed past threw his grenade into the uncleared room. "Frag out!" he yelled.

There stood Arellano, holding a live grenade. He wasn't about to try to put the pin back in, so he tossed his grenade into the room, too.

Arellano shouted, "Frag out!" only seconds after the first exclamation.

Because the first grenade had not yet exploded, Arellano feared that the Marines below would not realize that two grenades were cooking off. His mind raced as he scrambled for cover. Marines were trained to rush a room the instant their grenade detonated in order to take advantage of the stun effect of the explosion. Would the Marines charge up the stairs as soon as the first grenade blew? Arellano had to take action, and he would only have a split second after the first explosion to do so.

BOOM!

As soon as the first grenade went off, the Marines below did exactly as they were trained to do, and precisely what Arellano feared: they started up the stairs. The sergeant ran to the doorway to stop them. Glancing over, he spotted his own grenade in the room.

How could this be? he thought. Did the insurgents toss my grenade back toward the door? Did it bounce off something in the room, or did the first explosion blow my grenade into the open?

Arellano yelled, "Get back! There's another grena…"

BOOM!

Arellano's senses turned to slow motion. He saw everything clearly: the curtains rose in the room; smoke came through each crevice in the bricks, joined by sparks from the flesh-eating fragmentation pouring through the mud-brick wall. The force of the explosion spun Arellano onto his hands and knees. The loud boom echoed in his ears; he was certain he was deaf.

His world collapsed into a narrow unsteady focus, his mind racing: had he saved his Marines? Had he kept them from the door? And then another thought filled his consciousness. "I'm hit, I'm hit!"

A distant voice tried to encourage Arellano. "You're okay."

Arellano tried to move around, but his palms slipped in a pool of his own blood. Dazed, breathing hard, and feeling weak, he asked the Marine, "What do you mean I'm good?! Can't you see I'm bleeding to death?"

Arellano felt blood streaming from his neck, which had been shredded by shrapnel, and more metal fragments had ripped into his leg only millimeters from his femoral artery. When others rushed to try to help him to his feet, he crumpled like a rag doll. It felt as though he were being electrocuted, and the pain was excruciating. Still, he tried to remain as calm as possible and helped as best he could while Marines removed his flak jacket.

Kilo Company Marines quickly cleared the house and hoisted their wounded sergeant to carry him to safety. He was dead weight; Arellano couldn't do much to help as he was dragged down the stairs, head bouncing on each riser. Moaning in pain, he watched the wall, then the ceiling, then more Marines rushing into the house, and finally the dingy grey sky outside. He could still hear gunfire, but was now lying in the street with the mounting numbers of other wounded while a corpsman cut away his uniform. It was beautiful to be outside.

Lance Corporal Lenard had finally found his friend and squad leader. He rushed to Arellano's side and reached down to grab his hand. Arellano squeezed Lenard's hand as the corpsmen worked to stop the bleeding.

"They are going to have to put a tourniquet on your neck," Lenard joked.

"They better make it tight." Arellano replied. He pointed to his crotch. "How am I down there?"

Smiling, "It's gone, bro'!" Lenard quipped.

As he was rushed to the waiting AMTRAC, a cold chill engulfed Arellano's body. Marines placed him on the center bench, the back ramp was raised, and the vehicle lurched forward, racing to get Arellano to Bravo Surgical in Camp Fallujah before he really did bleed to death.

"Stop giving me morphine," he told First Sergeant Knox. "I want to feel the pain so I don't slip away."

Arellano reached to his chest and grabbed the cross dangling from his dog tag chain. He wondered if he would die, and tried to picture his family and Lindsey's beautiful face. Would he ever see her again? Arellano would fight for his life; he couldn't leave Lindsey behind.

The other wounded Marines moaned and groaned with every bump in the road on a journey that seemed to take forever. When the casevac finally ground to a stop and the ramp dropped, Arellano was whisked into the trauma unit.

Once all the casualties had been evacuated and the fallen Marines' bodies retrieved, Captain McNulty surrounded 915 Block with gun trucks, tracks, and tanks. He pulled his infantry back and proceeded to level the block, using precision 500-pound bombs to do so. The bombing continued until well after sunset, and 915 Block remained cordoned all night.

That night, Lieutenant Colonel Malay visited the mortuary unit to say his personal farewells to Blazer, Clairday, Kirk, Lopez, and Stewart. He also went to Bravo Surgical again. Of the twenty-five Marines who had been wounded that day, some remained in the fight, but many were still at the surgical unit. Arellano, groggy from the first of many surgeries, looked up and saw Lieutenant Colonel Malay and Sergeant Major Resto stopping at every bed. When they reached his, they told him that he had fought a good fight. Malay and Resto told the wounded about the day's events, and announced that not everyone who had been hit had survived. Sergeant Major Resto finished by reading the names of those who had fallen. Arellano closed his eyes and wept.

The next morning McNulty hit 915 Block again with tank main gun rounds and bombs. It took nine 500-pound bombs to complete the destruction. Despite the focused and overwhelming firepower, when Third Platoon moved in to clear the rubble it found four insurgents inside the first house. When they opened fire on the Marines, Yeager jumped into the fight and killed each in turn. By the time the fight was finally over, the Darkhorse Marines had lost five of their comrades in 915 Block, and fourteen more were seriously wounded.

It was not until December 13 that the block was free of enemy fighters. The Marines had killed thirty insurgents who were wearing green uniforms, assault vests, and pistol belts, had clean weapons, and were eating from food stores. These were seasoned soldiers, not ragtag thugs. It had been Darkhorse's most difficult fight yet, and the costliest single engagement since the VBIED attack on Ramos' Marines in the Zaidon.

And still more jihadists were waiting for their chance to kill Americans.

Cornered Jackals

On the morning of the December 14, the Darkhorse Marines moved to sweep the far eastern edge of the Askari District from MICHIGAN north. Kilo Company was several blocks inside the city on the battalion's left. With tanks, AAVs, machine gun teams, and snipers in overwatch, the Marines moved house-to-house, clearing in their now-familiar squeegee fashion. Although the tactics were familiar, after their last few encounters Malay's Marines went back to clearing with a renewed vigilance.

Sergeant Eric Copsetta had refused to leave the 915 Block fight despite taking a chunk of shrapnel in his jaw. Instead, he insisted on returning to his Marines after his injury was treated. When he returned with his face bandaged, his platoon commander asked, "Have they given you any meds?"[18]

"Yes, sir, they gave me these Vicodin," confirmed Copsetta. "But I can still shoot straight."

"OK, Sergeant, just don't shoot me."

Cragholm needed Copsetta. The fighting had reduced Third Platoon to two understrength squads. Copsetta, along with Corporal Michael Anderson, Jr., moved his squad across the rooftops, clearing buildings from the top down. They wanted to flush any enemy fighters into the streets instead of trapping them on top of barricaded buildings. At a one-story house, before moving from the roof to the ground floor, Corporal Anderson tossed a stun grenade down the stairwell. Lance Corporal Adam Rouse and an Iraqi Intervention Force soldier followed the grenade down the stairs and turned left into a large kitchen. Anderson, with a green Iraqi soldier in tow, raced down the stairs and moved to the first door on his right. The door was closed, so Anderson kicked it in. Unbeknownst to Anderson, eight insurgents had barricaded themselves in the room.

Shots rang out. One of the rounds narrowly missed Anderson's body armor and tore into his side under his arm, mortally wounding him. The Iraqi soldier turned and ran from the house.

Hospital Corpsman 2nd Class Nicholas Cook and Lance Corporal Bradley Balak were the next down the stairs. As soon as Anderson fell, Cook

---

18 Capt Michael Cragholm telephone interview, 03/01/08.

and Balak opened fire, shooting into the open doorway. The enemy's focus immediately turned to them, and bullets whizzed toward the stairway. Cook heard a snap and felt a slash across his lip. The round didn't break the skin, but had passed so close that it burned his lip. Another bullet ricocheted, hurling a small chunk of shrapnel into Balak's nose. Shocked more than injured, Balak and Cook retreated back up the stairs.

Corporal van Doorn and Lieutenant Cragholm were two houses down when the shooting broke out. Instead of racing to the fight, they methodically cleared both of the intervening houses so as to be in position to isolate the target house from the north and east, while Sergeant Copsetta moved his Marines into positions to isolate the building from the south and west. A machine gun team moved to a southern rooftop to cover the alleyways behind the house.

The enemy fighters were now surrounded, but Anderson was lying in the doorway. Sergeant Elber Navarro, Arellano's mentor and friend, moved his squad to the front side of the house, rammed the front gate with a 20-ton AAV, and pushed it into the courtyard. Navarro's Marines charged through the yard and into the house. All of the rooms were clear except for the one with Anderson's body in the doorway. Captain McNulty and Gunny Brockmann pulled up outside the house in their HMMWV. McNulty got a quick update from Cragholm and headed into the house.[19]

Navarro and McNulty rechecked the first room on their left, then Navarro moved to the bunkered room and fired through the doorway. He tossed grenade after grenade into the room—fragmentation, smoke, and incendiary, the latter triggering a fire. Navarro waited for several pounding heartbeats and then, weapon at the ready, stepped into the doorway to ensure he had killed the insurgents. To his surprise, three Muj were on their feet and heading for the door—fleeing the growing conflagration. Navarro squeezed his trigger, dropping all three enemy fighters before they could raise their weapons.

While Navarro was cleaning the room, McNulty moved past the open door and dragged Anderson's body out of the line of fire and into a small bathroom at the foot of the stairs. McNulty would have to cross the line of fire once more to get outside.

19 Maj Andrew McNulty telephone interview, 01/23/08.

Navarro retreated back into the hallway toward McNulty just as RPK machine gun rounds splintered the bedroom door. Another insurgent charged the door and Navarro cut him down as well. The enemy fighters tossed their own grenades toward the hallway and into the kitchen, wounding Rouse. Navarro, McNulty, and the other Marines in the house could do little more than hunker down through the enemy's grenade barrage. Once in the bathroom McNulty couldn't hear a thing; the repeated explosions and gunfire had temporarily taken out his hearing.

Lieutenant Colonel Malay moved to the sound of the guns. He was always in the city, and shifted to wherever his Marines were in contact with enemy fighters. Often he was just another Marine in the fight. Malay carried an M16, but no radio, choosing instead to monitor events from the radios hanging in his HMMWV. He didn't like to carry one himself because he knew he would have a tendency to get on and shoot off his mouth. Malay had confidence in his men and tried to let them do their jobs without his constant intervention, but he always moved to the point of action.

When Malay pulled up outside the house, he tried to get McNulty on the radio without success.[20] Concerned that he had lost one of his company commanders, Malay charged into the house just as another insurgent tried to flee the room. McNulty and Navarro cut him down, too.

Smoke from the fire was billowing into the hallway and Navarro was having trouble breathing. The situation was already bad enough when another enemy grenade flew out of the room toward McNulty and Navarro, bounced off the wall, and landed on one of the dead insurgents. Navarro scrambled backward toward the bathroom, landing on Corporal Anderson's legs. The three Marines were in a heap on the bathroom floor when the grenade exploded—BOOM!—and out ran a flaming Muj, AK in hand. The man tried to flee up the stairs to avoid Navarro's shots, but a Marine at the top of the stairs ended the enemy fighter's flight with a burst from his SAW.

Navarro decided to throw one last grenade into the room to buy time to drag Anderson's body past the open doorway and out of the house. When he reached down for it, however, he discovered he did not have any left.

"Someone give me a grenade!" he yelled.

"I got it," replied a Marine in the house. "Just get out of here."

---

20 Col Patrick Malay telephone interview, 11/04/07.

Navarro turned toward the voice only to discover it belonged to Lieutenant Colonel Malay. Navarro's battalion commander pulled the pin and pitched a final grenade into the room.

BOOM!

Navarro and McNulty crossed the line of fire and ran out of the house while Martinez and van Doorn rushed to pull Anderson's body into the street. With the house clear, the Marines circled the building and watched it burn to the ground.

Darkhorse Marines had encountered heavily armed, fanatic enemy fighters nearly every day since their arrival in the Askari District. They were supposed to be clearing caches and preparing to reopen the city to civilians. Instead, they were engaging in mortal combat with the hardest of the hardcore. And there were still the last few northeastern blocks to clear. Diehard jihadists were trapped there—and there is nothing more dangerous than cornered jackals.

Chapter 16

No Better Friend

"Sometimes, I would trade it all for a good night's sleep."

— Colonel Pat Malay, October 8, 2007

The Iraqi soldiers had divided up the city into its traditional districts and the Marines had numbered every block. The numbering system had been very helpful during the fight, and now it would be used in the repatriation of the population. If the city was simply opened and civilians were welcomed back quickly, humanitarian needs would be difficult to address, and it would be nearly impossible to block the return of enemy insurgents. As a result, several entry control checkpoints were set up at the edge of Fallujah and Humanitarian Assistance Centers were established in three of the four quadrants of the city. Each resident was given a Biometric Assessment Card. The card was required to pass through checkpoints and to receive humanitarian assistance at the distribution centers.

The Jolan District in the northwest was repopulated first. Shupp slated Humanitarian Assistance Centers for Dave's Field, Jolan Park, and in an open field near the flour factory that Buhl's Marines named Brahma Park. The Darkhorse Marines opened the first humanitarian site at Jolan Park. As the people showed up, each resident received an ID card and each family was given a wheelbarrow. The civilians loaded up their "shopping carts" with food, water, and fuel and then wheeled it home. By the time the repatriation

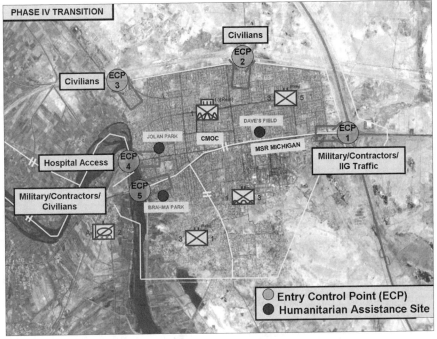

Phase IV Transition

Graphics from LtGen Richard F. Natonski's
PowerPoint presentation and are used with his permission

was complete, the Marines had handed out more than 65,000 humanitarian assistance packets.

With Fallujah cleared of nearly all enemy fighters, the Marines turned to cleaning up the war-torn city. They focused on gathering up enemy bodies, clearing debris from the streets, and removing all of the weapons and explosives from hundreds of caches. The streets were filled with the refuse of war: burned-out cars, dangling wires, and debris of all shapes and sizes. Feral dogs roamed the streets, and cats that once had slep on children's laps now dined on the bloated bodies of former fanatic fighters.

The Hydra Mosque and the nearby Cultural Center contained the "Home Depot" of caches. Inside both were rooms stacked to the ceiling with mortar rounds, rockets, and artillery shells. Janabi's Mosque was also loaded with weapons. Colonel Shupp ordered the ordnance removed and blown up in the street. Afterward, the Marines placed photographs of the weapons in the mosque, accompanied by the statement: "Look what was done in your

Mosque by the enemies of Iraq. Americans do not destroy Mosques."[1] The Marines finished clearing most of the caches by the 18th of December.

Task Force Bruno spent days clearing caches and fighting the last insurgent holdouts. Late in the afternoon of December 22 while clearing Sector 19 in the northeast section of Fallujah, Major Desgrosseilliers' Marines got into another fight and killed a couple more insurgents. When they ran out of daylight, Desgrosseilliers suspended his operation and planned to return the next day to finish up.

The Last Diehards

Desgrosseilliers had an established rotation, alternating his Marines so that they patrolled one day and rested the next. On December 23, Task Force Bruno returned to Sector 19, the same neighborhood they had been working the day before. Sergeant Jarrett Kraft, Corporals Jeremiah Workman and Raleigh Smith, and Lance Corporals Eric Hillenburg and James Phillips were in the city with other Marines and their platoon commander, 1st Lieutenant Al Butler, Jr. Workman cleared one side of the street while his friend Kraft worked the other.

The block they approached was infested with nearly thirty insurgents, and Butler's men came under heavy automatic weapons fire, followed by a flurry of grenades. As usual, the enemy had waited until the Marines were inside their stronghold before opening fire. They had learned the hard way that it was foolhardy to fight the Marines from afar. Their only real protection was to trap some within their own building, because the enemy knew more Marines would swarm into the structure to help their fallen brothers. They knew that death was certain eventually, but hoped they could kill more Americans on their way out of this world.

Smith, Phillips, and two more of Kraft's men climbed a staircase onto a landing, not knowing that eight insurgents were barricaded in the upstairs rooms. They were moving to check the first bedroom when an enemy fighter jumped out of a wardrobe and tossed a grenade onto the landing. The shrapnel killed Smith and seriously wounded two more Marines. Miraculously, Phillips emerged unscathed. Leaving Smith's body in the

---

1   Col Michael Shupp personal interview, 09/25/07.

doorway, the Marines retreated, bleeding, stumbling, staggering, and diving out onto a second-floor balcony.

Lieutenant Butler was standing in the street below when heard the fight break out. He moved into a nearby house with more Marines and raced to the roof. From that position he couldn't see the target house, but he could see where he needed to be: on the roof of a larger house next to the target house. From there, he would be able to look down into the insurgent-filled building. Butler left a couple of Marines on the first roof and took the rest to the building and raced up two flights of stairs.[2]

Workman was across the street when he heard the distinctive rattle of AK-47s and the burp of a SAW when the encounter began. He rushed from the house he was searching, crossed the street through a hail of grenades and gunfire, and raced into the fight.[3]

As Workman entered the house, he saw Kraft and Sergeant Samuel Guardiola on the stairs yelling at someone on the second floor. Enemy fire drilled the walls on the stairwell, turning concrete to a fine, misty powder. Reluctantly, Guardiola and Kraft retreated downstairs.

"Some of our guys are trapped up there!" Kraft shouted at Workman. He was referring to Smith (who was already dead), Phillips, and two other Marines.

Not knowing whether the men were wounded, dead, or unhurt, Workman, Kraft, and Guardiola pulled together a team to charge back into the house to rescue them. But no one wanted to take point. Workman watched for a few nervous seconds before blurting out, "Screw it! I'll go first!" He rushed back into the house, with eight or nine other Marines right behind him.

When Workman stopped at the foot of the staircase. One of the Marines behind him tossed a grenade onto the second floor. The Marines watched in surprise as it rolled back down the stairs, scattering for cover to avoid the coming blast.

BOOM!

The blast tore into the walls but no Marine was injured. Workman and the others regrouped at the base of the stairs. The Marine second in line

---

2   Capt Alfred Butler telephone interview, 06/03/09.

3   Sgt Jeremiah Workman telephone interview, 11/05/07.

encouraged Workman with a shove, indicating, "Go on, we're right behind you!"

Enemy bullets whizzed and snapped past Workman's head and pocked the wall behind him as he rushed up the first set of stairs. Halfway up at the landing the stairs turned ninety degrees and provided some cover. Workman paused there and looked back. No one had followed him up the stairs. Alone, he inched partway up the second flight to get a better look at what was waiting for him. Even though the firing remained intense, he could see two downed Marines. He could almost reach out and touch his friend, Raleigh Smith.

Workman turned and looked down. The Marines below were motioning and yelling at him: "Get back down here!"

"No—you get up here!" he shouted back.

Workman was sure he would be shot if he tried to run back down, but he returned to the landing. When it became clear that no one was coming up, he jumped down the entire first flight. Bullets whizzed past, but none so close to his head that he heard the tell-tale snapping of its passage.

Meanwhile, trapped upstairs, the uninjured Phillips covered the door while the two wounded Marines searched for a way off the flat roof. Bleeding badly, they decided to dangle off the balcony and drop to the ground. Phillips stayed behind to hold off the enemy while his wounded buddies fled. The two were hanging from the second floor when an insurgent raced into the doorway leading to the balcony, reached around the door jamb, and sprayed the rooftop patio with AK fire. One of the bullets hit Phillips in the head, killing him instantly.

By now, Butler and his Marines had made it to their new vantage point. From there, they could see down onto the second floor patio where Smith and Phillips lay dead. Butler left a couple of Marines on the roof to cover the patio door while he and a team jumped across to the target house and dragged the two fallen Marines out of the line of fire.

Downstairs, the Marines regrouped again, and this time the entire assault team rushed up the stairs—Workman again on point. Seeing the Marines charge, the enemy opened up with everything they had: automatic weapons fire filled the house as the Marines on the stairs lobbed grenades toward the upstairs bedrooms. The enemy fire continued unabated. Workman peeked around the corner to discover that Smith's body was gone.

From the front of the stack at the top of the stairs, Workman saw a yellow grenade bounce out of one of the bedrooms onto the landing.

"Grenade!" he shouted as he crunched his body up into a ball.

BOOM!

The room filled with flames. Shrapnel struck every Marine in the stack and knocked them back on the stairs. One chunk of hot metal seriously injured a Marine when it tore into his eye; he was helped out of the house for medical attention. Workman felt as if someone had smacked him in the leg with a baseball bat. As he would soon discover, metal was embedded in both legs and his left elbow, though he was not bleeding much. Satisfied that he was still in the fight, Workman charged back to the top of the stairs and fired into the bedrooms until he ran out of ammunition.

The Marines were forced to fall back again. When Workman reached the street, he saw the two wounded Marines who had dropped off the roof staggering out of an adjacent building. One was covered in blood and looked like a zombie. Workman rushed to his aid. The wounded infantryman could no longer walk, so Workman dragged him, through gunfire about 100 yards down the street to the casualty collection point. With his adrenalin pumping, Workman reached the corpsmen, handed over his wounded comrade, and charged back to the fight with more Marines.

When Major Desgrosseilliers heard the gunfire, he hopped into his truck and raced toward the fight. He knew exactly where to go and drove right to the buildings he had been in the day before. The major rolled up an alley in the middle of an escalating firefight. As the Marines were now discovering, the enemy was holed up in a group of five buildings. As soon as Desgrosseilliers came to a stop, his vehicle came under fire. When one of the rounds knocked his goggles from his helmet, the major hit the deck behind his vehicle and rolled to a wall. He looked up—and there was Workman.

"Hey, what's going on?" Desgrosseilliers asked.

Workman just stared blankly at his XO.

Desgrosseilliers rose, grabbed him by the shoulders, and slammed him into the wall. "Tell me what's going on!" he demanded.

Workman shook it off and came around, relating the story of the trapped Marines, the barricaded insurgents, and the hand grenades. Desgrosseilliers could hear Butler and his Marines yelling inside the building, but he didn't know exactly where they were. He knew they were alive, and that he had to do everything possible to get to them. Desgrosseilliers snapped at Workman and the other Marines standing in earshot, "We're going in there!"[4]

Desgrosseilliers decided to approach from the opposite side of the complex, hoping to divert the enemy's attention away from Lieutenant Butler and the isolated Marines. As he raced to flank the enemy, insurgents fired from rooftops and windows and tossed grenades into the street.

Desgrosseilliers led his men into the target building where Workman again led the stack up the stairwell, exchanging gunfire and grenades with the enemy. Several times, enemy grenades and automatic weapons fire drove Desgrosseilliers, Workman, and the others out of the building. Each time the determined Marines regrouped and reentered the house. Their goal was to get in behind the enemy to force them to break contact with Lieutenant Butler and his Marines.

The insurgents were operating as an organized military unit. They had set up ambush sites and fortified their positions, chiseled out rat holes that allowed them to move from building to building within their stronghold, and had guards well posted. The Marines outside were killing one or two insurgents at a time but, as Desgrosseilliers explained it, "there were more of them than there were of us."[5]

Workman was at the head of the stack but he had reached the limit of his endurance—throwing up, bleeding, and about to give in to exhaustion. It was then that he heard a bloodcurdling scream and he turned to find his friend, Lance Corporal Philip Levine, had been hit in the arm with an armor-piercing round. Major Desgrosseilliers, who was fighting right behind Levine when he was hit, had been splattered with so much blood and gore that the major thought that he himself had been shot in the face. What was left of Levine's arm was black and smoking. Workman stopped thinking of himself and reached down for another shot of endurance.

Although he was in real danger of bleeding to death, Levine continued trying to shoot his rifle with his good arm as Workman and the others dragged him from the fight. It was the commotion of the Marines dragging the screaming Levine from the building that distracted the enemy sufficiently for Lieutenant Butler and his men to get off the roof of the house,

---

4 LtCol Todd Desgrosseilliers telephone interview, 12/7/07.

5 *Ibid.*, 12/13/07.

with Butler carrying Smith's lifeless body. Workman rushed Levine to the corpsmen, who worked fast to bandage his severed arm. Levine kept insisting that he could continue the fight, and asked Sergeant Major Rudy Resto for a pistol.

"You are not going back," replied the sergeant major. "You've done your part."

Once Levine had been calmed, Workman noticed two of his friends lying in the back of a HMMWV. Neither was moving. Workman jumped up into the back of the truck to see how they were doing. Raleigh Smith was lying face-up with his arm resting across his forehead. To Workman, it looked as though he was shielding his eyes from the sun. He leaned over to give Smith a few words of encouragement.

"Raleigh," he said. Smith did not respond.

"Doc! Get over here!" Workman shouted to one of the corpsmen.

"Naw, man, he's all right, he's all right," Corpsman 3rd Class Rakesh Sundram responded.

Workman shook Smith once, then again—harder. "Doc, get over here! He's not moving."

"He's all right, Workman, he's all right."

Shaking uncontrollably, Workman leaned over and listened for a heartbeat or a breath. "Sonny! Get the fuck over here!" he yelled, refusing to understand what he knew was the truth.

"Workman—he's dead, man. He's gone."

He had seen many dead insurgents during the last few days, but he had never seen a dead Marine. Now, when the realization swept over him, a wave of anger gripped Workman. He turned to the second Marine. It was Eric Hillenburg, and he had a gaping bullet hole in his head.

Workman jumped from the back of the truck, gathered the remaining Marines, and ran back into the house, sprinting up the stairs determined to exact his revenge.

While Workman and the others were racing Levine to medical attention, Major Desgrosseilliers cordoned off the area and called for tanks and air power. He moved his Forward Air Controller into position and radioed Kilo Company, which sent a rifle platoon to reinforce the Marines who had been fighting now for more than an hour. Before long, Lieutenant Colonel Malay appeared with a bunch of satchel charges.

By now, most of Captain Bodisch's tanks were 10,000 hours past scheduled service and his mechanics were working day and night just to keep them rolling. Radios were out and numerous other systems were beyond repair, leaving many tanks little more than rolling pillboxes. But they still had their armor and guns, and they could still move. Two of Bodisch's tanks were still good to go.

Bodisch had been monitoring the escalating combat on his radio while sitting at Jolan Park with his XO and had already mapped out his route to the fight. When he heard Desgrosseilliers call for assistance, he and his XO hauled ass through the city, racing down MICHIGAN in their pair of tanks, traversing three miles in fewer than five minutes.

Meanwhile, back in the house at the top of the stairs, Workman said to himself, "Fuck it!" and moved to rush into the bedroom. Sergeant Jarrett Kraft grabbed the back of his web belt just as RPK rounds sprayed out the door. If not for Kraft, Workman would have been killed by the burst of machine gun fire.

Desgrosseilliers, meanwhile, had moved back into the building so that he could order Workman and the others out. The major didn't want to lose any more Marines in this stairwell slog. It was time to pull everyone outside so he could use bigger weapons against these diehards. In order to deliver the order, however, Desgrosseilliers had to get back in the stack with Workman.

When an insurgent popped out with a grenade, the Marines opened fire. One of the shots hit the Muj in the elbow and the grenade fell from his hand and bounced down the stairs, exploding close to Desgrosseilliers. Thankfully his body was protected, but the grenade tore a chunk out of his helmet and a few small pieces of shrapnel hit his leg. The concussion of the blast blew Workman down the top flight of stairs to the landing, knocking both Workman and Desgrosseilliers unconsciousness. The major came around first and moved to Workman, shaking him in the hope he had not lost another Marine. When Workman regained consciousness, they helped each other from the house. Desgrosseilliers ordered all the Marines from the buildings and Workman fell back for a final time.

Kilo Company had the stronghold surrounded, with Marines lining the rooftops and a CAAT section covering the road north of the enemy's hideout. Kraft showed up with an EOD sniper who had a rifle with a scope.

"Where in the hell did you get that?"[6] Desgrosseilliers asked.

"It was in my truck," the young Marine replied.

Desgrosseilliers immediately posted the sniper on a nearby roof.

It had been about fifteen or twenty minutes since Desgrosseilliers had called for tanks. Bodisch was just pulling up as everyone was pouring out of the building for the last time. Bodisch could see that a tough fight had been going on: the bodies of two Marines were visible in the back of a HMMWV, and the remaining Marines were still under heavy fire. Nonetheless, Desgrosseilliers rushed out into the street toward Bodisch's tank.

"Look at this crazy son of a bitch,"[7] Bodisch radioed Smithley.

The major ducked behind Bodisch's M1 and picked up the grunt phone. It was not until he heard the voice that Bodisch realized it was the battalion XO. Desgrosseilliers asked him to turn due north and to fire on the houses on the block.

Bodisch and Smithley slowly clanked forward as Desgrosseilliers walked behind the lead tank directing Bodisch's fire into the insurgent stronghold. Enemy fighters on the rooftops tried to kill Desgrosseilliers by lobbing grenades at the tank and firing wildly into the alley as he crouched behind the tank while rounds and shrapnel pinged off the armor. The young EOD sniper across the street picked off more than one insurgent as they popped up to take a shot. Once in position, Bodisch and Smithley fired main gun rounds into the buildings.

Each time Bodisch's tank fired up its engine to move, a huge plume of heat spewed out the rear vents and washed over Desgrosseilliers, melting his fleece vest under his body armor. At one point he was hit by a ricochet that added a superficial wound to his mounting injuries.

Lieutenant Colonel Malay barely recognized Desgrosseilliers, who had blood and who knows what splattered all across his face, with the rest of his body covered in soot, dust, and dirt-caked blood. He had a dent in his helmet,

---

6   LtCol Todd Desgrosseilliers telephone interview, 12/13/09.

7   Maj Robert Bodisch telephone interview, 1/7/08.

his clothes were melted, and his leg was bleeding. Because of the repeated shocks to his ears and brain he could not hear well, so he was yelling at the top of his lungs and did not even know it.

The tanks were running out of ammo but the insurgents refused to die. Around 1300, the Forward Air Controller took over, calling in circling aircraft, identifying and verifying the target buildings. He managed to "convince the Air Force pilot to drop his bombs even though we were only fifty or sixty feet away,"[8] remembered Desgrosseilliers. The Marines were so close that Desgrosseilliers recalls watching in amazement as the bombs flew into the windows of the buildings, the explosions rattling the tanks. The aircraft dropped fifteen JDAMS on the enemy complex.

The noise and concussion mellowed the jihadis for a short time, but the bombs didn't do as much damage as the Marines had hoped. Some of the insurgents were still alive and eager to continue fighting. It was starting to get late and Desgrosseilliers wanted to finish off these guys. The last thing he wanted was to give them time to regroup and return for a third day.

"Screw this," Desgrosseilliers thought.

The major decided to send in the engineers with Malay's satchel charges to level the buildings and kill the enemy inside, once and for all. The charges collapsed the structures around the remaining diehard insurgents. By now the Marines had used tanks, bombs, and had dropped the second floor of several buildings. Somehow, one last enemy fighter popped up out of the rubble like a "Terminator" with a machine gun and shot Lance Corporal Ilarraza in the leg.

Bodisch had been slowly slewing his turret to cover Ilarraza's stack as they rounded a corner into the driveway of one of the destroyed buildings. When he saw Ilarraza go down and the rest of the Marines in the stack fall back, Bodisch ordered his driver to reorient the tank. "HEAT round, on my command!" he yelled.

Bodisch kept his turret trained on the insurgent as his tank pivoted in place beneath him. When he noticed that he had awakened the sleeping behemoth, the enemy combatant shifted his fire toward the tank. Bodisch jerked back away from his shattered periscope as chips of glass brushed his face.

---

8 LtCol Todd Desgrosseilliers telephone interview, 12/13/07.

"Holy shit," Bodisch thought. "This guy is fucking nailing me!" Bodisch radioed Desgrosseilliers: "Clear your Marines."

Desgrosseilliers and Lieutenant Casey Brock rushed to Ilarraza to drag him to safety. Just as they reached the wounded Marine, a shot rang out and Lieutenant Brock went down. He had been hit squarely in the back in his SAPI plate. Brock shook it off, jumped back to his feet, and continued to help Desgrosseilliers. Together, they dragged Ilarraza out of the line of fire as the enemy hit the wounded Marine again and again.

Once behind the wall, Desgrosseilliers looked up at Bodisch and gave a thumbs-up.

"Fire!" Bodisch commanded.

The machine gun-toting insurgent saw the giant fireball erupt from Bodisch's main gun, may have felt the earth tremble, but never caught sight of the supersonic 120mm main gun round that blew him into oblivion.

Malay announced their success: "Pink mist, good job!"

This had been no rag-tag group. The entire block of buildings was fortified. The enemy fighters had even rolled up carpets and stacked them everywhere, and overturned the furniture and stacked that up, too. It had been a bitter, hard-fought, close-quarters battle.

The Marines found the bodies of at least thirty insurgents and uncountable body parts. No one really knows how many of them had made their last stand in these buildings. When all was said and done, the Marines found papers indicating that most of these men were not even Iraqis. They were hardcore foreign fighters who had come to Fallujah on a one-way ticket. Stuck in the city, they were going to either hijack the government or die as martyrs.

The last battle of the fight to free Fallujah claimed the lives of Raleigh Smith, James Phillips, and Eric Hillenburg, and wounded twenty other Marines.

The Marines found mountains of ordnance on pallets stacked to the ceilings throughout the Askari District. There were so many explosives that it was too dangerous to move it all, so senior leadership ordered it blown in place. The explosions destroyed six, eight, and even ten houses at a time.

When the detonations ended and the dust settled to the ground, the fight for Fallujah was over.

Unfinished Business

Miraculously, Colonel Larry Nicholson had recovered enough from the rocket attack on his office in Camp Fallujah to join the fight. He would need more surgery, but he arrived at Camp Fallujah on December 24 to take Joe L'Etiole's spot so that L'Etiole could return to the United States to assume command of his own battalion. On Christmas day, Colonel Nicholson and General Joe Dunford drove to an Entry Control Point north of the city to hand out candy to some of the local children. When Nicholson climbed out of his HMMWV on PL APRIL, Lieutenant Colonel Malay had difficulty believing his eyes: all he could remember was Nicholson being carried out of his office barely clinging to life. Not only had Nicholson survived the rocket attack, but he had kept his vow and made it back into the fight.

Colonel Shupp became the military governor of Fallujah. During the transition period he was responsible for security, cleanup, and the repatriation of Fallujah's civilian population. As the governor, Shupp walked the streets with his small security detachment, making himself accessible to the Iraqi civilians. He also attended the city council meetings every Monday. One day, an Iraqi complained to Shupp that he had been attacked by an American dog. On another occasion, an angry Iraqi arrived at the city council meeting with a strange accusation: "They shot and burned my motorcycle," the Iraqi explained through Shupp's interpreter.[9]

"They shot your motorcycle?" Shupp didn't understand why anyone would do that.

The incensed Iraqi led Shupp to one of the checkpoints. Apparently, the man had ignored orders to stop at a Marine traffic control point. The Marines hadn't opened fire on the man, but when they managed to finally stop him, an angry Marine emptied his M16 into the motorcycle and set it ablaze. Shupp chided the Marine for the wanton destruction of the man's bike and had the Iraqi compensated for the loss of his transportation.

The man left happy.

---

9 Col Michael Shupp personal interview, 09/25/07.

New Year's Day, 2005

Al Qaeda in Iraq and all of the anti-Iraqi forces had suffered a major defeat in Fallujah, but the insurgency in Anbar Province was not over; the fight just shifted to the Anbar countryside. Those insurgents not killed or captured scattered to the winds. Some went to Ramadi, and others to Hit, Karmah, Habbaniyah, and to Haditha—and especially Muj Island. They were far from defeated, but they were on the run and the Marines were in hot pursuit.

"Muj Island" was an insurgent stronghold in the fast-moving waters of the Euphrates River about eight kilometers south of the Haditha Dam. Wittnam's Small Craft Company had moved to Haditha Dam on December 22 to patrol the Euphrates and try to clear the river down to Muj Island. The water was shallow in this region. Because the older river craft drew too much water to safely navigate between Haditha Dam and Muj Island, previous commanders had restricted their water patrols to waters north of the dam. Wittnam wanted to start patrolling south of the dam with his new shallow-draft, Small Unit Riverine Craft. On New Year's Day, he sent his first patrol downriver.

Gunny Vinciguerra, Brian Parrello, and Juan Rubio were supposed to be off-duty. Vinciguerra was planning to chill out and do laundry, Rubio went to the computer center to check his email, and Parrello was just trying to get some rest. When they heard that Wittnam's first patrol had been ambushed and one of their Marines wounded, all three volunteered to go back out after the unseen insurgents near Muj Island.

Together, they raced to the boats with Lieutenant Andrew Thomas, 4th Platoon's Commander, and Captain Jonathan Kuniholm, an engineer who was along for the ride to familiarize himself with the area for future operations. As they were boarding someone exclaimed, "Wait! We didn't bring the radio." Without comment, Parrello sprinted away, returned with the radio, and jumped aboard the boat. He never asked, "Who's going to carry this thing?" He naturally assumed he would act as the radioman on this trip.

The boats sped downriver and put the Marines ashore 800 meters north of the first ambush site. The coxswains beached their boats and Thomas,

Rubio, Parrello, Kuniholm, Vasey, and Vinciguerra jumped to dry land with twelve other Marines to track the enemy down. They moved on foot south toward the original point of contact. It took them thirty minutes to reach the old water-pumping station from which the first ambush had originated.[10]

Sergeant Vasey noticed the blood first. "Sir, I've got blood and drag marks here," he told Thomas. It looked as if the Marines had hit an insurgent in the first ambush, and that he had been dragged away from the river.

The entire platoon spread out in a tactical formation and headed south. Vasey took point about 100 meters out front, Vinciguerra assumed rear security, and the other fire teams spread out around Lieutenant Thomas, Captain Kuniholm, Parrello (with the radio), and Rubio.

When the Marines passed a short wall, Captain Kuniholm noticed a five-gallon water can and issued a caution: "Those are the kind of cans the enemy has been using for IEDs," he told the group. Parrello, however, was on the radio reporting the ground unit's position to the boats and missed the warning. Everyone else moved away from the can except Parrello. Rubio noticed that he hadn't heard Kuniholm and tugged on his blouse. "Hey, brother, we need to get away from here." Parrello and Rubio turned to put distance between themselves and the can when their universe exploded.[11]

Parrello took the brunt of the blast and was slammed into Rubio, the force hurling both into a mud wall. The impact knocked Rubio unconscious. Rubio came to a minute later, his ears ringing and his wrist, elbow, and legs feeling as if they were on fire. He did a quick check to make sure he was okay. His arms were working, but he was still groggy and his senses rattled. After awhile he could make out the crack of Aks and the whoosh of RPGs being launched, and then the snap of M16s and 203s firing. About 100 feet behind Rubio, Gunny Vinciguerra was pumping out 40mm grenades as fast as he could, and all of the Marines were firing on the enemy.

As Rubio's vision cleared, he realized to his horror that the dirt around him was being kicked up by enemy fire: he was in the middle of a firefight and that the Muj were shooting at him! Before he could react, an RPG slammed into the wall and exploded right above him, sending two pieces of shrapnel into his head just under his helmet. He reached for the back of his

10 GySgt Brian Vinciguerra telephone interview, 02/05/08.

11 HM2 Juan Rubio telephone interview, 11/15/07.

head to check it as he remembered that Parrello and Captain Kuniholm had been right in front of him just a few minutes ago. "Where are they?" he wondered. His wounds were not important now; he had to find Kuniholm and Parrello.

The enemy fired an RPG in Vinciguerra's direction that detonated twenty-five meters to his left. The gunny continued firing his high-explosive grenades as a second RPG exploded just fifteen meters away. Unscathed by the initial blast, Lieutenant Thomas fell back to Vinciguerra's position at the base of an old foundation. "I've got two guys down," Thomas told Vinciguerra. A third RPG slammed into the foundation, this time only eighteen inches from Vinciguerra. Fortunately, he only had his arm exposed, but when he dropped his rifle and pulled his arm back, he saw a large hunk of gore and exposed bone. Vinciguerra wiggled his fingers and thought, "I'm good to go."

Rubio found the severely wounded Parrello lying nearby. Without thinking, Rubio sprayed shots from his M16 as he crawled toward the fallen Marine, emptying three magazines in the process. When he reached the wounded Marine, Rubio pulled him behind a wall to get him out of the line of fire.

Rubio pulled the mangled radio off Parrello's back, cut open his flak jacket, and did what he could to stabilize his friend. He could see that Parrello's chest was badly bruised, he was bleeding internally, and one of his arms was mangled. Parrello regained consciousness as Rubio was splinting the shattered limb. He complained that his chest, arm, and legs were all hurting. Rubio tightly wrapped Parrello's broken ribs and then dragged him to a safer location while other Marines within sight laid down covering fire.

Kuniholm had also been critically wounded by the IED blast. Rubio, wounded himself and running on adrenalin alone, left a Marine with Parrello and reentered the kill zone to help Kuniholm. The captain was bleeding badly from an arm that had been nearly blown off below the elbow. He was holding his wounded right hand in his left. Rubio applied a tourniquet to stop the bleeding and wrapped the mangled arm. Once Rubio had bandaged the wound, he instructed another Marine to continue caring for the captain and set out in search of more wounded Marines.

Rubio found Gunny Vinciguerra next. He applied a tourniquet, bandaged the wound, and started an IV. The gunny had little doubt that Rubio's actions saved his life. "I'd like to tell him he's my hero," Vinciguerra confirmed, "and without him I wouldn't be standing here today."[12] Rubio told Lance Corporal Kevin Powell to remain with Vinciguerra and get him down to the bank of the river.

With the radio destroyed, the Marines had no way to call the boats to come get them. Lance Corporal Rich Rupert, the company's fastest runner, volunteered to sprint north 800 meters to get word of the wounded Marines to the boat captains. He ran back to the boats as fast as he could, jumped aboard, and guided them down to the ambush site. As Rupert was running for the boats, Rubio grabbed a few Marines and told them to cover him while he ran back for Parrello and Sergeant Vasey. Thomas ordered his men to head for the boat landing: "Okay, guys, let's move back, let's move back."

Rupert was the first off the boats. He grabbed Parrello and dragged him down to the shoreline as the other Marines gathered their wounded aboard and then climbed aboard themselves. Even though he was wounded, Gunny Vinciguerra stood on the bank counting his Marines. Once he was sure that all of his men were accounted for, he boarded and the boats raced north toward the dam.

Vinciguerra yanked his dog tag off and gave it to Lance Corporal Stoddard. "Call this in as a medevac," he ordered. "You've got one urgent surgical, one urgent, and one routine." Vinciguerra didn't realize just how seriously wounded Parrello was. He considered his own wounds minor; after all, he could still wiggle his fingers. He was the most concerned about Kuniholm.

After Rubio checked Kuniholm to make sure he hadn't started bleeding again, he turned his attention to Parrello. Rubio knew he was bleeding internally, and he knew what he had to do—but he didn't have the equipment he needed. Rubio found the largest syringe he had and conducted a poor-man's thoracentesis by driving the needle in just below Parrello's lung in an effort to remove fluid. The procedure immediately relieved some of the pressure on Parrello's collapsed lung.

Still, Parrello was in dire need of a surgeon. His chest cavity was filling with blood, which soon would make it difficult for his heart to continue beating. Rubio needed a chest tube; if he had one, he knew he could keep Parrello alive another few precious minutes, and maybe long enough to get him to an operating room.

---

12 Philip Creed, "New Years Day – Corpsman Awarded the Silver Star," *Navy Times*, June 12, 2006.

"Doc, I can't breathe. I can't breathe! I CAN'T BREATHE!" Exclaimed the former radioman.

In the racing boat Rubio could do nothing else except continue to give him morphine. It took the coxswain less than fifteen minutes to get back to Haditha Dam. Parrello was rushed from the boat to a HMMWV ambulance that whisked him up to the top of the dam where an Army Black Hawk medevac helicopter was waiting with rotors turning.

Rubio remained at Parrello's side in the ambulance during the mad dash to the helicopter, cradling him, talking to him, and trying to keep him awake and alive. Just as they pulled up to the helicopter, Parrello looked up and asked, "Are you okay, Doc? I know you were right next to me."

"Don't worry about me, brother. We're going to get you home."

A calm look passed across Parrello's face, as if he was relieved that Rubio was not injured. "I'm getting sleepy," he said before taking in one last shallow breath—and then he stopped breathing.

Parrello was rushed into the waiting helicopter with Kuniholm; Vinciguerra was loaded last. As the Black Hawk lifted into the sky, Vinciguerra looked to his right and saw Rubio standing there, tears streaming down his face, repeating over and over, "I'm sorry. I'm sorry. I'm sorry."[13]

Vinciguerra looked away to the left. The medics had bagged Parrello and were frantically working to keep him alive. Vinciguerra knew Parrello would not survive, yet these medics refused to give up and kept working on Brian for the entire flight. When they landed, he was rushed into surgery but it was too late to save him. Lance Corporal Brian Parrello had lived a short life, but he died doing what he loved, and will forever be remembered as a United States Marine.

And what an honor that is. The Marines have defended the American people throughout our history, and have brought peace and stability to countless people in nations around the world. They are ferocious fighters yet compassionate human beings—"no worse enemy and no better friend."[14] It is amazing how quickly they can turn from full-scale combat to humanitarian assistance operations. By January 2005, the Marines were

---

13 GySgt Vinciguerra telephone interview, 2/5/08.

14 MajGen James Mattis, USMC.

working to help the citizens of Fallujah clean up their city and return to their homes.

The People of Fallujah

Colonel Michael Shupp insisted on knowing whenever there was a gathering inside the city of more than fifty people. Later that month he got a call that a large crowd was gathering at the Jolan Park humanitarian site. When he heard the news, the colonel called Major Arnold and told him to gather his Personal Security Detachment and they drove to the center of the city.

The citizens of Fallujah were normally compliant in the face of authority, but on this morning things had gotten out of hand. The women in their separate queue were pushing and shoving, old women were being crushed in the crowd, and people were being pushed into the concertina wire barriers.

"Sergeant Major," Shupp said, "we can't let this happen."[15]

Shupp and his Marines jumped over a sand-bagged wall and pressed into the crowd, pushing the Iraqis back with their rifles. They never fired a shot; they pressed forward. Shupp turned to his interpreter, Mohammed Hawlery, and told him to stay at his side and keep telling the crowd what he was saying: "Treat each other with dignity." "Help each other." "Don't push each other."

Mohammed continued yelling at the top of his voice to everyone in earshot while Shupp and his Marines pushed toward the concertina to break up the crowd and rescue the victims of the hysteria.

Shupp later recalled the incident:

I reached down and there was an old mother in her black robes. It was so bad that my bodyguard, Corporal [Cameron] Sims—he's just a moose of a man—he's holding people back. I say, "I gotta get my Leatherman out to cut her out." I pick her up, and as I'm picking her up, she grabs my hand and she kisses my hand and says, "God bless your mother and father."

15 Col Michael Shupp, personal interview, 9/25/07.

It wasn't just me. Every Marine out there was doing one thing. They weren't out there to hurt any of the Iraqi people; they were out there to protect them, to serve them, to give them a chance. And this little old lady captured it all in that one little moment.[16]

16 *Ibid.*

Epilogue

"In modern counterinsurgency, 'victory' may not be final . . ."

— David Kilcullen

Brian Parrello, Chris Adlesperger, Sean Sims, Antoine Smith, James "JP" Blecksmith, Rafael Peralta, Victor Lu, Lonny Wells, Joshua Palmer, Demarkus Brown, Eric Hillenburg, Michael Anderson, and seventy-three other soldiers, sailors, and Marines did not die in vain. Fallujah had been completely cleared of insurgents. Zarqawi and his al Qaeda thugs were on the run. Peace and security had been returned to the city and its citizens.

With Fallujah clear of its worst elements, the road to reconciliation was finally open. The Marines could now work to gain the respect and support of al Anbar's sheiks, imams, and everyday citizens. Fallujah would become a model for a modern-day, free and independent Iraq.

Still, the loss of nineteen Darkhorse Marines weighed heavy on Patrick Malay's heart. "Could he have trained them better?" he wondered. "Could he have been a better leader?" "Might they have lived?" He will never be able to fully answer these questions, but he will always remember his Marines who paid the ultimate price for freedom.

During the past few months, Lieutenant Colonel Malay had dedicated every waking moment to leading his battalion. As a result, he had neglected his routine paperwork. One evening in early January of 2005 he sat down to catch up on some of that work. It has been a longstanding tradition in the Marine Corps for the battalion commander to send a congratulatory letter home to the mothers of children newly born to deployed Marines. One of the tasks awaiting the lieutenant colonel that night was to sign a pile of newborn letters. He picked up the stack, and for some unknown reason decided to count them. When he had finished, a smile creased his face.

Nineteen.

There were nineteen babies born to Marines in his battalion. Nineteen children who would carry on. Nineteen new innocent souls.

Somehow, the loss of his nineteen men felt a little more distant, and the weight on his shoulders was a little lighter.

Victory in Iraq was still years away, and the Marines still had a long, hard grind ahead. But if any moment during these years can be called a turning point, it must be the successful conclusion of Operation al-Fajr.

For the people of Iraq, the transition from living under a ruthless dictator to living and working in a free society has been a long metamorphosis. Every success has ridden on the back of all the previous efforts. No single soldier, Marine, or military unit can claim the victory in Anbar Province. But that is as it always has been with the United States military: together, they cannot be defeated.

In 2005, the 1st Marine Division's main effort shifted to Ramadi, Western Anbar Province, and the restive Zaidon. The Marines worked hard to clear the remaining insurgent strongholds, and then to win the hearts and minds of the people. In the tradition of their WWI predecessors, Gary Patton's 2nd Infantry Division soldiers fought side-by-side with Marines in Ramadi. In the summer of 2005, Craig Tucker's RCT-7 Marines returned to the Zaidon region until the First Marine Division was relieved by Major General Huck and the 2nd Marine Division. The Camp Lejeune Marines carried on the fight, moving the province closer to peace and security by hunting down criminals, insurgents, and religious fanatics in Iraq's "Wild West."

It was a long time coming, but the sheikhs, imams, and citizens of al Anbar Province finally realized that the Marines were there to help the people and that the foreign insurgents were there to kill and oppress the population. After months of fighting, the people of Anbar changed sides and the "Anbar Awakening" began.

The mothers of Anbar offered up their sons to serve in the Iraqi security forces to help finally rid their land of the cancer that was the insurgency. Slowly, the Marines turned the responsibility for security back to the Iraqi government. Slowly, peace and stability returned to Anbar Province.

Today Fallujah, Ramadi, and Haditha show every sign of peace, stability, and prosperity. Parents can send their children to school, and families have hope for the future.

As goes Anbar, so goes Iraq.

Appendix 1

Fallujah Order of Battle

1st Marine Expeditionary Force
LtGen John Sattler

Task Force Blue Diamond – 1st Marine Division
Major General Richard F. Natonski – *Devil Dog 6*
Brigadier General Joseph Dunford ADC
LtCol George Bristol G-2
LtCol Joe L'Etiole G-3
LtCol Mike McCarthy FSC
LtCol Gary "Static" King, Air Officer

1st Marine Regiment
Regimental Combat Team 1
Colonel Mike Shupp – *Inchon 6*

7th Marine Regiment
Regimental Combat Team 7
Colonel Craig Tucker – *Ripper 6*

2nd Brigade Combat Team, 1st Cavalry Division US ARMY
"Black Jack Brigade"
Colonel Michael Formica – *Black Jack 6*

2d Radio Battalion
LtCol John Pollock

1st Marine Regiment – Regimental Combat Team 1
Colonel Mike Shupp – *Inchon 6*
LtCol Keil Gentry – XO
LtCol Jim Donlan – *POB 6*
LtCol Dave Bellen – S2
LtCol Jeffrey Chessani – S3
Gunner Chuck Carleton – Regimental Gunner
Sergeant Major Eduardo Leardo III – Regimental Sergeant Major

3d Battalion, 1st Marines
LtCol Willy Buhl – *Brahma 6*
Major Clark Watson – XO
Major Jeff McCormick – S2
Major Christian Griffin – S3
Captain David "Pork Chop" Smay – FAC
CWO3 Armando Garcia – Battalion Gunner
Sergeant Major Ed Sax

Weapons (George) Company – Rob Belnap

India Company – Capt Brett Clark – *Raider 6*
1st Platoon – 1stLt Timothy Strabbing

Kilo Company – Capt Timothy Jent – *Spartan 6*
1stLt Paul Vaughan – XO
1stSgt Allen Miller – *First Sergeant*

1st Platoon – 1stLt Adam Mathes
2d Platoon – 1stLt John Jacobs
3d Platoon – 1stLt Jesse Grapes

Lima Company – Capt Brian Heatherman – *Warrior 6*
1stLt Greg Jones – XO
1stSgt Wayne Hurt – *First Sergeant*
CAP India – 1stLt Zach Iscol

3d Battalion, 5th Marines
LtCol Pat Malay – *Darkhorse 6*
Major Todd Desgrosseilliers – XO
Major Robert Piddock – S3
CWO3 Stuart White II – Battalion Gunner
SgtMaj Rudy Resto – Sergeant Major

India Company – Capt Brian Chontosh/Leonard Coulman – *Diesel 6*
1st Platoon – Lt John Campbell
2nd Platoon – 2dLt Clint Alanis
3rd Plt – Lt J.P. Blecksmith/Jensen/MacIntosh
Weapons Platoon – 1stLt Sven Jensen

Kilo Company – Capt Andrew McNulty – *Samurai 6*
1stLt William "Ben" Diaz – XO
2dLt Duncan – FO
1stSgt Steven Knox – *First Sergeant*

1st Platoon – 2dLt Michael Cragholm
2nd Platoon – 2dLt Todd Moulder
3rd Platoon – 2dLt Colin Browning
Weapons Platoon – GySgt Cardenas

Lima Company – Capt Eduardo Bitanga – *Havoc 6*

Weapons Company – Capt Tom Knowl
Scout Platoon – 1stLt Samuel Rosales
81mm Mortars – 1stLt Alfred Lee Butler IV

Charlie Company, 2nd Tank Battalion
Capt Rob Bodisch – *Comanche 6*
1stLt Aaron Smithley – XO

Delta Company, 2d AMTRACS
Captain Medeo

Mike Battery, 14th Marine Regiment

2nd Battalion, 7th Cavalry Regiment US ARMY
Task Force 2-7
14 tanks, 30 Bradleys
LTC James Rainey – *Ghost 6*
MAJ Scott Jackson – XO – *Ghost 5*
CPT Dave Grey – S2
1LT Mike Erwin – Assistant S2
MAJ Tim Karcher – S3
CPT Coley D. Tyler – FSO
Sergeant Major Tim Mace - CSM

A Company, 2-7
CPT Edward Twaddell III – *Apache 6*
1LT Hank Wiley – *Apache 5*

1st Platoon – Bradleys – 1LT Daniel Kilgore
2nd Platoon – Bradleys – 1LT Michael Durant
3rd Platoon C/3-8 (attached) – tanks – 1LT Matt Wojcik

C Company, 2-7
CPT Chris Brooke – *Comanche 6*
10 Bradleys

C Company, 3rd Battalion, 8th Cavalry Regiment
CPT Peter Glass – *Cougar 6*
1LT Michael Throckmorton – XO
1st Sgt Robert Blakey

1st Platoon – tanks – 1LT Omari Tompson
2nd Platoon – tanks – 1LT John Baker
2nd Platoon C/2-7 (attached) – Bradleys – 2LT Benjamin Polanco

Bravo Company, 215th Forward Support Battalion
CPT Jake Brown

3d Light Armored Reconnaissance Battalion(-)(Rein.)
Task Force Wolfpack
LtCol Steve Dinauer – *Wolfpack 6*
Major Ken Kassner – XO
Major Innes Quiroz – S3
Major Rick "Rico" Uribe – FAC
Lt Greg Rockford USN – Surgeon
SgtMaj Leland Hatfield – SgtMaj

HQSVC(-)(Rein.), 3rd LAR Battalion
Captain Matthew Good

Company B, 1st Battalion, 23rd Infantry Regiment(Rein)
Major Michael Miller Jr. – *Cajun 6*

1st Platoon – Captain Ronald 'Shane' McGinty

Company C, 3rd LAR Battalion
Captain Scott Conway – *Comanche 6*

Company C(-)(Rein.), 1st Battalion, 9th Infantry Regiment, 2BCT, 2ID, USA
14 Bradleys, 4 tanks
CPT Victor Pirak USA – *Cobra 6*

Small Craft Company. HQBn, 2nd Marine Division
Major Dan Wittnam – *Game Warden 6*

Scout Sniper Platoon(-), HQSVC Co, BLT 1/4
1stLt Manerian

36 Commando, Iraqi Special Operation Forces (TACON)
CPT Trevor Driver USA – Team Leader SOF

Plat. Co A(-), Iraqi Intervention Force (TACON)
Captain Adam Collier (LNO)

Combat Service Support Company – 113(DS), 1st FSSG
Major Pat Sweeney

7th Marine Regiment – Regimental Combat Team – 7
Colonel Craig Tucker – *Ripper 6*
LtCol Robert Kosid - XO
Major Lawrence Hussey – S2
LtCol Nicholas Vuckovich – S3
Major Brent Norquist – S4
Major Jonathan Dunne – FCS
Cmdr Mark Hammett – Regimental Surgeon
SEAL Platoon Commander – *Neutron 6*
CW3 Jeffrey Eby – Regimental Gunner
SgtMaj Phillip Freed – Regimental Sergeant Major

1st Battalion, 8th Marines
LtCol Gareth Brandl – *Hunter 6*
Major Mark Winn – XO
Capt Gregory Starace – S2
Major Kevin Trimble – S3
Palmer Jones – AsstS3
Capt Bruce 'Link' Green – Air Officer
Capt Matt Nodine – JAG
Cmdr Richard Jadick USN – Surgeon
LCDR Denis Cox USN – Chaplain
SgtMaj Anthony Hope – SgtMaj
Company A – Capt Aaron Cunningham – *Avenger 6*
1stLt Doug Krugman – XO
Capt 'Jorge' Ramsey – FAC
1stSgt Derek Fry – First Sergeant

1st Platoon – 2dLt Elliot Ackerman
2nd Platoon – 2dLt Hunt
3rd Platoon – 2dLt Douglas Barnes
Weapons Platoon 1stLt Dan Malcom (KIA November 10)

Company B – Capt Read Omohundro – *Beowulf 6*
FAC – Capt Michael "Yuri" Stroud

Company C – Capt Theodore Bethea II – *Cajun 6*
1stLt Christopher Conner – XO
Lt Patrick O'Connor – FO
1stSgt Andrade – First Sergeant

1st Platoon – 2dLt Rhoades
2nd Platoon – 2dLt Turner
3rd Platoon – 2dLt Littell

Weapons Company – Captain Stephen Kahn – *Wolverine 6*
Weaps Platoon Leader – Lt Mathew Kutilek
Weaps Platoon Leader – Lt David Lee
Weaps Platoon Leader – Lt James Risler

1st Battalion, 3d Marines
LtCol Mike Ramos – *Bronco 6*
Maj. Aden Pfeuffeur – S3
"Crash" – Air Officer

Company A – Capt Lee Johnson – *Junkyard 6*

Company B – Capt Jay Garcia – *Blade 6*

Company C – Capt Thomas Tennant – *Spartan 6*
"Worm" and "Buzz" – FAC
1stSgt Michael Farrell – First Sergeant
Weapons Company – Capt Derek Wastilla

Charlie Company, 1st LAR (attached) – Captain Gilbert Juarez – *War Pig 6*
Forward Observer – 2dLt William Warkentin

1st Pltn. – Lieutenant Paul Webber
Raider Pltn. – 2d Lt Mike Aubry
AAV Platoon – *Gator 6*

2-2 Infantry Regiment US ARMY
Task Force 2-2
LTC Peter A. Newell – *Ramrod 6*
CPT Ray Pemberton – S2
MAJ John Reynolds – S3
MAJ (Dr.) Lisa Dewitt – Surgeon
CPT James Cobb – FSO
CSM Steve Faulkenberg/Darrin Bohn – Command Sergeant Major – *Ramrod 7*

A Company, 2nd Battalion, 2nd Infantry Regiment
CPT Sean P. Sims/CPT Doug Walter – *Terminator 6*
1LT Edward Iwan – XO
1LT Christopher Walls – Platoon Leader

1st Platoon – tanks – 1LT Jeff Emery
3rd Platoon – Bradleys – 1LT Joaquin Meno
Engineer Platoon

A Company, 2nd Battalion, 63rd Armored Regiment
CPT Paul Fowler

F Troop, 4th Cavalry Regiment
CPT Kirk Mayfield

Iraqi Intervention Force
Major Miller – LNO
2d Force Reconnaissance, 4th Platoon
Capt Jason Schauble

Alpha Company, 3d Light Armored Reconnaissance Battalion

Alpha Company, 2d Tank Battalion (-) ten tanks
Capt Christopher Meyers – *Panzer 6*
1stLt Mark Markley – XO
Company First Sergeant – 1stSgt Brant Young
Tank Leader – GySgt Frank Herbert

2d (WHITE) Platoon – Lt David Klingensmith
3d (BLUE) Platoon – 2dLt Jeffery Lee

Charlie Company, 2d AMTRACS

Charlie Battery, 1st Battalion, 12th Marine Regiment – *Steel Rain 6*

2nd Brigade Combat Team, 1st Cavalry Division US ARMY
"Black Jack Brigade"
COL Michael Formica – *Black Jack 6*

1st Battalion – 5th Cavalry Regiment
LTC Myles Miyamasu – *Black Knight 6*

A Company/2-12 Cavalry – tanks

1st Battalion, 5th Infantry Regiment (Stryker)
LTC Todd McCaffrey – *Bobcat 6*

2nd Battalion, 12th Cavalry Regiment (Tanks)
LTC Tim Ryan

Alpha Battery/3-82 Field Artillery
8 Paladin Guns

2nd Reconnaissance Battalion
LtCol Darric Knight – *Raider 6*
Major Timothy (Rich) Dremann Jr. – XO
Captain Travis Homiak – S3

A Company – Maj. Pat Simon – *Triton 6*
B Company – Maj. Mark Rainey/Maj. Kevin Hutchinson – *Plague 6*

A Company, 2nd Light Armored Reconnaissance Battalion
Captain John Griffin – *Apache 6*
Lt Philpot - XO
1stSgt Brian Link

1st Platoon
2nd Platoon
3rd Platoon – Lt Phares
Mortar Section

759th Military Police Battalion
LTC Byron Freeman

2nd Brigade Combat Team, 2nd Infantry Division US ARMY
Colonel Gary Patton
1/503 Parachute Infantry Regiment
1/506 Parachute Infantry Regiment
2nd Battalion, Fifth Marines
44th Engineer Battalion

4th Aviation Brigade, 1st Cavalry Division US ARMY
Colonel James C. McConville

1st Battalion, 227th Aviation Regiment (1-227) (attack)
LTC Ron Lewis – *Attack 6*

2nd Battalion, 227th Aviation Regiment (2-227) (lift)
LTC William K. Mooney
1st Battalion, 25th Aviation Regiment (1-25) (attached)
LTC Mike Lundy

615th Aviation Support Battalion
LTC Dave Parker

24th Marine Expeditionary Unit
Colonel Ron Johnson
Battalion Landing Team 1/2

31st Marine Expeditionary Unit
Colonel Lee Miller
Battalion Landing Team 1/3

3d Marine Air Wing
MajGen Keith Stalder

HMM-161

HMM 268

VMFA 242 – F/A18

HMLA-169
LtCol "Shooter" Wright

Appendix 2

Dramatis Personae
Operation Phantom Fury Participants

This alphabetical list is provided to make it easier for readers to keep track of the participants of Phantom Fury written about within these pages.

Abdelwahab, Akram "Abe" SGT, USA, 3d Squad, A Company, 2d Battalion, 7th Cavalry Regiment

Ackerman, Elliot 2dLt, USMC, *Avenger 1*, Platoon Commander, 1st Platoon, Company A, 1/8

Adlesperger, Christopher LCpl, USMC, Team Leader, 1st Squad, 1st Platoon, Kilo Company, 3d Battalion, 5th Marines

Alicea, Benny SPC, USA, 3d Squad, A Company, 2d Battalion, 7th Cavalry Regiment

Anderson, Michael Jr. Cpl, USMC, 1st Squad, 1st Platoon, Kilo Company, 3d Battalion, 5th Marines

Anderson, Nathan Cpl, USMC, Weapons Company, attached to 1st Platoon, Bravo Company, 1/8

Arellano, Jason Sergeant, USMC, Squad Leader, 3d Squad, 2d Platoon, Kilo Company, 3d Battalion, 5th Marines

Armendariz, George LCpl, USMC, Scout, 1st Platoon, Charlie Company, 1st LAR Battalion, BLT 1/3

Arnold, Bill Maj, USMCR, Scout Platoon Commander, RCT-1, Colonel Shupp's Personal Security Detachment Commander

Aylmer, John LCpl, USMC, 1st Squad, 1st Platoon, Kilo Company, 3/5

Baker, Jeremy Cpl, USMC, Fire Team Leader, 1st Squad, 1st Platoon, Kilo Company, 3/5

Ball, Jonathan Sergeant USMC, Tank Gunner, Headquarters Platoon, Alpha Company, 2d Tank Battalion (Meyers' gunner)

Barnes, Douglas Lt, USMC, *Avenger 3*, Platoon Commander, 3d Platoon, Company A, 1/8

Barreto, Travis CPL, USA, A Company, Task Force 2-2, Part of Captain Sims' Personal Security Detachment

Batalona, Wesley, Blackwater contractor, killed March 31, 2004

Bellavia, David SSG, USA, Squad Leader, 2d Squad, 3d Platoon, A Company, Task Force 2-2

Bellen, Dave LtCol, USMC, *Inchon 2*, Intelligence Officer, 1st Marine Regiment (RCT-1)

Bethea, Theodore II Capt, USMC, *Cajun 6*, Company Commander, Company C, 1st Battalion, 8th Marines

Bitanga, Eduardo Capt, USMC, *Havoc 6*, Company Commander, Lima Company, 3d Battalion, 5th Marines

Blazer, Melvin SSgt, USMC. Kilo Company, 3d Battalion, 5th Marines

Blecksmith, James "JP" Lt, USMC, *Diesel 3*, Platoon Commander, Third Platoon, India Company, 3/5

Bodisch, Robert Capt, USMC, *Comanche 6*, Company Commander, Charlie Company, 2d Tank Battalion

Brandl, Gareth LtCol, USMC, *Hunter 6*, Battalion Commander, 1st Battalion, 8th Marines (1/8)

Bremer, Lewis Paul, Ambassador to Iraq

Bristol, George LtCol, USMC, Intelligence Officer, 1st Marine Division

Brooke, Chris Capt, USA, *Comanche 6,* Company Commander, C Company, 2–7 Cavalry Regiment

Browning, Colin Lt, USMC, *Samurai 3*, Platoon Commander, 3d Platoon, Kilo Company, 3/5

Buhl, Willard LtCol, USMC, *Brahma 6*, Battalion Commander, 3d Battalion, 1st Marines (3/1)

Burns, Kyle LCpl, USMC, LAV Gunner, 1st Platoon, Charlie Company, 1st LAR Battalion, BLT 1/3 (Lt Paul Webber's gunner)

Butler, Alfred, Jr. Lt, USMC, Platoon Commander, 81mm Mortar Platoon, Weapons Company, 3/5 (member of Task Force Bruno)

Byrne, Brennan LtCol, USMC, Battalion Commander, 1st Battalion, 5th Marines (1/5) (April, 2004)

Carlisle, Cory Cpl, USMC, 3d Platoon, Kilo Company, 1st Battalion, 3d Marines

Casey, George GEN, USA, The first Commanding General, Multi-National Force – Iraq (MNF-I)

Cash, Joe Lt, USMC, Platoon Commander, Charlie Company, 2d Tank Battalion

Chambers, Ryan Cpl, USMC, 1st Platoon, Charlie Company, 1st Tank Battalion (Gunny Pop's gunner)

Chandler, Jon SSgt, USMC, 3d Platoon, Kilo Company, 3d Battalion, 1st Marines

Chessani, Jeffrey LtCol, USMC, Inchon 3, Operations Officer, 1st Marine Regiment (RCT-1)

Chontosh, Brian Capt, USMC, *Diesel 6*, Company Commander, India Company, 3d Battalion, 5th Marines

Christmas, George (Ron) Capt, USMC, Company Commander, Hotel Company, 2d Battalion, 5th Marines, Awarded Navy Cross and Purple Heart in Hue City, Vietnam

Cisneros, David Cpl, USMC, 1st Squad, 3d Platoon, Kilo Company, 3d Battalion, 5th Marines

Clairday, Jason Cpl, USMC, Team Leader, 1st Fire Team, 1st Squad, 2d Platoon, Kilo Company, 3/5

Clark, Brett Capt, USMC, *Raider 6*, Company Commander, India Company, 3d Battalion, 1st Marines

Cobb, James CPT, USA, Fire Support Officer, Task Force 2-2

Coduto, Gage Sgt, USMC, Squad Leader, 1st Squad, 2d Platoon, Kilo Company, 3d Battalion, 5th Marines

Colleton, Charles F, CW04, USMC, Regimental Gunner, 1st Marine Regiment (RCT-1)

Collier, Adam Capt, USMC, Liaison Officer to Co A, Iraqi Intervention Force (36 Commando)

Copsetta, Eric, Sgt, USMC, Squad Leader, 1st Squad, 1st Platoon, Kilo Company, 3d Battalion, 5th Marines

Cragholm, Michael Lt, USMC, *Samurai 1*, Platoon Commander, 1st Platoon, Kilo Company, 3/5

Cunningham, Aaron Capt, USMC, *Avenger 6*, Company Commander, Company A, 1st Battalion, 8th Marines

Desgrosseilliers, Todd Maj, USMC, *Darkhorse 5*, Executive Officer, 3d Battalion, 5th Marines 3/5 (commander, Task Force Bruno)

DeWitt, Lisa MAJ (Dr.), USA, Battalion Surgeon, Task Force 2-2

Diaz, William "Ben" Capt, USMC, *Samurai 5*, Executive Officer, Kilo Company, 3/5

Dinauer, Steve LtCol, USMC, *Wolfpack 6*, Battalion Commander, 3d Light Armored Reconnaissance Battalion

Distelhorst, Kenneth SSgt, USMC, Squad Leader, 2d Squad, 3d Platoon, Kilo Company, 3d Battalion, 5th Marines

Ducasse, Jose Sgt, USMC, Platoon Sergeant, 3d Platoon, Alpha Company, 2d Tank Battalion (Lee's wingman)

Dunford, Joseph BGen, USMC, Assistant Division Commander, 1st Marine Division

Escamilla, Herbierto Sgt, USMC, 1st Platoon, Charlie Company, 1st Tank Battalion (Gunny Pop's wingman)

Faulkenburg, Steve Command Sergeant Major, USA, Task Force 2-2

Fernandez, Jacob LCpl, 3d Squad, 2d Platoon, Kilo Company, 3d Battalion, 5th Marines

Fisher, Mason LCpl, USMC, 2d Squad, 3d Platoon, Kilo Company, 3d Battalion, 5th Marines

Fitts, Colin SSG, USA, Squad Leader, 1st Squad, 3d Platoon, A Company, Task Force 2-2

Formica, Michael Col, USA, *Black Jack 6*, Commanding Officer, 2d Brigade Combat Team, 1st Cavalry Division

Fowler, Paul CPT, USA, Company Commander, Alpha Company, 2d Battalion, 63d Armor Regiment, Attached to Task Force 2-2

Frias, Christopher LCpl, USMC, 1st Platoon, Charlie Company, 1st Tank Battalion (Gunny Pop's driver)

Fry, Derek 1stSgt, USMC, Company First sergeant, Alpha Company, 1/8

Gagucas, Joseph HN, USN, 3d Squad, 2d Platoon, Kilo Company, 3d Battalion, 5th Marines

Gantt, Anthony Cpl, USMCR, *White 3*, Tank Commander, 2d Platoon, Alpha Company, 2d Tank Battalion

Garcia, Jay Capt, USMC, *Blade 6*, Company Commander, Bravo Company, 1st Battalion, 3d Marines (1/3)

Guardiola, Samuel Sgt, USMC, Section Leader, 81mm Mortar Platoon, Weapons Company, 3/5, Member of Task Force Bruno

Glass, Peter CPT USA, *Cougar 6*, Company Commander, C Company, 3rd Battalion, 8th Cavalry Regiment

Gonzalez, Gerardo Pfc, USMC, 1st Squad, 1st Platoon, Kilo Company, 3d Battalion, 5th Marines

Gonzalez, Martin Sgt, USMC, Squad Leader, 2d Squad, 3d Platoon, Kilo Company, 3d Battalion, 5th Marines

Good, Mathew Capt, USMC, Company Commander, Headquarters Company, 3rd LAR Battalion

Grapes, Jesse Lt, USMC, *Spartan 3*, Platoon Commander, 3d Platoon, Kilo Company, 3/1

Griffin, Christian Maj, USMC, *Brahma 3*, Operations Officer, 3d Battalion, 1st Marines

Griffin, John Capt, USMC, *Apache 6*, A Company, 2nd Light Armored Reconnaissance Battalion

Harris, Albert SSG, USA, Senior Medic, A Company, Task Force 2-2

Hays, Alston LCpl, USMC, 1st Squad, 1st Platoon, Kilo Company, 3/5

Heatherman, Brian Capt, USMC, *Warrior 6*, Company Commander, Lima Company, 3d Battalion, 1st Marines

Helvenston, Scott, Blackwater contractor, killed March 31, 2004

Herbert, Frank GySgt, USMC, Tank Leader, Alpha Company, 2d Tank Battalion

Hernandez, Alex LCpl, USMC, 1st Platoon, Charlie Company, 1st Tank Battalion (Gunny Pop's loader)

Hillenburg, Eric LCpl, USMC, 81mm Mortar Platoon, Weapons Company, 3d Battalion, 5th Marines (member of Task Force Bruno)

Hodges, Erick LCpl, USMC, 1st Squad, 1st Platoon, Kilo Company, 3d Battalion, 5th Marines

Holder, Theodore S. II SSgt, USMC, Platoon Sergeant, 1st Platoon, Charlie Company, 1st LAR, BLT 1/3

Howard, Wayne SPC, USA, 3d Squad, A Company, 2d Battalion, 7th Cavalry Regiment

Hutchinson, Tim LCpl, USMC, H&S Company, 3d Light Armored Reconnaissance Battalion (Maj Ken Kassner's driver)

Icard, Travis LCpl USMC, 1st Fire Team, 1st Squad, 2d Platoon, Kilo Company, 3d Battalion, 5th Marines

Iversen, Joshua SSgt, USMC, Boat Captain, 4th Platoon, Small Craft Company

Iwan, Edward 1LT, USA, *Terminator 5*, Executive Officer, A Company, Task Force 2-2

Jacobs, John Lt, *Spartan 2*, Platoon Commander, 2d Platoon, Kilo Company, 3/1

Jadick, Richard CDR (Dr.), USN, Battalion Surgeon, 1st Battalion, 8th Marines

Jamison, Josh Lt, USMC, *Pale Rider 2*, Platoon Commander, 2d Platoon, Fox Company, 2/1

Jent, Timothy Capt USMC, *Spartan 6,* Company Commander, Kilo Company, 3d Battalion, 1st Marines

Johnson, Ron Col, USMC, Commanding Officer, 24th Marine Expeditionary Unit, 24th MEU

Juarez, Gilbert Capt, USMC, *War Pig 6,* Company Commander, Charlie Company, 1st LAR, BLT 1/3

Karcher, Tim MAJ, USA, *Ghost 3*, Operations Officer, 2d Battalion, 7th Cavalry Regiment (2-7)

Kasal, Brad 1stSgt, USMC, First Sergeant, Weapons Company, 3d Battalion, 1st Marines

Kassner, Kenneth Maj, USMC, *Wolfpack 5*, Executive Officer, 3d Light Armored Reconnaissance Battalion

Kielion, Shane LCpl, USMC, 2d squad, 1st Platoon, India Company, 3d Battalion, 5th Marines

Kilgore, Steven CW4, USA, Apache Copilot/Gunner with *Attack 6,* 1st Battalion, 227th Aviation Regiment

Kirk, Jeffrey Sgt, USMC, Squad Leader, 1st Squad, 3d Platoon, Kilo Company, 3d Battalion, 5th Marines

Klingensmith, David Lt, USMC, *Panzer 2*, Platoon Commander, 2d Platoon, Alpha Company, 2d Tank Battalion

Knight, Kristine SPC, North Carolina National Guard, Ambulance medic, attached to 1st Battalion, 8th Marines

Knight, Darric LtCol, USMC, *Raider 6,* Battalion Commander, 2nd Reconnaissance Battalion

Knospler, Jacob Cpl, USMC, Squad Leader, Bravo Company, 1st Battalion, 8th Marines

Knox, Steven 1stSgt, USMC, First Sergeant, Kilo Company, 3d Battalion, 5th Marines

Kirk, Jeffrey Sgt, USMC, Squad Leader, 3d Squad, 3d Platoon, Kilo Company, 3d Battalion, 5th Marines

Kraft, Jarrett Sgt, USMC, Squad Leader, 81mm Mortar Platoon, Weapons Company, 3/5 (member of Task Force Bruno)

LaPointe, Brian Lt, USMC, Platoon Commander, Engineer Platoon attached to 3/5

Lawson, Scott SSG, USA, 1st Squad, 3d Platoon, A Company, Task Force 2-2

Leardo, Eduardo III SgtMaj, USMC, Regimental Sergeant Major (member of Shupp's PSD), RCT-1

Lee, Jeffery Lt, USMC, *Panzer 3*, Platoon Commander, 3d Platoon, Alpha Company, 2d Tank Battalion

Lenard, William LCpl, USMC, 3d Squad, 2d Platoon, Kilo Company, 3d Battalion, 5th Marines

Leo, William Sgt, USMC, Squad Leader, 3d Platoon, Company A, 1st Battalion, 8th Marines

Levine, Philip LCpl, USMC, 81mm Mortar Platoon, Weapons Company, 3d Battalion, 5th Marines (member of Task Force Bruno)

Lopez, Hilario LCpl, USMC, 1st Squad, 2d Platoon, Kilo Company, 3d Battalion, 5th Marines

L'Etiole, Joe LtCol, USMC, Operations Officer, 1st Marine Division

Lewis, Ronald LTC, USA, *Attack 6,* Battalion Commander, 1st Battalion, 227th Aviation Regiment (1-227)

Malay, Patrick LtCol, USMC, *Darkhorse 6*, Battalion Commander, 3d Battalion, 5th Marines (3/5)

Malcom, Dan Lt, USMC, Platoon Commander, Weapons Platoon, Company A, 1/8

Markley, Mark Lt, USMC, *Panzer 5*, Executive Officer, Alpha Company, 2d Tank Battalion (Meyers' wingman)

Marquez, Christopher LCpl, USMC, 2d Platoon, Kilo Company, 3d Battalion, 1st Marines

McCaffrey, Todd LTC, USA, Battalion Commander, 1st Battalion, 5th Infantry Regiment

Mathes, Adam Lt, USMC, *Spartan 1*, Platoon Commander, 1st Platoon, Kilo Company, 3/1

Mattis, James MajGen, USMC, Commanding General, 1st Marine Division (until August 20, 2004)

Maxfield, Tristen SPC, USA, 1st Squad, 3d Platoon, A Company, Task Force 2-2

Mayfield, Kirk CPT, USA, Troop Commander, Brigade Reconnaissance Troop (BRT), F Troop, 4th CAV

McCaffrey, Todd LTC, USA, Battalion Commander, 1st Battalion, 5th Infantry Regiment

McCrum, Greg CPT, USA, Physician's Assistant, 2d Battalion, 2d Infantry Regiment

McNulty, Andrew Capt, USMC, *Samurai 6*, Company Commander, Kilo Company, 3/5

Meisenhalder, Michael Sergeant USMC, Platoon Scout, 3d Platoon, India Company, 3/5

Meno, Joaquin LT, USA, Platoon Leader, 3d Platoon, A Company, Task Force 2-2

Metz, Thomas LTG, USA, Commanding General, Multi-National Corps—Iraq (MNC-I), The first MNC-I commander

Meyers, Christopher Capt, USMC, *Panzer 6 also Black 6*, Company Commander, Alpha Company, 2d Tank Battalion (Markley's wingman)

Miller, Lee Col, USMC, Commanding Officer, 31st Marine Expeditionary Unit (MEU)

Misa, SPC, USA, 1st Squad, 3d Platoon, A Company, Task Force 2-2

Miska, Phillip LCpl, USMC, 2d Squad, 3d Platoon, Kilo Company, 3d Battalion, 5th Marines

Mitchell, Robert J. Jr. Cpl, USMC, Squad Leader, 3d Platoon, Kilo Company, 3d Battalion, 1st Marines

Miyamasu, Myles LTC, USA, *Black Knight 6,* Battalion Commander, 1st Battalion, 5th Cavalry Regiment

Moulder, Todd Lt, USMC, *Samurai 2*, Platoon Commander, 2d Platoon, Kilo Company, 3/5

Natonski, Richard MajGen, USMC, *Devil Dog 6*, Commanding General, 1st Marine Division

Navarro, Elber Sergeant, USMC, Squad Leader, 3d Squad, 1st Platoon, Kilo Company, 3/5

Newell, Peter LTC, USA, *Ramrod 6*, Commanding Officer, Task Force 2-2

Nicoll, Alexander Pfc, USMC, 3d Platoon, Kilo Company, 1st Battalion, 3d Marines

Nicholson, Larry Col, USMC, Regimental Commander (14 Sept Only), 1st Marine Regiment (RCT-1)

Norwood, Byron Sgt, USMC, CAAT Section Leader, Weapons Company, 3d Battalion, 1st Marines, Attached to 3d Platoon, Kilo Company, 3d Battalion, 1st Marines

O'Brien, Sean SGT, USA, Forward Observer, Task Force 2-2

Ohle, Lance SPC, USA, 1st Squad, 3d Platoon, A Company, Task Force 2-2

Olson, Gregg LtCol, USMC, Battalion Commander, 2d Battalion, 1st Marines (2/1) (April, 2004)

Omohundro, Read Capt, USMC, *Beowulf 6,* Company Commander, Company B, 1st Battalion, 8th Marines

Overbay, Greg SSGT, USAF, Joint Tactical Air Controller (JTAC), A Company, Task Force 2-2

Parrello, Brian Cpl, USMC, Team Leader and Boat Coxswain, 4th Platoon, Small Craft Company

Patton, Gary COL, USA, Commanding Officer, 2d Brigade Combat Team, 2d Infantry Division

Payton, George LCpl, USMC, 2d Squad, 3d Platoon, Kilo Company, 3d Battalion, 5th Marines

Pell, James HM3, USN, 2d squad, 1st Platoon, India Company, 3d Battalion, 5th Marines

Peralta, Rafael Sgt, USMC, Platoon Guide, 1st Platoon, Company A, 1st Battalion, 3d Marines

Phillips, James LCpl, USMC, 81mm Mortar Platoon, Weapons Company, 3d Battalion, 5th Marines (member of Task Force Bruno)

Pickering, Aaron LCpl, USMC, 2d Platoon, C Company, 1st Battalion, 3d Marines

Piddock, Robert Maj, USMC, *Darkhorse 3*, Operations Officer, 3d Battalion, 5th Marines

Pirak, Victor CPT, USA, *Cobra 6*, Company Commander, C Company 1st Battalion, 9th Infantry Regiment (attached to Task Force Wolfpack)

Pioske, Chad LCpl, USMC, 3d Squad, 3d Platoon, Kilo Company, 3d Battalion, 5th Marines

Popaditch, Nicholas GySgt, USMC, *Red 4*, Platoon Sergeant, 1st Platoon, Charlie Company, 1st Tank Battalion

Pruitt, Christopher Sgt, USMC, Platoon's Guide, 3d Platoon, Kilo Company, 3d Battalion, 1st Marines

Rainey, James LTC, USA, *Ghost 6*, Battalion Commander, 2d Battalion, 7th Cavalry Regiment

Ramos, Mike LtCol USMC, *Bronco 6*, Battalion Commander, 1st Battalion, 3d Marines

Read, Lucian, Freelance news photographer

Resto, Rudy SgtMaj, USMC, Battalion Sergeant Major, 3d Battalion, 5th Marines (3/5)

Reyes, Anibal SSG USA, *Red 2*, Tank Commander, 1st Platoon, C Company, 3rd Battalion, 8th Cavalry Regiment

Rios, Ricardo Cpl, USMC, Tank gunner, 3d Platoon, Alpha Company, 2d Tank Battalion (Lt Jeffery Lee's gunner)

Rodriguez, Rene Pvt, USMC, 3d Platoon, Kilo Company, 3d Battalion, 1st Marines

Rogero, Alonso HN, USN, Corpsman, 1st Squad, 1st Platoon, Kilo Company, 3d Battalion, 5th Marines

Rubio, Juan HM3, USN, Corpsman, 4th Platoon, Small Craft Company

Sanchez, Jose Cpl, USMC, 3d Platoon, Kilo Company, 3d Battalion, 1st Marines

Sanchez, Ricardo LTG, USA, Commanding General, Coalition Joint Task Force 7 (CJTF-7)

Santillana, Carlos SSG, USA, Squad Leader, 3d Squad, A Company, 2d Battalion, 7th Cavalry Regiment

Sattler, John LtGen, USMC, Commanding General, 1st Marine Expeditionary Force

Schaeffer, Dan LCpl, USMC, 2d Platoon, Kilo Company, 3d Battalion, 1st Marines

Sebastian, Ricardo SSgt, USMC, Machine Gun Section Leader, Weapons Platoon, Company A, 1st Battalion, 8th Marines (attached to 3d Platoon)

Sevald, Matthew LCpl, USMC, Loader, 3d Platoon, Alpha Company, 2d Tank Battalion (Lt Jeffery Lee's loader)

Severtsgard, Samuel LCpl, USMC, 3d Platoon, Kilo Company, 3d Battalion, 1st Marines

Seyford, Joseph SPC, USA, A Company, Task Force 2-2, Part of Captain Sims' Personal Security Detachment

Shane, Ryan GySgt, USMC, Bravo Company, 1st Battalion, 8th Marines

Shea, Kevin Maj, USMC, Communications Officer, 1st Marine Regiment (RCT-1)

Shupp, Michael Col, USMC, *Inchon 6*, Regimental Commander, 1st Marine Regiment (RCT-1)

Silcox, William Jr. Cpl, USMC, Team Leader, 2d Squad, 3d Platoon, Kilo Company, 3d Battalion, 5th Marines

Sims, Sean CPT, USA, *Terminator 6*, Company Commander, A Company, 2-2 Infantry Regiment

Sites, Kevin, Freelance NBC correspondent with 3d Battalion, 1st Marines

Skaggs, Michael Capt, USMC, Company Commander, Charlie Company, 1st Tank Battalion

Smith, Antoine LCpl, USMC, 1st Platoon, India Company, 3d Battalion, 5th Marines

Smith, Mathew SSG, USA, *Red 3*, Tank Commander, 1st Platoon, C Company, 3rd Battalion, 8th Cavalry Regiment

Smith, Peter 1SG, USA, First Sergeant, A Company, 2-2 Infantry Regiment

Smith, Raleigh Cpl, USMC, 81mm Mortar Platoon, Weapons Company, 3d Battalion, 5th Marines, Member of Task Force Bruno

Smith, Wes SGT, USA, Medic, 2-2 Infantry Regiment

Smithley, Aaron Lt, USMC, Comanche 5, Executive Officer, Charlie Company, 2d Tank Battalion (Bodisch's wingman)

Solis, Adam LCpl, USMC, LAV Gunner, 1st Platoon, Charlie Company, 1st LAR Battalion, BLT 1/3 (SSgt Holder's gunner)

Spencer, Rhyne Sgt, USMC, Vehicle Commander, 1st Platoon, Charlie Company, 1st LAR Battalion, BLT 1/3 (see front jacket photo)

Stalder, Keith MajGen, USMC, Commanding General, 3d Marine Air Wing

Stewart, Ian Cpl, USMC, 3d Squad, 3d Platoon, Kilo Company, 3d Battalion, 5th Marines

Stoddard, Kyle Capt, USMC, *Pale Rider 6*, Company Commander, Fox Company, 2d Battalion, 1st Marines

Sunnerville, Ryan Cpl, USMC, Team Leader, 1st Squad, 1st Platoon, Kilo Company, 3d Battalion, 5th Marines

Teague, Michael, Blackwater contractor, killed March 31, 2004

Tennant, Thomas Capt, USMC, *Spartan 6,* Company Commander, Company C, 1/3

Thomas, Andrew Lt, USMC, *Game Warden 4*, Platoon Commander, 4th Platoon, Small Craft Company

Toolan, John Col, USMC, Regimental Commander, 1st Marine Regiment (April 2003 – September 2004)

Trimble, Kevin Maj, USMC, *Hunter 3*, Operations Officer, 1st Battalion, 8th Marines (1/8)

Tucker, Craig Col (ret.), USMC, *Ripper 6*, Regimental Commander, 7th Marine Regiment, RCT-7

Twaddell, Edward III CPT, USA, *Apache 6*, Company Commander, A Company, 2-7 Cavalry Regiment van Doorn, Terrence Cpl, USMC, Squad Leader, 3d Squad, 1st Platoon, Kilo Company, 3/5

Vanhove, Michael LCpl, USMC, 3d Platoon, Kilo Company, 3d Battalion, 1st Marines

Vasey, Andrew Sgt, USMC, Boat Captain, 4th Platoon, Small Craft Company

Velez, Jose SPC, USA, 3d Squad, A Company, 2d Battalion, 7th Cavalry Regiment

Vinciguerra, Brian GySgt, USMC, Platoon Sergeant, 4th Platoon, Small Craft Company

Volpe, Paul Pfc, USMC, Bravo Company, 1st Battalion, 8th Marines

Webber, Paul Lt, USMC, *War Pig 1*, Platoon Commander, 1st Platoon, Charlie Company, 1st LAR, BLT 1/3

Wells, Lonny Sgt, USMC, 3d Platoon, Bravo Company, 1st Battalion, 8th Marines

Weemer, Ryan Cpl, USMC, 3d Platoon, Kilo Company, 3d Battalion, 1st Marines

Willis, David Cpl, USMC, Squad Leader, 3d Squad, 3d Platoon, C Company, 1/3

Winn, Mark Maj, USMC, *Hunter 5*, Executive Officer, 1st Battalion, 8th Marines (1/8)

Wittnam, Dan Maj, USMC, *Game Warden 6*, Company Commander, Small Craft Company, 2d Marine Division, Small Unit Riverine Craft on the Euphrates

Woods, Julian HM3, USN, 3d Squad, 3d Platoon, C Company, 1/3

Workman, Jeremiah Cpl, USMC, Squad Leader, 81mm Mortar Platoon, Weapons Company, 3/5 (member of Task Force Bruno)

Yeager, Kip LCpl, USMC, 2d Squad, 3d Platoon, Kilo Company, 3d Battalion, 5th Marines

Zovko, Jerry, Blackwater contractor, killed March 31, 2004

Appendix 3

Award Citations

The President of the United States Takes Pleasure in Presenting The Navy Cross
To
Christopher S. Adlesperger
Lance Corporal, United States Marine Corps
For Services as Set Forth in the Following

CITATION:

The President of the United States takes pride in presenting the Navy Cross (Posthumously) to Christopher S. Adlesperger, Private First Class, U.S. Marine Corps, for extraordinary heroism while serving as a Rifleman, Company K, Third Battalion, Fifth Marines, Regimental Combat Team 1, First Marine Division in support of Operation IRAQI FREEDOM on 10 November 2004. As Private First Class Adlesperger made entry into a house in the Jolan District of Al Fallujah, during Operation AL FAJR, his squad received a heavy volume of enemy machinegun fire from a well-prepared entrenched machine gun position. These fires instantly killed the point man, and injured another Marine and the platoon corpsman. Exposed to heavy enemy machine gun fire and grenades, Private First Class Adlesperger immediately attacked the enemy with rifle fire. While doing so, he suffered a fragmentation wound from enemy grenades. With the majority of his platoon pinned down by insurgent positions, Private First Class Adlesperger single—handedly cleared stairs and a roof top to move the injured to a rooftop where they could receive medical attention. On his own initiative, while deliberately exposing himself to heavy enemy fire, he established a series of firing positions and attacked the enemy, forcing them to be destroyed in place or to move into an area where adjacent forces could engage them. Disregarding his own wounds and physical exhaustion, Private First Class Adlesperger rejoined his platoon and demanded to take the point for a final assault on the same machine gun position. Once an Assault Amphibian Vehicle created a breach in the wall adjacent to the enemy's position, Private First Class Adlesperger was the first Marine to re-enter the courtyard where he eliminated a remaining insurgent at close range. When the fighting finally ceased, a significant number of insurgents from fortified positions had been eradicated. Through his actions, Private First Class Adlesperger destroyed the last strongpoint in the Jolan District of Al Fallujah, and saved the lives of his fellow Marines. By his outstanding display of decisive leadership, unlimited courage in the face of heavy enemy fire, and utmost devotion to duty, Private First Class Adlesperger reflected great credit upon himself and upheld the highest traditions of the Marine Corps and the United States Naval Service.

The President of the United States Takes Pleasure in Presenting The Navy Cross
To
Jason S. Clairday
Corporal, United States Marine Corps
For Services as Set Forth in the Following

CITATION:

For extraordinary heroism as Fire Team Leader, 1st Squad, 2nd Platoon, Company K, 3rd Battalion, 5th Marines, Regimental Combat Team 1, 1st Marine Division, during Operation Iraqi Freedom on 12 December 2004. While conducting a security sweep in the Askari District of al Fallujah, a platoon-sized insurgent force engaged 3rd Platoon. Corporal Clairday immediately repositioned his men and jumped a four foot gap three stories up onto the roof of the enemy stronghold where a mortally wounded Marine lay, isolated by the enemy. After throwing several fragmentation grenades, Corporal Clairday fiercely led the attack into the house. He was immediately hit with AK-47 rifle fire in both legs and fell into the kill zone. Under heavy enemy fire, he continued to aggressively engage the enemy while extracting himself from the doorway. Without regard for his own wounds, he rejoined the squad making entry and entered the house a second time. Once inside, he took control of the stack and repositioned himself in the front while suppressing the enemy using fragmentation grenades and his rifle. Again, without concern for his own safety, Corporal Clairday led the Marines into the room where he single-handedly attacked the insurgents and received mortal wounds. His courageous actions enabled reinforcing assault elements to destroy the insurgent position. By his outstanding display of decisive leadership, unlimited courage in the face of heavy enemy fire, and utmost devotion to duty, Corporal Clairday reflected great credit upon himself and upheld the highest traditions of the United States Marine Corps and the United States Naval Service.

The President of the United States Takes Pleasure in Presenting The Navy Cross
To
Dominic D. Esquibel
Corporal, United States Marine Corps
For Services as Set Forth in the Following

CITATION:

For extraordinary heroism while serving as Scout Sniper, Company B, 1st Battalion, 8th Marine Regiment, Regimental Combat Team 7, 1st Marine Division, I Marine Expeditionary Force, U.S. Marine Corps Forces, Central, in support of Operation Iraqi Freedom on 25 November 2004. After an enemy ambush on 3d Platoon nearby, Lance Corporal Esquibel quickly moved to an overwatch position and spotted five wounded Marines in a building courtyard. He courageously low-crawled close to the enemy stronghold to gain intelligence and then ran through the rooftops under intense enemy fire to relay the intelligence to the 3d Platoon Commander. With total disregard for his own safety, he re-occupied his position and threw a grenade, destroying several enemy insurgents and silencing one of the enemy's machine guns. After eliminating part of the threat, he low-crawled to another area and dropped a grenade through a hole in the roof, eliminating several more enemy personnel and silencing another enemy machine gun. As a tank breached the courtyard wall, 3d Platoon began suppressing the target building. He seized this opportunity and quickly moved to the courtyard while under enemy machine gun fire, dragging out a wounded Marine. He re-entered the courtyard to retrieve a second wounded Marine. Still under enemy fire, he moved through the open area a third time, extinguished a fire that had mortally wounded the third casualty, and swiftly carried out his body. Due to his heroic efforts, two Marines survived the devastating enemy ambush. By his outstanding display of decisive leadership, unlimited courage in the face of heavy enemy fire, and utmost devotion to duty, Lance Corporal Esquibel reflected great credit upon himself and upheld the highest traditions of the Marine Corps and the United States Naval Service.

The President of the United States Takes Pleasure in Presenting The Navy Cross
To
Bradley A. Kasal
First Sergeant, United States Marine Corps
For Services as Set Forth in the Following

CITATION:

The President of the United States takes pleasure in presenting the Navy Cross to Bradley A. Kasal, First Sergeant, U.S. Marine Corps, for extraordinary heroism while serving as First Sergeant, Weapons Company, Third Battalion, First Marine Regiment, Regimental Combat Team 1, FIRST Marine Division, I Marine Expeditionary Force, U.S. Marine Corps Forces Central Command in support of Operation IRAQI FREEDOM on 13 November 2004. First Sergeant Kasal was assisting 1st Section, Combined Anti-Armor Platoon as they provided a traveling over watch for 3d Platoon when he heard a large volume of fire erupt to his immediate front, shortly followed by Marines rapidly exiting a structure. When First Sergeant Kasal learned that Marines were pinned down inside the house by an unknown number of enemy personnel, he joined a squad making entry to clear the structure and rescue the Marines inside. He made entry into the first room, immediately encountering and eliminating an enemy insurgent, as he spotted a wounded Marine in the next room. While moving towards the wounded Marine, First Sergeant Kasal and another Marine came under heavy rifle fire from an elevated enemy firing position and were both severely wounded in the legs, immobilizing them. When insurgents threw grenades in an attempt to eliminate the wounded Marines, he rolled on top of his fellow Marine and absorbed the shrapnel with his own body. When First Sergeant Kasal was offered medical attention and extraction, he refused until the other Marines were given medical attention. Although severely wounded himself, he shouted encouragement to his fellow Marines as they continued to clear the structure. By his bold leadership, wise judgment, and complete dedication to duty, First Sergeant Kasal reflected great credit upon himself and upheld the highest traditions of the Marine Corps and the United States Naval Service.

The President of the United States Takes Pleasure in Presenting The Navy Cross
To
Jarrett A. Kraft
Sergeant, United States Marine Corps
For Services as Set Forth in the Following

CITATION:

The President of the United States takes pleasure in presenting the Navy Cross to Jarrett A. Kraft, Sergeant, U.S. Marine Corps, for extraordinary heroism while serving as Squad Leader, 81-millimeter Mortar Platoon, Weapons Company, Third Battalion, 5th Marine Regiment, Regimental Combat Team 1, FIRST Marine Division, I Marine Expeditionary Force, U.S. Marine Corps Forces, Central, in support of Operation IRAQI FREEDOM on 23 December 2004. As numerically superior insurgent forces attacked Sergeant Kraft and the Marines in Al Fallujah, Iraq, he quickly organized and fearlessly led three assault forces on three separate attacks to repel the insurgents and ensure the successful advance of the battalion. With complete disregard for his own life, he placed himself between intense enemy fire and the men during each attack providing suppressive fire and leadership to sustain the fight and eliminate the enemy. Although grenades thrown by the insurgents rendered him momentarily unconscious during one assault, this did not dampen his spirit or determination. Undeterred, Sergeant Kraft continued to lead from the front, despite being wounded himself. On two more occasions, he was knocked down stairwells by enemy grenade blasts and finally while emplacing a sniper in a critical location, Sergeant Kraft was knocked down by the blast from a friendly M1A1 tank main gun. He demonstrated courageous leadership with a complete disregard for his own safety, during this desperate two-hour battle as he personally braved multiple enemy small arms kill zones to render assistance and guidance to his Marines. By his outstanding display of decisive leadership, unlimited courage in the face of heavy enemy fire, and utmost devotion to duty, Sergeant Kraft reflected great credit upon himself and upheld the highest traditions of the Marine Corps and the United States Naval Service.

The President of the United States Takes Pleasure in Presenting The Navy Cross
To
Aubrey L. McDade
Sergeant, United States Marine Corps
For Services as Set Forth in the Following

CITATION:

For extraordinary heroism while serving as Machine Gun Squad Leader attached to 1st Platoon, Company B, First Battalion, Eighth Marines, Regimental Combat Team &, First Marine Division, in support of Operation IRAQI FREEDOM on 11 November 2004. Shortly after departing a platoon firm base and proceeding south toward Phase Line Grace, 1st Platoon entered an alley and encountered an immediate heavy volume of small arms and machine gun fire. In the opening seconds of the engagement, three Marines were seriously wounded as the well positioned and expecting enemy pinned others down. On contact, Sergeant McDade rushed from the rear of the platoon column toward the kill zone and immediately deployed a machine gun team into the alley to provide suppressive fire on the enemy. After several attempts to reach casualties in the alley were met with heavy, well-aimed machine gun fire, he showed total disregard for his own safety by moving across the alley and successfully extracting the first of three wounded Marines from the kill zone. Aware of the fact that there were still two wounded Marines in the alley, Sergeant McDade dashed through the heart of the kill zone two more times, each time braving intense enemy fire to successfully retrieve a Marine. After extracting the last casualty from the kill zone, he assisted in the treatment and medical evacuation to these Marines. His quick thinking and aggressive actions were crucial in saving the lives of two of the three casualties. Sergeant McDade's undaunted courage, fighting spirit and total devotion to duty reflected great credit upon him and were in keeping with the highest traditions of the Marine Corps and of the United States Naval Service.

The President of the United States Takes Pleasure in Presenting The Navy Cross
To
Robert J. Mitchell, Jr.
Corporal, United States Marine Corps
For Services as Set Forth in the Following

CITATION:

The President of the United States takes pleasure in presenting the Navy Cross to Robert J. Mitchell, Jr., Corporal, U.S. Marine Corps, for extraordinary heroism while serving as Squad Leader, Company K, Third Battalion, First Marine Regiment, Regimental Combat Team 1, 1st Marine Division, I Marine Expeditionary Force, U.S. Marine Corps Forces, Central, in support of Operation IRAQI FREEDOM on 13 November 2004. During a ferocious firefight with six insurgents fighting inside a heavily fortified house, Corporal Mitchell courageously attacked the enemy strongpoint to rescue five wounded Marines trapped inside the house. Locating the enemy positions and completely disregarding his own safety, he gallantly charged through enemy AK-47 fire and hand grenades, in order to assist a critically wounded Marine in an isolated room. Ignoring his own wounds, he began the immediate first aid treatment of the Marine's severely wounded leg. Assessing that the Marine needed immediate intravenous fluids to survive, he suppressed the enemy, enabling a Corpsman to cross the impact zone. Once the Corpsman arrived, he moved to the next room to assist other casualties. While running across the impact zone a second time, he was hit in the left leg with a ricochet off of his weapon and with grenade shrapnel to the legs and face. While applying first aid, he noticed a wounded insurgent reach for his weapon. With his rifle inoperable, he drew his combat knife, stabbed the insurgent, and eliminated him instantly. Demonstrating great presence of mind, he then coordinated the casualties' evacuation. Limping from his own wounds, Corporal Mitchell assisted in the evacuation of the last casualty through the impact zone under enemy fire, ultimately saving the lives of multiple Marines. By his bold leadership, wise judgment, and complete dedication to duty, Corporal Mitchell reflected great credit upon himself and upheld the highest traditions of the Marine Corps and the United States Naval Service.

The President of the United States Takes Pleasure in Presenting The Navy Cross
To
Rafael Peralta
Sergeant, United States Marine Corps
For Services as Set Forth in the Following

CITATION:

For extraordinary heroism while serving as Platoon Guide with 1st Platoon, Company A, 1st Battalion, 3d Marines, Regimental Combat Team 7, 1st Marine Division, in action against Anti-Coalition Forces in support of Operation AL FAJR, in Fallujah, Iraq on 15 November 2004. Clearing scores of houses in the previous three days, Sergeant Peralta asked to join an under strength squad and volunteered to stand post the night of 14 November, allowing fellow Marines more time to rest. The following morning, during search and attack operations, while clearing the seventh house of the day, the point man opened a door to a back room and immediately came under intense, close-range automatic weapons fire from multiple insurgents. The squad returned fire, wounding one insurgent. While attempting to maneuver out of the line of fire, Sergeant Peralta was shot and fell mortally wounded. After the initial exchange of gunfire, the insurgents broke contact, throwing a fragmentation grenade as they fled the building. The grenade came to rest near Sergeant Peralta's head. Without hesitation and with complete disregard for his own personal safety, Sergeant Peralta reached out and pulled the grenade to his body, absorbing the brunt of the blast and shielding fellow Marines only feet away. Sergeant Peralta succumbed to his wounds. By his undaunted courage, intrepid fighting spirit, and unwavering devotion to duty, Sergeant Peralta reflected great credit upon himself and upheld the highest traditions of the Marine Corps and the United States Naval Service.

The President of the United States Takes Pleasure in Presenting The Navy Cross
To
Jeremiah W. Workman
Corporal, United States Marine Corps
For Services as Set Forth in the Following

CITATION:

The Navy Cross is presented to Jeremiah W. Workman, Corporal, U.S. Marine Corps, for extraordinary heroism while serving as Squad Leader, Mortar Platoon, Weapons Company, 3d Battalion, 5th Marine Regiment, Regimental Combat Team 1, 1st Marine Division, U.S. Marine Corps Forces, Central Command in support of Operation IRAQI FREEDOM on 23 December 2004. During clearing operations in Al Fallujah, Iraq, Corporal Workman displayed exceptional situational awareness while organizing his squad to enter a building to retrieve isolated Marines inside. Despite heavy resistance from enemy automatic weapons fire, and a barrage of grenades, Corporal Workman fearlessly exposed himself and laid down a base of fire that allowed the isolated Marines to escape. Outside the house, he rallied the rescued Marines and directed fire onto insurgent positions as he aided wounded Marines in a neighboring yard. After seeing these Marines to safety, he led another assault force into the building to eliminate insurgents and extract more Marines. Corporal Workman again exposed himself to enemy fire while providing cover fire for the team when an enemy grenade exploded directly in front of him causing shrapnel wounds to his arms and legs. Corporal Workman continued to provide intense fire long enough to recover additional wounded Marines and extract them from the besieged building. Although injured, he led a third assault into the building, rallying his team one last time to extract isolated Marines before M1A1 tanks arrived to support the battle. Throughout this fight, Corporal Workman's heroic actions contributed to the elimination of 24 insurgents. By his bold leadership, wise judgment, and complete dedication to duty, Corporal Workman reflected great credit upon himself and upheld the highest traditions of the Marine Corps and the United States Naval Service.

To All Who Shall See These Presents Greeting:
This is to Certify that
The President of the United States of America
Authorized by Act of Congress July 9, 1918
Has Awarded The

To:
Elliot L. Ackerman
Second Lieutenant, U.S. Marine Corps (Reserve)
Company A, 1st Battalion, 8th Marines, RCT 7, 1st Marine Division, I MEF

CITATION:

The President of the United States takes pleasure in presenting the Silver Star Medal to Elliot L. Ackerman, Second Lieutenant, U.S. Marine Corps (Reserve), for conspicuous gallantry and intrepidity in action against the enemy while serving as Platoon Commander, First Platoon, Company A, First Battalion, Eighth Marines, Regimental Combat Team 7, FIRST Marine Division in support of Operation IRAQI FREEDOM II from 10 to 15 November 2004. During a ferocious enemy counter-attack in the insurgent stronghold of Fallujah, with complete disregard for his own safety, Second Lieutenant Ackerman twice exposed himself to vicious enemy fire as he pulled wounded Marines out of the open into shelter. When the amphibious tractors sent to evacuate his wounded men could not locate his position, he once again left the safety of his covered position and rushed through a gauntlet of deadly enemy fire to personally direct the amphibious tractors towards his wounded Marines. On 11 November as the battle continued, Second Lieutenant Ackerman recognized the exposed position of his Marines on the rooftops and ordered them to seek cover in the buildings below. Shortly afterwards, he personally assumed the uncovered rooftop position, prompting a hail of deadly fires from the enemy. With rounds impacting all around him, he coolly employed an M240G machine gun to mark targets for supporting tanks, with devastating effects on the enemy. Throughout the battle and despite his own painful shrapnel wounds, he simultaneously directed tank fires, coordinated four separate medical evacuations, and continually attacked with his platoon directly into the heart of the enemy with extreme tenacity. Second Lieutenant Ackerman's bold leadership, personal initiative, and total devotion to duty reflected great credit upon him and were in keeping with the highest traditions of the United States Naval Service.

To All Who Shall See These Presents Greeting:
This is to Certify that
The President of the United States of America
Authorized by Act of Congress July 9, 1918
Has Awarded The

Silver Star Medal
To:
Benny Alicea
Specialist, U.S. Army
Company A, 2d Battalion, 7th Infantry Regiment, 1st Cavalry Division

CITATION:

The President of the United States of America, authorized by Act of Congress July 9, 1918 (amended by an act of July 25, 1963), takes pleasure in presenting the Silver Star to Sergeant [then Specialist] Benny J. Alicea, United States Army, for conspicuous gallantry and intrepidity in action while serving with Company A, 2d Battalion, 7th Infantry Regiment, 1st Cavalry Division, during combat operations in support of Operation IRAQI FREEDOM, on 4 November 2004, in Iraq. Sergeant Alicea, then a Specialist serving as a rifleman and grenadier in Company A, demonstrated gallantry in the face of the enemy during Operation PHANTOM FURY. While injured and under extreme pressure, he saved the lives of his squad mates. Specialist Alicea's super size fires curtailed the enemy's ability to accurately engage multiple wounded soldiers through an intense firefight. His actions are a testament to his love for his comrades and demonstrate the "Never Quit" attitude of a First Cavalry Division soldier. His actions reflect great credit upon himself, Alpha Company 2-7 Cavalry, the "Ghost" Battalion, the First Cavalry Division, and the United States Army.

Synopsis:

Sergeant Alicea, then a Specialist serving as a rifleman and grenadier in Company A, was part of a door-to-door sweep to round up terrorist suspects when his squad was ambushed at a two-story house along the primary north-south road in Fallujah. Dropping back into the courtyard, with gunfire spraying out of the house and from across the street, Sergeant Alicea was struck in the hip and buttocks by shrapnel from two grenades that had been rolled through the front door. Moving away from the courtyard, the squad headed for the street. After continuing to fire on the house, Sergeant Alicea was the last to emerge. When his wounded leg gave out, he huddled into a position alongside three wounded comrades in the middle of the road as multiple rounds flew all around them. He continued firing his weapon at the insurgent forces until his own ammunition was exhausted. He then grabbed magazines from the wounded and managed to protect the position until another Bradley fighting vehicle arrived on the scene. He helped load the most seriously injured soldiers before finally being taken away himself. By his heroic actions he Sergeant Alicea saved the lives of three of his comrades.

To All Who Shall See These Presents Greeting:
This is to Certify that
The President of the United States of America
Authorized by Act of Congress July 9, 1918
Has Awarded The

Silver Star Medal
To:
David Bellavia
Staff Sergeant, U.S. Army

Company A, Task Force 2-2, 1st Infantry Division, RCT 7, 1st Marine Division, I MEF

CITATION:

The President of the United States of America, authorized by Act of Congress July 9, 1918 (amended by an act of July 25, 1963), takes pleasure in presenting the Silver Star to Staff Sergeant David Bellavia, United States Army, for conspicuous gallantry and intrepidity in action while serving with Company A, Task Force 2-2, 1st Infantry Division, during combat operations in support of Operation IRAQI FREEDOM during the battle for Al Fallujah, Iraq, on 10 November 2004. Staff Sergeant Bellavia's personal bravery and selfless actions are in keeping with the highest traditions of the military service and reflect great credit upon himself, 1st Infantry Division and the United States Army.

NARRATIVE TO ACCOMPANY AWARD:

Staff Sergeant David Bellavia distinguished himself by conspicuous gallantry and intrepidity in action while serving with Company A, Task Force 2-2, 1st Infantry Division, in support of Operation IRAQI FREEDOM during the battle for Al Fallujah, Iraq, on 10 November 2004. On that date Sergeant Bellavia's platoon was ordered to clear a block of 12 buildings from which Jihadists were firing on American forces. The first nine buildings were unoccupied, but were found to be filled with enemy rockets, grenade launchers and other kinds of weapons. When Bellavia and four others entered the tenth building, they came under fire from insurgents in the house. Other soldiers came to reinforce the squad and a fierce battle at close quarters ensued. Many American soldiers were injured from the gunfire and flying debris.

At this point, Sergeant Bellavia, armed with a M249 SAW gun, entered the room where the insurgents were located and sprayed the room with gunfire, forcing the Jihadists to take cover and allowing the squad to move out into the street. Jihadists on the roof began firing at the squad, forcing them to take cover in a nearby building. Sergeant Bellavia then went back to the street and called in a Bradley Fighting Vehicle to shell the houses. After this was done, he decided to re-enter the building to determine whether the enemy fighters were still active. Seeing a Jihadist loading an RPG launcher, Sergeant Bellavia gunned him down. A second Jihadist began firing as the soldier ran toward the kitchen and Bellavia fired back, wounding him in the shoulder. A third Jihadist began yelling from the second floor. Sergeant Bellavia then entered the uncleared master bedroom and emptied gunfire into all the corners, at which point the wounded insurgent entered the room, yelling and firing his weapon. Sergeant Bellavia fired back, killing the man.

Sergeant Bellavia then came under fire from the insurgent upstairs and the staff sergeant returned the fire, killing the man. At that point, a Jihadist hiding in a wardrobe in a bedroom jumped out, firing wildly around the room and knocking over the wardrobe. As the man leaped over the bed he tripped and Sergeant Bellavia shot him several times, wounding but not killing him. Another insurgent was yelling from upstairs, and the wounded Jihadist escaped the bedroom and ran upstairs. Sergeant Bellavia pursued, but slipped on the blood-soaked stairs. The wounded insurgent fired at him but missed. He followed the bloody tracks up the stairs to a room to the left. Hearing the wounded insurgent inside, he threw a fragmentary grenade into the room, sending the wounded Jihadist onto the roof. The insurgent fired his weapon in all directions until he ran out of ammunition. He then started back into the bedroom, which was rapidly filling with smoke.

Hearing two other insurgents screaming from the third story of the building, Sergeant Bellavia put a choke hold on the wounded insurgent to keep him from giving away their position. The wounded Jihadist then bit Sergeant Bellavia on the arm and smacked him in the face with the butt of his AK-47. In the wild scuffle that followed, Sergeant Bellavia took out his knife and slit the Jihadist's throat. Two other insurgents who were trying to come to their comrade's rescue, fired at Bellavia, but he had slipped out of the room, which was now full of smoke and fire. Without warning, another insurgent dropped from the third story to the second-story roof. Sergeant Bellavia fired at him, hitting him in the back and the legs and causing him to fall off the roof, dead. At this point, five members of 3d Platoon entered the house and took control of the first floor. Before they would finish off the remaining Jihadists, however, they were ordered to move out of the area because close air support had been called in by a nearby unit.

To All Who Shall See These Presents Greeting:
This is to Certify that
The President of the United States of America
Authorized by Act of Congress July 9, 1918
Has Awarded The

Silver Star Medal
To:

Dale Allen Burger, Jr.
Corporal, U.S. Marine Corps
Company I, 3d Battalion, 1st Marines, RCT 1, 1st Marine Division, I MEF

CITATION:

The President of the United States takes pride in presenting the Silver Star Medal (Posthumously) to Dale Allen Burger, Jr., Corporal, U.S. Marine Corps, for conspicuous gallantry and intrepidity in action against the enemy while serving as Squad Leader, Company I, Third Battalion, First Marine Regiment, Regimental Combat Team 1, FIRST Marine Division, I Marine Expeditionary Force, in support of Operation IRAQI FREEDOM II from 9 to 14 November 2004. During an intense firefight, Corporal Burger's squad leader was knocked unconscious and suffered a concussion from a rocket-propelled grenade. Realizing the platoon's attack was losing momentum, Corporal Burger immediately assumed the squad leader's responsibilities and quickly directed his fire teams to establish positions in nearby buildings. Displaying heroic leadership and tactical proficiency, he personally led a team to a rooftop and neutralized several enemy sniper positions with accurate fire, enabling the Platoon to regain critical momentum. Despite withering enemy fire and with total disregard for his personal safety, Corporal Burger employed his M-203 grenade launcher and two AT-4 rockets, eliminating enemy insurgents operating in adjacent buildings. Leading the squad in an assault against a large group of insurgents occupying a building, he was seriously wounded and evacuated. Disregarding his wounds, he volunteered to return to the Platoon three days later. During an ensuing firefight, Corporal Burger encountered three severely wounded Marines inside a house where numerous insurgents were barricaded behind fortified positions. Again disregarding his own safety, and under heavy enemy fire, he charged into the house to recover his fellow Marines. While valiantly returning fire and calling for the wounded Marines, he received enemy fire and fell mortally wounded. By his bold leadership, wise judgment, and complete dedication to duty, Corporal Burger reflected great credit upon himself and upheld the highest traditions of the Marine Corps and the United States Naval Service.

To All Who Shall See These Presents Greeting:
This is to Certify that
The President of the United States of America
Authorized by Act of Congress July 9, 1918
Has Awarded The

Silver Star Medal
To:
Chad Cassady
Sergeant, U.S. Marine Corps
Company L, 3d Battalion, 1st Marines, RCT 1, 1st Marine Division, I MEF

CITATION:

The President of the United States takes pleasure in presenting the Silver Star Medal to Chad Cassady, Sergeant, U.S. Marine Corps, for conspicuous gallantry and intrepidity in action against the enemy while serving as Scout Sniper Team Leader, Company L, 3d Battalion, 1st Marine Division, I Marine Expeditionary Force, U.S. Marine Corps Forces, Central, in Al Fallujah, Iraq, in support of Operation IRAQI FREEDOM on 9 November 2004. Sergeant Cassady demonstrated extraordinary leadership, undaunted bravery, and tactical expertise in the execution of his duties. During the multiple engagements, he consistently displayed courage under fire through his rapid decision-making and confident actions. Under sustained, heavy, and highly accurate enemy direct and indirect fire he repeatedly exposed himself to save the lives of several wounded Marines who were trapped in the open, pulling them to safety despite his own multiple, serious wounds. Sergeant Cassady refused to accept medical aid until all other wounded Marines were treated. Throughout the intense urban combat, his judgment and tactical proficiency were unrivaled. His presence of mind and physical courage while under fire were inspiring and undoubtedly saved lives. By his bold leadership, resolute determination, and complete dedication to duty, Sergeant Cassady reflected great credit upon himself and upheld the highest traditions of the Marine Corps and the United States Naval Service.

To All Who Shall See These Presents Greeting:
This is to Certify that
The President of the United States of America
Authorized by Act of Congress July 9, 1918
Has Awarded The

Silver Star Medal
To:
Timothy Connors
Corporal, U.S. Marine Corps
Company A, 1st Battalion, 8th Marines, RCT 7, 1st Marine Division, I MEF

CITATION:

The President of the United States takes pleasure in presenting the Silver Star Medal to Timothy Connors, Corporal, U.S. Marine Corps, for conspicuous gallantry and intrepidity in action against the enemy while serving as Third Squad Leader, Second Platoon, Company A, First Battalion, Eighth Marine Regiment, Regimental Combat Team 7, FIRST Marine Division, I Marine Expeditionary Force, U.S. Marine Corps Forces, Central, in support of Operation IRAQI FREEDOM from 10 to 15 November 2004. As Second Platoon came under heavy enemy fire from concealed positions on three sides, Corporal Connors effectively directed the fire of the squad as the platoon attempted to move into surrounding buildings for cover. When the squad entered a building for cover, the first Marine in the door was mortally wounded by several enemies who were defending a heavily fortified machine gun position. Corporal Connors and his fellow non-commissioned officers re-entered the building only to be forced back by a tenacious enemy. He directed the use of improvised explosive devices and a shoulder-launched multi-purpose assault weapon to create a secondary breach and eliminate the enemy position. When it was evident the improvised explosive devices and rocket failed to penetrate the enemy stronghold, Corporal Connors led a group of non-commissioned officers of Second Platoon into the enemy stronghold. Under intense enemy machine gun fire and without regard to his own personal safety, Corporal Connors eliminated the enemy with hand grenades and deadly accurate small arms fire at close proximity. By his bold leadership, wise judgment, and complete dedication to duty, Corporal Connors reflected great credit upon himself and upheld the highest traditions of the Marine Corps and the United States Naval Service.

To All Who Shall See These Presents Greeting:
This is to Certify that
The President of the United States of America
Authorized by Act of Congress July 9, 1918
Has Awarded The

Silver Star Medal
To:
Todd S. Desgrosseilliers

Major, U.S. Marine Corps
Task Force Bruno, 3d Battalion, 5th Marines, RCT 1, 1st Marine Division, I MEF

CITATION:

The President of the United States takes pleasure in presenting the Silver Star Medal to Todd S. Desgrosseilliers, Major, U.S. Marine Corps, for conspicuous gallantry and intrepidity in action against the enemy while serving as Officer-in-Charge, Task Force BRUNO, Third Battalion, Fifth Marine Regiment, Regimental Combat Team 1, FIRST Marine Division, I Marine Expeditionary Force, U.S. Marine Corps Forces, Central Command, in support of Operation IRAQI FREEDOM II from 12 to 23 December 2004. On 12 December, Major Desgrosseilliers was leading Task Force BRUNO in clearing operations when several Marines became trapped inside a building by intense enemy fire. During the engagement, an enemy grenade landed in the midst of the Marines. With complete disregard for his own safety, Major Desgrosseilliers shielded them from the explosion with his own body. Ignoring shrapnel wounds, he rallied his Marines and directed grenade, heavy machine gun and tank fire to destroy the 15 insurgents in the house. On 23 December, Task Force BRUNO came under heavy enemy fire while conducting operations in hostile territory. Throughout the firefight, he personally cleared several rooms and eliminated insurgents with rifle and grenade fire. When one of the Marines was seriously wounded he exposed himself to direct enemy fire and helped drag him to safety. Despite being wounded again with shrapnel during the firefight, he remained in the open to direct a devastating volume of tank main gunfire until the enemy was destroyed. In this engagement, 30 insurgents were killed including key terrorist leadership. By his bold leadership, wise judgment, and complete dedication to duty, Major Desgrosseilliers reflected great credit upon himself and upheld the highest traditions of the Marine Corps and the United States Naval Service.

To All Who Shall See These Presents Greeting:
This is to Certify that
The President of the United States of America
Authorized by Act of Congress July 9, 1918
Has Awarded The

Silver Star Medal
To:
Paul A. Fowler
Captain, U.S. Army
Company A, 2d Battalion, 63rd Armor Regiment, Task Force 2-2,
1st Marine Division

Synopsis:

The President of the United States takes pleasure in presenting the Silver Star Medal to Paul A. Fowler, Captain, U.S. Army, for conspicuous gallantry and intrepidity in action while Commanding the 2d Battalion, 63rd Armor Regiment, during combat operations in support of Operation IRAQI FREEDOM, during November 2004, in Iraq. During the battle for Fallujah, Captain Fowler executed a successful armored assault against several hundred enemy fighters in the northeastern part of the city, securing the flanks of battalions on either side. During a 14-hour firefight, he remained in position at the head of his company during house-to-house fighting in which nearly all of his tanks were attacked with grenades and small arms. On the third night of the operation, Captain Fowler led a house-to-house assault in southeast Fallujah that ended after 12 hours when his company destroyed a strong point occupied by 30 enemy fighters.

To All Who Shall See These Presents Greeting:
This is to Certify that
The President of the United States of America
Authorized by Act of Congress July 9, 1918
Has Awarded The

Silver Star Medal
To:
Samuel Guardiola
Sergeant, U.S. Marine Corps
Weapons Company, 3d Battalion, 5th Marines, RCT 1, 1st Marine Division,
I MEF

CITATION:

The President of the United States takes pleasure in presenting the Silver Star Medal to Samuel Guardiola, Sergeant, U.S. Marine Corps, for conspicuous gallantry and intrepidity in action against the enemy as Section Leader, Mortar Platoon, Weapons Company, Third Battalion, Fifth Marine Regiment, Regimental Combat Team 1, FIRST Marine Division, U.S. Marine Corps Forces, Central Command, in support of Operation IRAQI FREEDOM on 23 December 2004. While searching for enemy weapons caches, Sergeant Guardiola's section was ambushed by insurgents occupying well-fortified positions. Realizing that they were trapped in the impact zone, he exposed himself to intense enemy fire in order to reorganize and consolidate his Marines. Upon discovering two of his Marines were isolated inside a building, he gathered an assault force to recover them. Sergeant Guardiola used the adjacent rooftop to access the building and reach the Marines inside, while constantly under small arms and grenade fire. Once inside, he found his fallen comrades and immediately planned their evacuation. As the enemy assaulted with a fragmentation grenade, he covered the Marines with his own body to shield them from the enemy grenade, which did not detonate. Despite intense enemy fire, Sergeant Guardiola carried one fallen Marine down three flights of stairs, clearing rooms along the way with his 9 millimeter pistol. Although exhausted and dehydrated, he continued to carry his comrade to the evacuation point. By his bold leadership, wise judgment, and complete dedication to duty. Sergeant Guardiola reflected great credit upon himself and upheld the highest traditions of the Marine Corps and the United States Naval Service.

To All Who Shall See These Presents Greeting:
This is to Certify that
The President of the United States of America
Authorized by Act of Congress July 9, 1918
Has Awarded The

Silver Star Medal
To:
Theodore S. Holder, II
Staff Sergeant, U.S. Marine Corps
Light Armored Reconnaissance Company, Battalion Landing Team 1/3,
Regimental Combat Team 7, 1st Marine Division, I MEF

CITATION:

The President of the United States takes pride in presenting the Silver Star Medal (Posthumously) to Theodore S. Holder, II, Staff Sergeant, U.S. Marine Corps, for conspicuous gallantry and intrepidity in action against the enemy while serving as Platoon Sergeant, Light Armored Reconnaissance Company, Battalion Landing Team 1/3, Regimental Combat Team 7, FIRST Marine Division, I Marine Expeditionary Force, U.S. Marine Corps Forces Central Command in support of Operation IRAQI FREEDOM on 11 November 2004. While conducting a movement to contact through the city of Al Fallujah, Iraq, Staff Sergeant Holder and his Light Armored Reconnaissance Company was ambushed from the front and right flank. A heavy volume of enemy small arms and rocket-propelled grenade fire hit the lead vehicle, severely wounding one of the scouts. With no way for the scouts to remount their vehicle without exposing themselves to a devastating wall of machine gun fire, Staff Sergeant Holder, with complete disregard for his own safety, skillfully maneuvered his vehicle directly into the enemy's line of fire in order to protect them. Even as a burst of machine gun fire hit the turret wounding him, he continued to remain exposed and guide the fires of the gunner onto the enemy positions. As the enemy fire began to concentrate on the vehicle, he continued to fire an M-240G machine gun and control the fires of the vehicle's main gun. As the enemy fire continued to build, he was seriously wounded once again. Despite the severity of his wounds, he continued to man the machine gun and return fire upon the enemy, eventually succumbing to his fatal injuries. By his bold leadership, wise judgment, and complete dedication to duty, Staff Sergeant Holder reflected great credit upon himself and upheld the highest traditions of the Marine Corps and the United States Naval Service.

To All Who Shall See These Presents Greeting:
This is to Certify that
The President of the United States of America
Authorized by Act of Congress July 9, 1918
Has Awarded The

Silver Star Medal
To:
Kristopher D. Kane
Corporal, U.S. Marine Corps
Company C, 1st Battalion, 3d Marines, RCT 7, 1st Marine Division, I MEF

CITATION:

The President of the United States takes pleasure in presenting the Silver Star Medal to Kristopher D. Kane, Corporal, U.S. Marine Corps, for conspicuous gallantry and intrepidity in action against the enemy while serving as Squad Automatic Weapon Gunner, Second Platoon, Company C, Battalion Landing Team, First Battalion, Third Marine Regiment, Regimental Combat Team 7, FIRST Marine Division, I Marine Expeditionary Force, U.S. Marine Corps Forces, Central, in support of Operation IRAQI FREEDOM on 10 November 2004. During Operation AL FAJR, insurgent forces engaged a squad from Second Platoon as they moved up the stairs of a house. Responding to a call for assistance, Corporal Kane entered the building amidst a hail of enemy armor piercing rounds fired at him through the ceiling and dodged hand grenades that were tossed down the stairs. When he observed wounded Marines trapped in the enemy line of fire, Corporal Kane immediately positioned himself to provide covering fire for the Marines attempting to pull the wounded to safety all the while remaining dangerously exposed to the enemy's impact zone. He repeatedly thwarted insurgent attempts to fire their machine guns down the stairs at the fellow Marines with accurate and deadly fire from his Squad Automatic Weapon. He held his ground, in the direct line of enemy fire, even as a D-9 armored bulldozer punched a hole in an adjacent wall and the building began collapsing around him. As the last of the wounded were being evacuated, portions of the building fell on top of him, crushing his leg. His heroic actions and selfless devotion inspired all who observed him and were instrumental in the evacuation of Marines needing urgent medical care, and in the destruction of an enemy stronghold. By his bold leadership, wise judgment, and complete dedication to duty, Corporal Kane reflected great credit upon himself and upheld the highest traditions of the Marine Corps and the United States Naval Service.

To All Who Shall See These Presents Greeting:
This is to Certify that
The President of the United States of America
Authorized by Act of Congress July 9, 1918
Has Awarded The

Silver Star Medal
To:
Jeffrey L. Kirk
Sergeant, U.S. Marine Corps
Company K, 3d Battalion, 5th Marines, RCT 1, 1st Marine Division, I MEF

CITATION:

The President of the United States takes pride in presenting the Silver Star Medal (Posthumously) to Jeffrey L. Kirk, Sergeant, U.S. Marine Corps, for conspicuous gallantry and intrepidity in action against the enemy while serving as First Squad Leader, Third Platoon, Company K, Third Battalion, Fifth Marine Regiment, Regimental Combat Team 1, First Marine Division, I Marine Expeditionary Force, U.S. Marine Corps Forces, Central, in support of Operation IRAQI FREEDOM on 10 November 2004. While Sergeant Kirk and his squad gained entry into a building, insurgents threw a grenade from a room containing a hardened machine gun position. Sergeant Kirk quickly organized and led Marines from multiple squads across an open courtyard to eliminate the threat. Effective enemy small arms fire forced him and the other Marines to withdraw to a covered position while returning fire with grenades and small arms. Unfazed, Sergeant Kirk re-grouped his men behind cover and attacked the building a second time. Although wounded as he approached the position, he continued to attack by throwing a grenade into the room and then eliminating the enemy machine gunner with a rifle. Enemy fire and grenades again erupted from the same room. Sergeant Kirk and the Marines withdrew once more, throwing grenades in their wake. Refusing medical attention, he remained as the point man and led the Marines in for a third assault on the enemy position. He quickly overwhelmed and destroyed the remaining insurgents, clearing the building to the roof. His extraordinary actions in the face of great danger destroyed a key defensive position and prevented the enemy from inflicting serious casualties on other Marines. By his outstanding display of decisive leadership, unlimited courage in the face of heavy enemy fire, and utmost devotion to duty, Sergeant Kirk reflected great credit upon himself and upheld the highest traditions of the Marine Corps and the United States Naval Service.

To All Who Shall See These Presents Greeting:
This is to Certify that
The President of the United States of America
Authorized by Act of Congress July 9, 1918
Has Awarded The

Silver Star Medal
To:
Jeffrey T. Lee
First Lieutenant, U.S. Marine Corps
Company A, 2d Tank Battalion, RCT 7, 1st Marine Division, I MEF

CITATION:

The President of the United States takes pleasure in presenting the Silver Star Medal to Jeffrey T. Lee, First Lieutenant, U.S. Marine Corps, for conspicuous gallantry and intrepidity in action against the enemy as Third Platoon Commander, Company A, Second Tank Battalion, Regimental Combat Team 7, First Marine Division, I Marine Expeditionary Force, U.S. Marine Corps Forces Central

Command in support of Operation IRAQI FREEDOM II from 8 to 11 November 2004. Second Lieutenant Lee's aggressive leadership and bold decisions provided the catalyst for the Regiment's success during two major firefights. While attached to Company C, he destroyed numerous enemy, allowing the infantry company to take their objective. Operating for more than 12 hours and desperately low on fuel, he accepted great tactical risk and continued to destroy the enemy. This decision led to the successful taking of the Battalion's objective. While attached to Company A, Task Force 1/8, he led an attack south. While eliminating numerous insurgents all around him, he was shot through his right arm. Refusing medical attention, he continued to fight the enemy and help Company A achieve success. In spite of his gunshot wound, he pushed the assault two more city blocks to reach the battalion phase line. At this time, the tank was critically exposed in a courtyard while the infantry developed positions in the buildings. He continued to eliminate insurgents who attacked the tenuous infantry position. His aggressiveness and bravery broke the enemy's will, and were critical to the success of the Company as it attacked into the heart of the enemy defenses. By his bold leadership, wise judgment, and complete dedication to duty, Second Lieutenant Lee reflected great credit upon himself and upheld the highest traditions of the Marine Corps and the United States Naval Service.

To All Who Shall See These Presents Greeting:
This is to Certify that
The President of the United States of America
Authorized by Act of Congress July 9, 1918
Has Awarded The

Silver Star Medal
To:
Kirk Mayfield
Captain, U.S. Army
Troop F, 4th Cavalry, 1st Infantry Division

Synopsis:

The President of the United States takes pleasure in presenting the Silver Star Medal to Kirk Mayfield, Captain, U.S. Army, for conspicuous gallantry and intrepidity in action while Commanding Troop F, 4th Cavalry, 1st Infantry Division, in combat against enemy forces in support of Operation IRAQI FREEDOM, in November 2004, in Iraq. At the beginning of the attack on Fallujah, Captain Mayfield occupied an attack-by-fire position on the northeast edge of the city. From there he spent eight hours directing artillery; mortar and direct fire against an entrenched enemy platoon while himself under constant small-arms, grenade, sniper and mortar attack. His unit ultimately destroyed the enemy position, killing 30 insurgents just before the main attack. Once the assault began, he maintained his position ahead of the force and continued to direct fire against the enemy. His unit killed 75 insurgents during the first 30 hours of battle. Early in the battle, his unit opened a key highway and cut off the line of retreat for the insurgents. On the fourth day, he volunteered his troops in an 18-hour effort to clear 60 houses, battle enemy fighters literally room-to-room, killing 25 insurgents.

To All Who Shall See These Presents Greeting:
This is to Certify that
The President of the United States of America
Authorized by Act of Congress July 9, 1918
Has Awarded The

Silver Star Medal
To:
Peter Newell
Lieutenant Colonel, U.S. Army
2d Battalion, 2d Infantry Regiment, 1st Infantry Division

Synopsis:

The President of the United States takes pleasure in presenting the Silver Star Medal to Peter Newell, Lieutenant Colonel (Infantry), U.S. Army, for conspicuous gallantry and intrepidity in action while commanding the 2d Battalion, 2d Infantry Regiment, 1st Infantry division, during combat action against enemy forces in support of Operation IRAQI FREEDOM, in November 2004, at Fallujah, Iraq. Lieutenant Colonel Newell deployed a 550-soldier mechanized task force on 72 hours' notice to Fallujah in November 2004, leading a continuous 12-day attack in the heavily fortified Askari district. His forces overwhelmed resistance in the first 14 hours, ultimately killing 330 enemy fighters, capturing 48 others, destroying 38 weapons caches, two roadside- bomb factories and one car-bomb factory while becoming the first battalion in the division to achieve its objective. On 12 November Lieutenant Colonel Newell was caught in an ambush following an 11-hour night attack. Narrowly escaping enemy fire, he left his tracked vehicle and personally assisted in the evacuation of a mortally wounded officer.

To All Who Shall See These Presents Greeting:
This is to Certify that
The President of the United States of America
Authorized by Act of Congress July 9, 1918
Has Awarded The

Silver Star Medal
To:
Traver D. Pennell
Sergeant, U.S. Marine Corps
Company I, 3d Battalion, 1st Marines, RCT 1, 1st Marine Division, I MEF

CITATION:

The President of the United States takes pleasure in presenting the Silver Star Medal to Traver D. Pennell, Sergeant, U.S. Marine Corps, for conspicuous gallantry and intrepidity in action against the enemy while serving as Squad Leader, Company I, Third Battalion, First Marines, Regimental Combat Team 1, FIRST Marine Division, I Marine Expeditionary Force, in support of Operation IRAQI FREEDOM on 14 and 15 November 2004. Sergeant Pennell displayed unyielding personal courage while leading his attacking squad through sustained high intensity urban combat in south Fallujah, Iraq. As an adjacent squad entered a house occupied by nine fanatical insurgents, the squad came under heavy enemy fire and sustained numerous casualties. Demonstrating great presence of mind, he unhesitatingly led his squad in an assault into the house to assist his fellow Marines. Locating a Marine shot in the face, Sergeant Pennell, under intense grenade and small arms fire, rescued the Marine and carried him to safety. He immediately called for assistance and courageously re-entered the house with another Marine. With bullets impacting all around them, Sergeant Pennell directed his Marines to lay down suppressive fire as he searched for the remaining wounded. Immediately, the enemy PKM machine gun fire struck Sergeant Pennell's comrade. Ignoring this intense machine gun fire, he proceeded to suppress the enemy with lethally accurate fire of his own, rescue his fellow Marine and carry him to safety. Sergeant Pennell's multiple attacks and accurate fire repeatedly drew the enemy's attention and allowed a supporting attack from an adjacent platoon to clear the house and rescue the remaining wounded. By his bold leadership, wise judgment, and complete dedication to duty, Sergeant Pennell reflected great credit upon himself and upheld the highest traditions of the Marine Corps and the United States Naval Service.

To All Who Shall See These Presents Greeting:
This is to Certify that
The President of the United States of America
Authorized by Act of Congress July 9, 1918
Has Awarded The

Silver Star Medal
To:
Richard Pillsbury
Staff Sergeant, U.S. Marine Corps
Company A, 1st Battalion, 8th Marines, RCT 7, 1st Marine Division, I MEF

CITATION:

The President of the United States takes pleasure in presenting the Silver Star Medal to Richard Pillsbury, Staff Sergeant, U.S. Marine Corps, for conspicuous gallantry and intrepidity in action against the enemy while serving as Platoon commander with Second Platoon, Company A, First Battalion, Eighth Marines, Regimental Combat Team 7, FIRST Marine Division, in support of Operation IRAQI FREEDOM from 10 November to 10 December 2004. In Fallujah on 10 November, after successfully taking the eastern sector of the Mayor's complex and evacuating his Platoon Commander, Staff Sergeant Pillsbury found himself thrust into the role of Platoon Commander in what would turn out to be two weeks of intense house-to-house fighting. Leading with great skill, presence of mind, and calm effectiveness, he repeatedly directed his Marines and supporting arms in attacks on many buildings, under heavy enemy fires, and in direct, close combat. On one tragic occasion during a firefight, an errant 500-pound bomb landed 20 meters from his building. Although his platoon suffered three casualties, he calmly orchestrated the evacuation while continuing to fight. On 15 November, approximately 50 meters short of the limit of advance, one of his squads entered a house to clear it. As the squad came under intense small arms and machine gun fire, one of his Marines was killed. Realizing that he could easily lose his entire platoon piece by piece if they continued to enter the house, he utilized the tank main gun to destroy the house and insurgents. He then orchestrated a heroic entry into the house and was able to destroy remaining enemy fighters, and retrieve the body of the fallen Marine. Staff Sergeant Pillsbury's calmness in the face of impending hardship inspired absolute trust and loyalty from his platoon. By his courageous actions, zealous initiative, and total devotion to duty, Staff Sergeant Pillsbury reflected great credit upon himself and upheld the highest traditions of the Marine Corps and the United States Naval Service.

To All Who Shall See These Presents Greeting:
This is to Certify that
The President of the United States of America
Authorized by Act of Congress July 9, 1918
Has Awarded The

Silver Star Medal
To:
Nicholas A. Popaditch

Gunnery Sergeant, U.S. Marine Corps
Company C, 1st Tank Battalion, 2d Battalion, 1st Marines,
1st Marine Division,
I MEF

CITATION:

The President of the United States takes pleasure in presenting the Silver Star Medal to Nicholas A. Popaditch, Gunnery Sergeant, U.S. Marine Corps, for conspicuous gallantry and intrepidity in action against the enemy while serving as Tank Platoon Sergeant, First Platoon, Company C, First Tank Battalion, Second Battalion, First Marine Regiment, FIRST Marine Division, I Marine Expeditionary Force, in support of Operation IRAQI FREEDOM from 6 to 7 April 2004. While on patrol in the city of Al Fallujah, Iraq, Fox Company came under heavy enemy fire and without hesitation, Gunnery Sergeant Popaditch surged his two tanks into the city to support the Marines under fire. He led his tank section several blocks into the city, drawing enemy fire away from the beleaguered Marines. His decisive actions enabled Fox Company to gain a foothold into the city and evacuate a critically wounded Marine. For several hours, enemy forces engaged his tank section with withering rocket-propelled grenade fire until they were destroyed by accurate machine gun fire. Acting as the forward observer for an AC-130 gunship, Gunnery Sergeant Popaditch directed fire onto enemy targets effecting their annihilation. With complete disregard for his personal safety, he moved his tank forward to draw the enemy from their covered and concealed positions allowing the AC-130 to engage them. On the morning of 7 April, Gunnery Sergeant Popaditch was severely wounded by a rocket-propelled grenade blast while fighting insurgents. Blinded and deafened by the blast, he remained calm and ordered his crew to a medical evacuation site. By his bold leadership, wise judgment, and complete dedication to duty, Gunnery Sergeant Popaditch reflected great credit upon himself and upheld the highest traditions of the Marine Corps and the United States Naval Service.

To All Who Shall See These Presents Greeting:
This is to Certify that
The President of the United States of America
Authorized by Act of Congress July 9, 1918
Has Awarded The

Silver Star Medal
To:
Juan M. Rubio

Hospital Corpsman Third Class, U.S. Navy
Small Craft Company, 1st Marine Division, I MEF

CITATION:

The President of the United States takes pleasure in presenting the Silver Star Medal to Juan M. Rubio, Hospital Corpsman Third Class, U.S. Navy, for conspicuous gallantry and intrepidity in action against the enemy while serving as a Platoon Corpsman attached to the 4th Platoon, Small Craft Company, FIRST Marine Division, I Marine Expeditionary Force, U.S. Marine Forces Central Command, in support of Operation IRAQI FREEDOM on 1 January 2005. During a dismounted patrol along the Euphrates River, 4th Platoon was ambushed in a complex attack by a well-emplaced and determined enemy. As Petty Officer Rubio and an assault element swept through the ambush site, insurgents detonated an improvised explosive device. Rocket- propelled grenades, machine gun, and small arms fire followed immediately after the explosion wounding three Marines. Realizing the severity of the Marines' wounds, and although bleeding profusely from wounds to his wrist and elbow, Petty Officer Rubio low-crawled across open terrain, exposing himself to enemy fire to provide triage. Working simultaneously on three urgent surgical casualties, Petty Officer Rubio coached his fellow Marines who were assisting other casualties as the volume of incoming fire intensified. Upon stabilizing the wounded for casualty evacuation, he directed the Platoon to provide covering fire as he and several Marines began moving the casualties back towards the watercraft. Without regard for his own life, he once again exposed himself to the heavy and accurate enemy fire moving the Marines from the ambush site to the shoreline. By his bold leadership, wise judgment, and complete dedication to duty, Petty Officer Rubio reflected great credit upon himself and upheld the highest traditions of the United States Naval Service.

To All Who Shall See These Presents Greeting:
This is to Certify that
The President of the United States of America
Authorized by Act of Congress July 9, 1918
Has Awarded The

Silver Star Medal
To:
Sean P. Sims
Captain, U.S. Army
Company A, 2d Battalion, 2d Infantry Regiment, 1st Infantry Division

Synopsis:

The President of the United States takes pride in presenting the Silver Star Medal (Posthumously) to Sean P. Sims, Captain (Infantry), U.S. Army, for conspicuous gallantry and intrepidity in action while serving with the 2d Battalion, 2d Infantry Regiment, 1st Infantry Division, during combat action against enemy forces in support of Operation IRAQI FREEDOM near Fallujah, Iraq, during November 2004. Captain Sims planned and executed the task force's main attack against entrenched enemy forces, then held position under constant fire to establish a foothold in northeast Fallujah. He led a 14-hour house-to-house fight, frequently leaving the safety of his Bradley fighting vehicle, then led a fight to seize, then hold Highway 10 against constant enemy counterattack. His company killed more than 40 enemy fighters, destroyed 35 homemade bombs and a dozen weapons caches. He was shot and killed while clearing a building in Fallujah November 13.

To All Who Shall See These Presents Greeting:
This is to Certify that
The President of the United States of America
Authorized by Act of Congress July 9, 1918
Has Awarded The

Silver Star Medal
To:
Peter L. Smith
First Sergeant, U.S. Army
Company A, 2d Battalion, 2d Infantry Regiment, 1st Infantry Division

Synopsis:

The President of the United States takes pleasure in presenting the Silver Star Medal to Peter L. Smith, First Sergeant, U.S. Army, for conspicuous gallantry and intrepidity in action while serving with the 2d Battalion, 2d Infantry Regiment, 1st Infantry Division, during combat operations in support of Operation IRAQI FREEDOM, in Fallujah, Iraq. Under heavy fire during the battle for Fallujah on 12 November 2004, Smith organized the evacuation of his company executive officer, who was fatally wounded. The next day he led the company during 18 hours of intense house-to-house fighting after the company commander also was killed in action.

To All Who Shall See These Presents Greeting:
This is to Certify that
The President of the United States of America
Authorized by Act of Congress July 9, 1918
Has Awarded The

Silver Star Medal
To:
Sean A. Stokes
Corporal, U.S. Marine Corps
Company L, 3d Battalion, 1st Marines, 1st Marine Division, I MEF

CITATION:

The President of the United States takes pride in presenting the Silver Star Medal (Posthumously) to Sean A. Stokes, Corporal, U.S. Marine Corps, for conspicuous gallantry and intrepidity in action against the enemy while serving as Rifleman, 1st Platoon, Company L, Third Battalion, First Marines, FIRST Marine Division, I Marine Expeditionary Force, from 9 November 2004 to 18 November 2004, in support of Operation IRAQI FREEDOM 03-05. Throughout nine days of high intensity urban combat in Fallujah, Corporal Stokes fought as his unit's point man, requiring him to repeatedly be the first man to engage enemy forces. On 9 and 11 November, Corporal Stokes led a four man element into a building held by armed enemy. As they entered the building, his element was engaged with automatic rifle fire from within. Fearless in the face of danger, Corporal Stokes pressed forward in the close confines of the building against the enemy fire and killed the insurgent before his fellow Marines could be injured. On 17 November, an enemy hand grenade exploded beneath Corporal Stokes as he cleared a small house, severely wounding him. Though dazed and wounded from the blast, and rather than attempting to save himself and exit the building, he chose to ensure the Marines around him were protected and began suppressing the enemy within the house with his rifle. The fire he provided allowed the rest of his team to reach a covered position outside the house, where they organized an assault and reentered the building, killing the enemy in a counterattack. Corporal Stokes fought through Fallujah with the resolve of closing on the enemy, while protecting the Marines around him at all costs. By his extraordinary heroism in the face of extreme danger, zealous initiative, and exceptional dedication to duty, Corporal Stokes reflected great credit upon himself and upheld the highest traditions of the Marine Corps and the United States Naval Service.

To All Who Shall See These Presents Greeting:
This is to Certify that
The President of the United States of America
Authorized by Act of Congress July 9, 1918
Has Awarded The

Silver Star Medal
To:
Jose "Freddy" Velez
Corporal, U.S. Army
Company A, 2d Battalion, 7th Infantry Regiment, 1st Cavalry Division
Specialist, U.S. Army
CITATION:

The President of the United States of America, authorized by Act of Congress July 9, 1918 (amended by an act of July 25, 1963), takes pleasure in presenting the Silver Star to Specialist Jose A. Velez, for meritorious achievement in the face of the enemy during Operation Phantom Fury. Specialist Velez, while under extreme enemy fire, saved the lives of his squad mates. As the squad automatic rifleman, Specialist Velez' suppressive fire diminished the enemy's ability to accurately engage his squad through two intense firefights. His valorous actions reflect great credit upon himself, 1st Cavalry Division, Multi-National Corps Iraq, and the United States Army.

Synopsis:

The President of the United States takes pride in presenting the Silver Star Medal (Posthumously) to Jose "Freddy" Velez, Corporal, U.S. Army, for conspicuous gallantry and intrepidity in action while serving with Company A, 2d Battalion, 7th Infantry Regiment, 1st Cavalry Division, during combat operations in support of Operation IRAQI FREEDOM on 4 November 2004. When his unit was attacked in Fallujah, Iraq, Corporal Velez was killed by a sniper as he stood over wounded comrades in efforts to shield them from enemy fire.

Bibliography

Barnard, Anne. "Inside Fallujah's War." *The Boston Globe*, November 28, 2004.

Bellavia, David, with John R. Bruning. *House to House*. New York: Free Press, 2007.

Bossie, David, "Perfect Valor." Citizens United, 2009.

Blanding, Michael. "The Opposite of Fear." *Tufts Magazine*, Boston, Spring 2007.

Carlson, Peter. "A Hero Who Didn't Save Himself." *The Washington Post*, March 4, 2007.

Cobb, Capt James T., USA, 1stLt Christopher A. LaCour, USA, and William H. Height, SFC USA. "The Fight for Fallujah – TF 2-2 in FSE AAR: Indirect Fires in the Battle for Fallujah." *Field Artillery Magazine*, March-April, 2005, pp. 22-28.

Creed, Philip. "Corpsman Awarded Silver Star." *Navy Times*, June 12, 2006.

Filkins, Dexter. "Disguised in Iraqi Uniforms, Rebels Kill a Marine." *The New York Times*, November 13, 2004.

Flight 33 Productions. "SHOOTOUT! Return to Fallujah." The History Channel, December 15, 2006.

Helms, Nathaniel R. *My Men are My Heroes*. Des Moines, Iowa: Meredith Books, 2007.

Jadick, Richard, with Thomas Hayden. *On Call in Hell*. New York: NAL Caliber, 2007.

Kaemmerer, Lance Corporal T. J. "A Hero's Sacrifice." *Marine Corps News*, December 2, 2004.

Kjeilen, Tore. "Iraq: History." *Encyclopedia of the Orient*, http://i-cias.com/e.o/iraq_5.htm

Krulak, Gen. Charles C. *Marine Corps Doctrinal Publication 1 – Warfighting*. Washington, D.C.: Department of the Navy, Headquarters United States Marine Corps, June 20, 1997.

———. "The Three Block War: Fighting in Urban Areas." *Vital Speeches of the Day*. Vol. 64, Iss. 5 (December 15, 1997), pp. 139-142.

Lidden, Jennifer. "Tracing the History of Fallujah." Interview with Annas Shallal, National Public Radio, November 13, 2004.

Natonski, LtGen Richard, USMC. *Operation Al Fajr – The Battle for Fallujah.* (PowerPoint Briefing.) 2007.

O'Donnell, Patrick K. *We Were One*. Cambridge, Massachusetts: Da Capo Press, 2006.

Perry, Tom. "His Corps Value Was Bravery." *Los Angeles Times*, October 3, 2006.

Popaditch, Nicholas, with Mike Steere. *Once a Marine: An Iraq War Tank Commander's Inspirational Memoir of Combat, Courage, and Recovery*. New York: Savas Beatie LLC, 2008.

Ripley, J.W., Colonel, U.S. Marine Corps (Ret). *Marine Corps Historical Center Writing Guide.* Washington Navy Yard, Washington, D.C.: History and Museums Division, Marine Corps Historical Center, 2004.

Robinson, Linda. *Masters of Chaos – The Secret History of the Special Forces*. New York: Public Affairs, 2004.

Roux, Georges. *Ancient Iraq*. New York: Penguin Books, 1992.

Sheeler, Jim. "Remembering the Brave." *Rocky Mountain News*, July 22, 2006.

Sparks, Maj Daniel B., USMCR, ed. *Small Unit Actions*. Quantico, VA: History Division, Marine Corps University, 2007.

Webber, Paul. "What Veterans Day Means to Me." Www.crashfistfight. blogspot.com, November 11, 2007.

West, Bing. *No True Glory*. New York: Bantam Dell, 2005.

Background Material

While the following documents were not specifically cited, they provided essential background material that enabled me to pull the entire story together.

Bethea, Maj Theodore C., II, USMC. *Company Summary of Events During Phantom Fury Phase IIIB, 1st Battalion, 8th Marines*. United States Marine Corps.

Bodisch, Capt Robert, USMC. *Operation AL FAJR Combat Chronology of Company C, 2d Tank Battalion – 7-20 November 2004 Al Fallujah Iraq.*

———. *Charlie Company, 2d Tank Battalion After Action Report, Operation Al Fajr.*

Christmas, Maj Ron, USMC. "A Company Commander Remembers the Battle of Hue." *Marine Corps Gazette*, February 1977, pp. 19-26.

Dinauer, LtCol Steven, USMC. *Task Force Wolfpack: Operation Al Fajr (Phantom Fury) After Action Report.* (Power Point Presentation.) December 15, 2004.

Estes, LtCol Kenneth W. USMC (ret.). *U.S. Marine Corps Operations in Iraq, 2003-2006.* Washington, D.C.: History Division, United States Marine Corps, April 2008.

Griffin, Capt John F., USMC. *Monthly Report, September 2004, Company A 2d Light Armored Reconnaissance Battalion.* United States Marine Corps.

———. *Monthly Report October 2004, Company A 2d Light Armored Reconnaissance Battalion.* United States Marine Corps.

———. *Monthly Report November 2004, Company A 2d Light Armored Reconnaissance Battalion.* United States Marine Corps.

———. *Monthly Report December 2004, Company A 2d Light Armored Reconnaissance Battalion.* United States Marine Corps.

Glubb, Sir John. *A Short History of the Arab Peoples.* New York: Stein and Day, 1970.

Hollis, Patricia Slayden. "Second Battle of Fallujah – Urban Operations in a New Kind of War – Interview with LtGen John F. Sattler." *Field Artillery Magazine*, March-April 2006.

Knight, LtCol Darric M., USMC. *Command Chronology Report for November 2004, 2d Reconnaissance Battalion.* United States Marine Corps.

———. "The Three Block War: Fighting in Urban Areas." *Vital Speeches of the Day.* Vol. 64, Iss. 5 (December 15, 1997), pp. 139-142.

Matthews, Matt. *Operation AL FAJR: A Study in Army and Marine Corps Joint Operations.* Global War on Terrorism Occasional Paper 20. Fort Leavenworth, Kansas: Combat Studies Institute Press, 2006.

McDonnell, Patrick J. "Fallujah Insurgency Chaotic, Persistent." *The Los Angeles Times*, November 12, 2004.

McNulty, Capt Andrew, USMC. *Operation Order 3-04: Phantom Fury.*

Meyers, Capt Christopher V., USMC. *Operation Phantom Fury Chronology, Company A, 2d Tanks.*

Price, Jay, Joseph Neff and Charles Crain. "Chapter 6: Fury Boils to Surface." *The News and Observer*, www.newsobserver.com, October 23, 2005.

Sattler, LtGen John F., USMC. *I MEF Command Chronology, July – December, 2004.* United States Marine Corps.

Shupp, Col Michael, USMC. *1st Marines, 1st Marine Division Command Chronology, September – December, 2004.* United States Marine Corps.

Tracy, Gunnery Sergeant Patrick, USMC. *Street Fight in Iraq*. Oceanside: Leatherneck Publishing, 2006.

Interviews

Operational Leadership Experiences in the Global War on Terrorism, Combat Studies Institute, Fort Leavenworth, Kansas.

LtGen Richard Natonski, USMC, with Laurence Lessard, 04/05/06
LTC Peter Newell, USA, with Matt Matthews, 03/23/06
LTC James Rainey, USA, with Matt Matthews, 04/19/06
Major Robert Bodisch, USMC, with Jenna Fike, 10/26/09
MAJ (Dr.) Lisa DeWitt, USA, with Matt Matthews, 03/23/06
CPT Chris Brooke, USA, with Matt Matthews, 05/01/06
CPT James Cobb, USA, with Matt Matthews, 06/02/06
CPT Peter Glass, USA, with Matt Matthews, 03/29/06
CPT Edward Twaddell, III, USA, with Matt Matthews, 02/28/06

Personal Interviews

Lt General (ret.) Ron Christmas, USMC, Telephone Interview, 12/05/07
Lt General Thomas F. Metz, USA, Personal Interview, 05/20/08
Lt General Richard F. Natonski, USMC, Telephone Interview, 10/11/07
Lt General Richard F. Natonski, USMC, Telephone Interview, 03/11/07
Lieutenant General John F. Sattler, USMC, Telephone Interview, 12/03/07
Lieutenant General Keith J. Stalder, USMC, Telephone Interview, 11/20/07
Lieutenant General Keith J. Stalder, USMC, Telephone Interview, 08/08/07
Major General Richard Formica, USA, Personal Interview, 05/23/08
Brigadier General Larry Nicholson, USMC, Telephone Interview, 03/10/08
Brigadier General Gary Patton, USA, Telephone Interview, 02/01/08
Brigadier General Joseph Dunford, USMC, Telephone Interview, 11/16/07
Colonel Gareth Brandl, USMC, Telephone Interview, 11/20/07
Colonel Willard Buhl, USMC, Telephone Interview, 12/04/07
Colonel Joseph (Jay) A. Bruder, USMC, Telephone Interview, 10/10/07
Colonel Steve Dinauer, USMC, Personal Interview, 09/24/07

Colonel James Donlan, USMC Personal Interview, 09/26/07

Colonel Michael Formica, USA, Telephone Interview, 11/06/07

Colonel Keil Gentry, USMC, Personal Interview, 05/19/08

Colonel Darric Knight, USMC, Telephone Interview, 03/03/08

Colonel Ronald Lewis, USA, Telephone Interview, 02/15/08

Colonel Patrick Malay, USMC, Telephone Interview, 10/05/07

Colonel Patrick Malay, USMC, Telephone Interview, 11/04/07

Colonel Peter Newell, USA, Telephone Interview, 10/29/07

Colonel James Rainey, USA, Telephone Interview, 11/07/07

Colonel Mike Ramos, USMC, Telephone Interview, 03/04/08

Colonel Michael Shupp, USMC, Telephone Interview, 09/03/07

Colonel Michael Shupp, USMC, Personal Interview, 09/25/07

Colonel Michael Shupp, USMC, Telephone Interview, 01/21/07

Colonel (ret.) Craig Tucker, USMC, Telephone Interview, 01/10/08

Lt Colonel George Bristol, USMC, Telephone Interview, 11/07/07

Lt Colonel Todd Desgrosseilliers, USMC, Telephone Interview, 12/07/07

Lt Colonel Tim Karcher, USA, Telephone Interview, 02/15/08

Lt Colonel Kenneth Kassner, USMC, Telephone Interview, 11/04/07

Lt Colonel Jay Kopelman, USMC, Telephone Interview, 05/22/08

Lt Colonel Joe L'Etiole, USMC, Telephone Interview, 10/29/07

Lt Colonel Chris Mahoney, USMC, Telephone Interview, 12/27/07

Lt Colonel Myles Miyamasu, USA, Telephone Interview, 11/06/07

Lt Colonel Brent Norquist, USMC, Telephone Interview, 11/28/07

Lt Colonel Francis Piccoli, USMC, Telephone Interview, 12/04/07

Lt Colonel Robert Piddock, USMC, Telephone Interview, 04/10/08

Lt Colonel Nicholas Vuckovich, USMC, Telephone Interview, 11/21/07

Lt Colonel Nicholas Vuckovich, USMC, Personal Interview, 05/22/08

Lt Colonel Jack Waldron, USA, Telephone Interview, 10/06/07

Lt Colonel Mark Winn, USMC, Personal Interview, 05/19/08

Major Bill Arnold, USMCR, Telephone Interview, 01/09/08

Major Theodore Bethea II, USMC, Personal Interview, 05/20/08

Major Eduardo Bitanga, USMC, Telephone Interview, 02/15/08

Major Robert Bodisch, USMC, Telephone Interview, 01/07/08

Major Chris Brooke, USA, Telephone Interview, 01/11/08

Major Aaron Cunningham, USMC, Telephone Interview, 07/09/08

Major (Dr.) Lisa DeWitt, USA, Telephone Interview, 12/22/07

Major Kevin Forkin, USMCR, Telephone Interview, 10/05/07

Major Mathew Good, USMC, Telephone Interview, 10/29/07

Major John Griffin, USMC, Telephone Interview, 11/04/07
Major Travis Homiak, USMC, Personal Interview, 01/16/08
Major Scott Jackson, USA, Telephone Interview, 12/17/07
Major Timothy Jent, USMC, Telephone Interview, 03/24/08
Major Gilbert Juarez, USMC, Telephone Interview, 02/21/08
Major Andrew McNulty, USMC, Telephone Interview, 01/23/08
Major Christopher Meyers, USMC, Telephone Interview, 05/01/08
Major Christopher Meyers, USMC, Personal Interview, 05/19/08
Major Aiden Pfeuffer, USMC, Telephone Interview, 02/08/08
Major Derek Price, USAF, Telephone Interview, 04/30/08
Major Patrick Simon, USMC, Telephone Interview, 06/21/08
Major Michael Skaggs, USMC, Telephone Interview, 09/18/09
Major Kyle Stoddard, USMC, Telephone Interview, 09/22/09
Major Thomas Tennant, USMC, Telephone Interview, 02/19/08
Major Kevin Trimble, USMC, Telephone Interview, 11/21/07
Major Dan Wittnam, USMC, Telephone Interview, 10/08/07
Captain Clint Alanis, USMC, Telephone Interview, 08/04/08
Captain Alfred Butler, USMC, Telephone Interview, 06/03/09
Captain John Campbell, USMC, Telephone Interview, 08/25/08
Captain Brian Chontosh, USMC, Telephone Interview, 12/08/07
Captain Leonard Coulman, USMC, Telephone Interview, 11/20/07
Lieutenant Denis Cox, USN, Telephone Interview, 09/19/08
Captain Michael Cragholm, USMC, Telephone Interview, 03/01/08
Captain Mike Cundiff, USAF, Telephone Interview, 11/19/07
Captain William "Ben" Diaz, USMC, Telephone Interview, 02/25/08
Captain Michael Erwin, USA, Personal Interview, 01/30/08
Captain Peter Glass, USA, Telephone Interview, 12/23/07
Captain Cheree Kochen, USAF, Telephone Interview, 04/30/08
Captain Brian LaPointe, USMC, Telephone Interview, 06/09/09
Captain Jeffery Lee, USMC, Telephone Interview, 07/10/08
Captain Todd Moulder, USMC, Telephone Interview, 03/31/08
Captain David "Scotty" Tompkins, USAF, Telephone Interview, 04/30/08
Captain Paul Vaughan, USMC, Telephone Interview, 04/02/08
Captain William Warkentin, USMC, Telephone Interview, 07/10/08
Captain Paul Webber, USMC, Telephone Interview, 11/10/09
1st Lieutenant Douglas Barnes, USMC, Telephone Interview, 08/07/08
1st Lieutenant Sven Jensen, USMC, Telephone Interview, 10/15/08
Gunner Jeffery Eby CWO4, USMC, Telephone Interview, 11/28/07

CW4 Steven Kilgore, USA, Telephone Interview, 03/12/08

Sergeant Major Michael Berg, USMC, Telephone Interview, 02/19/08

Sergeant Major Derek Fry, USMC, Telephone Interview, 07/29/08

Sergeant Major Eduardo Leardo III, USMC, Telephone Interview, 10/01/07

Sergeant Major Brian Link, USMC, Telephone Interview, 10/25/07

Sergeant Major Rudy Resto, USMC, Telephone Interview, 10/04/07

First Sergeant Michael Farrell, USMC, Telephone Interview, 02/27/08

First Sergeant Frank Herbert, USMC, Telephone Interview, 06/03/08

Gunnery Sergeant Nicholas Popaditch, USMC, Telephone Interview, 09/10/09

Gunnery Sergeant Nicholas Popaditch, USMC, Telephone Interview, 09/11/09

Sergeant First Class Larriva Santiago Jr., USA, Telephone Interview, 03/23/08

Gunnery Sergeant Ricardo Sebastian, USMC, Telephone Interview, 07/24/08

Gunnery Sergeant Paul Starner, USMC, Telephone Interview, 03/05/08

Gunnery Sergeant Brian Vinciguerra, USMC, Telephone Interview, 02/05/08

Staff Sergeant Matt Anderson, USMC, Telephone Interview, 02/25/08

Staff Sergeant David Bellavia, USA, Telephone Interview, 07/18/09

Staff Sergeant Kenneth Distelhorst, USMC, Telephone Interview, 03/18/08

Staff Sergeant Joshua Iversen, USMC, Telephone Interview, 10/29/07

Staff Sergeant Beau Mattioda, USMC, Telephone Interview, 07/26/08

Staff Sergeant Anibal Reyes, USA, Telephone Interview, 02/12/08

Technical Sergeant James Monk, USAF, Telephone Interview, 06/06/09

Sergeant Jason Arellano, USMC, Telephone Interview, 03/10/08

Sergeant Jonathan Ball, USMC, Telephone Interview, 07/15/08

Sergeant Nathan Medinger, USMC, Telephone Interview, 06/21/08

Sergeant Michael Meisenhalder, USMC, Telephone Interview, 03/03/08

Sergeant Elber Navarro, USMC, Telephone Interview, 02/24/08

Sergeant Rhyne Spencer, USMC, Telephone Interview, 10/20/09

Sergeant Jeremiah Workman, USMC, Telephone Interview, 11/05/07

Hospital Corpsman 2 Juan Rubio, USN, Telephone Interview, 11/15/07

Corporal Jeremy Baker, USMC, Telephone Interview, 06/22/08

Corporal Anthony Gantt, USMCR, Telephone Interview, 06/10/08

Corporal Terrence van Doorn, USMC, Telephone Interview, 03/03/08

Corporal David Willis, USMC, Telephone Interview, 02/21/08

Lance Corporal John Aylmer, USMC, Telephone Interview, 07/08/08

Lance Corporal Alston Hays, USMC, Telephone Interview, 07/14/08

Lance Corporal Travis Icard, USMC, Telephone Interview, 07/24/08

Lance Corporal Shane Olden, USMC, Telephone Interview, 02/18/08

Lance Corporal Robert Weeks, USMC, Telephone Interview, 11/20/09

Private First Class William Berry III, USMC, Telephone Interview, 07/27/08

Dr. Richard Jadick, Telephone Interview, 07/09/08

Ms. Christine Knight, Telephone Interview, 05/20/09

Mr. Ranan Lurie, Telephone Interview, 02/24/08

Ms. Shirley Parrello, Telephone Interview, 02/09/08

Mr. Lucian Read, Telephone Interview, 03/25/08

Mr. Stu Segall, Telephone Interview, 11/19/07

Websites

www.fas.org/man/dod-101/sys/land/at4.htm   (Federation   of   American Scientists – Military Analysis Network)

www.newsobserver.com (November 28, 2005)

www.globalsecurity.org

www.icasualties.org

www.defense.gov/specials/insignias/officers.html

www.defense.gov/specials/insignias/enlisted.html

Index